IFIP Advances in Information and Communication Technology 541

Editor-in-Chief

Kai Rannenberg, Goethe University Frankfurt, Germany

Editorial Board

IFIP – The International Federation for Information Processing

IFIP was founded in 1960 under the auspices of UNESCO, following the first World Computer Congress held in Paris the previous year. A federation for societies working in information processing, IFIP's aim is two-fold: to support information processing in the countries of its members and to encourage technology transfer to developing nations. As its mission statement clearly states:

> IFIP is the global non-profit federation of societies of ICT professionals that aims at achieving a worldwide professional and socially responsible development and application of information and communication technologies.

IFIP is a non-profit-making organization, run almost solely by 2500 volunteers. It operates through a number of technical committees and working groups, which organize events and publications. IFIP's events range from large international open conferences to working conferences and local seminars.

The flagship event is the IFIP World Computer Congress, at which both invited and contributed papers are presented. Contributed papers are rigorously refereed and the rejection rate is high.

As with the Congress, participation in the open conferences is open to all and papers may be invited or submitted. Again, submitted papers are stringently refereed.

The working conferences are structured differently. They are usually run by a working group and attendance is generally smaller and occasionally by invitation only. Their purpose is to create an atmosphere conducive to innovation and development. Refereeing is also rigorous and papers are subjected to extensive group discussion.

Publications arising from IFIP events vary. The papers presented at the IFIP World Computer Congress and at open conferences are published as conference proceedings, while the results of the working conferences are often published as collections of selected and edited papers.

IFIP distinguishes three types of institutional membership: Country Representative Members, Members at Large, and Associate Members. The type of organization that can apply for membership is a wide variety and includes national or international societies of individual computer scientists/ICT professionals, associations or federations of such societies, government institutions/government related organizations, national or international research institutes or consortia, universities, academies of sciences, companies, national or international associations or federations of companies.

More information about this series at http://www.springer.com/series/6102

Denis Cavallucci · Roland De Guio
Sebastian Koziołek (Eds.)

Automated Invention
for Smart Industries

18th International TRIZ Future Conference, TFC 2018
Strasbourg, France, October 29–31, 2018
Proceedings

 Springer

Editors
Denis Cavallucci
Institut National des Sciences Appliquées
Strasbourg, France

Sebastian Koziołek
Wrocław University of Technology
Wrocław, Poland

Roland De Guio
Institut National des Sciences Appliquées
Strasbourg, France

ISSN 1868-4238   ISSN 1868-422X   (electronic)
IFIP Advances in Information and Communication Technology
ISBN 978-3-030-13210-1   ISBN 978-3-030-02456-7   (eBook)
https://doi.org/10.1007/978-3-030-02456-7

This Springer imprint is published by the registered company Springer Nature Switzerland AG
The registered company address is: Gewerbestrasse 11, 6330 Cham, Switzerland

Preface

Industry is constantly changing. But the recent changes it has to face are of a completely different magnitude compared with previous ones. If improving quality, avoiding unnecessary expense, producing in time and as ecologically as possible have been the main difficulties that industry has had to face in the past 60 years, the challenge it faces today is different.

The notion that an inventor (or a brainstorming group) in a company is enough to constantly feed it with new ideas is a model that has lived. The abundance of knowledge freely available to consumers and inventors forces companies to design differently, especially when searching for innovation. We must now deal with the digital availability of knowledge, its versatility, and the fact that it is available in abundance for a world where intelligence is linearized and where competition to be the first with the best possible ideas is both more complex and more ephemeral.

Artificial intelligence (AI) could not dream of better conditions to get back in the spotlight. The first experiences in the 1970s were encouraging but of little value. Today AI benefits from the appetite of companies to process the abundance of data, boosted by the fact that computing power has increased tenfold in the past ten years. In addition, the industrial giants of the Web have for the most part freely offered their algorithms for computer researchers to make use of. We are facing a new era: the era of digital intelligence driven by AI advances and the impact they will have on the world.

Our association, ETRIA (European TRIZ Association) has been working for two decades for the advancement of TRIZ and its penetration in academic, scientific, educational, and industrial circles. ETRIA organizes, through one of its members, its annual congress in a different city and country every year. This 18th edition took place at INSA in Strasbourg and was organized by the CSIP team of the I-Cube Laboratory (UMR CNRS 7357) and sponsored scientifically by IFIP. More particularly within IFIP, its TC5 is composed of working groups and one of them, working group 5.4, is entirely dedicated to computer-aided innovation. This edition of the TRIZ Future Conference (TFC 2018) was once again an opportunity to take stock of the main advances made by major contributors to the progress of this theory.

In view of the facts described above and the theme of ETRIA, which is associated with the progress of TRIZ in the world, this edition raised the question of invention and its digitization. In a digital world where industry increasingly aspires to automate its global operation and the way in which it responds with agility to the versatility of customer requirements, how are the recent developments of TRIZ contributing to this?

This book contains 27 articles divided into seven themes. The first theme is dedicated to the teaching of TRIZ. It includes two articles dealing with gamification, continuing education, or the development of education systems. The second theme includes three articles. It is dedicated to contributions that link TRIZ to knowledge representations. A third theme is dedicated to biomimicry, either in software or methodological terms. Here again three articles comprise this theme. The following theme leads us toward the strategic management of the company. The implications of the use of TRIZ are discussed, and this year this theme includes five articles. The fifth is dedicated to associations between TRIZ and other methods. Whether it is a question of experimental design, design thinking, or even of new approaches such as the FORMAT method, this theme is covered in six articles and constitutes the most extensive part. Perhaps we can see this as a way to extend TRIZ beyond its intrinsic capabilities. A little as if the association with other approaches constituted an undeniable way of evolution toward ever more potentialities. The sixth theme is presented in a series of four articles that address the sometimes close, sometimes contradictory links between the TRIZ and the functional approach. Finally, the seventh theme brings together four articles and addresses the use of patent or text populations as a data source to feed projects, whether upstream to capture knowledge or further downstream for a strategic purpose. In this section we find the most obvious link between TRIZ and IA through machine learning.

As we see year after year, TRIZ continues to initiate new thematic orientations while reinforcing older ones. This shift the world is making toward digitization is a tremendous opportunity for TRIZ. By extending beyond its usual scope to other approaches, by offering its ontology as a potential database architecture, TRIZ has been able in recent years to continue its evolution to stay tuned with the requirements of our world.

What challenges are then still facing us? To convince, through excellence, again and again. By observing what characterizes the longevity of TRIZ we notice that its two fundamentals (the notion of contradiction and the notion of laws of evolution of technical systems) continue to question other fields. Whether it is a question of observing biomimicry in the light of contradiction or making use of machine learning as a way of extracting information likely to give rise to contradictions, we always find in current research the two fundamentals of TRIZ. Its future will thus lie in the resolution of both extending toward novelty while preserving its fundamentals.

The leitmotiv this year was "Automated Invention for Smart Industries." It prefigures a theme that is not new to the world of TRIZ. The oldest remember the catchy title "invention machine" and software that later became a company. But perhaps it was too early to make such a statement three decades ago. Today, the rise in the frontline of AI, the supercomputers, the considerable financial efforts of leading countries not to lose in advance the world battle of AI, allows us to envisage a completely different future for systematic invention than being once more forgotten.

For its part, ETRIA will have contributed to it once again this year by offering the TRIZ world the opportunity to meet and share our progress in all the subjects that make it up. To welcome newcomers, ensure that they are in contact with their older colleagues, learn about the latest developments of teams, and leave the edition more motivated than ever to continue this wonderful adventure called research. And there is nothing more beautiful than research that turns into something useful for society and more particularly for industry. ETRIA provides a forum for these two worlds (research and industry) to meet, discuss, understand, share, and produce new knowledge together.

September 2018

Denis Cavallucci
TFC2018 Chair

Organization

Local Organizing Committee

Denis Cavallucci (Conference Chair)	INSA Strasbourg
Hicham Chibane	INSA Strasbourg
Amadou Coulibaly	INSA Strasbourg
Roland De Guio (Scientific Chair)	INSA Strasbourg
Sébastien Dubois	INSA Strasbourg
Roger Dumont	Socomec
Sara Ghabri	INSA Strasbourg
Jean-Marc Hornsperger (Professional Chair)	Socomec
Rémy Houssin	INSA Strasbourg
Jean-François Rapp	INSA Strasbourg
Ivana Rasovska	INSA Strasbourg
Betty Rayapen (Administrative Assistant)	INSA Strasbourg
Jean Renaud	INSA Strasbourg
Michael Rosfelder	Socomec
Achille Souili	INSA Strasbourg
Jean-Marc Voirpin	Socomec
Pei Zhang	INSA Strasbourg

List of Reviewers

Oleg Abramov	Algorithm, Ltd., Russia
Robert Adunka	Siemens, Germany
Dmitriy Bakhturin	RosAtom, Russia
Rachid Benmoussa	ENSA Marrakech, Morocco
Tiziana Bertoncelli	GE, Germany
Yuri Borgianni	Free University of Bozen-Bolzano, Italy
Aurelien Brouillon	INSA Strasbourg, France
Gaetano Cascini	Politecnico di Milano, Italy
Michel Chaux	Michelin, France
Hicham Chibane	INSA Strasbourg, France
Dobrusskin Christoph	Phillips, Holland
Guillermo Cortes Robles	Instituto Tecnológico de Orizaba, Mexico
Marco Aurelio De Carvalho	Universidade Tecnologica Federal do Parana, Brazil
Ellen Domb	trizgroup, USA
Roger Dumont	Socomec, France

Contents

TRIZ Combined with other Approaches

Biomimicry and TRIZ

Design Entity Recognition for Bio-inspired Design Supervised State of the Art

Davide Russo[1], Pierre-Emmanuel Fayemi[2(✉)], Matteo Spreafico[1], and Giacomo Bersano[2]

[1] Bergamo University, 24044 Dalmine, BG, Italy
[2] IKOS Consulting, Levallois-Perret, France
p.fayemi@aim-innovation.com

Abstract. In the last years the efforts spent for the enhancement of parsing engines led to several software more performant, in terms of both effectiveness in identification of syntax modules and speed of elaboration of the text, than the previous generation ones. Exploiting the benefits coming from such a new generation of software, nowadays the patent search can overcome the limits due to the classic FOS approach and performs it in a quasi-real-time way. This paper focuses on technical-problems identification methods based on syntactic dependency patterns, for ameliorating supervised state of the art and patent intelligence. Through parsing the patent text, very precise lists of technical problems are automatically extracted without the user being an expert in the problems of the sector. An exemplary case dealing with bio-inspired design is proposed, stressing what types of engineering problems are nowadays benefitting the most from the approach.

Keywords: Biomimetics · Biomimicry software · Triz · Syntactic parser

1 Introduction

Over the last years there has been an increment of papers regarding both TRIZ and biomimicry. The greatest efforts were produced to introduce TRIZ fundamentals, like technical contradictions or function modeling as tools for knowledge transfer of biological organisms, in order to solve technical problems.

A vast literature has been produced about this topic, even if spread under different labels (biomimetics, bionics, bio mimesis, biomimicry, bio gnosis, biologically inspired design).

The main part of these works is focused on new methods for searching biological literature for functional analogies to implement, while only few papers such as [1] suggest how to make successful the transfer of a concept from living to non-living systems. As Vincent said in [2] "a simple and direct replica of the biological prototype is rarely successful, even if it is possible with current technology".

There are many reasons for explaining these difficulties that we summarized in two main aspects: interdisciplinarity and function modelling.

In the first case there is a communication problem, in fact the most acknowledged database of biomimetics knowledge are run by biologists, which not necessarily

© IFIP International Federation for Information Processing 2018
Published by Springer Nature Switzerland AG 2018. All Rights Reserved
D. Cavallucci et al. (Eds.): TFC 2018, IFIP AICT 541, pp. 3–13, 2018.
https://doi.org/10.1007/978-3-030-02456-7_1

describe a living organism for technicians looking for functions and the most appropriate biological resources suitable for addressing an engineering problem. However, it is not only a language problem, that could be partially solved by Bridging cross-domain terminology for biomimetic design [3], but what is intimately different is the way a biologist and an engineer look at the solution. For example, while an engineer describes a material in terms of performance or technical specifications and manufacturing requirements, biologist take into account how in natural systems a long-term evolution allows a homogeneous material to change locally and temporally its structure variables, expanding the design space of homogeneous materials and allowing the creation of new materials with specific property profiles [4]. From the nature perspective, instead of developing new materials each time we want new functionality, we should adapt and combine the materials we already have. Bogatyrev in [2, 5] contributed to prove this thesis demonstrating how technology solves problems largely by manipulating usage of energy, while biology uses information and structure, two factors largely ignored by technology.

The second bottleneck consists of creating efficient functional models for describing the complexity of natural system. Several attempts have been produced starting from implementing models from conceptual design as Energy Material Signal model [19], cause effect [6], functional basis [7] or Function Behavior Structure model [8]. Also, TRIZ community provided a significant contribution on this topic.

TRIZ was developed as a systems approach for engineering; biology is, itself, a system. Starting from this assumption, the conflicting functions are similarly classified into the standard TRIZ [9] features, which now allow the conflicts to be treated in the standard TRIZ system. Many authors [2, 5, 10] provided several works about conflicts identification in biomimicry, trying to interpret natural phenomena as technical contradiction and identifying resources and inventive principles adopted for overcoming the technical conflicts.

The article presents a synthesis of the major features characterizing a natural system in order to fix what entities has to be highlighted during biology transfer in Sect. 2. In Sect. 3, it illustrated the methodological proposal to retrieve the state of the art and the way of proceeding conducted in this study. After, in Sect. 4, an example of the methodology through a case study is provided. Section 5 presents the results achieved from the case study. In closing, Sect. 6, the conclusion.

2 Software for Biomimetics

While several computerized solutions have emerged over the years [12], two of them, i.e. AskNature and DANE, seems to prevail among the bioinspired design software.

2.1 Asknature

AskNature is a well establish tools within the bio-inspired design toolset. Known for being the largest database related to bio-inspiration, the tool aims at initiating pathways between natural phenomena, living organisms presenting such phenomenon and potential experts of the considered organisms [13].

To enable this, the database behind the AskNature website articulates itself around a specific ontology, called Biomimicry Taxonomy, based on a classification of functional keywords. This classification scheme is organized according to three hierarchical levels: eight categories (e.g. get, store, or distribute resources), thirteen sub-groups (e.g. capture, absorb, or filter, expel) and 162 functions (e.g. organisms, solid particles, chemical entities) [14]. By focusing on organizing biology by challenge, the taxonomy enables designers to translate their technical problematic, usually formalized with their specific professional jargon, to biological ones [15].

Through this mechanism of classification, the Biomimicry Taxonomy has been thought to be a key entry point of AksNature which encompasses descriptions of the biological strategies organisms use to tackle the problems they encounter [13].

AskNature has been at the forefront of the bio-inspired design tools for approximately a decade, and as such is part of the 48% of BID tools available as open source [12]. Its free access to its content

As one of the first biomimetics tools with a free and publicly access to its content as a constitutive element [13]. AskNature is one of the tool to have initiated the remaining trend toward open-source among the BID tools [12]. The combination of AskNature and its Biomimicry Taxonomy has been identified as one of the simplest and quickest way to implement biomimicry [16]. This accessibility seems to have made a difference regarding its use, with AskNature website being the only tool mentioned in interviews with biomimetic products developers [17].

Being for approximately a decade at the forefront of the bio-inspired design tools, AskNature has acted over the years as a catalyst in the expansion of the biomimetic toolset (e.g. BIOPS, a tool guiding the user to the websites asknature.org, to a patent database (freepatentsonline.com) and/or to scientific literature (sciencedaily.com) in order to find more information.; the Scalable Systematic Biologically-Inspired Design approach [18].

2.2   DANE

Functional modelling has been a major way of describing investigated systems for the bioinspired design process [16]. In 2007, Tinsley et al. have introduced a new way to convert biological knowledge, and especially design solutions, into valuable input for problem solving. This conversion, based upon functional language modeling has been pushed forward in the early 2010's by [19] who proposed general guidelines to formalize a biological system according to a functional representation integrating criterion such as its inspirational type and its scale.

Biological functional models offer the possibility to easily compile them into databases. Designer would thus be able to look for and identify analogous biological model relevant to their initial problematic. [20] have defined a problem-driven biologically inspired design process which provides iterative feedback and refinement loops. The process founds its foundations within the analysis of how students from the interdisciplinary course on biologically inspired design at Georgia Institute of Technology (ME/ISyE/MSE/PTFe/BIOL 4803) were implementing their BID approach throughout the progress of their case study.

Projects analysis lead to a synthetic 6-steps process, as shown in the following figure (Fig. 1):

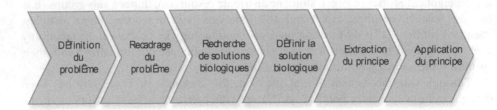

Fig. 1. Problem-driven biologically inspired design process [20].

In order to make this analogical reasoning accessible for the designers who do not possess any biological background, [8] have developed both a computer aided design knowledge-based software and a representation scheme called DANE (Design by Analogy to Nature Engine). This approach focuses on generating a custom-built database, which is, de facto, dependent on the addition of new engineering and biologically representations.

The specificity of DANE generated models is their main focuses on describing in a detailed way the internal structure and functions of a system. Within the representation scheme, functions are modeled through a progression of states, linked together by behavioral causal explanations, along with structure box diagrams, highlighting the physical parameters involved in each of them.

DANE representation mainly focuses on two distinct designers' need: find a biological analogy relevant to a given design context and facilitate the understanding of biological systems so that anyone can extract then transfer the key functional principles.

In this model, the function is represented by means of a schema that specifies "initial" and "final" conditions of the system, with the aim of representing what the system actually does.

The function (defining the "why" of a system) is accomplished through a progression of states through which the system evolves, each described by a set of physical variables defining the relevant properties of the system.

The behavior (defining the "how" of a system) consists of this sequence of states, together with the causal explanation of the transition between them (Design & Intelligence Laboratory - Georgia Tech, 2011). Usually, these explanations consist in a physical phenomenon or principle that governs the state transition (Fig. 2).

Finally, the structure (defining the "what" of a system) is represented by means of a box diagram.

The compiled representation defines the computer aided design software called DANE 2.0. The tool focuses on establishing structured descriptions of biological systems and offering creative triggers by allowing designers to tap into a database of DANE representations of both engineering and biological examples.

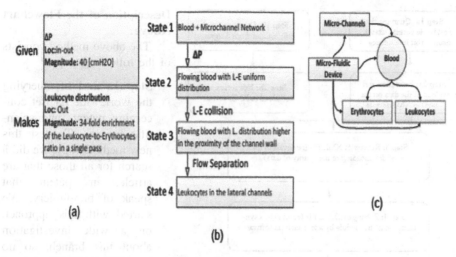

Fig. 2. DANE representation model applied to micro-fluidic device [11]

3 Proposal

As a means to test the method proposed in this work, the authors have considered the extraction in full text (i.e. title, abstract, description, claims and priority dates) regarding the whole patent set and all scientific publications (from scientific journals, books and conference proceedings) concerning the field of biomimicry. They are interested on a wide investigation about this branch, so no specific topics was defined to limit the number of documents analyzed.

Extraction of the Scientific Paper and the Patent Corpus

The authors used Orbit Intelligence (www.orbit.com) to querying the worldwide patent DB and Scopus (www.scopus.com) in order to interrogate scientific literature.

The goal is to extract the largest set of documents with the aim to study the problem in a complete and exhaustive way. It follows a schematic representation of the search queries with the results obtained.

The patent corpus considered for this study is a collection of 20770 patents belonging to different application fields and 46612 scientific publications owning searched with the following query: "(biomimicry) or (biomimetic+) or (bio_inspir+)".

Below is a flowchart that describes, schematically, the way of proceeding conducted in this study (Fig. 3):

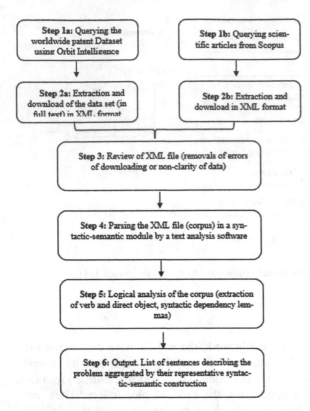

Step 1a: Querying the worldwide patent Dataset using Orbit Intelligence

Step 1b: Querying scientific articles from Scopus

Step 2a: Extraction and download of the data set (in full text) in XML format

Step 2b: Extraction and download in XML format

Step 3: Review of XML file (removals of errors of downloading or non-clarity of data)

Step 4: Parsing the XML file (corpus) in a syntactic-semantic module by a text analysis software

Step 5: Logical analysis of the corpus (extraction of verb and direct object, syntactic dependency lemmas)

Step 6: Output. List of sentences describing the problem aggregated by their representative syntactic-semantic construction

Fig. 3. Graphical representation of the operations performed in this study from the interrogation of worldwide scientific paper or patent databases to the output list of sentences.

Description of the Flowchart Above:

The above method consists of the following steps:

– **Step 1a and b:** Querying the worldwide dataset concerning patents and scientific articles. To test this new methodology, we did a search for all those that are articles and patents that speak of biomimicry. We started with this approach on a wide investigation about this branch, so no specific topics was defined to limit the number of documents analyzed. The ultimate goal is to work with a dataset containing only biological documents.

– **Step 2a and b:** The extraction of the files took place using the xml format, a structural document with pre-defined tags, XML is a document that acts as a container to store data that can be used by other software and easy to open.

– **Step 3 and 4:** Revision of the file from a semantic point of view in order to prepare the file to be searched according to complex and linguistically motivated queries. The procedure starts analysing the raw text through a set of algorithmic operations that enrich the above-mentioned text with additional features.

   With more detail, the procedure is as follows:
   • Conversion of the corpus text into a series of single words (tokens).
   • Generation of a tag by the text analysis software that represents the part-of-speech (PoS) of that token.
   • In this way, the model becomes able to discriminate similar words with different meanings from a logical and syntactic point of view.

– **Step 5:** Extrapolation, from the corpus, of syntactic lemmas in order to provide a sample to be read list of functions. In order to extract only the useful information from the entire corpus set, the method gives to the searcher the list of sentences aggregated by their representative syntactic-semantic construction.

– **Step 6:** The proposal aims to give a sample to be read list of functions and technical problems through the parsing of the patent and scientific articles dataset. The tool gives, as a final output, a list of sentences describing the problem aggregated by their representative syntactic-semantic construction.

4   Case Study

In the following, a comparative analysis between ASKNATURE and semantic tools is presented. The selected input function has been the conductivity of electrical impulses. The topic selection has been made arbitrarily on the basis of the importance of electrical impulse in both living and technical systems.

4.1   AskNature

The biomimicry taxonomy possessed a specific entry related to electrical conductivity:

– Group: Modify
– Subgroup: Modify chemical/electrical state
– Function: Modify conductivity.

This "modify conductivity" has been used has the input to tap into the AskNature dat-base. AskNature offered two "solutions" in the form of two distinct strategies.

The first one is the inner-ear cells from vertebrates which convert sound signal to electrical current. The second one is the microbial nanowires of geobacter which transfer electrons in order to "breathe" mineral instead of oxygen.

A second function, belonging to the same "Modify chemical/electrical state" subgroup, could have been relevant considering the initial query: "Modify electron transport". However, result of this specific function within the database exclusively shows the geobacter solution which was already identified.

4.2   Scientific Paper and the Patent Corpus

The patent corpus & scientific publications set was trimmed down from the previous set, i.e. ((biomimicry) or (biomimetic+) or (bio_inspir+)), with the following results (Table 1):

Table 1. List of queries and related results

	Search queries	# of results
Patent corpus	((biomimicry) or (biomimetic+) or (bio_inspir+))/TI/AB/IW/TX	20770
Scientific publication set	((biomimicry) or (biomimetic+) or (bio_inspir+))	46612

According to author's strategies, all sematic network among words has been extracted. In order to retrieve interesting documents acting on "electrical conductivity" applications, a list of verbs having "electrical conductivity" as object has been produced as shown in Table 2.

Table 2. List of lemmas related to "electrical conductivity" as objects

	Occurrence	Rank
verbs with "electrical conductivity" as object	230	36.86
have	72	8.49
improve	25	6.84
....	......	....
include	10	6.4
measure	8	5.93
maintain	8	5.6
increase	8	5.31
enhance	7	5.03
provide	6	4.59
exhibit	6	4.38
....	......	....
achieve	3	3.37
impart	2	3.34
decrease	2	3.03
....	......	....
reduce	1	1.99
promote	1	1.76
lower	1	1.7
involve	1	1.64
incorporate	1	1.57
evaluate	1	1.52
enable	1	1.38
....	......	....

The documents analyzed are those containing propositions having actions dealing with improvement task (i.e. improve, increase, enhance, provide, upgrade, etc.) as object.

5   Results

Results from the case study, summarized in Table 3 stressed differences between the use of AskNature and the semantic research tool which could be classified according to two categories: quantity and quality.

Table 3. Summary of "conductivity of electrical impulses" from both AskNature, scientific papers and patent corpus

Ask Nature		Non-patent literature		
Sensor	**Nanowires**	**Nanofiber**	**Doped carbon**	**Microelectrodes**
Inner-ear cells convert sound signal to electrical current	Microbial nanowires transfer electrons	Tough and flexible CNT-polymeric hybrid scaffolds for engineering cardiac constructs Kharaziha et al.	Transforming Hair into Heteroatom - Doped Carbon with High Surface Area Chaudhari Kn, Song My, Yu Js	Electrically engineered Robots — Micro Driven Bioinspired Soft — Su Ryon S., Migliori B., Miccoli B.
		Bioinspired Hierarchical Nanofibrous Silver-Nanoparticle/Anatase-Rutile Titania Composite as an Anode Material for Lithium-Ion Batteries Luo Y et al.		
Ion channels in inner-ear receptor cells switch electrical conductivity depending on lateral deflection of the sensors where they are located	Geobacter species "breathe" minerals instead of oxygen by transferring electrons along protein nanowire "pilli" via "electron hopping"	Fiber-alignment and **improved** the *electrical conductivity* and toughness of the scaffolds	Our unique synthesis strategy involving moderate activation and further graphitization **enhances** the *electrical conductivity*, while still maintaining the precious heteroatoms.	Flexible microelectrodes are embedded into the biomimetic scaffold, which **increase** its *electrical conductivity*. After culturing and maturation of cardiomyocytes on the biomimetic scaffold.
		The high loading content of the silver component in the composite **improves** the *electrical conductivity* of the electrode		

Patent literature

Electro spraying	Aerogel	Carbon nanotubes	Polymer actuators
WO2014193995 Title of invention: Electro spraying systems and associated methods	US 20160361464 Title of invention: Biomimetic Hydrogel Scaffolds and Related Methods	CN107337198 Title of invention: Cobweb-like structural material based on single-walled carbon nanotubes and preparation method of material	US8907050 Title of invention: Polymeric additive for strength, deformability, and toughness enhancement of cementitious materials and composites
A thin film of titanium/gold was sputtered onto the grid dies to **increase** their *electrical conductivity*	Incorporation of graphene as an array is likely to **improve** the *electrical conductivity* of fibrous hydrogel scaffolds.	Conductivity and transmittance, combined with a rigid substrate not only can increase its mechanical strength, it is also possible to **increase** its *electrical conductivity*; this "spider web structure material imitation spider"	The broken cube fragments were first oven dried at 60 deg. C. to remove most of the moisture content followed by gold coating of the fragment exposed surfaces with sputter coater to **increase** *electrical conductivity*
	WO 201760719 Title of invention: Aerogels		WO 2017132763 Title of invention: Bio-inspired polyflavin electrodes for energy storage devices
	Graphene aerogel is a polymer aerogel with improved properties due to the presence of the graphene, e.g. **improved** *electrical conductivity* or structural strength		R9 and R10 are independently a hydrogen atom, alkyl group, a polyether chain to **improve** *ionic conductivity* or a conjugated polymer chain to **improve** *electrical conductivity*
			US9147825 Title of invention: Methods of fabricating multi-degree of freedom shaped electroactive polymeractuators/sensors for catheters
			The electroactive polymers that are typically used in connection with the present disclosure are ionic EAPs, more typically those that feature an ion-exchange capable polymer network and have the ability to **increase** *electrical conductivity* under oxidation or reduction

With a quantity focus, AskNature has shown its limitation in enlarging designer's scope of knowledge with only two highlighted possible solution, labelled "sensor" and "nanowires". This identified weakness seems to be induced by the design of the tool. In order to be populated, AskNature requires biologists to formalize content from their expertise. The process of mobilizing these biologists proves to be tedious as well as time consuming. This limits the tool's exhaustiveness compared to tools capable of automatically screening scientific literature. From its largest scope of investigation, the semantic tool has been able to identify seven possible solutions, labelled "Nanofiber", "Doped carbon", "Microelectrodes", "Electro spraying", "Aerogel", "Carbon nanotubes" and "polymer actuators".

On the quality aspect, the semantic tool's approach tends to offer better results. Compared to AskNature, the semantic approach offered a largest variety of solutions typology. While AskNature specifically promoted "technological solutions", the semantic tool highlighted almost 60% (4 results) of "technological solution" for around 40% (3 results) of "strategic principles". In addition to this, both volume and precision of the available information were higher through the semantic approach. Information gathered through ask nature consisted of an average 436 words resulting from a popularization of scientific content, which significantly less than any patent or scientific article both in number of words or comprehensiveness.

6 Conclusion

Test on a database that already has examples of bio-inspiration "written by engineers".

The limit of this case study relates to understand what is the organism that serves as inspiration. One must read the title of the article or the patent because, so far, it is necessary to read the title of the article or the patent because one does not have the preposition with which electrical conductivity and the organization relate directly.

If a scholar reads an article in biology, we can identify that we speak of improvement of electrical conductivity in an article about a fish. The relationship is much easier to find. But to begin with, it was easier to skew the experience because it ensured a certain number of results with more writing by engineers and not biologists, reducing the semantic bias.

Future development does not use the database on biomimetics but uses the articles of biology. In the future we can use directly in biological databases to find strategies to solve problems.

References

1. Sartori, J., Pal, U., Chakrabarti, A.: A methodology for supporting transfer in biomimetic design. Artif. Intell. Eng. Des. Anal. Manuf. **24**, 483–505 (2010)
2. Vincent, J.F.V., et al.: Biomimetics: its practice and theory. J. R. Soc. Interface **3**(9), 471–482 (2006)

3. Chiu, I., Shu, L.H.: Bridging cross-domain terminology. In: ASME 2005 International Design Engineering Technical Conferences and Computers and Information in Engineering (2005)
4. Wegst, U.G.K., Ashby, M.F.: The mechanical efficiency of natural materials. Phil. Mag. **84**, 2167–2186 (2004)
5. Bogatyrev, N.R.: Ecological Engineering of Survival. Publishing house of SB RAS, Novosibirsk (2000)
6. Chakrabarti, A., et al.: A functional representation for aiding biomimetic and artificial inspiration of new ideas. AIE EDAM **19**(02), 113–132 (2005)
7. Stroble, J.K., et al.: Modeling the cellular level of natural sensing with the functional basis for the design of biomimetic sensor technology. In: 2008 IEEE Region 5 Conference. IEEE (2008)
8. Vattam, S., Wiltgen, B., Helms, M., Goel, A., Yen, J.: DANE: fostering creativity in and through biologically inspired design. In: Taura, T., Nagai, Y. (eds.) First International Conference on Design Creativity, pp. 115–122. Springer, London (2011). https://doi.org/10.1007/978-0-85729-224-7_16
9. Altshuller, G.S.: Creativity as An Exact Science. Gordon & Breach, New York (1988)
10. Vincent, J.F.V., Mann, D.L.: Systematic technology transfer from biology to engineering. Philos. Trans. R. Soc. Lond. A: Math. Phys. Eng. Sci. **360**(1791), 159–173 (2002)
11. Shevkoplyas, S.S., Yoshida, T., Munn, L.L.: Biomimetics design of a microfluidic device for auto-separation of leukocytes from whole blood. Am. Chem. Soc. **77**, 933–937 (2005)
12. Wanieck, K., Fayemi, P.-E., Maranzana, N., Zollfrank, C., Jacobs, S.: Biomimetics and its tools. Biomim. Tools **6**(2), 53–66 (2017)
13. Baumeister, D., Tocke, R., Dwyer, J., Ritter, S.: Biomimicry Resource Handbook: A Seed Bank of Best Practices. Biomimicry 3.8, Missoula (2013)
14. Deldin, J.-M., Schuknecht, M.: The AskNature database: enabling solutions in biomimetic design. In: Goel, A.K., McAdams, D.A., Stone, R. (eds.) Biologically Inspired Design, pp. 17–27. Springer, London (2014). https://doi.org/10.1007/978-1-4471-5248-4_2
15. Hooker, G., Smith, E.: AskNature and the biomimicry taxonomy. Insight **19**(1), 46–49 (2016)
16. Fayemi, P.E., Wanieck, K., Zollfrank, C., Maranzana, N., Aoussat, A.: Biomimetics: process, tools and practice. Bioinspiration Biomim. **12**(1), 011002 (2017)
17. Jacobs, S.R., Nichol, E.C., Helms, M.E.: Where are we now and where are we going? The BioM innovation database. J. Mech. Des. **136**(11), 111101 (2014)
18. Vandevenne, D., Verhaegen, P.A., Dewulf, S., Duflou, J.R.: Product and organism aspects for scalable systematic biologically-inspired design. Procedia Eng. **131**, 784–791 (2015)
19. Nagel, R.L., et al.: Exploring the use of functional models in biomimetic conceptual design. J. Mech. Des. **130**(12), 121102 (2008)
20. Helms, M., Vattam, S.S., Goel, A.K.: Biologically inspired design: process and products. Des. Stud. **30**(5), 606–622 (2009)
21. Bogatyreva, O., Shillerov, A., Bogatyrev, N.: Patterns in TRIZ contradiction matrix: integrated and distributed systems. In: Proceedings of ETRIA World Conference TRIZ Future 2004, Florence, Italy, 5 November 2004

Development of an Ontology of Biomimetics Based on Altshuller's Matrix

Julian Vincent[1](✉) and Denis Cavallucci[2]

[1] Nature Inspired Manufacturing Centre, Heriot-Watt University,
Edinburgh, UK
jv21@hw.ac.uk
[2] CSIP @ ICube (UMR-CNRS 7357), 67084 Strasbourg Cedex, France

Abstract. The discovery of novel solutions in engineering is critical for most industries. Largely inspired by TRIZ, practical solutions can be found beyond engineering. In the wider search, the tradition of looking to biology for solutions (biomimetics) is well founded but little exploited. It turns out to be a non-trivial exercise, requiring a bridge between largely descriptive biology (functioning primarily at the molecular level) and engineering which is predictable (but at a more statistical level). We propose that the bridge is best built at the level of design, more particularly in the behaviour of solving well-defined problems, an aspect at which TRIZ excels. We postulate that an ontology is an excellent medium for this bridge. The central theorem is that there is a finite number of design problems expressed as trade-offs (Altshuller's Matrix) and that the same (or very similar) trade-offs can be identified in biology. The ontology enables the identification and alignment of these trade-offs, thus marrying a problem in engineering with its solution in biology and referential expression in a (possibly) novel engineering material, structure or device.

Keywords: Ontology · TRIZ · Contradiction · Biomimetics · Trade-off

1 A World of Differences

1.1 Different but not Incompatible Sciences

Biomimetics requires the fusion of biology (currently a largely descriptive science) and engineering (almost entirely analytical) [1]. This can be achieved at the level of design. Using elements of TRIZ [2], one of the authors (JV) has shown that biology and engineering can be brought together in an ontology [3]. Ontologies are in common usage for the digital storage and integration of design information in medicine, architecture, engineering, materials science, and a number of other areas [4]. With access to enough information, an ontology can become a research tool at the heart of an AI system [5]. The intention is that the ontology of biomimetics should drive agents capable of forming structures, controlling systems and developing new materials, based on the types of interaction and change found in biological systems. Biomimetics (= biomimicry = bionics = bio-inspired design = …) relies on transforming and transferring information that we glean from biology into information that can be used in design, development and manufacture (whatever is appropriate) of something man-made [6].

Published by Springer Nature Switzerland AG 2018. All Rights Reserved
D. Cavallucci et al. (Eds.): TFC 2018, IFIP AICT 541, pp. 14–25, 2018.
https://doi.org/10.1007/978-3-030-02456-7_2

Physics and chemistry provide us with tools with which we measure (and therefore classify and make predictions about) phenomena in general, and with such clear models we can unravel many of the complexities of our surroundings and separate effect from cause. But physics (and maths) fail when faced with life and living things. There must therefore be parts of biology that are currently unknown and unrecognised, even though we can observe the effects of those parts, since we inevitably view most of biology through the prism of physics. Our temptation will then be to ascribe those effects to candidate causes with which we are familiar, even if those causes are not appropriate and out of context. The distinction of a successful model is its ability to quantify and predict. There is currently no way that biological events such as speciation and morphological changes can be predicted. At its root, current understanding of biology is unquantifiable in terms of constitutive models. There is no basic theory of biology; biological phenomena cannot be predicted from first principles; we cannot make an egg. Biology is in the alchemical stage, where experiments can accumulate information but the basic general principles are obscure. Biology awaits its Newton.

1.2 Short Summary of Current Research Limits

There have been several efforts to enlarge the capacities of TRIZ to identify solutions from biology [6–12]. Whatever this method is called (Eco-TRIZ, Bio-TRIZ etc.) it always relies on associating functions originating in engineering with function of a specific natural body. In many cases, the achievements of nature are superior to the capabilities of engineering, especially under conditions of global accounting. Most current biomimetic concepts have previously been explored at a basic level (such as hydrophobic surfaces of plants); a few present basic problems to be solved (such as absorption of water from a dry atmosphere) if they are to be reproduced artificially. There are biological phenomena that will need new discoveries in physics before they can be transferred biomimetically [13]. Our conclusion is that there is limited utility in these simple methods.

2 Describing and Aligning Domains Using an Ontology

2.1 A Description of Biomimetics Bridged by TRIZ "Contradictions"

We are thus left with the central problem in biomimetics. How to bridge the gap between technology (quantifiable) and biology (descriptive)? At present it seems that the bridge can be only partial [13–15]; currently the most useful answer must, at least initially, recognise the limitations imposed by physics [16]. Thus, we can define a target in general terms. As a criterion of success, if only partial, we need to produce one kind of structure (e.g. biological theory) [17] in the context of another (e.g. engineering or design theory), and *vice versa*. If we could do this in such a way that the resulting pair of operations were mutually inverse, then we would have grounds for saying that the two theories were equally general; if we could say one and not the other, we could rank one theory more general than the other; if we can say nothing at all, then the generality of the two formalisms cannot be compared—they are of different generality.

Viewed like this, biomimetics falls into the second category. Much, though not all, of the mechanisms of biology can be described (though not necessarily explained) by physics, engineering and chemistry. The inverse is less easy or possible, despite the efforts of 2,000+ years of biological inspiration in technology. So biology and technology are of different generality. Nonetheless, the effort should be concentrated on selecting one or more design or descriptive system in common use in engineering and seeing how far that system can describe biology as well.

TRIZ is a good candidate for this exercise because it is a systematic approach to complexity and is used by engineers and designers for solving problems in a creative manner. If this system can describe biology, even at a utilitarian level, then we have a possible model for biomimetics. We need to find or define a level at which it is possible to transfer parameters and observations. The place of TRIZ in biomimetics is argued in the following section.

2.2   How TRIZ Decomposes a Problem

Ideally, TRIZ helps in dissecting a problem, removing confusion, distilling it down to its essentials, and suggesting solutions derived from the study of a wide range of successful patents. The completeness of the description and abstraction of the problem that this produces makes it possible to compare the problem with a much wider range of solutions than is available with most other problem-solving systems. This range of solutions must necessarily include the living world. Thus it is necessary to expose biology to the same general system of reduction and classification that has been used with patents. This has not yet been done, although a number of studies have used different modules of TRIZ as a mirror for biology [e.g. 12]. For this study we have chosen to develop an ontology based on the well-known Contradiction Matrix.

The Contradiction Matrix is often regarded more as toy than tool, but this view can be considered due to a general misunderstanding of its structure and therefore of its possibilities and use. Whether or not Altshuller was aware of the internal structure of the Contradiction Matrix that we will illustrate is probably not known. However, it's a fair guess that it was strongly influenced by the concepts of Hegelian philosophy, widely taught in continental Europe during the last century and beyond. But we must dig deeper, into the Dialectic and its origins, in order to derive a more balanced and critical understanding.

2.3   The TRIZ Matrix is Dialectic: Not a New Thought!

The concept of the Dialectic has its origins with the Greek philosopher Heraclitus of Ephasus, who said that everything is in constant change as a result of inner strife and opposition (unfortunately, Heraclitus never published his ideas formally). The concept was popularised by Plato's Socratic dialogues, that in order to establish a truth it is necessary to have two or more people with opposing views to engage in dispassionate discussion until a resolution is reached. This unity of opposites is now known as the Dialectic. In practical terms this equates to making a statement of some sort, questioning the statement with counter-arguments, then working towards some sort of agreed truth.

Over the years, many forms of dialectic have arisen; the one most familiar to Europeans is the Hegelian Dialectic, although Hegel said that he got the idea from Kant. Kant named the two opposites thesis and antithesis, and the resolution he called the synthesis. The synthesis can then become the thesis in a new dialectic. This, however, is a formalism. As Karl Popper gleefully pointed out, advance is more likely to be made with the rather messy 'trial-and-error', much closer to Socratic dialogue.

But there is a basic problem with the Hegelian Dialectic. Although in its ideal form merit is recognised in both thesis and antithesis, and preserved in the synthesis (an example is the argument between wave and corpuscular theories of light, in which the synthesis has to accommodate both models), there is a great tendency for muddle arising from the loose way in which dialecticians speak of contradictions. Criticism, which forms the basis of the antithesis, invariably points out a contradiction. But this can lead to the impression that thesis and antithesis are essentially contradictory, such that any synthesis will have to challenge the law of the exclusion of contradictions of traditional logic. This law asserts that two contradictory statements can never be true together, such that any dialectic synthesis derived from such an argument must be rejected as false on purely logical grounds. But Hegelian dialecticians claimed that this law of traditional logic has been subverted by the Dialectic and must be discarded. This action totally destroys the logical argument and renders admissible and valid any statement whatsoever. We need to step back from this brink.

In fact, as Popper recommends, it would be best not even to use the term 'dialectic'. He would use the clearer terminology of the method of trial-and-error. However, it seems to us that the concept of the dialectic needs to be understood since it appears to have played an important role in the development of TRIZ [18]. In Russia both the Hegelian Dialectic and TRIZ are taught at kindergarten level and upwards and may even be important in everyday thinking. But in Europe, Cartesian rationalism has very much been confined to the Continent; in the UK, a nation of pragmatists, the main thrust has been empiricism. Without the burden of Hegel's tradition, it is easier to be antithetical about the Dialectic!

2.4 Altshuller's Proposition: Place Opposites into a Matrix

It is obvious with a little study that the Contradiction Matrix is assembled using the rules of dialectic discourse [19]. A collection of carefully selected parameters describes the conditions and characteristics of materials and systems. The instructions for use say that two of these parameters must be chosen - one that describes the end goal (i.e. the ideal solution) and one that describes the characteristic that is frustrating or contradicting the achievement of this goal. Respectively these are Hegel's Thesis and Antithesis. These two parameters, both drawn from the same list of 39, are arranged along two orthogonal sides of a matrix, and suggestions for a synthesis of each pair of parameters defined at the crossing points in the body of the matrix, drawn from patents in which this particular problem was solved, are plotted at that point. Since the two parameters are essentially different in character (basically positive or negative) the Matrix appears well populated, with no intended symmetry about the diagonal. However, simple analysis of the Matrix shows that there is a very significant symmetry about the diagonal (Fig. 1). 27% of the suggested syntheses are totally symmetrical (no

cant   symmetry   about   the   diagonal

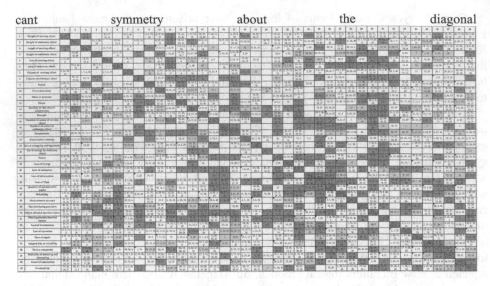

Fig. 1. The standard TRIZ Contradiction Matrix. Identical squares coloured yellow (Color figure online)

disparity across the diagonal, with the suggested Inventive Principles not differing) and a further 25% differ in only one suggested Inventive Principle out of a common maximum of four. So the Matrix is heavily populated with Socratic rather than Hegelian syntheses; half of it is displaying the characteristics of a balanced trade-off rather than an Hegelian argumen2. Taking this into account, the suggested Inventive Principles appear to fall into a number of categories, as yet unanalysed. Some of them, where the dialectic is in the form of a problem to be solved, will prescribe real solutions to the problem; some, also aiding the generation of a practical synthesis, will suggest novelty that can introduce a new dimension to the problem without necessarily providing a solution; a third category, more closely associated with the ~50% or trade-offs, will suggest changes that manipulate the trade-off such that its inherent variability can be harnessed in the provision of an adaptive response to changing internal or external conditions. Since living organisms are open and adaptive systems, it seems reasonable to suggest that this form of synthesis of the trade-off will be more common in biology since it allows and underpins adaptation in general.

Usefully, trial-and-error provides the basic variability for natural selection in biology, genetic and phenotypic variations being exposed to the selection pressures of the environment, physical and biotic. But the trial-and-error of natural selection, whose product is evolution, is different from the Socratic and Hegelian versions of the dialectic in at least one major factor. Socrates could argue only about what was known, and Hegel's formalism was even more limiting. Natural selection works on variants of organisms that have some novelty about them, and the selection pressures are similarly lacking in control, although they may be circumscribed by context (environment, heredity, etc.). Scientific research is much the same - you may have an inkling of what the answer has to be, but the journey you take to get there is unlikely to be direct. It is also very likely that your imagined end-point will turn out to have been illusory, and the new reality is more interesting and convincing than was initially conceived. In science, therefore, and especially in biology (biologists love surprises), the Hegelian Dialectic is not an appropriate model for research since at least half of the argument cannot be predicted since there is no coherent model in biology that will support such prediction.

The resolution of the Contradiction Matrix and biological systems may be likely to lie mainly in the 50% of the Matrix that is symmetrical and Socratic. This may or may not turn out to be true, but it suggests that the most productive area for the discovery and analysis of valid comparisons will be in the area of trade-offs whose symmetry and adaptiveness are well understood both in biology and in engineering.

It is important that biological trade-offs are assessed independently of any consideration of physics or engineering. The literature of biomimetics has many examples of a biomimetic transfer where the assessment of the biology has been made from the point of view of engineering or physics [7, 14, 20]. This is largely because the biological information is being interpreted by an engineer—more a reflection of the low number of biologists involved in biomimetics. This has the unwanted result of a strong bias towards engineering, leading to the deduction in one case [21] that some 95% of biological 'innovations' for inclusion in the Contradiction Matrix are not novel to engineering. This is not necessarily a result of the way that biology works, but a result of sampling bias of individual cases which have been interpreted by an engineer rather than taking the biologist's independent assessment of the trade-off. Unfortunately, although many biological studies successfully identify the trade-off under investigation, only some 40% of these identify the factors involved. It is these factors, equivalent to the Inventive Principles of TRIZ, that are the agents of change and control, and that therefore supply the iconoclastic impulse.

2.5 Using Established Tools of Computer Science to Build a Framework

In order for these insights and ideas to be brought to fruition, they have to be arranged in a logical and dynamic framework. The ubiquitous data base is incapable of a dynamic response, but the terms in a data base, arranged hierarchically and with their relationships mapped simply, can be arranged into a Simple Knowledge Organisation System (SKOS) [22] that can be developed within the editing environment of Protégé, an open source editor more commonly used for developing ontologies [23]. Since the relationships in a SKOS are relatively broad and unruly, it is possible to generate a network of terms in a fairly short time; this network can be displayed in Protégé and explored interactively easily. But it is not easy to use such a network for analysis and prediction; it can possibly stimulate creativity but it cannot establish facts or laws. For this we need an ontology.

In its simplest form, an ontology is a standardised vocabulary. Connectivity of the items in that vocabulary is more easily obtained since computers can be programmed to deal with the logical web of reasoning that the ontologist creates.

The ontology is written in OWL2, the main language of the semantic Web, using the editor Protégé, available from Stanford University. It follows the organisation of the Basic Formal Ontology (BFO) thus ensuring that it can be integrated with other ontologies following the same, widely adopted, format. The BFO has as its primary classification 'continuants' (things which persist through time) and 'occurrents' (events which occur in time and space) [24]. The main continuants are objects, which exist in the absence of any other characteristics. They are therefore independent of those characteristics. However, they have descriptors of one sort or another, such as size, colour, mechanical properties and inbuilt tendencies. These descriptors would not exist without the objects they describe, and so they are dependent continuants. In this ontology, the objects are animals and plants and the things of which they are composed. The 39 Engineering Parameters are descriptors of the objects, and so they are dependent continuants. They have been modified from the TRIZ originals to give them relevance to biology. Thus, Parameter number 31, usually entitled 'harmful side effects', now includes autoimmunity as a possible side effect of the immune system, an essential component of the organism's defence system (Fig. 2). Parameter number 39, 'productivity', includes growth, fecundity and rate of foraging (Fig. 3).

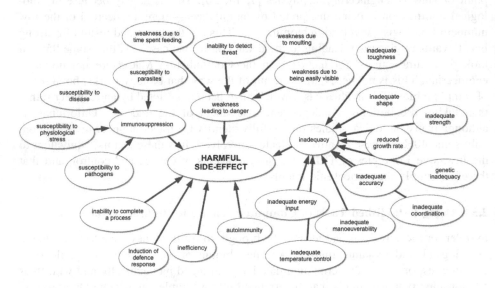

Fig. 2. Structure of class and sub-classes of Parameter 31, Harmful Side-effect

The Inventive Principles are the means of change or adaptation, and so they are events which occur in time – that is, they are occurrents. These principles have been adapted and reformatted to accommodate principles of biological control and change. Thus, principle 26, 'copying', includes reproduction, camouflage and substitution (as when a male spider gives the female a faux prey item during courtship, or a cuckoo lays its egg in an alien nest) (Fig. 4); principle 22, 'convert harm to benefit', includes altruism and sacrificial bonds in the matrix of ceramic composites such as bone (Fig. 5).

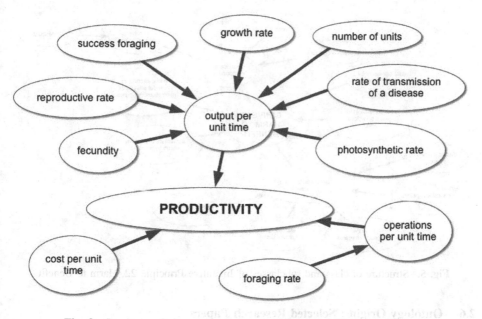

Fig. 3. Structure of class and subclasses of Parameter 39, Productivity

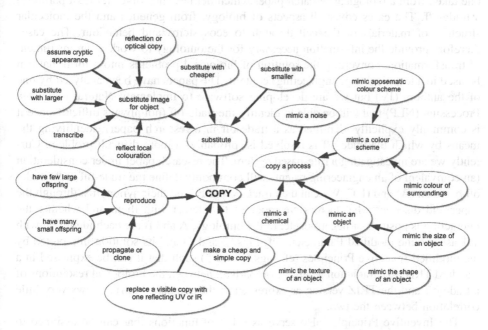

Fig. 4. Structure of class and subclasses of Inventive Principle 26, Copying

Fig. 5. Structure of class and subclasses of Inventive Principle 22, Harm to Benefit

2.6   Ontology Origins: Selected Research Papers

The ontology in its present condition derives its information from some 400 cases, each one taken from a biological research paper which defines and solves (at least partially) a trade-off. The cases cover all aspects of biology, from genetics and the molecular structure of materials of the cell through to ecosystems and behaviour. The cases therefore provide the information necessary for the ontology to work as an instrument of transformation, converting the solution of biological problems into a form that can be used in a technical (e.g. engineering) context. The papers have been analysed by one of the authors (JV) but we are developing software to implement Natural Language Processing (NLP) that will be able to identify the trade-off (not always difficult since it is commonly explicitly identified as a trade-off in a research paper); identifying the means by which the trade-off is resolved is (probably) a more difficult problem. Currently we are investigating a rule-based system. The research paper under consideration (an equivalent of an engineering patent) will commonly define the trade-off as "a trade-off between (A) and (B)". We can then track A and B, and their synonyms, through the paper and discover what factors are reported to interact with them and whether the interaction is positive or negative, etc. In the ontology, A and B are each identified with at least one the modified Parameters (cf. Figs. 2 and 3) and its solution interpreted by the modified Inventive Principles (cf. Figs. 4 and 5) such that it can be expressed in a standard TRIZ Contradiction Matrix. Comparison between the biological resolutions of a trade-off and the TRIZ version as expressed in the standard Matrix shows very little correlation between the two.

The Inventive Principles also serve as a list of functions that can be assigned to biological objects. Thus, it is possible to identify biological structures that can serve as instances of various functions (Fig. 6). The tube foot of an echinoderm is both a deployable structure (principle: dynamism) and a hydraulic dynamic effector (principle:

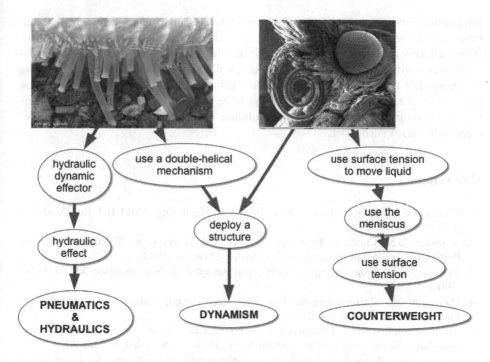

Fig. 6. Characterisation of echinoderm tube feet and butterfly proboscis

pneumatics and hydraulics). Another deployable structure – the proboscis of lepi-dopterous insects uses surface-tension forces to move a liquid (surface-tension effect in the principle: counterweight). Thus we have a more phenomenological access to functionality in biology, available for biomimetics that is directly available for the interpretation of trade-offs.

3 Next Steps

The ontology is built, but only as proof of concept in that it needs more data from solved biological trade-offs and (probably) additions to the list of biological continu-ants. The computerised analysis of relevant research papers will speed up collection of data. Currently we are investigating NLP, but it is possible that machine learning could prove useful, although since each biological trade-off is necessarily considered as an individual item. this requirement might not fit with the more statistical approach taken by machine learning.

Next we need to design interfaces that allow the ontology to be interrogated by both humans and by autonomous agents. The former is not too difficult; Protégé already has several graphical interfaces that can display inter-relationships and results of searches. It's the way autonomous agents will be able to interact that's exciting and some way off. The scenario is as follows: An agent has a problem of some sort which it defines as a trade-off. It goes to the ontology informing it of the trade-off plus any contextual information. The ontology searches for all examples of that trade off, then matches all or some of the contextual information, and identifies cases that match these conditions. It then informs the agent of the Inventive Principles that resolved that particular trade-off, together with information about the biological components that were active during resolution. It's then up to the agent to select from this information what changes are relevant for it to resolve or manipulate the trade-off. Further research may orient us towards a complete AI system for the resolution of technical problems with a biomimetic solution, if such exists.

References

1. Vincent, J.F.V.: Biomimetics - a review. Proc. Inst. Mech. Eng. PART H-J. Eng. Med. **223** (H8), 919–939 (2009)
2. Altshuller, G.S.: Creativity As an Exact Science: The Theory of the Solution of Inventive Problems. Gordon and Breach Science Publishers, London (1984)
3. Vincent, J.F.V.: Biomimetics: its practice and theory. J. R. Soc. Interface **3**(9), 471–482 (2006)
4. Darlington, M.J.: Investigating ontology development for engineering design support. Adv. Eng. Inform. **22**(1), 112–134 (2008)
5. Artificial Intelligence - foundations of computational agents – 13.3 Ontologies and Knowledge Sharing. http://artint.info/html/ArtInt_316.html. Accessed 08 May 2018
6. Fayemi, P.E., Wanieck, K., Zollfrank, C., Maranzana, N., Aoussat, A.: Biomimetics: process, tools and practice. Bioinspir. Biomim. **12**(1), 011002 (2017)
7. Abdala, L.N., Fernandes, R.B., Ogliari, A., Löwer, M., Feldhusen, J.: Creative contributions of the methods of inventive principles of TRIZ and BioTRIZ to problem solving. J. Mech. Des. **139**(8), 082001 (2017)
8. Chen, J.L., Hung, S.C.: Eco-innovation by TRIZ and biomimetics design. In: 2017 International Conference on Applied System Innovation (ICASI), pp. 40–43 (2017)
9. Chen, J.L., Yang, Y.-C.: Eco-innovation by integrating biomimetic with TRIZ ideality and evolution rules. In: Hesselbach, J., Herrmann, C. (eds.) Glocalized Solutions for Sustainability in Manufacturing, pp. 101–106. Springer, Berlin, Heidelberg (2011). https://doi.org/10.1007/978-3-642-19692-8_18
10. Cohen, Y.H., Reich, Y., Greenberg, C.S.: Integrating TRIZ knowledge through biomimetic design, p. 2
11. Kamps, T., Münzberg, C., Stacheder, L., Seidel, C., Reinhart, G., Lindemann, U.: TRIZ-based biomimetic part-design for Laser Additive Manufacturing, p. 10
12. Kobayashi, T., Isono, Y., Arai, K., Yamauchi, T., Kobayashi, H.: Bio-TRIZ database for sustainable lifestyle technology transfer from nature to engineering. In: 2017 International Electronics Symposium on Knowledge Creation and Intelligent Computing (IES-KCIC), pp. 276–280 (2017)
13. Trotta, M.G.: Bio-inspired design methodology. Int. J. Inf. Sci. **1**(1), 1–11 (2011)
14. Badarnah, L., Kadri, U.: A methodology for the generation of biomimetic design concepts. Archit. Sci. Rev. **58**(2), 120–133 (2015)
15. Cohen, Y.H., Reich, Y.: The Biomimicry discipline: boundaries, definitions, drivers, promises and limits. Biomimetic Design Method for Innovation and Sustainability, pp. 3–17. Springer, Cham (2016). https://doi.org/10.1007/978-3-319-33997-9_1
16. Barth, F.G., Humphrey, J.A.C., Secomb, T.W.: Sensors and Sensing in Biology and Engineering. Springer, Berlin (2012). https://doi.org/10.1007/978-3-7091-6025-1

17. Mercer, E.H.: The Foundations of Biological Theory. Wiley, Hoboken (1981)
18. Rousselot, F., Zanni-Merk, C., Cavallucci, D.: Towards a formal definition of contradiction in inventive design. Comput. Ind. **63**(3), 231–242 (2012)
19. Dubois, S., Eltzer, T., de Guio, R.: A dialectical based model coherent with inventive and optimization problems. Comput. Ind. **60**(8), 575–583 (2009)
20. Lindemann, U., Gramann, J.: Engineering design using biological principles. The Design Society - a Worldwide Community 2004. (2004) https://www.designsociety.org/publication/19775/ENGINEERING+DESIGN+USING+BIOLOGICAL+PRINCIPLES. Accessed 08 May 2018
21. Vincent, J.F.V., Mann, D.L.: Systematic technology transfer from biology to engineering. Philos. Trans. R. Soc. Math. Phys. Eng. Sci. **360**(1791), 159–173 (2002)
22. Miles, A., Appleton, C.R., Brickley, D.: SKOS Core: Simple Knowledge Organisation for the Web, p. 8 (2005)
23. Noy, N.F., Sintek, M., Decker, S., Crubezy, M., Fergerson, R.W., Musen, M.A.: Creating semantic web contents with protege-2000. IEEE Intell. Syst. **16**(2), 60–71 (2001)
24. Arp, R., Smith, B.: Function, role and disposition in basic formal ontology. In: Proceedings of Bio-Ontologies Workshop, Intelligent Systems for Molecular Biology (ISMB), Toronto, pp. 45–48 (2008)

Education

GamiTRIZation – Gamification for TRIZ Education

Claudia Hentschel[1(✉)], Christian M. Thurnes[2], and Frank Zeihsel[3]

[1] University of Applied Sciences HTW Berlin, Berlin, Germany
claudia.hentschel@htw-berlin.de
[2] UAS Kaiserslautern, Competence Centre OPINNOMETH,
Zweibruecken, Germany
[3] Synnovating GmbH, Kaiserslautern, Germany

Abstract. TRIZ provides tools and methods to meet complex challenges. Since most TRIZ-capabilities are based not only on theory but also on practical application, today's challenge is to make people not just learn about the TRIZ-method, but to learn actual skills and to get something done with them in a given time frame.

Learning TRIZ needs interactive settings to quickly transfer knowledge and methods into action. TRIZ-experts usually can rely on a long-term practice. Games and cases allow to teach and multiply this experience by activating learners and emphasizing individual capabilities – even by adding a fun factor. That is why gamification actually is a recognized learning and teaching approach.

The authors have compiled, reviewed and analyzed a number of games and cases that offer playful learning and teaching of a variety of different TRIZ tools. The article gives an overview about the used settings and types of games and cases.

Keywords: Game · Case · Gamification · GamiTRIZation · TRIZ education

1 Introduction

Consider the intensity with which students engage in activities during their leisure time, such as sports, music, photography and video games. Motivation, learning and education seem to reach their peak in such situations, as engagement is coupled with intense personal commitment and involvement. This is why the authors felt that motivation and learning are but two sides of the same issue.

Play plays an important role in learning, and "Games are perhaps the first designed interactive system our species invented." [1, p. 1]. The number of new contents, subjects and fields to attain competences in is rising. So is the complexity in which competencies have to be conveyed, e.g. within a limited time frame and to groups of people from a wide variety of technical and cultural backgrounds. Within this setting, play is more and more recognized as an answer to learning [2].

The authors' interest in using playful elements for education is derived from their outstanding objective guided by the question of how to promote situations in where

- students from various backgrounds (e.g. kids and adults, different cultures, technical and non-technical, …)

D. Cavallucci et al. (Eds.): TFC 2018, IFIP AICT 541, pp. 29–39, 2018.
https://doi.org/10.1007/978-3-030-02456-7_3

- are motivated to learn,
- engage in the (learning and teaching) act,
- are ensuring that learning will occur and willing to reflect their learning act and
- find the learning process – not just the learning outcome – to be satisfying.

These goals seem largely unattainable at the same time. However, this is a common challenge, which teachers and trainers experience every day. Teachers, instructional designers, and trainers should not refrain from encouraging or expecting play behavior in their students when they wish to sustainably reach these goals for their attendees, never mind what the field is. The purpose of this article is to propose play in general and games and cases as special goal for learning and teaching TRIZ – considered a "hard nut to crack" for learners and teachers alike.

The authors compiled the best TRIZ games and cases known at the moment (status: **April 2018**) to transfer each learning and teaching act into an interactive situation, where the process and outcome produces high sustainability within the players. They go even further and suggest that learning environments that conjure up playful situations deserve recognition especially for spreading the TRIZ method, its tools and applications – due to the contradictory condition that TRIZ itself comprises. It is considered as highly fruitful and efficient in solving difficult, risk-creating problems, but at the same time is difficult, risky and time-consuming to learn in a way that it can be fruitfully and efficiently applied. To overcome this contradiction, play is considered a compromise-avoiding and at the same time contemporary answer; it shows contradictory elements itself.

2   The Paradox of Play

The English language distinguishes clearly between the words "play" and "game", while in German (the authors' mother tongues) this distinction does not exist. It is simply to be translated as "Spiel". Exploring the English sources, it turns out, that two basic relationships between the terms play and game can be found [3, p. 72, 73]:

1. Play is a component of games: Games are complex phenomena and there are many ways to frame them and understand them.
2. Games are a subset of play: Play represents many kinds of playful activity. Some of these activities are games, but some are not.

As it looks, both terms can be used interchangeably; nevertheless, the authors have decided to follow the second, in which play is considered as highlighting the wider sense of the issue, and games being one component of it. Other sub-components, the authors are familiar with in their business affiliations and especially in their field of production management issues, are cases and simulations, e.g. to perfectly convey the ideas of lean production [4]. For their current research highlighted in this paper, they have restricted to games and cases, the latter being considered here as another subset of the wide definition of play.

Cases highlight given situations, in which the player has to solve some problem or fulfill some task, usually in a given time frame. In many situations, it is hard to decide whether a game or a case is at hand, as also a game may contain case-elements, and vice-versa. The authors sometimes intuitively decided about a repartition based on their experience in training issues, with heavily considering the main aspect underlying each of them: the fun-factor and that it would work interactively for the participants. These considerations paved the way for a newly published book entitled "Playing TRIZ – Games and Cases for learning and teaching inventiveness" [5]. This paper here more or less tells the story why the authors came up with such a publication.

For going deeper into the issue, various elements of the definitions of games and play are available (for an overview, see again [3]). The main author herewith deliberately selected some elements of play and games, and complemented the authors' own thoughts on cases, which led to a better understanding of the three (Table 1).

Table 1. Selected elements of a play, game and case (as understood by authors), '++' = applies fully, '+' = applies.

Element of understanding	Play	Game	Case
Proceeds according to rules limiting players		++	+
Goal-oriented/Outcome-oriented		+	++
For its own sake	++		
Activity, process or event (time frame)		+	++
Commitment		+	+
Conflict to be solved		+	++
Task to be fulfilled			++
Involves decision-making/influence		+	++
Entertaining and fun	++	+	+
Artificial/Safe, outside ordinary life	++	+	+
Creates special (social) groups	+		
Cooperation/Connection between people		++	++
Competition between groups/Players		++	+
System of parts/Resources and tokens		+	++
Absorbing, energy taking	++	+	+
...			

At a brief glance one could state that play is ideally considered as something free, without limitation and without being taken "serious", as they work for its own sake. It sometimes even works without any material or physical token, and may just be fired by phantasy and imagination. Games and cases are more goal-oriented and limited, either by rules and/or by time, and in many cases require or offer game pawns or tokens. Perhaps, play is the ideal (according to the understanding of Ideality in TRIZ) as it constitutes human's life right after birth, needs nothing and is thus essential for human development [6].

This can easily be understood when we observe children playing. They may be engaged or even engrossed (which is called "Flow", see [7]) in an activity which for them is pleasurable for its own sake. At the same time, nobody would doubt that they are not learning anything. They might behave cooperatively and connectedly or working for oneself and for their or its own sake – just for the fun of it. Even if they are willing to commit a great amount of time and energy, they are enjoying themselves and even accept false starts and frustration, e.g. for not proceeding faster or achieving some result. They simply try again and see how it works. Being called to stop might be the only frustration they encounter. With such behavior, they are learning a lot, but for them it does not feel so.

Adults, on the other hand, have mostly internalized that analytical thinking is worthwhile; but possessing a lot of knowledge and/or life experience might be a hindrance when encountering new situations or solving complex problems, in which thriving through could be a much better approach [8]. Nevertheless, the prevailing logic especially in groups and when there is limited time is, that outcomes are much better when everybody follows rules.

Paradoxically, rules can also help to break rules, contributing to new, innovative ideas and outcomes. Rules, as limiting as they may seem, may also open possibilities and make broaden our perspectives, which again is the beginning of exploration – and then play. With a closer look on the elements' column above, apart from these contradictions, many others could be enumerated, with parameter 1 as the one we would like to achieve, but parameter 2 considered as the possible deteriorating one (Table 2).

Table 2. Selected (technical) contradictions of play(-ful situations) for learning.

Contradiction #	Parameter 1	Parameter 2
1	Entertainment	Serious (learning) outcome
2	Enjoyment, fun	Engagement
3	For one's own sake, for it's own sake	Engaged for an outcome, for an activity, for competition,...
4	Cooperation and connection	Competition
5	Team-building/belonging/(social) groups	Working for oneself/achievement/working for a task
6	Winning	Losing
7	Exploring/Thriving through a given (new) situation	Gaining influence on and control over a given situation
8	Nobody forcing, free will, ...	For an outcome, for an objective, ...
9	Freedom, anarchy, creativity,...	Limitation of players, rules, structure, organization, ...
10	Rules (to break (former) rules)	Rising complexity
11	Ignorance if own knowledge will be helpful	Commitment
12	Real-life situation	Artificial/Story telling
13	...	...

Altogether, play as an activity for children always sounded fine, but adults often bristle at the thought, that play would describe something that they do, especially when we leave leisure aside and come to work or even education. For very long, work was considered the opposite of play [2].

This is the reason, why the term play nowadays seems to cheapen or degrade a learning experience, especially if it is for work purposes, and if so, the entertaining element is not taken serious. So it is no wonder, that in many sources we read about "serious play" to indicate all kinds of so-called real and hard learning, innovation and training outcomes achieved by playful elements [2, 9–11].

Fortunately, some recent authors are heavily calling for returning to more play in our (children's and adult's) life again, and even state that playfulness is the key to everything, not just creativity and inventiveness [12–14]. This trend is also supported by the growing market of digital computer games that frequently convey the term "gamification" not only in education, but in all aspects of life [15, 16].

The paradoxical and even contradictory situation of play being at once too complex to fully understand, and predicting yet an everyday phenomena just waiting to emerge, is why the authors have taken such an interest in games and cases to transfer knowledge in their classes and trainings [4, 17]. Fortunately, play nowadays is more and more considered a suitable goal for learning situations that demand creative higher-order thinking and a strong sense of personal commitment and engagement [2, 10, 18]. Play is doing something right, and that "something" involves a complex set of conditions, especially when it comes to the comparatively difficult subject to learn – TRIZ.

3   Playing TRIZ – Overcoming Contradictions

3.1   Learning and Teaching TRIZ with Games and Cases

Learning TRIZ is not easy – but teaching TRIZ is even more difficult. Ellen Domb already explained this problem in detail [19]. Her thoughts in part were based on the "revised bloom's taxonomy for learning" [20]. This taxonomy contains the following levels of learning: the first (or lowest) level is "remembering", followed by "understanding", "applying", "analyzing", "evaluating" and "creating" the last or highest level. Of course there are also many other models of individual and group learning in classical and newer learning theories and considerations on how these theories can be used in teaching [21].

Many classical teaching approaches are based on taxonomies or classifications such as the one mentioned above. If teaching methods are dedicated to address only one certain level, it is easy to understand that different teaching methods may be better suited for one of these levels than for another one [19].

Teaching TRIZ typically addresses several levels of such taxonomies. In many cases the underlying learning theory is more process-oriented than leveled. The models of single-loop, double-loop and deutero-learning [22], e.g. can be used to design cases or simulations for learning (and also teaching) the proper usage, evaluation, reflection and further development of methods and processes. The design of cases based on these learning models, for example, is used to enable students at the university to deeply understand and learn TRIZ-forecasting [23].

Games, cases and simulations fit very well to the requirements that are often placed on the teaching and learning of TRIZ. If we think in terms of learning models such as the above taxonomy, games and cases offer the possibility to combine several specific methods for the learning objectives on specific levels by combining different phases, game situations etc. If one thinks in terms of more systemic or process-oriented learning models, games, cases and simulations deliver the loops for e.g. single- and double-loop learning, as well as the experience for deutero-learning.

Many teachers, consultants and professors use project- or problem-based tasks, case-studies for teaching TRIZ – a look at the proceedings of international TRIZ-conferences shows a wide range of specific teaching concepts. Problem- and project-based learning is a traditional learning-method in TRIZ-learning – even classical TRIZ books use many real-world examples to explain and illustrate knowledge, see e.g. [24].

The usage of games and the enrichment of case-studies towards more activating cases without pre-defined solutions fit also very well to these teaching thoughts and go hand in hand with the rising significance of gamification-approaches. There are certainly many interesting games and cases for learning and teaching TRIZ – some approaches have already been presented at conferences, e.g. in [23, 25]. However, since many treasures are still hidden, the authors have launched a call for papers to make successful games accessible to the general public, and thus support a stronger growth of gamification in the field of TRIZ.

3.2   Dealing with the Paradox in Play – Some Examples

In chapter 2 some paradoxes and contradictions in the use of games as learning methods were mentioned. Some games deliberately use such contradictions. The following examples will illustrate this:

The presented game "Umbrella 5.0" [5] is a game for children, which is held at the university as a learning event for school children. They work together in groups and these groups compete with each other. This competition ensures a high level of commitment and motivates the children very strongly. However, experience has shown that at the end of the game the disappointment is very big among the groups that cannot consider themselves winners. However, if the competition is waived, motivation and activity of the children are lower as in the competition scenario.

This contradiction can be treated as a physical contradiction (in terms of TRIZ): There should be some competition between the groups so that the children are highly motivated AND there should be no competition between the groups so that the children are not frustrated in the end. In this case, the contradiction seems to have been resolved by separation in time, but with a closer view it is resolved by separation in relation: In the first phase of the game, the children get the impression that the groups compete with each other – this gives them great fun and motivation to be better than other groups. At the same time, however, the competition does not already name winners or losers – instead, it just prepares them for a "big final".

With this feeling and mindset, the children start into the second and final phase. However, due to an almost imperceptible change in the rules, the groups no longer compete with each other in the end. Instead, the solution ideas (of all group members) compete for the favor of each single child. While in the first phase, the evaluation is (apparently) the responsibility of the professor, in the second phase it is transferred to each individual child. That is why, in the end, there are no *children* that are winners or losers – the winners are not human, the winners are *ideas*. The gentle change of the rules leads to a first phase with different conditions and relationships than in the second phase [5].

A much simpler contradiction in the same game arose initially from the grouping of the teams. The grouping was necessary in order to create a competitive structure. But the grouping required a lot of time, because the children do not know each other and sometimes are shy. In total, however, only a very short period of about 90 min is available for the whole event. This contradiction was solved by separation in time, or specifically "preliminary action". Today the tables and chairs are already arranged to groups *before* the children arrive and they automatically build the groups when they sit down [5].

The contradiction between rules (as a means of reducing complexity), and the necessity of being able to deal with growing complexity can be found in the game "TRIZmeta" by Darell Mann and Cara Faulkner [5]. Changing the rules of the game in parlour games (using TRIZ rules) creates a deep understanding of the TRIZ rules on the one hand and of reacting to changes and the individual learning process on the other. The learning models of single-loop and double-loop learning explained above can clearly be recognized in this game.

4 Compilation of TRIZ Games and Cases

4.1 Call for Papers for Chapter Creation

In order to show the already existing variety of games for TRIZ training and to increase their distribution, the authors launched a "call for chapter" in 2017. The submissions would be reviewed and published in a book in the autumn of 2018.

The aim was to provide as broad an overview as possible. Therefore, no narrow classifications regarding "game, play, case, simulation…" was asked for. Conversely, however, the collection may be used to develop such classifications for TRIZ-games or game-like forms of TRIZ-learning.

The call for chapter asked the authors to describe their game. Information on the practical implementation was also requested, e.g.: duration, number of attendees, materials, educational objectives/competencies and the areas of TRIZ addressed by the game or simulation.

There have been many requests of interested authors. Finally, 19 abstracts were submitted. It is expected that 13 of these games and cases will be described in detail in the book [5]. All examplified hints for games and cases given here will make part of the book, but not all games and cases could be referred to herewith, as the work in progress and the deadline for this paper more or less fall together.

4.2   Characteristics of the Games and Cases

Gamification maybe defined in various ways. With regard to the authors' goal to explore the variety of games in the TRIZ environment, a very broad definition of gamification may be helpful as a basis to explore the collected games and cases: "The application of gaming metaphors to real life tasks to influence behavior, improve motivation and enhance engagement" [26, p. 4].

In all submitted games "influence behavior, improve motivation and enhance engagement", is of major concern to increase the ability to solve problems with the help of TRIZ-tools or -principles. The "application of gaming metaphors" is very different for each individual contribution. This is illustrated below, using quality criteria for games as they are identified by the successful German game developer Kramer [27]: Originality, Replay, Chance to win, Surprise, Timing, Consistency and Quality of Materials, Influence, Target Group, Easy Start and Rule Complexity [acc. to 27].

Originality. Almost every game contains new elements. In some games, well known TRIZ-tools are used to solve witty problems. Some games invite the player to bring in his or her own problems – in these cases the rules of the game are the main aspect of novelty. Besides that, the criterion "originality" is always in relation with the target audience: people that never worked on Ellen Domb's (the author of, among TRIZniks very well-known "Titanic TRIZ", see her experience in learning and teaching TRIZ in [19]) Titanic-TRIZ-Case (see as well in [5]) will find it a very witty and entertaining endeavor.

Replay. According to Kramer [27], a good game should provide incentives for its replay. This only partially applies to the collected TRIZ games and cases. Some games are generic – they introduce general rules and procedures, but deal with individual problems and can be repeated by the same person for many problems. Other games, on the other hand, deal with specific problems and therefore offer little incentive to be used several times by the same person in exactly this form. Such specific schemes can of course be used to develop further games and/or cases in analogy. An algorithmic computer game does not offer these possibilities – it is certainly attractive to play this one, two or three times, after that the player should look forward to some new levels or another program.

Chance to Win. In many games, there are winners and losers. In other games, all participants win – for example, in the fight against a threatening situation, as is the case with the Titanic problem.

Surprise. Good games contain surprising elements. Many of the collected TRIZ games contain elements based on chance that deliver surprises. The course of the game is therefore not exactly predictable, but suddenly shows variations. These variations are realized, for example, by drawing cards: Using the 40 innovation principles (IP) in a Lean TRIZ game, IP cards are drawn randomly. In a TRIZ-Bionics board game by Nick Eckert, see in [5], the game pieces are moved because of dice results and another action follows depending on the field reached on the board.

Timing. If several groups or single players take part in a game, the game sequence should ensure that the game ends for all at the same time. If one is finished much earlier than others, these players would have to wait, which does not have a positive effect on motivation and makes it difficult to facilitate the game. Some games with several groups therefore have a stock of problems that is larger than the amount of problems expected to be solved. In this way, faster groups can be employed with additional tasks or rounds, as long as slower groups also finish.

Consistency and Quality of Materials. The materials should be consistent. The Apollo 13 TRIZ-Case [see in 5], for example, remains consistently with its topic throughout the entire process and uses photos and other media from the original situation.

Influence. Players should be able to influence the game and be able to involve themselves to a certain extent. In most TRIZ games, this is at least done by generating solutions with the help of TRIZ tools. In other cases, various elements, such as the selection of problems to be solved or even the rules of the game, can also be influenced by the players.

Target Group. All TRIZ-games and cases submitted have defined certain target groups. These are, for example, job-related target groups, such as production workers looking for waste elimination or age-specific target groups such as children between the ages of 8 and 12. Other target groups are defined by the level of knowledge or ambition – so a computer game on the 40 innovation principles is mainly aimed at TRIZ beginners (although TRIZ professionals may also enjoy this).

Excitement. TRIZ-games and cases should not be boring. Excitement and suspense can be controlled through the game play. Many of the games collected rely on consciously controlled processes with phases of high tension and rather relaxing phases.

Easy Start Many of the collected TRIZ games and cases allow a very easy start of the game. In these games, required TRIZ knowledge is built up during the course of the game. However, this is difficult if the game requires very extensive TRIZ knowledge and experience. In such games, the leaders of the game often switch to more extensive instructional TRIZ sessions before or during the game. The games can therefore not be judged as "good" or "bad" on this criterion, because it also depends very much on whether the games are played separately or are integrated into a larger context.

Rule Complexity. Kramer [27] emphasizes, that the complexity of the rules of the game should correspond to the complexity of the content. So simple games should also have simple rules. This is often the case with the collected TRIZ games. In some games, however, the complexity of the rules of the game overlaps with the complexity of TRIZ methods to be applied. This increases the complexity in certain game situations very much.

5   Outlook

The actual collection of TRIZ Games and Cases is the beginning of an empirical research in terms of analysis and synthesis of this topic. The Call for Chapter deliberately formulated only very vaguely what "games, cases, and simulation" is all about. As there have been numerous expressions of interest from further authors, national and international, volume 2 of the book is envisaged to continue the collection of existing approaches.

If a larger number of examples would have been collected, research activities can be carried out further. Based on a broader collection of examples, classifications and investigations can be developed with regard to various criteria. It will then be easier to define which special features gamification has in the area of TRIZ education – which are therefore special characteristics of "GamiTRIZation", for the first time coined as a term within this paper here.

References

1. Zimmerman, E.: Manifesto for a Ludic Century. https://kotaku.com/manifesto-the-21st-century-will-be-defined-by-games-1275355204. Accessed 09 Mar 2018
2. Rieber, L.P., Smith, L., Noah, D.: The value of serious play. Educ. Technol. **38**(6), 29–37 (1998)
3. Salen, K., Zimmerman, E.: Rules of Play – Game Design Fundamentals. MIT Press, Cambridge (2004)
4. Bicheno, J., Thurnes, C.M.: Lean Simulationen und Spiele. Synnovating GmbH, Kaiserslautern (2016)
5. Thurnes, C.M., Hentschel, C., Zeihsel, F. (eds.): Playing TRIZ – Games and Cases for Teaching and Learning Inventiveness. Synnovating GmbH, Kaiserslautern (2019)
6. Huizinga, J.: Homo Ludens – Um Ursprung der Kultur im Spiel, 24th edn. Rowohlt Taschenbuch Verlag, Reinbek bei Hamburg (2015). Original Version (1938)
7. Csikszentmihalyi, M.: Flow: The Psychology of Optimal Experience. Harper & Row, New York (1990)
8. Czinki, A., Hentschel, C.: Solving complex problems and TRIZ. In: Belski, I. (ed.) Structured Innovation with TRIZ in Science and Industry – Creating Value for Customers and Society, pp. 27—32. Elsevier, Amsterdam (2016)
9. Hohmann, L.: Innovation Games: Creating Breakthrough Products through Collaborative Play. Addison Wesley, New York (2007)
10. Michael, D., Chen, S.: Serious Games: Games that Educate, Train, and Inform. Thompson Course Technlogy PTR, Boston (2006)
11. Schrage, M.: Serious Play: How the World's Best Companies Simulate to Innovate. Harvard Business School Press, Boston (2000)
12. Hüther, G., Quarch, C.: Rettet das Spiel – Weil Leben mehr als Funktionieren ist. HANSER Verlag, München (2016)
13. Kelley, D., Kelley, T.: Creative Confidence: Unleashing the Creative Potential Within Us All. HarperCollins Publishers, New York (2015)
14. Henderson, S.J., Moore, R.K.: Fostering Inventiveness in Children. Library of Congress, North Charleston (2013)

15. Busch, C.: Gamification – technologies and methods of digital games as innovation drivers in creative and other industries. In: Holl, F., Kiefer, D. (eds.) Creative Sprint – A Collaborative View on Challenges and Opportunities in the Creative Sector, pp. 112–130. University of Applied Sciences Brandenburg, Brandenburg (Havel) (2014)

16. McGonigal, J.: SuperBetter – a revolutionary approach to getting stronger, happier, braver and more. In: German: Gamify Your LIFE – Durch Gamification Glücklicher, Gesünder und Resilienter Leben. Herder Verlag, Freiburg (2016)

17. Hentschel, C.: EduGames for complex problem solving – play or pray for innovation. In: Knaut, M. (ed.) Industrie von morgen. Beiträge und Positionen der HTW Berlin, pp. 18–25. BWV Berliner Wissenschafts-Verlag, Berlin (2017)

18. Werbach, K., Hunter, D.: For the Win – How Game Thinking can Revolutionize Your Business. Wharton Digital Press, Philadelphia (2012)

19. Domb, H.: Teaching TRIZ is not learning TRIZ. TRIZ-J. (2008). https://triz-journal.com/teaching-triz-does-not-equal-learning-triz/. Accessed 05 Apr 2018

20. Anderson, L., Krathwohl, D.R. (eds.): A Taxonomy for Learning, Teaching and Assessing: A Revision of Bloom's Taxonomy of Educational Objectives. Longman, New York (2001)

21. Bates, B.: Learning Theories Simplified: … and how to apply them to teaching. Sage, Thousand Oaks (2015)

22. Argyris, C., Schoen, D.A.: Die lernende Organisation, 3rd edn. Klett-Cotta, Stuttgart (2008)

23. Thurnes, C.M., Zeihsel, F., Fuchs, R.: Competency-based learning in TRIZ – Teaching TRIZ forecasting as example. Innov. – J. Eur. TRIZ Assoc. 1(02), 128–133 (2016)

24. Altshuller, G.S.: Creativity as an Exact Science: The Theory of the Solution of Inventive Problems. Gordon and Breach, London (1984)

25. Cascini, G., Saliminamin, S., Parvin, M., Pahlavani, F.: OTSM-TRIZ games: enhancing creativity of engineering students. Procedia Eng. 131, 711–720 (2015)

26. Marczewski, A.: Gamification: A Simple Introduction. Amazon Media, Seattle (2013)

27. Kramer, W.: Was macht ein Spiel zu einem guten Spiel? http://www.kramer-spiele.de/vortraege/vortrag2.htm. Accessed 05 Apr 2018

Paradoxes and Organizational Learning in Continuous Improvement Approaches: Using the TRIZ Principles for Developing Problem Solving Performance in a Michelin Plant

Zahir Messaoudene[✉]

ECAM Lyon, 40 Montée Saint Barthélemy, 69321 Lyon, France
zahir.messaoudene@ecam.fr

Abstract. Continuous improvement approaches advocate the development of organizational learning to support the system of problem solving. For this, companies use different strategies for implementing of continuous improvement. A survey has been conducted showing that these strategies can have a paradoxical impact on the performance of problem solving. How can we explain the difficulties faced by companies in the development of problem solving? The classical learning model used by the majority of companies generates contradictions called "empirical". To provide an innovative contribution to the problem-solving learning problematic, TRIZ theory and paradox theory are used to characterize a problem model (in the form of paradoxes and organizational tensions) and a solution model (in the form of paradoxical practices). Finally, a case study in the form of experimentation in one of the Michelin factories is realized. The specific problem is modeled using TRIZ and the paradoxical approach. An organizational innovation called "problem solving pull (PSP ©)" has been developed. This specific solution made it possible to eliminate some of the tensions and make the problem-solving learning system more dynamic.

Keywords: Paradoxes management · Problem solving
Learning organizational

1 Introduction

For more than 30 years, continuous improvement initiatives (CII) such as Lean Management have been very successful in improving industrial performance. CII advocate the development of problem solving by operational teams. However, companies do not always achieve the expected results [1, 2]. Several studies have identified sustainability difficulties [3–5]. *If more and more organizations are deploying of problem-solving practices, how can we explain the difficulties faced by companies? What are the contradictions that justify these difficulties?*

To answer these first questions, we conducted a survey of operational teams in several companies. The contradictions that come from the speeches of production agents and managers will be exposed. Their impacts on the learning process of problem solving will be formalized.

© IFIP International Federation for Information Processing 2018
Published by Springer Nature Switzerland AG 2018. All Rights Reserved
D. Cavallucci et al. (Eds.): TFC 2018, IFIP AICT 541, pp. 40–51, 2018.
https://doi.org/10.1007/978-3-030-02456-7_4

Learning about problem solving is seen as a process of change management [5]. Change is a major theme in the universe of organization. In order to better understand the current problem of organizations in the face of change management, the literature has seen the concept of ambivalence [6]. Ambivalence suggests that people may be simultaneously in favor of and against change [7]. This is why the paradoxical approach seems particularly enlightening in formulating our research problem. *What are the organizational paradoxes in processes of problem-solving learning? What are the opposing trends that generate underlying organizational tensions within the operational teams?*

To answer these questions, our work will provide a brief study of the modeling of the problem of organizational change proposed by Perret [8]. We will use this model for our problem as a set of ambivalent behaviors according to the organizational contradictions and their interactions. The TRIZ will be used to reformulate this model [9].

Advocating for paradoxical management to respond to these challenges is however insufficient if we do not enter into a reflection on its implementation. Identify practices and the processes that underpin them; identifying the organizational mechanisms upon which these processes of change can be based are equally important steps. *What are the paradoxical organizational practices?*

Thus, we propose to use a model of solutions that characterizes a grid of paradoxical organizational practices analysis proposed by scientific literature. In order to formalize a frame of reference for the analysis of our scientific problematic, we will base ourselves on the paradigm of thought resulting from the TRIZ [9].

Finally, we will propose to use our paradoxical approach on a study case. This last part will propose a modeling of our approach with the help of the TRIZ Theory [9] on a specific problematic related to the processes of problem solving. A specific implementation condition will illustrate our study using a specific solution called "Problem Solving Pull" adapted to our organizational study case.

2 Formulation of Specific Problem to Learning Problem Solving

A survey on the performance of CII was conducted [5]. We collected responses from 37 companies. 20% of companies have fewer than 50 employees, 44% of these companies have fewer than 100 employees and 36% have fewer than 200 employees. The companies surveyed are divided into several sectors of activity: the manufacture of equipment for the automotive sector, the manufacture of industrial equipment, and outsourcing of the aerospace and mechanical sector. The survey was conducted from September 2015 to February 2017. The selection of the sample was based on SMEs having started a continuous improvement process for at least three years. The sample of interviewees is 370 people, 40% of whom are agents of production and 60% of managers.

2.1   The Empirical Contradictions Within Continuous Improvement Initiatives

This study confirms the problem of sustainability of problem-solving approaches within the CII. It identified four generic difficulties that explain the barriers within companies to "learn by solving problems". These difficulties have been translated into the following empirical contradictions (C1-4):

- C1: Continuous improvement generates problems and affects their resolution (75% of the people interviewed);
- C2: Continuous improvement is not used as a source of acquisition of new skills for problem solving (64% of the people interviewed);
- C3: The visual management spaces is not exploited as an axis of progress for the problem solving organization (77% of the people interviewed);
- C4: Organizational strategy is unfavorable for learning of problem solving (78% of people interviewed).

The results of this analysis are justified by the fact that 90% of companies use traditional learning approaches. These models develop a diffusion of continuous improvement approaches in a mechanistic way. This strategy prevents the individual and collective learning of problem solving. Indeed, traditional approaches to learning continuous improvement approaches go through two phases of diagnosis (Fig. 1). The first diagnosis concerns the organization of problem solving (A). The second diagnosis is dedicated to problem-solving skills (B).

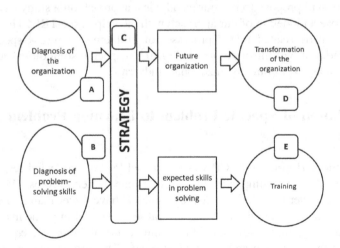

Fig. 1.   Classical model of learning of problem solving.

2.2   The Impacts on Learning of Problem Solving

Argyris and Schön describe three loops of learning of problem-solving [10]. The simple loop consists of adapting to changes in the environment. Individuals respond to results by a simple feedback loop connecting the detected error to action strategies

(Fig. 2). The double-loop induces a change in the values of use strategies. The double loop refers to the two feedback loops that link the observed effects of the action to values and paradigms. Thus, individuals perform a double-loop learning when their investigation generates changes in the values of the use theory (Fig. 2). Argyris and Schön have also highlighted a third type of learning to emphasize the possibility of learning about one's own way of learning. It can lead to the formation of new learning strategies, learning itself becoming a learning object (Fig. 2). This figure also shows the location of the impact of the empirical contradictions within the learning loops.

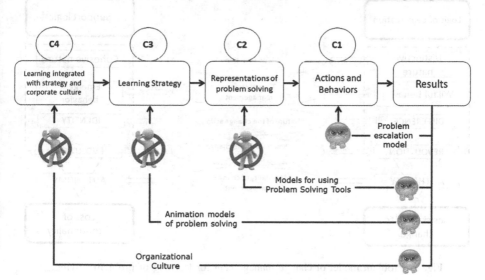

Fig. 2. The impact of contradictions on single-double-triple loop learning.

3   Formulation of the Problem Model

Perret [8] proposes a framework of analysis in which two logics of contradictory actions coexist by recognizing reciprocal interactions between the action and the context. The first logic is the logic of demarcation. For this author, the intentional change aims to act on an organizational context and seeks to transform it. For the second logic, which the author calls logic of support, the intentional change can only act according to a given organizational context to which he must conform and adapt. For the logic of demarcation, the action of the leader is characterized by two essential elements: distinctive nature and deliberate behavior. This logic confronts leaders with resistance to change. For the logic of support, the action of the leader is characterized by two essential elements: cohesive nature and emergent behavior. This second logic constrains the leaders with the risks of losing the intentionality of their actions. Table 1 shows the conflicts and tensions that arise from the coexistence of these two logics.

The Fig. 3 illustrates the paradoxical paradigm of the antagonistic pair (demarcation logic/support logic).

Table 1. Ambivalent behavior of the change according to Perret [8].

	Logic of demarcation	Logic of support
The nature of the action of change	Difference	Identity
The dynamics of the action of change	Revolution	Evolution
The modalities of the change management	Autority	Autonomy

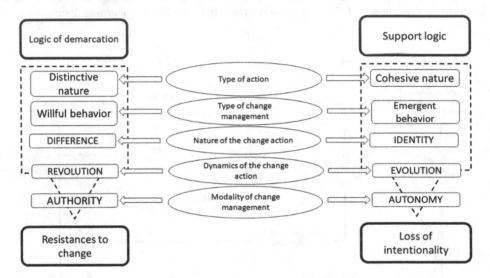

Fig. 3. Problem model of change management for learning of problem solving.

4   A Model of Solutions in the Form of Paradoxical Organizational Practices

Josserand and Perret [11] say that an organization practices a paradoxical management if it is able to reconcile the constraints perceived usually as opposed. The paradoxical organizational practices are characterized by the ability to master a self-equilibrium. Josserand and Perret [11] identifies six types of practices according to two dimensions (Table 2). The first dimension corresponds to a mode of articulation of the dualities of the antagonistic couples. The analyzed practices can play on a temporal or spatial articulation of the two lemmas of the paradox. The second dimension is that of the logic overcoming the paradox: differentiation, dialogue and disappearance.

In this article, in connection with our problematic, we will focus on describing the change of frame of reference in a logic of disappearance. This organizational practice will be experienced in our case studies.

4.1   The Logic of Disappearance and Framing

In the logic of disappearance, the paradox no longer exists: the individuals no longer live in a situation of double constraints; they have integrated the two contradictory

Table 2. Organizational practices and solution model from Josserand and Perret [11].

		Logic….		
		of differentiation	of dialogue	of disappearance
Organizational practices	Diachronic dimension (time)	Sequential practices	Stratification oscillation	Framing
	Synchronic dimension (space)	Subdivision	Local construction	

dimensions. The disappearance of the paradox can be explained by the transition from one logical level to another. In the reframing, a new element is introduced in a situation that allows the logical jump, which allows to get out of the contradiction [12, 13]. It is frequent that the change of logical level is made possible by the intrusion into our world of a new object, a third element that enriches or disturbs our representation of reality. An object, a concept or a person then allows the reconciliation of the two opposites [14].

4.2   Change of Reference Frame in a Logic of Disappearance

The practice of reframing is based on a cognitive leap. The reframing presents a difficulty related to the inability to project outside the frames [16]. Barriers generate this difficulty.

The first typology of barriers is linked to the often-insufficient knowledge of managers to leave the framework. The imperfection of the knowledge of the real pushes the organization towards the cognitive biases described by Lambert [15]: focusing on certain solutions, illusion of control. Eby and Adams [16] stress the importance of informal and regular meetings. These meetings are opportunities for sharing experiences.

The second barrier is psychological type. The question of reframing is then about techniques to ensure that people can receive knowledge that is useful to them in the context they are facing. Behavioral concerns are central to Argyris' methods of promoting organizational learning [10].

The last barrier that constrains the possibilities of reframing is that related to the organizational culture. Knowledge can be irreconcilable with culture or organizational routines. These routines enclose the company in a single thought. The managers defend these routines without questioning. The structure of the organization leads to a routine of choices that further reinforces uniformity. It becomes impossible to change the perceptions of a situation or a problem. The individual can also express defensive routines in the form of resistance to change [6, 16]. For this, it is necessary to introduce a kind of logic of questioning in the company. One of the essential vectors of renewal lies in a permanent contact between the managers with operational agents.

We propose to use the formalism resulting from the TRIZ to formulate our model of solutions in connection with the specific problematic and the model of problem (Fig. 4).

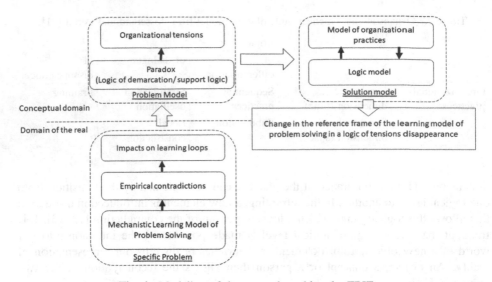

Fig. 4. Modeling of the research problem by TRIZ.

To illustrate our approach, we will use a case study that will allow us to explain our approach in the search for an organizational innovation of learning of problem solving.

5   Case Study and Experimentation of the Paradoxical Approach

We conducted an experiment with our paradoxical approach on a Michelin production factory located in Le Puy en Velay between December 2016 and October 2017. The approach was tested on two-production workshops with 12 production agents associated with their manager.

5.1   Background of the Experiment

Michelin is a leading group in the design, industrialization and production of pneumatic products. For years, this company has developed a program of development of empowerment and autonomy for its production agents. The company wants to develop the concept of the learning organization to strengthen its initial program. The central service has created problem-solving tools as well as training and support for operational staff in the use of these tools.

5.2   Formulation of the Problem of Learning Problem Solving

To test our paradoxical approach, we modeled our problem using TRIZ. The system studied is the learning of problem solving of production agents. In order to discover the organizational paradoxes and the associated tensions, we used two typological models, the level of maturity of the current system and the approach by the Vepoles, which are respectively, represented by the Figs. 5 and 6. The names of the parties are as follows:

– SE (Energy source) = operating standards (quality, inventories, security)
– CC_RdP (Engine) = Skills and knowledge in problem solving
– O_RdP (Transmission) = Problem solving tools
– F_RdP (Control) = Training for problem solving tools
– AP (Work) = Production Agent
– Pb (Object) = Problem (operating deviations)

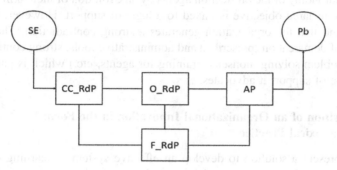

Fig. 5. Current system of problem solving learning.

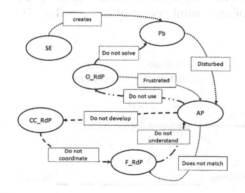

Fig. 6. Vepole model of the specific problem.

It follows from this first diagnosis with the agents of production and their manager that the system of learning of the resolution of problems contains organizational tensions, which are {authority/autonomy}, and {revolution/evolution}. Subsequently using semi-structured interviews, we were able to capture a series of ambivalent discourses that confirm these paradoxes. Below are some examples of these speeches:

– Authority/autonomy: "*I am trained to use these tools to develop my problem solving skills, but I do not use them because it is too administrative and complicated to complete. I fill them a posteriori or I forget to fill them because I do not have time"-* *"I solve my problems not to penalize production but I do not develop my skills or I do not know if the solutions are effectives"*

- Revolution/evolution: *"I have followed training on problem solving tools that I do not use and I'm told you do not solve problems then? – "I solve problems, it's my daily work and so I do not need problem-solving tools".*

These two analyzes validate the fact that within these two production workshops, the current system of learning of problem solving is not effective because it contains organizational paradoxes that generate tensions. Indeed, the organization wants to develop the autonomy of the production agents by an evolution of their skill in problem solving. This declared objective is linked to a logic of support. However, in fact and reality, we find that the organization generates a strong contradiction. The company uses a logic of demarcation (prescribed and administrative tools, strong control over the actions of problem solving, nonsense training for agents, etc.) which is paradoxically with the logic of support it advocates.

5.3   Proposition of an Organizational Innovation in the Form of Paradoxical Practice

In order to present a solution to develop an effective system of learning of problem solving, we have developed a model of evolution specific to this study case by increasing its level of ideality. This model proposes to reduce the irregularities of evolution of the parts by the integration of a logic of framing. The aim is to increase the degree of dynamism of the control system of learning (Fig. 7).

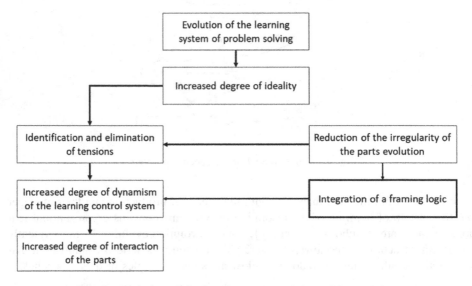

Fig. 7. Evolution of the learning system of the problem solving

We propose an innovative framing logic for the development of problem solving for production agents (Fig. 8). This logic is named "Problem Solving Pull © (PSP)". This is about needs of learning for problem solving. In fact, learning dimensions must take into account individual, collective, managerial and organizational realities. The diagnosis of individual and collective learning requires an evaluation of lived experiences: the actual work of problem solving [A], the work of team between individuals and managerial practices used by leaders [B]. These experiences are used later to guide the strategies of training [C] and finally to improve the learning organization of problem solving [D].

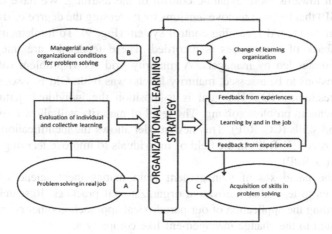

Fig. 8. Organizational innovation (Problem Solving Pull)

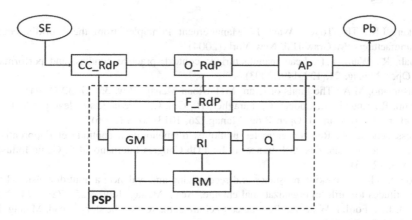

Fig. 9. Integration of the PSP into the learning control system of problem solving

6 Conclusion

This research work had several objectives. First, it was a question of identifying the empirical contradictions, which justify the difficulties of the companies to perpetuate the learning of problem solving of the operational teams. We have shown that these contradictions stem from a set of organizational paradoxes (opposing tendencies that generate tensions within the agents of production). The scientific literature resulting from the paradoxes theories associated with TRIZ helped us to formulate a model of the problem as well as a generic solution model. These models were tested on a concrete case and creates an organizational innovation. The new logic has helped to evolve the current system towards more dynamic control of the learning. We have developed a new logic (PSP) that helps to remove tensions by increasing the degree of dynamism of the production agents (AP) learning control system (Fig. 9). To implement this logic, frequent feedback of experiences is recorded. These feedbacks are integrated into managerial routines led by managers. A maturity grid (GM) problem solving capabilities (dimensions to be assessed, maturity levels) was built. GM is associated with a system of questioning (Q). The goal is to position the individual maturity of the production agents in problem solving. The level of maturity will allow developing the knowledge and skills (CC_RdP). This new model allows the identification of training and coaching needs (F_RdP) in the field of individuals to improve learning of problem solving tools (O_RdP).

Linking the paradoxes of management from management sciences with TRIZ should allow us to test other innovative organizational practices. Research is in perspective regarding the application of our paradoxical approach in other companies with problems related to the change management like company 4.0.

References

1. Liker, J.K.: The Toyota Way: 14 Management Principles from the World's Greatest Manufacturers. McGraw-Hill, New York (2004)
2. Shah, R., Ward, P.T.: Lean manufacturing: context, practice bundles, and performance. J. Oper. Manag. **21**, 129–149 (2003)
3. Cusumano, M.A.: The limits of Lean. MIT Sloan Manag. Rev. **35**, 27–32 (1994)
4. Conti, R., Angelis, J., Cooper, C., Faragher, B., Gill, C.: The effects of lean production on worker job stress. Int. J. Oper. Prod. Manag. **26**, 1013–1038 (2006)
5. Messaoudene, Z.: Relation entre les pratiques d'amélioration continue et l'apprentissage organisationnel dans des PME française. In: 11th Congrès International de Génie Industriel, Canada (2015)
6. Piderit, S.K.: Rethinking resistance and recognizing ambivalence: a multidimensional view of attitudes towards an organizational change. Acad. Manag. Rev. **4**(25), 783–794 (2000)
7. Ford, J.D., Ford, L.W., et al.: Resistance to change: the rest of the story. Acad. Manag. Rev. **33**(2), 362–377 (2008)
8. Perret, V.: Les paradoxes du changement organisationnel, Le paradoxe: penser et gérer autrement les organisations, pp. 253–297. Ellipses, Paris (2003)
9. Altshuller, G.S.: Creativity as an Exact Science – the Theory of the Solution of Inventive Problem. Gordon and Breach Publishers, Philadelphia (1984)

10. Argyris, C., Schon, D.A.: Apprentissage organisationnel. Théorie, méthode et pratique. De Boeck, Paris (2002)
11. Josserand, E., Perret, V.: Pratiques organisationnelles du paradoxe: Le paradoxe – Penser et gérer autrement les organisations, Chapitre 7, pp. 165–187. Ellipses (2012)
12. Westenholz, A.: Paradoxical thinking and change in the frame of reference. Organ. Stud. **14** (1), 37–58 (1993)
13. Morin, P.: Le développement des organisations. Dunod, Paris (1989)
14. Ford, J., Backoff, R.: Organizational change in and out of dualities and paradox. In: Quinn, R., Cameron, K. (eds.) Paradox and Transformation: Toward a Theory of Change in Organization and Management, pp. 81–121. Ballinger, Cambridge (1988)
15. Lambert, G., Ouédraogo, N.: L'apprentissage organisationnel et son impact sur la performance des processus, Revue française de gestion 2006/7, no. 166, pp. 15–32 (2006)
16. Eby, L.T., Adams, D.M., et al.: Perceptions of organizational readiness for change: factors related to employees' reactions to the implementation of team-based selling. Hum. Relat. **53**(3), 419–442 (2000)

Managing with TRIZ

TRIZ – Develop or Die in a World Driven by Volatility, Uncertainty, Complexity and Ambiguity

Martin Kiesel[1]([⊠]) and Jens Hammer[2]

[1] Siemens AG, DF MC TTI, Erlangen, Germany
martin.kiesel@siemens.com
[2] School of Business and Economics, Friedrich-Alexander-University
Erlangen-Nuremberg, Erlangen, Germany
jens-hammer@gmx.de

Abstract. Across industries, companies face the need to increase development speed in a volatile and uncertain market environment, and digitalization, cloud computing, and artificial intelligence are game-changing. Classical theory of inventive problem-solving (TRIZ) is derived from patent analysis and based on technical/mechanical problem-solving. Many TRIZ methods and tools exist to address the changing and difficult-to-predict marketplace. However, in a VUCA (volatility, uncertainty, complexity, and ambiguity) world, we face situations that are increasingly complex and potentially require different approaches. This paper discusses the extent to which TRIZ methods and tools are helpful in a "VUCA world" and how TRIZ should be adapted in this changing environment. The authors investigate when TRIZ can provide helpful direction and in which dimensions it should evolve. A potential "TRIZ Picture of the Future" is presented based on a literature review and long-term experience in Lean development, TRIZ, and foresight technologies.

Keywords: TRIZ · VUCA · Cynefin Framework
Three-Layered product architecture

1 Introduction

In industry, companies must face the need for increasing developing speed in a volatile and uncertain market environment. We live in a world where companies must reinvent faster than ever before. Digitalization, cloud computing and artificial intelligence introduce a game changing situation. In the last 15 years, 52% of the fortune 500 companies have disappeared. In contrast, classical TRIZ was derived from patent analysis, based on technical/mechanical problem solving. There is a bunch of methods and tools available for these issues. However, in a VUCA (Volatility, Uncertainty, Complexity, Ambiguity) world we face situations which are increasingly complex and potentially require different approaches. In the VUCA World which is more or less addressing software, the development approaches are moving to Lean, Agile, Design Thinking, User Experience and other methodologies. The paper discusses to which extent the TRIZ methods and tools are helpful in a VUCA world and how TRIZ should

D. Cavallucci et al. (Eds.): TFC 2018, IFIP AICT 541, pp. 55–65, 2018.
https://doi.org/10.1007/978-3-030-02456-7_5

develop to fit into the changing environment. The authors investigate where classic and modern TRIZ can provide helpful directions and in which dimensions TRIZ should evolve. A potential "TRIZ Picture of the Future" based on literature review and long-term experiences in Lean development, TRIZ and foresight technologies was derived.

2 Literature Review

2.1 Changing Environment

"Across many industries, a rising tide of volatility, uncertainty, and business complexity is roiling markets and changing the nature of competition." [1].

New technologies are changing industry boundaries and the nature of products, processes, and services (e.g., a competitive landscape created by digitalization and Industrie 4.0) [2]. Industries, businesses, and customer needs used to be clearly delineated—for example, in markets such as education, consumer electronics, computers, communication devices, software, music, and movies [2]. Twenty years ago, organizations in each of these industries had individual, established competitors and competitive dynamics [2]. It was an ecosystem of certainty in which features and functionality were embedded in the product and developed over relatively known steps. Digitization has empowered industries and products to combine features and functions in many new ways [2]. Over time, companies have seen technological skills such as miniaturization as among their core competencies; from that perspective, miniaturization's primary benefit to consumers has been portability, and companies have thus focused innovation in the product space on making as many products as possible smaller and lighter [2]. However, current consumer perspectives might frame the challenge differently [2].

Employing an acronym for volatility, uncertainty, complexity, and ambiguity—VUCA—organizations have asserted that we now live in a "VUCA world" [2], which creates potential challenges for companies, leaders, and employees. "Volatility" refers to unclear, unforeseeable, and rapidly changing market conditions, and "uncertainty" addresses user acceptance of implemented features or new business models. "Complexity" is related to complex development conditions (e.g., teams worldwide and new technologies), and "ambiguity" focuses on unclear direction, lack of stable forecasting, and unclear cause-effect chains. However, optimists see companies' opportunities if their leaders master the accompanying challenges. For example [3]:

- Volatility provides profit opportunity [4];
- Uncertainty is an opportunity [5];
- Simplifying IT complexity is a major opportunity for all companies [6]; and
- Ambiguity equals opportunity [7].

Nevertheless, volatility and uncertainty increase the demand for short development cycles and customer-driven development, and complexity requires greater system knowledge and partner approaches. Particularly in terms of ambiguity, there is a significant need for experimentation, although only intelligent experimentation can determine what the customer values and what benefits the company—and what does not. In the "VUCA world," development approaches are moving to methodologies such as Lean, Agile, Design Thinking, and User Experience.

2.2 Evolution of TRIZ

The TRIZ methodology was derived from the analysis of the world patent collection [9] and established a bunch of tools shown in Fig. 1 (frequently used tools MATRIZ). These tools cover, problem identification (analysis), problem solving (ideation), forecasting for technical evolutions and solutions selection. TRIZ provides different methods for these processes (e.g. technical and physical contradictions for modelling of inventive problems) and forecasting methods like 9-Screen Approach or TESE (Trends of Engineering System Evolution).

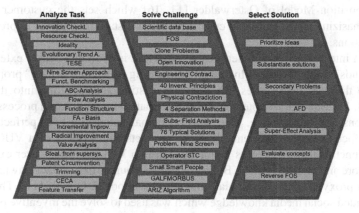

Fig. 1. Classification of TRIZ tools [9, 10]

The methodology has always had a strong focus on identifying available resources in the environment especially in the super-system which might support the problem solving. In recent years the TRIZ toolset increases its portfolio and its application fields. However, within TRIZ, the product and potential next development steps are main reasons for its application. Moreover, the main application field is for hardware development or optimization.

TRIZ and the related tool set developed over years. Different research contributions show first steps for a shift from hardware to software products and services. The latest TRIZ developments have extended the scope of TRIZ from technical systems to business systems [11] and introduced extended fields:

- Voice of the product
- Voice of the market
- Voice of the business

Based on this, new tools emerged addressing "blocking contradictions" [11] on this extended field

- Value-Conflict Mapping (VCM) [12]
- Value-Conflict Mapping Plus (VCM+) [13]

These tools expand the scope of analysis and contradiction resolving process by considering the entire business system comprising [11]

- **products** (classical TRIZ) with value proposition and goods & services
- **business organization and ecosystem** with the business requirements and the approach the product is brought to market
- **market** with market requirements, market methods and customers & users

Boka applied the TRIZ method in business systems combining TRIZ with the Value Proposition Model of Osterwalder [11, 16] which sets the customer into the center emphasizing pains, gains and customer jobs as a starting point for improvements and innovations.

"Human interactions" is another area where TRIZ is evolving. Mayer extended the existing trends by the "Trend of Increased Addressing of Human Senses" proposing to incorporate the near field senses like Sensing, Tasting and Smelling into the TESE toolbox [14, 15]. Sun [25, 26] integrated user information into the design process to solve contradictions in product usage. The focus on human interactions fits perfectly to the increasing focus on user experience (UX) in products and services of a VUCA environment. Functional completeness is not enough in a VUCA world – user experience becomes more and more important. Boka used new resources like a "data crawler" which presented a proxy to social media platforms like Facebook & Google [11]. These platforms provided social media knowledge which was used to solve the inventive problems. Litvin [17] provides in his paper "Open Innovation: TRIZ Approach vs. Crowdsourcing" [17] key principles for efficient usage of open innovation. "First, focus on key problems, not on initial ones. Second search on functions not on specific designs."

In "Main Parameters of Value (MPV): TRIZ-based Tool Connecting Business Challenges to Technical Problems in Product/Process Innovation" [18] Litvin provides approaches how MPVs can be used to develop a business with a clear direction. This can also be incorporated into a Lean development setup.

Halas investigated the combination of TRIZ, Design Thinking (DT) & Lean [19]. He concluded, that TRIZ supplements these tools by providing methods and tools for the ideation phase [19]. DT and Lean tools provide approaches for human interaction, empathy, experimentation and for getting fast feedback from the customer. According to Abramov [8], other creativity approaches like Design Thinking become more popular then TRIZ in a Lean and Agile development environment. Moreover, there is a higher demand for customer driven and customer focused methods.

3 Methodology

For a structured discussion the authors used a Cynefin Framework and a Three-Layer Product Model to characterize the status of the TRIZ methodology and derive actions. The Cynefin Framework [20] is a reference for classification of system/problem types and Three-Layer Product Model of Bosch [21] supports in discussion with an architecture model for products & services in a VUCA world.

Introduction of Cynefin Framework as a Reference for Classification of Problem Types

Dave Snowden provides with the Cynefin Framework (see Fig. 2, [20]) a generic framework which classifies systems/problems and provides approaches how to deal with them.

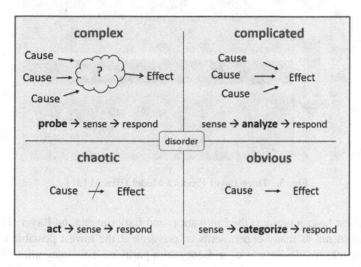

Fig. 2. Cynefin Framework [20]

The classification defines obvious problems, complicated problems, complex problems and chaotic ones.

Simple problems show a clear cause – effect relation. Complicated problems require a more analytical view on the system. Complex problems have no clear analyzable cause-effect-chain. For chaotic problems the Framework recommends fast acting without any analyzing. The disorder area tags systems/problem which can't be clearly classified and mapped to one of the four areas.

Introduction of Three-Layer Product Model as an Architecture Model for Products and Services in a VUCA World

Bosch recommends a Three-Layer Product Model which provides a solution approach for addressing different needs in a VUCA word (see Fig. 3) [21]. The product architecture is divided into three layers (innovative principle #1: segmentation).

The lowest layer covers the Commoditized Functionality. The major optimization criteria for this layer is cost. The usage of open source and components of the shelf (COTS) is strongly recommended.

The middle layer covers the Differentiation Functionality. This is the area where the Unique Selling Proposition (USP) is in. The major investment should be focused in this area.

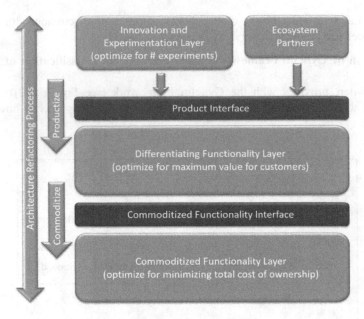

Fig. 3. Three-Layer Product Model (Bosch) [21]

The highest layer represents the Innovation and Experimentation Layer. This Layer is optimized to run as many experiments as possible at the lowest possible costs.

The product provides interfaces to Ecosystem partners. This integration allows the leverage of ecosystems for raising the overall value of the product. This kind of architecture supports speed, keeps the USP of a product in a dedicated layer and leverages existing resources like Open Source, Components of the Shelf (COTS) and ecosystems to the best possible extent. According to the model there are continuous Architecture Refactoring measures in place to move the functionality from the top layer to the bottom layer of the Architecture over time. New valuable functionality explored in the Innovation Layer moves to the Differentiating Layer. USP Features of the Differentiating Layer move to the Commodized Layer when the functionality is regarded as Standard and is no longer a USP of the product.

For each of the identified discussion areas we used reflection of the current state and definition of the target state to verify the current status and derive possible next development steps. The current and target state are based on a literature review and trends in research development.

4   Results and Discussion

A "VUCA world" signifies increasingly complex scenarios that potentially require new approaches to problem-solving across industries. In terms of TRIZ's future and development, key drivers include volatile and uncertain markets/outcomes, as well as product complexity. The use of the Cynefin framework and Three-Layer Product

Model has led to the following findings regarding the classification of problems and the product model.

Cynefin Framework

Simple problems show a clear cause-effect relationship. Rational judgment is the proposed method to find a suitable measure for solving the problem. TRIZ and its 40 Innovative Principles (40iP) are appropriate to solve the problem, although other classical tools are also suitable.

Complicated problems require a more analytical view of the system, and several causes typically exist for an effect. This type of problems can be analyzed by methods such as Root Cause Analysis. Classical TRIZ analysis tools focus on complicated problems that can be understood through analytical tools.

Complex problems have no clear analyzable cause-effect chain. They require a different solution approach, such as building a hypothesis for a possible solution and testing it; analytical approaches based on theory are not suitable. This is the typical area of uncertainty in determining the right solutions for a "VUCA world." Complex problems cannot be analyzed using analytical tools without experiments. TRIZ foresight tools like the Nine-Screen Approach or TESE provide helpful direction for deriving solution hypotheses that are beyond the obvious solution approaches derived from brainstorming, and they can be used for complex problems as well.

For chaotic problems, the framework recommends acting rapidly without analysis. The disorder area tags systems/problem that cannot be clearly classified and mapped to one of the four areas.

The transfer of problems from a complex space to a complicated one and then to a simple one can be supported by TRIZ integrating the newly explored findings and by successfully integrating new technologies into the existing TRIZ knowledge base (e.g., adding new innovation principles, new resources that can solve the problems, or new TESE). Moreover, TRIZ's scope can be extended (e.g., from products to services and approaches including new business models, customer interaction, and feedback).

Three Layer Product Model

The Three-Layer Product Model demonstrates that TRIZ tools can be applied to support the evolution process in different ways (e.g., supporting the problem analysis process with Root Cause Analysis, identifying contradictions in the current product architecture, formulating necessary functions, and searching with Function-Oriented Search). Generating a Picture of the Future for the Product is addressing the changing environment by using Ideality, the Nine-Screen Approach, and TESE and determining requirements for the next evolution of the product architecture. generates additional value. Moreover, the authors recommend discussing application fields, technical and ecosystem resources, and TRIZ in a Lean and Agile working environment. The application field describes areas in which TRIZ methods and tools should be used to meet the demands of the "VUCA world." Resources play a major role in the TRIZ toolset and are one basis of the methodological approach.

Besides the Cynefin framework and the Three-Layer Product Model, further key topics to develop TRIZ in a "VUCA world" include application fields, technical and ecosystem resources, and working models.

Application fields. Currently, TRIZ tools focus on technical systems and processes. Regarding future requirements, the methodology needs to extend its scope to the following aspects, which are to some extent already in development or addressed in some articles:

- Technical systems with increasing software, human interaction, and information technology-related aspects and technologies (e.g., cloud computing and blockchain);
- Business systems/models;
- Service-oriented business models (covering the trend from products to services);
- User experience-related aspects (potentially in combination with Design Thinking approaches); and
- Emergent optimization of the product architecture to cover new upcoming demands (e.g., based on the Three-Layer Product Model [21])

This extended scope is necessary to meet current demands. The intention and philosophy of existing TRIZ tools remain valid—for instance, for key problem analysis, required function analysis for Function-Oriented Search, and formulating contradictions. However, tools such as function analysis must be extended to cover this wider scope.

Technical and ecosystem resources. The current array of technical resources is based on elementary effects (i.e., physical, chemical, and biological). They are often abbreviated as "MATCHEMIB," an acronym for the eight TRIZ "fields": mechanical, acoustic, thermal, chemical, electric, magnetic, intermolecular, and biological. Although the MATCHEMIB fields were introduced as stimuli during the idea-generation phase of Substance-Field Analysis, they can be used independently.

Development is needed in terms of successes in sensors and new application fields. In particular, data (data analytics) in the field of cloud computing, artificial intelligence, and deep learning are upcoming resources that must be covered in the future.

Ecosystems are part of the super-system, and, relevant ecosystems should be visible as resources (e.g., digital platforms from Microsoft Azure and Amazon AWS or open-source assets on the market).

TRIZ in a Lean and Agile working environment. Guidelines currently exist on how to apply TRIZ in an iterative and timeboxed-driven environment [17, 18, 22, 23]. Solution algorithms such as the algorithm for inventive problem-solving (ARIZ) are complex and rarely used in Lean development setups. Moreover, retrospectives and incremental improvements in TRIZ application have not been established. An investigation into the opportunities for integrating TRIZ into the large-scale Agile software development framework (SAFe) proposed applying TRIZ to drive innovation on different layers of the framework (portfolio, program, and team) [24]. According to the authors, one goal of TRIZ in a Lean and Agile working environment is that main parameters of value use and thinking is deeply integrated into the Lean development process; main parameters of value can be used to define overall project goals and serve as a frame for unfolding the intended values into specific Epics in a Product Backlog. TRIZ is heavily used in suggesting solution alternatives, especially "disruptive" approaches derived from TESE or radical trimming changing the problem situation. TRIZ use and further development is driven by retrospectives optimizing TRIZ application, and moreover, TRIZ is used and accepted as a learning and thinking tool for accelerated learning on the team and/or project level. Iteration is key for development in an uncertain world. Analysis of key problems and formulation of necessary functions (for Function-Oriented Search) are still necessary, but early user-centric testing and feedback is becoming increasingly important for early validation of feature hypothesis.

Solution algorithms like ARIZ are complex and are rarely used in Lean development setups. Moreover, retrospectives and incremental improvements concerning the application of TRIZ are not established.

In [24], the authors investigated the opportunities of integrating TRIZ into the large scale Agile software development Framework (SAFe). They propose to apply TRIZ to drive innovation on different layers of the Framework (Portfolio, Program and Team level).

One target of TRIZ in a Lean & Agile working environment is, according to the authors, that MPV-usage and-thinking is deeply integrated in the Lean development process. MPV can be used to define the overall project goals. MPVs serve as a frame for unfolding the intended values into specific Epics in a Product Backlog. TRIZ is heavily used in suggesting solution alternatives especially "disruptive" approaches derived from TESE or radical trimming changing the problem situation. TRIZ usage and further development is driven by retrospectives optimizing the application of TRIZ. And moreover, TRIZ is used and accepted as a learning & thinking tool for accelerated learning on team and/or project level. Iteration is key for a development in an uncertain world. Analysis of key problems, formulation of necessary functions (for function oriented search) are still very important, but early user centric testing and feedback becomes more and more important for early verification of feature hypothesis.

5   Conclusion

TRIZ has already developed in different application fields and optimized the known toolset. However, there is a need for improvement, which can be broken into four main areas as part of a "TRIZ Picture of the Future": **create new application fields, create new resources, simplify and adapt applicability, and foster emergent development.**

In terms of **new application fields**, technical systems must include increasing software-, human-, and information technology-driven aspects to cover the complete value of a product or service. Business systems and models should be considered in the TRIZ approach to cover the product or service's complete value proposition, as should user experience (including human interactions) and information technology areas (including software and Internet-related areas such as ecosystems and cloud computing). Moreover, tools must be adapted to cover the extended scope and to solve complex problems with experimental approaches.

Creating new resources is necessary to remain relevant in the face of new developments; new technical and ecosystem resources must be established. Moreover, there is a need to **simplify and adapt applicability** for TRIZ; incorporating Lean practices for improvement and further development (e.g., use retrospectives) will help to reflect on and improve TRIZ application. Finally, we must **foster emergent**

development of TRIZ, ensuring there is a shift from centralized development (Alt-shuller, TRIZ Master) to decentralized, autonomous, operationally driven development with clear focus (success criteria) on "value add" for innovation speed and quality in a "VUCA world." Figure 4 summarizes the core concepts of this "TRIZ Picture of the Future."

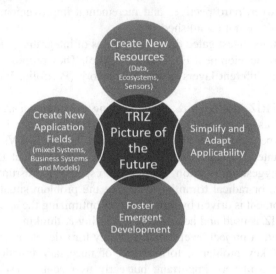

Fig. 4. TRIZ Picture of the Future

References

1. Doheny, M., Nagali, V., Weig, F.: Agile operations for volatile times. McKinsey Q. (2012). https://www.mckinsey.com/business-functions/operations/our-insights/agile-operations-for-volatile-times
2. Bennett, N., Lemoine, G.J.: What a difference a word makes: understanding threats to performance in a VUCA world. Bus. Horiz. **57**(3), 311–317 (2014)
3. Prahalad, C.K., Ramaswamy, V.: The new frontier of experience innovation. MIT Sloan Manag. Rev. **44**(4), 12–18 (2003)
4. Warwick-Ching, L.: Currency wars: volatility provides profit opportunity. The Financial Times. https://www.ft.com/content/e17e1ab0-8714-11e2-9dd7-00144feabdc0. Accessed 25 Mar 2013
5. Hemingway, A., Marquart, J.: Uncertainty is opportunity: engage with purpose. Edelman. http://www.edelman.com/post/uncertainty-is-opportunity-engage-with-purpose/. Accessed 27 June 2013
6. Boston Consulting Group: Simplifying IT complexity a major opportunity for many companies (press release). http://www.bcg.com/media/PressReleaseDetails.aspx?id=tcm:12-130333. Accessed 21 Mar 2013

7. Amerasia Consulting Group: Ambiguity equals opportunity: the story of the new HBS application.   http://www.amerasiaconsulting.com/blog/2013/6/3/ambiguity-equals-opportunity-the-story-of-the-new-hbs-application. Accessed 3 June 2013
8. Abramov, O., Sobolev, S.: Why TRIZ popularity is declining. In: TRIZ Future Conference, Wroclaw, Poland (2016)
9. Ikovenko, S., Bradley, J.: TRIZ as a lean thinking tool. In: 4th TRIZ Future Conference, Florence, Italy, February 2004
10. Adunka, R.: MA TRIZ Level 1 Training: Script; 2015; triz-online.de (2014). TRIZ online. http://www.triz-online.de/. Accessed 30 May 2014
11. Boka, S., Kuryan, A., Ogievich, D.: Applications of TRIZ in business systems. In: TRIZfest 2017, Krakow, Poland (2017)
12. Souchkov, V. http://www.xtriz.com/publications/Souchkov_Value_Conflict_Mapping.pdf
13. Kurjan, A., Souchkov, V.: Value-Conflict Mapping Plus (VCM+): adding business dimensions. In: TRIZfest-2014 Conference Proceedings (2014)
14. Mayer, O.: Trend of increased addressing of human senses – focus on near senses. In: 2016 TRIZ Etria Conference, Wroclaw, Poland (2016)
15. Mayer, O.: Increased addressing of human senses as a trend. In: TRIZfest 2017, Krakow, Poland (2017)
16. Osterwalder, A., Pigneur, Y.: Value Proposition Design: How to Create Products and Services Customers Want. Wiley, Hoboken (2014)
17. Litvin, S., Rutten, P.: Open innovation: TRIZ approach vs. crowdsourcing. In: TRIZfest 2017, Krakow, Poland (2017)
18. Litvin, S.: Main parameters of value: TRIZ-based tool connecting business challenges to technical problems in product/process innovation. http://www.triz-japan.org/PRESENTATION/sympo2011/Pres-Overseas/EI01eS-Litvin_(Keynote)-110817.pdf. Accessed 16 Mar 2018
19. Halas, M.: Lessons for TRIZ from design thinking & lean 3P. In: 2016 TRIZ Future Conference, Wroclaw, Poland (2016)
20. Snowden, D.: The cynefin framework. http://www.cognitive-edge.com
21. Bosch, J. https://www.researchgate.net/publication/260584542_Achieving_Simplicity_with_the_Three-Layer_Product_Model
22. Kiesel, M., Hammer, J.: Applying TRIZ and lean tools for improving development processes. A case study from industry: improving the testing process for SW and HW-related products. In: TRIZ Future 2016, Wroclaw, Poland (2016)
23. Hammer, J., Kiesel, M.: Applying TRIZ to improve lean product lifecycle management processes. In: TRIZfest 2017, Krakow, Poland (2017)
24. Opportunities for integrating TRIZ and systematic innovation tools into large scale Agile software development. In: 2016 TRIZ Future Conference, Wroclaw, Poland (2016)
25. Sun, X., et al.: Integrating user information into design process to solve contradictions in product usage. In: 2015 TRIZ Future Conference (2015). https://www.sciencedirect.com/science/article/pii/S2212827116001980
26. Sun, X., et al.: Innovative interaction design approach based on TRIZ separation principles and inventive principles. In: 2017 TRIZ Future Conference, Lappeenranta, Finland (2017)

Market Complexity Evaluation to Enhance the Effectiveness of TRIZ Outputs

Paolo Carrara[1]([⊠]) (iD), Davide Russo[1] (iD), and Anna Rita Bennato[2]

[1] Università degli Studi di Bergamo, 24044 Dalmine, Italy
{paolo.carrara,davide.russo}@unibg.it
[2] Loughborough University, Loughborough LE11 3TU, UK
a.bennato@lboro.ac.uk

Abstract. In the context of innovation consulting activity, it may happen working in technical fields characterized by a high competitiveness level. Although TRIZ allows reaching innovative ideas in any kind of industry, it does not suggest any tool in order to evaluate the success rate of the invention in the reference market. During the last years, TRIZ got methodological contributes to sharpen the matching between the inventive idea and the actual needs of the market, for example the market potential tool. In order to support TRIZ experts in selecting the best innovation strategy, this paper introduces a new tool for the TRIZ toolbox that takes into account the competitiveness level of the market. Several economics works disclose the correlation between the patent-citation triadic relationships and the presence of dominant positions of few competitors. A patent analysis, focused on triads in patent citation, can inform the TRIZ expert about potential critical situation able to prevent the success of an inventive solution. It can generate an important indicator that helps him in selecting the most promising innovation strategy. The method could be integrated in a classic TRIZ activity, using commercial patent searching tools. The case study shows how to extract this kind of indicator from patent citation environment in Machine Learning field.

Keywords: TRIZ · Patent · Patent thicket · Business Intelligence
Market structure

1 Introduction

Business Intelligence (BI) comprises the strategies and technologies used by enterprises for the data analysis of business information, in order to identify new business opportunities with a competitive market advantage [1–4]. Firms make use of BI strategies to support a wide range of business decisions, which include both operational (i.e. production, and distribution) and technical (i.e. analysis of data) procedure able to improve their own efficiency. In the most recent times, it has been adopted to support the product innovation process, minimizing the risk-management decisions about R&D to the minimum.

D. Cavallucci et al. (Eds.): TFC 2018, IFIP AICT 541, pp. 66–74, 2018.
https://doi.org/10.1007/978-3-030-02456-7_6

In this paper, with the aim to define the structure of the market *for* innovation, we investigate a large pool of patents extracted from Machine Learning field. It is useful for ranking of the list of product requirement with highest market potential [5].

The market for innovation is particularly characterized by the use of licensing and sale of patents which negotiations could both either promote or prevent the diffusion of a specific technology, affecting firms' incentive to invest in further innovation [6].

In order to take into account the market structure, while ranking the market potential of product/process requirements, we present a new method able to incorporate both characteristics. By using patent counts as a measure of innovation, in this article we propose a procedure which by identifying the presence of possible patent thickets we are able to pinpoint the major market players, and all possible constrains faced by a new innovator entering into the market. [7] (see Sect. 2). Patent thickets are a peculiar characteristic of complex industries. According to the claims made in the patents about both physical and methodological components of the patented product or process it is likely that the ownership of the exclusive intellectual property right can overlap across different economics agents (i.e. firms), preventing their use and creating a proper barrier, especially for the follow-on innovation [7].

Knowing whether or not there is a patent thicket, before starting the problem solving or product innovation activity, is pivotal, as it allows to anticipate and readjust the BI strategy before the launch of the product will occur into the market.

Currently there are no tools able to automatically extract the data necessary to unveil the risk to meet with patent thicket; however, there are strategies based on backward and forward citations with which it is possible to obtain indications regarding any priority relations between patent pairs (or applicant pairs) [8]. Other useful information can be derived from the co-applicant and co-inventors maps, which show collaboration and relationships even between different companies [9] that are assumed to be competition within the same market, unless R&D cooperation agreements have been signed, and then emerging from the co-patenting measurement. A simple indication of the presence of patent thickets it is not informative *per se*, and for that reason the approach we propose would instead suggest the major players in the market, highlighting also the relative structure of the market.

2 Patent Thicket as Measure for Market Structure

The patent thicket is "a dense web of overlapping intellectual property rights that a company must hack its way through in order to actually commercialize new technology" [7]. It affects the structure of the market, usually characterized by cumulative or complementary technologies [10], defending against competitors designing around a single patent [11] and/or building hindrances to the innovation [12–16].

A potential new entrant in a specific technological market might be discouraged by the presence of a thicket, simply because of the high cost related to the bargaining process which is requested to advance further the innovation. This is even more evident when the market is characterized by few big players which may have a dominant position by owning a large pool of patent, and then conditioning the access to the market. According to the complexity of the patent thickets, the new entrant can be discouraged by the sticky and costly process, and as a result it would not undertake any further investment in the advancement of the new technology [17]. Alternatively, whether the investment takes place by licensing agreements and a new technology is proposed, due to the initial high cost its diffusion will be limited, preventing future advancement in the innovation process [7]. Galasso and Schankerman [18] show how the presence of patent thickets obstruct follow-on research especially in the complex industries (for example in information and communications technology, electrical–electronics and medical instruments). Once we accept that innovation depends mainly on the paradigm which sees it as a cumulative process upon which new ideas are generated, in Gallini [19] we could find a comprehensive review of the literature which highlights the issues yielded by the presence of patent thickets.

2.1 A Method for Identifying Patent Thicket

The strategy to measure the density of a patent thicket proposed by von Graevenitz [8] relies on the patent literature cited by the examiner in the search report having kind X or Y. He uses the triple (see Fig. 1) of applicants involved in mutual blocking citation relationships as a unity of measure of the thicket density. Higher the number of triples, worse the hacking through the thicket.

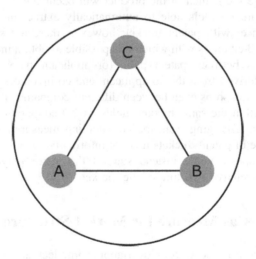

Fig. 1. Schematic presentation of the structure of triple. A, B and C circles identifies the firms involved in triple; the straight lines represent the mutual blocking relationships between firm couples (Source von Graevenitz [8])

Given the complexity of such a type of dimension, it finds some limitation for application to BI analysis. The required skills ranging from IT field, especially SQL language to querying PATSTAT, the statistical DB published by EPO (www.epo.org/searching-for-patents/business/patstat.html), to patent procedural knowledge. This makes hard to reproduce the analyses available in literature.

Furthermore, the method has been proposed in an economical context. It tend to make an economic analysis of the market for the main classes of OST-INPI/FhG-ISI technology nomenclature [20]. The typical dimension of the patent pools used by von Graevenitz is excessively large in order to give an information exploitable by decision makers concerning the reference market structure of a specific technical solution.

Moreover, although the triples count is an interesting method to measure the thicket density, it does not take into account the inner balance (or imbalance) of the patent portfolios, which explains the effective polarization toward one or two competitors in the triple.

In this article, the authors introduce an algorithm able to automatize the triples extraction process in a delimited technology environment. The output is a navigable network of citation links, in which the user can identify the main players, taking into account the contribution of the balance/imbalance information.

3 Triples Extraction Method for Identify Patent Thicket

To extract the information about the possible presence of patent thicket in a techno-logical domain related to a patent application, we suggest a modified triples evaluation algorithm.

It works in a patent pool selected in a more refined way than OST-INPI/FhG-ISI (or NACE) classification, considering the reference application field only. Thereby the measure of thicket density is 'local' and the approach can index the main players involved in thickening.

The algorithm gives three different indexes about the triple inner imbalance.

First it shows the number of citations for each couple in both directions (see Fig. 2). This might unveil that one (or two) of the player involved in the triple is not effectively disturbing the other two because its blocking patents are limited in number. Therefore, the other two applicants might not actually worry about the triple and control the market as a duopoly (or monopoly).

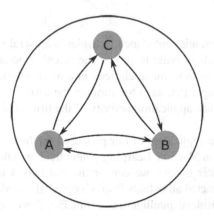

Fig. 2. A generic triple schema showing all citation relationships between the players. The arrows start from the cited player and go to the citing one (blocking direction).

The second index refers to the inner relative strength due to the portfolios size comparison of the triple players. The triples with an important imbalance due to this reason may suffer the effect of dominant positioning of one (or two) player. Thus, the actual configuration of the thicket tends to become a monopoly (or duopoly).

The last index measures the ratio between the target-technology-related portfolio of a firm in the triple and its whole patent portfolio. It indexes which is the effective interest of a single player involved in the triple to the target technology, and its relative market. A high ratio means the player considers strategic the target technology and the involving in triples could be a great fail risk.

The second index gives us the information about the inner imbalance between the players in a triple, while the third index shows the importance/interest of the target technology for each player (see Fig. 3).

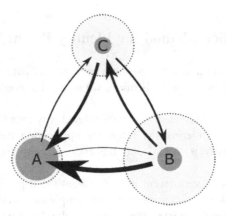

Fig. 3. A visualization of the imbalances inside a triple. The arrow thickness indexes the weight to the bilateral citation relationship, starting from the blocking player and pointing to the blocked one. The dotted circles indicate the dimension of the patent portfolios, related to the target technology. The number of the documents involved in the triple is proportional to the area of the grey circle.

The assessment on potential imbalance in triples is a useful indication that could be integrated into the BI tools in order to unveil the actual structure of the market to the decision makers and let them to make choices in a more informed way.

Figure 4 shows the algorithm used to compute the triples, considering filters in the choice of patent documents, application activity of the firms and inner imbalance in the triples.

As an example of the application of our proposed method we present the case of a pool of patent extract from Machine Learning patent field, and due to possible time lags in the patent office register update, we censor the last two years as suggested by the patent literature. We extracted all patents from Google, IBM and Microsoft focusing on machine learning and artificial intelligence. From Fig. 5 we can observe this market segment is dominated by the presence of three major players, Google, IBM, and Microsoft Technology. We use citation as a measure of a patent market value [21], and

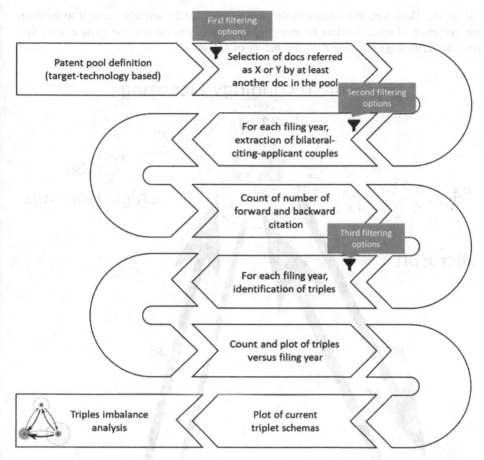

Fig. 4. The algorithm for the extraction from a technology-based patent pool of triples and related data. The first filtering option filters documents by filing year and applicants by minimum number of applications [10]. Second filter acts on the lifetime (in years) of a bilateral citation [10]. Filter 3 considers the imbalance parameters (relative portfolios dimension, documents involved in triple and number of bilateral citations)

in particular number of co-citation to identify the extent of the patent thickets among the major players. It emerges clearly that both Google and IBM tend to interact and make citation in a reciprocal relationship mainly with Microsoft Technology Licensing. Whereas the co-co-citation numbers between Google and IBM drop by almost 30 per cent compare to the same measure they have with Microsoft Technology. From this scenario it looks like that Microsoft Technology Licensing play a role as a leader controlling the number of citations which the other two players. This very preliminary analysis would suggest an oligopoly given the presence of three firms (with other two very small), where the one which owns the larger number of patents might play an important role in controlling the market entrants. Of course, a furthermore details analysis is needed to be able to understand if any illegal behaviour is in place (i.e.

collusion). However, from this simple picture would it be already enough to confirm the presence of high barriers to entry which could discourage the progress of this specific technology, leaving if in the hands of few actors.

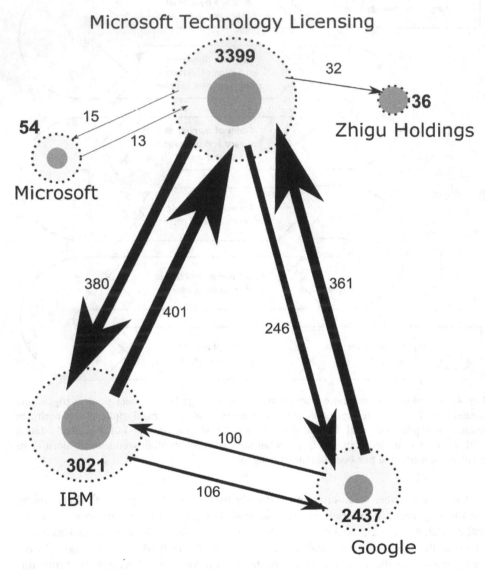

Fig. 5. Most interesting triple isolated by the algorithm in Machine Learning sector involving Google, IBM and Microsoft. The numbers near the circles indicate the number of patents held by the firm, while number on arrows shows blocking patents (or cited patents): e.g. IBM cited Google 100 times.

4 Conclusions

Due to the influence the competitiveness level might exert onto the success/failure of an inventive solution, its assessment is an important and strategic information for innovation activities.

This article gives to TRIZ experts a new tool that aims to assess the competitiveness level of the reference market. Using quantitative data from patents in the target technology field, the tool supports the choice of the innovation strategy for a firm that is looking for a new technology, especially when it operates in a complex market.

Although an economical research would be more accurate than the proposed method, the latter is very cheaper. In fact, while the first needs a high expertise in both economics and patents, the proposed method can run on currently available patent searching tools. This allows the TRIZ experts to carry out this analysis by themselves. Whether the result would be highlight a critical situation, a deeper analysis would be appropriate.

The method extracts citations data from patent database in order to compute triples and measure their inner balance. A great relative difference might highlight a dominant position.

It has been tested in machine learning field and it shown a dominant positioning of Microsoft, IBM and Google. The experimentation proves and highlights the risk for an unaware entrant to incur in unexpected extra charge due to the hard licensing bargaining.

The method is valid for any technical domain involved in patents.

References

1. Brannon, N.: Business intelligence and E-discovery. Intellect. Prop. Technol. Law J. **22**, 1–5 (2010)
2. Alaskar, T., Poulis, E.: Business intelligence capabilities and implementation strategies. Int. J. Glob. Bus. **8**, 34–45 (2015)
3. Marchand, M., Raymond, L.: Researching performance measurement systems. Int. J. Oper. Prod. Manag. **28**, 663–686 (2008). https://doi.org/10.1108/01443570810881802
4. Walsh, J.P., Lee, Y.-N.N., Jung, T.: Win, lose or draw? the fate of patented inventions. Res. Policy **45**, 1362–1373 (2016). https://doi.org/10.1016/j.respol.2016.03.020
5. Livotov, P.: Using patent information for identification of new product features with high market potential. In: TRIZ Future Conference. Elsevier B.V. (2014)
6. Arora, A., Fosfuri, A., Gambardella, A.: Markets for technology and their implications for corporate strategy. Ind. Corp. Chang. **10**, 419–451 (2001). https://doi.org/10.1093/icc/10.2.419
7. Shapiro, C.: Navigating the patent thicket: cross licenses, patent pools, and standard-setting. In: Jaffe, A.B., Lerner, J., Stern, S. (eds.) Innovation Policy and the Economy, pp. 119–150. MIT Press, Cambridge (2001)
8. Von Graevenitz, G., Wagner, S., Harhoff, D.: How to measure patent thickets-a novel approach. Econ. Lett. **111**, 6–9 (2011). https://doi.org/10.1016/j.econlet.2010.12.005

9. Ijichi, T., Yoda, T., Hirasawa, R.: Mapping R&D network dynamics: analysis of the development of co-author and co-inventor relations. J. Sci. Policy Res. Manag. **8**, 263–275 (1994). https://doi.org/10.20801/jsrpim.8.3_4_263

10. Von Graevenitz, G., Wagner, S., Harhoff, D.: Incidence and growth of patent thickets: the impact of technological opportunities and complexity. J. Ind. Econ. **61**, 521–563 (2013). https://doi.org/10.1111/joie.12032

11. Rubinfeld, D., Maness, R.: The strategic use of patents: implications for antitrust. Antitrust, patents Copyright - EU US Perspect, pp. 85–102 (2004)

12. Sabety, T.: Nanotechnology innovation and the patent thicket: which IP policies promote growth. Albany Law J. Sci. Technol. **15**, 477 (2004)

13. Bawa, R., Bawa, S.R., Maebius, S.B.: The nanotechnology patent "gold rush". J. Intellect. Prop. Rights **10**, 426–433 (2005)

14. D'Silva, J.: Pools, thickets and open source nanotechnology. Eur. Intellect. Prop. Rev. **31**, 300 (2009)

15. Clarkson, G., DeKorte, D.: The problem of patent thickets in convergent technologies. Ann. N. Y. Acad. Sci. **1093**, 180–200 (2006). https://doi.org/10.1196/annals.1382.014

16. Hargreaves, I.: Digital opportunity (2011)

17. Hall, B., Helmers, C., von Graevenitz, G.: Technology entry in the presence of patent thickets, Cambridge, MA (2015)

18. Galasso, A., Schankerman, M.: Patent thickets, courts, and the market for innovation. RAND J. Econ. **41**, 472–503 (2010). https://doi.org/10.1111/j.1756-2171.2010.00108.x

19. Gallini, N.: Do patents work? Thickets, trolls and antibiotic resistance. Can. J. Econ. **50**, 893–926 (2017). https://doi.org/10.1111/caje.12312

20. OECD: The Measurement of Scientific and Technological Activities Using Patent Data as Science and Technology Indicators. OECD Publishing, Paris (1994)

21. Hall, B.H., Jaffe, A.B., Trajtenberg, M.: Market value and patent citations. RAND J. Econ. **36**, 16–38 (2005). https://doi.org/10.1007/s00216-009-2643-x

Method of Innovation Assessment of Products and Processes in the Initial Design Phase

Bartosz Pryda, Marek Mysior[(⊠)], and Sebastian Koziołek

Department of Machine Design and Research, Wroclaw University of Science and Technology, Lukasiewicza 7/9, 50-371 Wroclaw, Poland
marek.mysior@pwr.edu.pl

Abstract. A key for economic success of an enterprise is proper decision making regarding product and process planning. The aim of this study was to develop a method of innovation assessment of products and processes that will be applicable at early stage of design and throughout life cycle of a product. The effectiveness of proposed method was examined on real-life case studies. The method is based on systematic, quantitative analysis of parameters, unlike current approaches that concentrate rather on subjective opinions or assessment of the design process, not the design itself. Proposed method comprises some already known tools regarding functional modelling including TRIZ and adopts them to innovation assessment environment. Innovation assessment using proposed method allows to facilitate decision making process regarding choice of concept to be further developed at an early stage of a design process, reducing cost and time of development of new products and processes.

1 Introduction

One of the conditions for maintaining global, economic growth is systematic, innovative and conceptual design of new products. It should be remembered that every invention ceases to be an innovation over time. Maintaining a high level of system usefulness in the long-term is associated with maintaining its stable level of ideality [1]. Furthermore in TRIZ, ideality is the factor that determines the development of technical systems. According to [2], ideality is defined as the ratio of benefits to costs and harms. It means that the bigger the benefit, the bigger the ideality of the system providing minimal costs and harms. Because of this, technical systems that can be described in terms of the ideality can be compared and thus assessed even at an early stage of the design process. In the system used, the proportion of useful to useless functions is changeable. This is due to a change in the need for the operation of this system and a partial change in its design assumptions. In practice, this is visible by the constant adaptation of elements of a given technical object to new design assumptions. When this adaptation ceases to be possible or is too expensive, new technology is implemented. Furthermore, according to one of the TRIZ trends of evolution [2, 3] ideality increases in time, which does not necessarily mean that the technical system will achieve market success. There are many examples of technical systems having high level of ideality and not being implemented to the market. In this article authors present a new method of innovation assessment of products and processes that take into

D. Cavallucci et al. (Eds.): TFC 2018, IFIP AICT 541, pp. 75–83, 2018.
https://doi.org/10.1007/978-3-030-02456-7_7

account the ideality as specified in TRIZ, but also takes into account several other factors that are important in terms of commercialization.

2 Problem Description

Innovation assessment of product and services is connected with the possibility of the product to be successfully introduced to the market. There are many methods on how to measure innovation in conceptual design among which some of them concentrate on the assessment of the system functions [1, 4–6] and some on the economic aspects of innovation [7–10]. From the point of view of an ideality of technical systems, the better the system the more useful functions it has providing minimal harm. It can be described by the equation [1]:

$$I = \frac{\sum_{i=1}^{n} F_u}{\sum_{j=1}^{n} F_b} \tag{1}$$

Where:
I -   System ideality
F_u -   Useful function
F_b -   Useless function

Taking into consideration only ideality of the system it can be observed that through elimination of harmful functions and addition of useful functions by application of 40 inventive principles of TRIZ [2], functional analysis and trimming [11] and other TRIZ tools continuous development of products is achieved. Nevertheless, manipulation of functions of the technical system is not directly related to the economic result of commercialization, that is why authors have deepen the analysis to include financial factors in innovation assessment by modifying Eq. 1.

According to [12], useful function presented in eq. 1. can be divided into three factors presented by [13], what makes a direct link between the parameters of technical system and market response.

$$Fu = \sum_{k=1}^{n} Fu_A + \sum_{l=1}^{o} Fu_{LQ} + \sum_{m=1}^{p} Fu_{MB} \tag{2}$$

According to the Eq. (2), useful function can be described as a sum of three separate set of functions. The first one is associated with attractive functions, which describe novel, unexpected features technical system delivers that are directly related to development trends and customer needs. The second one, called "linear-quality functions" is connected with performance of technical system- the better the system performs, the bigger usefulness is provided. The last set of useful functions is called "must-be requirements" and represents all features of the system that are necessary and vital for a technical system for the customer to be satisfied with the product. Relation of attributes assigned to each category with customers' satisfaction is presented on Fig. 1.

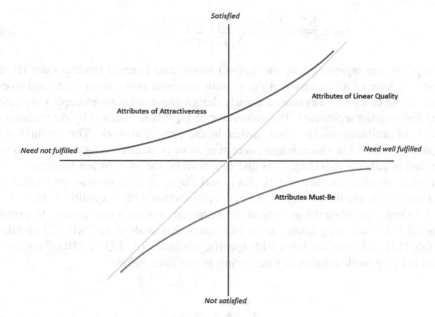

Fig. 1. Relation between fulfillment of needs and customers' satisfaction according to the KANO model [13]

As shown in [12], proportion of attractiveness, linear quality and must-be attributes in technical system is changing in time and thus the innovativeness of technical system.

3 New Innovativeness Metrics

According to [2], ideality can be increased either by introducing new useful functions to the system or by reduction of expenses and harms through elimination of harmful functions. It was observed however, that even if the ideality of the system grows through reduction of costs, it is not enough for the system to remain innovative and commercially attractive to customers. It means, that maintaining the same level of ideality of the system is not enough for the product to remain on the market. Based on Fig. 2 from [12] one may conclude, that a particular function (taking pictures by mobile phone for example) is changing in time from an attractive function, through linear-quality function to the must-be function. Comparing this with profit the system delivers, it decreases in time even though costs of manufacturing are decreasing. Taking into account Eq. (2) one may conclude, that the value of Fu does not change (the sum is constant, not even one function is neither removed nor added to the system). Providing constant costs of manufacturing, the ideality of the system remains stable and yet profits are decreasing. This means, that attractive, linear quality and must be attributes influence innovativeness in a different way. The proposed innovativeness metrics is presented in Eq. (3)

$$Inn = \frac{\sum_{k=1}^{n} Fu_A + \sum_{l=1}^{o} Fu_{LQ} + \sum_{m=1}^{p} Fu_{MB}}{\sum Expenses} \tag{3}$$

where profits are represented by the KANO model and harmful functions are represented as a sum of all expenses in the system (material costs, labor costs and overheads). Those costs can be evaluated at early design phase using for example Computer Aided Engineering techniques. The numerator of Eq. (3) is obtained by determination of fields of attributes, as described further in the presented work. This method is a comparative method in which design concept at an early stage is being compared to the other design concept providing costs and functions of the systems are known.

In order to obtain values of Fu_A, Fu_{LQ} and Fu_{MB}, authors propose adaptation of Fig. 1 that will relate the novelty of the analyzed function with its quality, as shown on Fig. 2. In order to obtain the novelty of the technical system, it is necessary to extract all useful functions using known tools like functional analysis in TRIZ [2] or other methods [14] and associate them with specific attributes (A, LQ or MB). This association is being made heuristically according to the rules below:

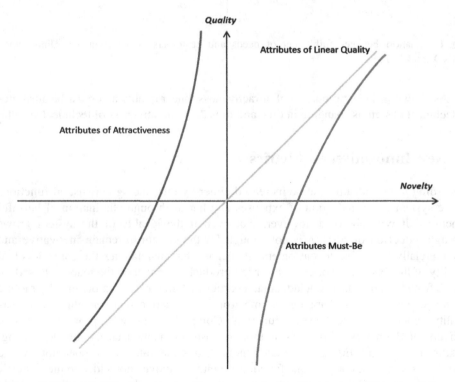

Fig. 2. Graph for obtaining fields of attributed that are used in innovativeness metrics

A - the attribute of a new design solution that so far has not been applied for purposes similar to the one implemented in the system under study. Often this attribute represents the introduction of new functions within the system,

Lq - a linear quality attribute, it includes design solutions that have been developed and applied earlier than in the examined system, however with an increased or reduced efficiency compared to previously known solutions design,

M - attribute of basic requirements, it includes such design solutions, which have been developed and applied earlier than in the examined system and defines the compliance only with the basic expectations of users,

Fb - the attribute of a useless function, it includes design solutions that in no way affect the operation of the system relative to the considered innovation assessment criterion.

For each function presented, it is necessary to evaluate quality of the function by comparing numerical parameters that describe the outcome of a particular function. For example, one of a possible useful function of a car is to give possibility to drive long distance. Outcome of this function can be described using such parameter as distance travelled [km], which is a numerical attribute. Scaling of the axis can be done by normalization methods in which the minimum value on axis "quality" is 0 and the maximum is 1. Placing those values on vertical axis of Fig. (2) and placing them on appropriate attribute (LQ, A, MB) gives novelty value (also normalized from −1 to 1) that is included in evaluation of the innovativeness metrics according to the Eq. 3.

4   Innovation Assessment of Thermal Insulation Systems

In this example, shortened innovation assessment method is presented based on the thermal insulation systems example. Numerical results of evaluation are not presented in this case study, because what is important is the method itself and not the result.

At the beginning of innovation assessment process, it is necessary to extract all useful functions related to the technical system being analyzed. For example, in the case of thermal insulation systems, those functions are:

- Insulating buildings
- Ensuring durability of outer building structure
- Decorating

With each function being analyzed, there is set of requirements that have to be fulfilled in order to realize the function, such as:

- Thermal insulation ability
- Installation (easiness of installation)
- Environmental protection
- Resistance to fire
- Resistance to external factors
- Resistance to water and moisture
- Attractiveness

Each of these conditions should be now marked by subordinate numbers. The technical requirements of the process, such as, for example, thermal insulation ability (condition 1.1) can be met by applying a low by using insulating materials (method 1.1.1). Next, the parameters of the insulating materials are identified as parameters

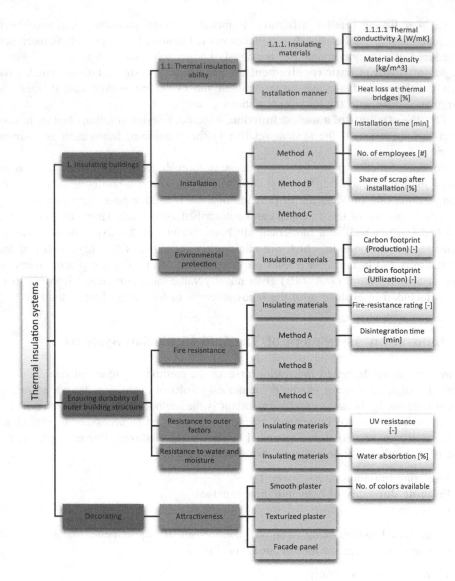

Fig. 3. Model of extraction of quality attributes in which useful functions are shown in red, requirements for the particular function are in green, technical methods of requirement fulfillment are in blue and the quality parameters are in white (Color figure online)

responsible for meeting the condition of the superior process. Figure 3 Presents all functions in red, requirements in green, methods in blue and parameters in white together with their numbers for clarification. Each of the applied methods receives innovation attributes assigned to the parameters responsible for meeting the superior condition (A, LQ, MB). For example, using thermal insulating materials method receives the innovation attributes assigned to the parameters: 1.1.11., 1.1.1.2, 1.1.1.3, …

These parameters are responsible for the fulfillment of the superior function, which is thermal insulation.

The basic element of measuring the level of system innovation is assignment of proper attributes to methods and parameters responsible for superior conditions of the system. Attributes of innovation are the features of the system's functions assigned to methods operation of the system and its parameters according to the innovation assessment criteria.

As a result, the level of system innovation is determined on the basis of system parameters that are scaled according to the characteristics of the attribute they received. Based on the scaled process parameters, the initial level of innovation is pre-identified. Then it is known whether the system parameters in the attribute characteristics are given a positive or negative quality value. In addition, the presented model identifies extreme levels of system parameters' quality marked with points on the relevant characteristics of the innovation attribute (Fig. 4). Next, the points of the extreme values of the process parameters represented by the unit of quality on the attribute curves should be combined. As a result, the indicated areas of quadrilateral surfaces (Fig. 4) determine the level of system innovation. The surface area P1 (green) is the scope of effective innovation and/or highly optimized known technology. The P2 (blue) area represents the scope of application of these design solutions that have elements of innovation. However, these solutions are not very effective and do not improve the users' satisfaction. Nevertheless, the P2 field is extremely important in studying the level of innovation because it sets the direction of product development. Field P3 (yellow) defines the scope of applied design solutions in the system, which are only the basic requirements of users. This area of evaluation indicates the lack of innovation, but also the high level of meeting the basic user requirements. The P4 field (red) indicates the use of risky design solutions. These solutions do not meet the basic user requirements or are extremely inefficient.

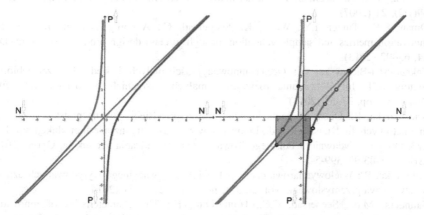

Fig. 4. Model of determining the level of system innovation. Fields: P1 (green), P2 (blue), P3 (yellow), P4 (red). (Color figure online)

At the end of the assessment process, values of obtained fields are summed together in specific categories and when costs are added to Eq. (3), level of innovativeness is obtained.

5 Conclusions

The presented Innovation assessment method finds its application in the design of interdisciplinary systems and their evaluation at an early stage of the design process as soon as the costs can be estimated. Due to its versatility it is possible to apply this method across various areas. The tools implemented within the theory can be implemented accordingly to the specific problems, both simple and complex systems. The direction of further development of this method is connected with more accurate evaluation of costs since most of them are very inaccurate at an early design stage. It is the basis for defining the technical specifications of new systems. Proposed innovation assessment method however makes it possible to compare several design concepts together and to choose the one that has a biggest potential to become profitable product on the market that is addressing needs of customers in a right way.

References

1. Zlotin, B., Zusman, A.: Directed Evolution: Philosophy, Theory and Practice. Ideation International Inc. (2001)
2. Gadd, K.: TRIZ for Engineers: Enabling Inventive Problem Solving. Wiley, Hoboken (2011)
3. Rantanen, K., Domb, E.: Simplified TRIZ. New Problem-Solving Applications for Engineers and Manufacturing Professionals. Taylor & Francis (2002)
4. Arafat, G.H., Goodman, B., Arciszewski, T.: RAMZES: a knowledge-based system for structural concepts evaluation. Comput. Syst. Eng. 4(2–3), 211–221 (1993)
5. Shelton, K.A., Arciszewski, T.: Formal innovation criteria. Int. J. Comput. Appl. Technol. 30(1/2), 21 (2007)
6. Oman, S.K., Tumer, I.Y., Wood, K., Seepersad, C.: A comparison of creativity and innovation metrics and sample validation through in-class design projects. Res. Eng. Des. 24, 65–92 (2013)
7. Zakrzewska-Bielawska, A.: Ocena innowacyjności małych i średnich przedsiębiorstw sektora ICT. In: Wyzywania rozwojowe małych i średnich przedsiębiorstw. Difin, Warszawa, pp. 37–53 (2011)
8. Kaczmarska, B.: Ocena poziomu innowacyjnosci przedsiebiorstw na podstawie zasobów internetowych. In: Knosali, R. (ed.) Innowacje w zarzadzaniu i inzynierii produkcji, pp. 112–123. Oficyna Wydawnicza Polskiego Towarzystwa Zarzadzania Produkcja, Opole (2013). ISBN 978-83-930399-5-1
9. Sitkowska, R.: Wielowymiarowa ocena potencjału innowacyjnego wytypowanych działów przetwórstwa przemysłowego, vol. 2/2011, no. 2, pp. 215–231 (2014)
10. Saunders, M.N., Seepersad, C.C., Holtta-Otto, K.: The characteristics of innovative, mechanical products. In: ASME IDETC Design Theory and Methodology Conference, no. 512, pp. 1–38 (2009)
11. Boratyńska-Sala, A.: Współczesny TRIZ- analiza funkcjonalna i trimming. In: Konferencja Innowacje w Zarządzaniu i Inżynierii Produkcji, pp. 26–37 (2011)

12. Koziołek, S.: Design by analogy: synectics and knowledge acquisition network. In: Rusiński, E., Pietrusiak, D. (eds.) RESRB 2016. LNME, pp. 259–273. Springer, Cham (2017). https://doi.org/10.1007/978-3-319-50938-9_27
13. Kano, N., Seraku, N., Takahashi, F., Tsuji, S.: Attractive quality and must-be quality. J. Jpn. Soc. Qual. Control **14**(2), 39–48 (1984)
14. Arciszewski, T.: Successful Education. How to Educate Creative Engineers. Successful Education LLC (2009)

Agile'TRIZ Framework: Towards the Integration of TRIZ Within the Agile Innovation Methodology

Didier Casner[1], Achille Souili[1,2], Rémy Houssin[1(✉)],
and Jean Renaud[2]

[1] ICube – CSIP Team, 24 boulevard de la Victoire,
67084 Strasbourg Cedex, France
remy.houssin@icube.unistra.fr
[2] INSA Strasbourg, 24 boulevard de la Victoire,
67084 Strasbourg Cedex, France

Abstract. Applying TRIZ is difficult, time-consuming and therefore requires implies important development costs: designers spend a lot of time to analyze the problem, to identify the contradictions, and then to develop innovative concepts and propose technical solutions. The efficiency of TRIZ strongly depends on the level of completeness of the problem and the experience of the designer with TRIZ tools. Agile methodologies are commonly used to efficiently develop new products toward an iterative, incremental and adaptive development cycle. They allow to rapidly provide a first technical solution and break the product development work into small increments for minimizing the amount of up-front planning and design. Agile'TRIZ is an Agile-based framework for TRIZ intended for enhancing the innovative skills and the efficiency of the designers, and to provide an efficient approach for quickly analyzing a problem and rapidly developing new innovative solutions using TRIZ tools through an iterative development cycle.

Keywords: TRIZ · Agile development · Agile framework
Concurrent engineering

1 Introduction

Customers nowadays have highly specific but also rapidly changing needs; although they still want high-quality and low-cost products. In order to stay competitive, the R&D engineers should on one hand integrate more technical innovations and on the other hand reduce their development time and costs.

The organization of the R&D teams within a company is so that the development process of complex products, such as vehicles, trains, aircrafts, is not performed by a single development team. The development is split into several teams (one team in charge of the development of the engine, one of the binnacle, ...) and the design activities are all be occurring at the same time, i.e., concurrently. The systems developed by the several development teams should then be integrated into a global super-system that should be homogeneous and optimal.

© IFIP International Federation for Information Processing 2018
Published by Springer Nature Switzerland AG 2018. All Rights Reserved
D. Cavallucci et al. (Eds.): TFC 2018, IFIP AICT 541, pp. 84–93, 2018.
https://doi.org/10.1007/978-3-030-02456-7_8

In order to deal with this competitive environment, current product design strategies tend to be more flexible, adaptive and involve agile frameworks [1]. Agility is the capability to react, and adopt to expected and unexpected changes within a dynamic environment constantly and quickly; and to use those changes (if possible) as an advantage [2]. An agile framework comprises agile values and principles as well as methods, which are commonly coupled through a process [3].

In order to integrate more innovation technologies, TRIZ is today regarded as one of the most comprehensive, systematically organized invention knowledge and creative thinking methodologies [4], it however has some drawbacks that have an impact on the introduction of TRIZ within the R&D teams in the industry. First of all, TRIZ is not an ideal theory as it does not guarantee a solution and then the feasibility or the success of the solution [5]. It does not provide finite and directly implementable solutions, only ideas or concepts: it does not provide tools for concretizing a standard solution [6]. It gives a very important number of ideas after the analysis phase. TRIZ tools are somehow difficult, time-consuming (especially the problem-analysis step) and can hardly be error-freely applied without prior expertise with TRIZ [7, 8]. The integration of TRIZ within an Agile innovation framework could solve those problems and offer a flexible, adaptive environment for rapidly developing innovative technologies and products.

The research work outlined in this paper aims to deal with such agility problems and aims to propose a first drawing for the integration of TRIZ in an Agile framework. The paper outlines a very first version of this framework which will be improved and tested in the future and will be presented in future communications.

This paper deals with the innovation design process and aims to propose a first concept of such an Agile framework, entitled Agile'TRIZ. The paper is organized in six sections. In Sect. 2, the Agile design strategy is introduced. The Sect. 3 discusses the interests and advantages of integrating TRIZ in an agile framework. In Sect. 4, a first concept of our Agile'TRIZ framework is presented. In Sect. 5, the concept is analyzed, and some research perspectives outlined. Finally, the conclusion presents some research perspectives in Sect. 6.

2 Agile Product Development Process

Agile is a microplanning project management methodology [9]. The Agile design strategies were first developed as software development strategies by seventeen software developers which published the Manifesto for Agile Software Development in 2001 [10]. However, iterative and incremental development methodologies are much older, with for example the evolutionary project management [11] and the adaptive software development [12, 13] process emerging in the 1970s. Several frameworks were designed for software development, like Scrum [3, 14, 15] or Kanban [16, 17].

Focusing on the innovation development process of new products, several frameworks were identified by [2, 3, 18]:

– Scrum [3], also used for software development, that structures the development process starting with Sprint Planning for each Sprint, Daily Scrums – brief daily

team meetings during which the progress is analyzed and the remaining hours of work are recorded –, Sprint Review and Sprint Retrospectives,
– Kanban, considered as an agile framework by Highsmith [13], which optimizes the current processes by mapping them, limiting work in progress and eliminating waste [19],
– Lean Startup [20], following the Build, Measure, Learn cycle actions according to [21], to develop businesses and products by adopting a combination of business-hypothesis-driven experimentation, iterative product releases, and validated learning.
– Design Thinking contains a process which comprises the phases understand, observe, define point of view, ideate, prototype and test [18, 22]. The Design Thinking framework stops with the concept development process and does not provides methods or tools for concept test, development, …
– Makeathons or Hackathons focus on iterative prototyping. After a set time the functions demonstrating the product's concept and its value will be presented [23],
– Agile–Stage-Gate Hybrids, developed by Cooper [23], which combines the Agile approach with the Stage-Gate innovation process model.

Figure 1 classifies the frameworks along the stage-gate innovation process model [24].

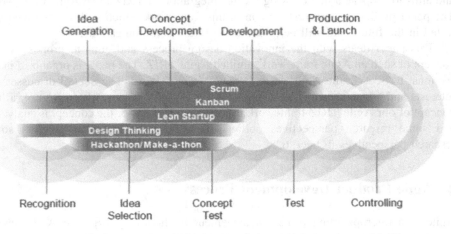

Fig. 1. Agile frameworks within the generic innovation process model [2]

Despite linear or iterative process models, an agile model passes several process phases at the same time with main aspect being to give priority to the innovation object within the innovation process. Starting with just a vision, the minimum feature set is derived to build a prototype and will lead to a first minimum viable product and a user interaction [2].

An agile innovation framework needs to be complemented with a systematic approach regarding physical product development. TRIZ presents a systematic approach for understanding and defining challenging problems and provides a range of strategies and tools for finding these inventive solutions [25–27]. TRIZ may then be applied for providing an organized approach for creative thinking and problem solving, as well as rapidly develop new innovative products if it were combined with an Agile innovation framework.

In the next section, the interest and advantages of developing an Agile framework integrating TRIZ as a problem-solving tool is discussed.

3 Why Integrating TRIZ in an Agile Framework?

Before presenting the Agile'TRIZ framework which aims to integrate TRIZ within an Agile innovation strategy, it can be interesting to understand how this idea emerged and what the foundations of the framework.

The framework emerged from the statement based on our own experience regarding the application of TRIZ with industrials and non-TRIZ experts that, during or before the workshops for idea generation, the design team spends a huge amount of time for analyzing the initial situation and its problem to draw the problem graph with hundreds of technical problems and partial solutions. And the design team will then decide, eventually using some evaluation tools such as [28], to focus the problem-solving activities on one or two problems or contradictions only (usually the most significant ones or the problems with the highest innovation potential). In other words, the design team spends more time in analyzing its problem than to develop new ideas and concepts but finally skip most of the identified problems or tasks. From this statement emerged two main questions:

1. Could the design team spend less time in analyzing the problem and more time on creativity tasks?
2. How could we speed up the creativity tasks to quickly develop implementable innovative products?

Based on the statement that several design teams should work in parallel and develop innovative technologies which should than be integrated into a global super-system that should be as optimal as possible, the classical linear design approaches imply that this combination occurs at the end of the development cycle and some subsystems may be incompatible, not fit properly with the other subsystems. This problem will imply that the design teams will then have to adjust the subsystems in order to correct those problems. This development strategy then leads to global super-systems integrating optimal subsystems but without optimal interactions which are often the source of further failures or dysfunctions. From this other statement, one additional question:

3. How could we improve the interaction of the design teams during the innovation development and eventually rapidly correct the interaction problems as soon as possible?

To solve these research questions, the idea of integrating TRIZ within an agile innovation strategy emerged. On one hand, the agile innovation strategy uses an iterative and incremental development strategy which would allow the design teams to rapidly develop new innovative products and to learn the positive and negative effects from the review of the prototype; but it does not provide tools for generating ideas and solving contradictions. On the other hand, TRIZ can be used for such purpose.

In comparison with the original TRIZ approach, a TRIZ-based agile framework would provide an iterative and incremental development strategy that should allow the designers to:

- Spend less time for analyzing the initial situation, as the designers may start the development with a minimal problem, which will be complemented in the next iterations,
- Use some TRIZ tools, such as the 40 inventive principles or the TRIZ database of technological effects, to provide a limited number of ideas for solving its problem,
- Rapidly go through the development of a first prototype,
- Learn the positive and negative effects from the evaluation, the review of the prototype,
- Improve the prototype during the further iterations (#2, #3, …),
- Improve the interactions between the different design teams and reduce the interaction problems of the final product.

The Agile'TRIZ framework, whose first concept is presented in the next section, is our response to those statements and research questions.

4 Concept of Agile'TRIZ

Agile'TRIZ represents the combination of the agile development strategy and TRIZ, as a process from idea to prototype through an adaptive, iterative and incremental innovation design strategy.

Figure 2 presents a functional diagram of the Agile'TRIZ framework.

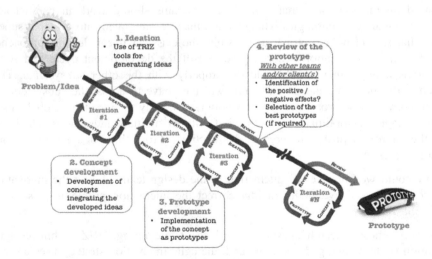

Fig. 2. Agile'TRIZ framework (concept)

Agile'TRIZ is based on the following strategy:

1. The design team comes with a user demand and analyzes it.
2. During the first iteration (Iteration #1), the design team uses the TRIZ tools (the TRIZ database of technological effects) or some other tools to develop a first virtual prototype. The team analyzes the positive and negative effects of the first prototype, eventually with the other teams (for highlighting eventual integration problems) and the client.
3. During the next iterations (Iteration #2, #3, ...), the design team develops new improved versions of the prototype (Version #2, ...) using some TRIZ problem-solving tools, such as the inventive principles, the standard solutions, ... and reviews the prototype.

The framework includes, for each iteration, the following four steps:

1. **Ideation step.** The designer uses TRIZ tools to generate new ideas and summarizes the idea generation in a morphological matrix (see Table 1). Each row contains the several ideas generated for a single problem. If different inventive principles can be applied, the ideas are presented with each row representing an idea using one inventive principle.

Table 1. Morphological matrix from the ideation step

Functions /problems	TRIZ inventive principle	Ideas		
Problem A	1. Segmentation	Idea A1	Idea A2	...
	3. Local quality	Idea A3	Idea A4	...
...				
Problem Z	23. Feedback	Idea Z1	Idea Z2	...

2. **Concept development step.** The design team develops concepts by combining at least one idea from each row. This step can be computerized with the use of combinatorial optimization algorithms. An example of such approach has been previously presented in [29] (Table 2).

Table 2. Concept development step

Functions /Problems	TRIZ inventive principle	Ideas		
Problem A	1. Segmentation	Idea A1	Idea A2	...
	3. Local quality	Idea A3	Idea A4	...
...				
Problem Z	23. Feedback	Idea Z1	Idea Z2	...

Concept C1   Concept C2

3. **Prototype development step.** The design team develops prototypes that implements the concepts developed during the previous step.
4. **Review of the prototype.** The design team, together with the other development teams and the client/user, reviews the developed prototypes and extracts the positive and negative effects of each prototype. A possible approach for concept evaluation was proposed by [30] and can be adapted for our framework.

They also analyze with the other teams the implementation and interaction problems that may occur from the integration of the prototypes within the global super-system by considering the prototypes developed by the other teams. During this step, they may also be requested to select the most significant prototype(s) if the number is too important or if the overall prototypes cannot be processed (with the use of computer-aided innovation tools for example).

An example of such collaborative teamwork is shown in Fig. 3.

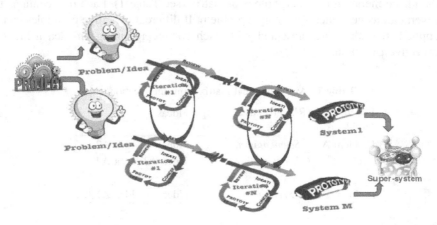

Fig. 3. Example of teamwork between different design teams within a project with Agile'TRIZ

At the end of each iteration, the positive and negative effects and other results from the review step are used as a basis for improving the prototype during the different steps.

This section proposed a first concept of the Agile'TRIZ framework we developed as an answer to the questions related with the integration of TRIZ within the agile innovation process in order to help the designers or the design team in rapidly develop a new innovative prototype and improve the prototype through an iterative and incremental strategy allowing better interactions with design teams (collaborative development strategy) and user interactions (the user can take part of the review of the prototypes at the end of each iteration).

The framework is discussed in the next section and some research perspectives related with the improvement of its integration with TRIZ and its evaluation are introduced.

5 Discussions and Research Agenda

With Agile'TRIZ and starting with just a vision, the minimum feature set is derived to build a prototype and will lead to a first minimum viable product and a user interaction. The several iterative steps allow to rapidly improve the prototype.

After a limited amount of iterations and time, the design team is able to provide a viable innovative solution to a set of user requirements, efficiently ensure that the product satisfies them by allowing regular user interactions through all the process (ideally after each iteration, during the review step) and rapidly change and correct the prototype regarding the report defined during the review step.

Agile'TRIZ also improves the ability of collaborative work and the possibility of the several design teams to work within a common project and simultaneously develop a portion of the global super-system. The review step indeed allows the teams to discuss and expose their prototypes and identify the interaction and integration issues. These issues can then rapidly be taken into account during the process.

In the future research work, the following tasks will be performed

- **Improvement of the framework.** The framework will be improved, and specific TRIZ-based tools be developed to improve the integration and compatibility of TRIZ with the Agile innovation strategy.
- **Experimentation and evaluation.** The framework will then be experimented in practice, first with our students and later with our industrial partners, in order to evaluate the framework regarding the Innovative Design Methodology based on TRIZ and the ability of the students/partners to rapidly develop viable prototypes as well as working in collaborative design teams. The quality of the process regarding its impact of the proposed approach on the outcomes of new problem development or the problem-solving process based on TRIZ.
- **Implementation and software development.** The framework will finally be implemented as a software platform to guide the designers through the framework and computerize some steps of the framework, such as the concept development and review steps. Some text-mining tools could also be integrated in the software to automate several steps, such as the analysis of the initial situation [31]; as well as some optimization tools to computerize the evaluation, the selection and the development of the concepts and technical solutions [29] or integrating product usage [32] and safety into the innovative design process [33].

6 Conclusion

This paper dealt with the innovation development process and aimed to provide a first concept of a TRIZ-based agile framework that integrates the advantages of TRIZ as a systematic problem-solving approach and the Agile innovation strategy as an adaptive, iterative and incremental development model.

After an introduction on the Agile development process, the interests and advantages of combining both approaches were discussed. Then, a first concept of the

Agile'TRIZ framework allowing the integration of TRIZ in an agile innovation process was presented. The framework was discussed, and some research agenda outlined.

References

1. Link, P.: Agile Methoden im Produkt-Lifecycle-Prozess – Mit agilen Methoden die Komplexität im Innovationsprozess handhaben. In: Schoeneberg, K.P. (ed.) Komplexitätsmanagement in Unternehmen, pp. 65–92. Springer Gabler, Wiesbaden (2014). https://doi.org/10.1007/978-3-658-01284-7_5
2. Böhmer, A., et al.: Think.make.start. - an agile framework. In: 84 Proceedings of the DESIGN 2016 14th International Design Conference (2016). Accessed 12 Apr 2018
3. Brandes, U., Gemmer, P., Koschek, H., Schültken, L.: Management Y: Agile, Scrum, Design Thinking & Co.: So gelingt der Wandel zur attraktiven und zukunftsfähigen Organisation. Campus Verlag (2014)
4. Cavallucci, D., Cascini, G., Duflou, J., Livotov, P., Vaneker, T.: TRIZ and knowledge-based innovation in science and industry. Procedia Eng. **131**, 1–2 (2015). https://doi.org/10.1016/j.proeng.2015.12.341
5. Robles, G.C., Negny, S., Lann, J.M.L.: Case-based reasoning and TRIZ: a coupling for innovative conception in Chemical Engineering. Chem. Eng. Process. Process Intensif. **48**, 239–249 (2009). https://doi.org/10.1016/j.cep.2008.03.016
6. Houssin, R., Renaud, J., Coulibaly, A., Cavallucci, D., Rousselot, F.: TRIZ theory and case based reasoning: synergies and oppositions. Int. J. Interact. Des. Manuf. IJIDeM **9**, 177–183 (2014). https://doi.org/10.1007/s12008-014-0252-1
7. Casner, D., Livotov, P., Mas'udah, Kely da Silva, P: TRIZ-based approach for process intensification and problem solving in process engineering: concepts and research agenda, Wroclaw, Poland (2016)
8. Casner, D., Livotov, P.: Advanced innovation design approach for process engineering. In: 21st International Conference on Engineering Design (ICED 17), Vancouver, Canada, pp 653–662 (2017)
9. Cooper, R.G.: Agile–stage-gate hybrids. Res-Technol. Manag. **59**, 21–29 (2016). https://doi.org/10.1080/08956308.2016.1117317
10. Martin, R.C.: Agile Software Development: Principles, Patterns, and Practices. Pearson Education (2003)
11. Woodward, S.: Evolutionary project management. Computer **32**, 49–57 (1999). https://doi.org/10.1109/2.796109
12. Edmonds, E.: A process for the development of software for non-technical users as an adaptive system. Gen. Syst. **21**, 215–218 (1974)
13. Highsmith, J.: Adaptive Software Development: A Collaborative Approach to Managing Complex Systems. Addison-Wesley (2013)
14. Rubin, K.S.: Essential Scrum: Umfassendes Scrum-Wissen aus der Praxis. MITP Verlags GmbH & Co. KG (2014)
15. Stark, E.: Scrum Quickstart Guide: A Simplified Beginner's Guide to Mastering Scrum. Createspace Independent Pub (2014)
16. Brechner, E.: Agile Project Management with Kanban. Microsoft Press (2015)
17. Cimorelli, S.: Kanban for the Supply Chain: Fundamental Practices for Manufacturing Management, 2nd edn. CRC Press (2016)
18. Taherivand, A., Schaefer, H., Kerguenne, A.: Design Thinking: Die agile Innovations-Strategie. Haufe Lexware (2017)

19. Anderson, C.: Makers: The New Industrial Revolution. Crown Publishing Group (2012)
20. Ellis, S.: Lean Startup Marketing: Agile Product Development, Business Model Design, Web Analytics, and Other Keys to Rapid Growth: A Step-By-Step Guide to Successful Startup Marketing. Hyperink (2012)
21. Ries, E.: The Lean Startup: How Today's Entrepreneurs Use Continuous Innovation to Create Radically Successful Businesses. Crown Publishing Group (2011)
22. Burba, D.: Agile by Design: Integrating Design Thinking and Agile Approaches Helps Organizations Find and Build the Right Customer-focused Solution (2016)
23. Komssi, M., Pichlis, D., Raatikainen, M., Kindström, K., Järvinen, J.: What are hackathons for? IEEE Softw. **32**, 60–67 (2015). https://doi.org/10.1109/MS.2014.78
24. Cooper, R.G.: Perspective third-generation new product processes. J. Prod. Innov. Manag. **11**, 3–14 (1994). https://doi.org/10.1016/0737-6782(94)90115-5
25. Cascini, G., Rissone, P., Rotini, F., Russo, D.: Systematic design through the integration of TRIZ and optimization tools. Procedia Eng. **9**, 674–679 (2011). https://doi.org/10.1016/j.proeng.2011.03.154
26. Brad, S., Mocan, B., Brad, E., Fulea, M.: Leading innovation to improve complex process performances by systematic problem analysis with TRIZ. TRIZ Knowl.-Based Innov. Sci. Ind. **131**, 1121–1129 (2015). https://doi.org/10.1016/j.proeng.2015.12.430
27. Terninko, J., Zusman, A., Zlotin, B.: Systematic Innovation: An Introduction to TRIZ, 1st edn. CRC Press, Boca Raton (1998)
28. Livotov, P.: Method for quantitative evaluation of innovation tasks for technical systems, products and processes. In: ETRIA World Conference 2008 "Synthesis in Innovation". University of Twente, Entschede, The Netherlands, pp. 197–199 (2008)
29. Casner, D., Houssin, R., Renaud, J., Knittel, D.: A multiobjective optimization framework for the embodiment design of mechatronic products based on morphological and design structure matrices. In: Bouras, A., Eynard, B., Foufou, S., Thoben, K.-D. (eds.) PLM 2015. IAICT, vol. 467, pp. 813–825. Springer, Cham (2016). https://doi.org/10.1007/978-3-319-33111-9_74
30. Chinkatham, T., Cavallucci, D.: Early feasibility evaluation of solution concepts in an inventive design method framework: approach and support tool. Comput. Ind. **67**, 1–16 (2015). https://doi.org/10.1016/j.compind.2014.11.004
31. Souili, A., Cavallucci, D., Rousselot, F., Zanni, C.: Starting from patents to find inputs to the problem graph model of IDM-TRIZ. TRIZ Knowl.-Based Innov. Sci. Ind. **131**, 150–161 (2015). https://doi.org/10.1016/j.proeng.2015.12.365
32. Sun, X., Houssin, R., Renaud, J., Gardoni, M.: Integrating user information into design process to solve contradictions in product usage. Procedia CIRP **39**, 166–172 (2016). https://doi.org/10.1016/j.procir.2016.01.183
33. Houssin, R., Coulibaly, A.: An approach to solve contradiction problems for the safety integration in innovative design process. Comput. Ind. **62**, 398–406 (2011). https://doi.org/10.1016/j.compind.2010.12.009

Discovery on Purpose?
Toward the Unification of *Paradigm Theory* and the *Theory of Inventive Problem Solving* (TRIZ)

Justus Schollmeyer[1(✉)] and Viesturs Tamuzs[2(✉)]

[1] Second Negation, Berlin, Germany
justus@secondnegation.com
[2] Altshuller Institute, Worcester, MA, USA
viesturs.tamuzs@gmail.com

Abstract. This essay relates Thomas Kuhn's Paradigm Theory with Genrich Altshuller's Theory of Inventive Problem Solving (TRIZ for short). Despite their clearly divergent cultural roots, both understand paradigm shifts as the result of problem-solving processes—Kuhn in science and Altshuller in technology. In contrast to Kuhn, Altshuller used paradigm shifts to study creative problem solving in technology in order to make invention on purpose possible. He summarized his finding in the *Algorithm of Inventive Problems Solving* (ARIZ), which, as we will show, can be made explicit in a more general system theoretical framework. This allows for its application outside of the technological domain without relying on crutches such as metaphorical analogies. In order to demonstrate the application of this generalized version of ARIZ, we reconstruct one of the most famous paradigm shifts in the history of science—the shift from the Ptolemaic geo-centric system to Copernicus' helio-centric one.

Keywords: ARIZ · Paradigm shift · Science

1 Introduction

From an epistemological point of view, Genrich Altshuller's *Theory of Inventive Problem Solving*—TRIZ—[1] is built upon four crucial decisions:

- (i) Technological objects are viewed from a system perspective.
- (ii) The focus of attention is on the development of these objects as systems.
- (iii) The development is studied in terms of concrete changes within the inner-systemic hierarchy.
- (iv) These changes are reconstructed as if they were the results of intentional problem solving.

Altshuller assumed that studying the development of technological systems in this way could serve as a suitable window into the black box of *creative problem solving*.

D. Cavallucci et al. (Eds.): TFC 2018, IFIP AICT 541, pp. 94–109, 2018.
https://doi.org/10.1007/978-3-030-02456-7_9

What is more, he showed that a clear understanding of the logic that underlies these processes can make creative problem solving teachable. The further TRIZ developed, the more the character of Altshuller's epistemological decisions crystalized. This can be best appreciated by following the roughly 30-year development of the *Algorithm for Inventive Problem Solving*—starting in 1956 and ending in 1985—with Altshuller's final version: ARIZ-85C [2]. In contrast to the earlier versions [3], the latest has almost entirely stripped off any reminiscence of its original domain: technology. Only a few terms, such as "tool," are reminiscent of the engineering discourse. Upon closer examination, however, they turn out to be placeholders for more abstract vocabulary concerning systems in general. We will call it *vocabulary for systemic thinking*.

The goal of our paper is to bridge the gap between the application of ARIZ in technology and other domains—particularly science. To do so, we will develop the *vocabulary of systemic thinking* as far as it is needed to express the structure of ARIZ in more general terms.[1] Then, we will address development in science much as Altshuller addressed development in technology. For this purpose, we introduce Thomas Kuhn's famous three phase distinction of *pre-normal, normal* and *revolutionary science* [4] and draw the attention to Altshuller's distinction of two different types of scientific discoveries—*new explanations* and *new detections* [5]. After matching Kuhn's distinction with Altshuller's, we will limit our attention to the application of ARIZ to explanatory discoveries alone. Having outlined to which extent explanations can be understood as *explanatory systems*, we will finally apply ARIZ, in its system theoretical form, to one of the most famous paradigm shifts in the history of science: the transition from the Ptolemaic to the Copernican planetary system. We conclude with suggesting the unification of both paradigm theory and TRIZ within a system theoretical framework. Since the goal of our paper is to show why and how ARIZ can be used in science, we will say very little about its application to technology. For a deeper understanding, we recommend the study of Altshuller's own example [2, 6].

2 Elements of a Vocabulary for Systemic Thinking

Systems can be described as finite sets of elements that are organized according to certain rules. These elements stand in relation to one another such that the system is more than the mere sum of its parts. The set that comprises the set of all elements of a

---

[1] At first sight, it might seem that a similar effect could be achieved by comparing the TRIZ-specific ontology with the specific ontology of the target domain. This, however, would only forge the foundation for an application of TRIZ in this specific target domain. In contrast to this strategy, we claim that TRIZ is itself an application of a more general framework of system thinking in the field of technology. Its ontology can be seen as an effect of this application. By spelling out this general way of thought, we hope to provide a framework for its application beyond the technical sphere.

system and the set of all the relations between them is called the *system structure*. While this structure determines the system's (context-dependent) behavior—i.e., the set of all of its states over time—, the same behavior might be realizable by alternative system structures [7].

That the concept of systems is primarily a pragmatic methodological category that helps to describe, explain and control subjects of our interest can be seen from the way the term *element* is used. Whether or not it is convenient to consider an element of a system to be (i) *elementary* and not in the need for further decomposition or (ii) itself a system with its own *system structure* depends upon the pragmatic context of the analysis. An element of a system S that has its own *system structure* is called a *sub-system* of S. In return, a system S that has another system S' as one of its elements, is called a *super-system* of S'.

From a subjective standpoint, a system's behaviour—or parts of it—can appear to be desirable or undesirable in certain contexts. Although most artificial—i.e. human-made—systems are designed for a purpose that is desired by someone, parts of their behaviour can be undesirable. A purpose can be described as a hierarchically ordered system of aims [7], where primary aims can be distinguished from secondary ones. Primary aims are expressed in the form of answers to the question of what the system was designed (or put into place) for, while secondary aims play an auxiliary role. The latter are either means to the end of achieving other aims, or they express a certain desirable behaviour of the system—for example, the elimination of some undesirable side-effect.

Thanks to their *system structure*, systems have the capacity to achieve primary and secondary aims. A system's capacity to achieve a primary aim will be called a *primary function* of the system and its capacity to achieve a secondary aim a *secondary function*. Note that, according to this definition, the term function is only used for capacities that are considered desirable (which does not exclude the possibility that the enabling structure might be the cause for effects that are considered undesirable). As a consequence, a change in the structure of a system that results in the loss of a function without further compensation yields undesirable effects (since a desirable effect can be understood as the negation of an undesirable effect).

The phenomenon of pragmatic relativity that shows in the use of the term *element* also applies to the distinction between the terms *primary function* and *secondary function*. On the one hand, the primary function of a system might only be a secondary function when viewed from the perspective of its super-system. On the other hand, a sub-system might only be in charge of a secondary function within a wider system.

However, when only looking at the very same sub-system, the former secondary function might turn out to be the primary function.[2]

Sub-systems (or elements) that provide a primary function will be called *primary sub-systems* and those providing secondary functions will be called *secondary sub-systems*.

3   Thomas Kuhn's Distinction of Pre-normal, Normal and Revolutionary Science

Having developed the vocabulary needed to view Altshuller's approach from a *systemic perspective* we can now turn our attention towards the concept of *development* by building upon Thomas Kuhn's *Structure of Scientific Revolutions* [4]. Summarising the findings from his studies in the history of science, Kuhn describes a pattern of evolution in science by distinguishing three phases: (i) Pre-Normal Science, (ii) Normal Science, and (iii) Revolutionary Science. Drawing on the tradition of American pragmatism, Kuhn explains these three different phases in terms of different types of problem solving. During the first phase, it is not yet clear how to best frame the problem. Consequently, different schools develop their own explanatory strategies, which compete with one another until an explanatory paradigm is developed that outcompetes alternative approaches such that researchers now rely on this paradigm

---

[2] This relativity of the terms primary and secondary function points to a deeper problem in approaches of systemic functional analysis in non-artificial systems such as [8] and [9]. Analyzing an object as a system is, in the first place, a methodological choice made by an inquiring subject for the sake of explaining some phenomenon. What the roles of a system's parts are (and the way in which these parts are individualized, too) partly depends on the explanatory choice of the inquiring subject. Take for example a human's heart: If we choose to consider its role in the context of blood circulation, we will conclude its role is to pump blood. If, however, we want to explain the entire sound spectrum in human bodies, the role of the heart will consist in creating a more or less rhythmical beat. This criticism of arbitrariness in systemic approaches has been prominently articulated by proponents of etiological theories [10, 11]. Moreover, etiologists argue that because of its dependency on subjective explanatory choices, systemic functional analysis cannot account for the normative dimension of *proper functioning*. In other words, whether or not a system's part works well cannot be judged on the basis of systemic approaches alone. All they explain is how the system actually behaves. Whether or not a heart, for example, beats too quickly or too slowly, too much or too little, exceeds the limits of the explanatory framework. As a consequence, the value judgement becomes again a matter of subjective consideration. Etiologists try to solve both of these problems by including the dimension of history into their understanding of functionality. Looking for the proper function of some part P in a system S, they argue, means to ask the question: *How come that P is a part of S?* Take for example a breathing apparatus that contains a filter. One could ask: *How come this filter is part of the breathing apparatus?* Moreover, they argue it can be said that the proper function of P in S is the effect E if and only if *P was selected to be a part of X, because of having the effect E in X*. In the breathing apparatus, the proper function of the filter is to filter the air just because the designer of the breathing apparatus put it in for the sake of achieving exactly this effect. In engineering this selection implies conscious decision-making, while it is a matter of natural selection when it comes to biological systems [11]. In other words, the proper function of the heart — to pump blood —, etiologists would argue, is the effect for the sake of which it has been picked by natural selection. Note that this framework also allows to assign multiple proper functions to a system's part in case that this part was selected for multiple effects (for a more detailed discussion of this debate see [12]).

when coping with the problems in their field. Kuhn calls this phase *normal science*. For example, when the Ptolemaic model was established, the European history of astronomy entered such a phase of normal science. By sticking to this paradigm, astronomers were able to solve well-defined problems, such as predicting the position of certain *vagabonds* at a given time (*vagabonds* was the term for moving celestial bodies at this time). Accordingly, one major parameter for the model's improvement was the accuracy of predictions. Among other things, the vagabonds moving on spheres around the Earth were themselves placed on further spheres in order to account for the appearance of planets moving backward. The more the model's accuracy was improved, the more obvious an internal contradiction in the model became: minor improvements in accuracy caused major deterioration in simplicity, even though full accuracy could not be achieved. When the Ptolemaic geo-centric paradigm was replaced by Copernicus' heliocentric one, the model's simplicity improved dramatically. Kuhn calls such replacements *paradigm shifts*. They are the result of problem-solving processes during the phase of *revolutionary science* and foster a redefinition of a discipline's paradigm, yielding a new phase of *normal science*.

4   Discoveries as *Detections* or *Explanations*

During all three phases, scientists aim at producing knowledge—some of it being called *discovery*. As Altshuller points out in a paper on creative problem solving in science [5], the term "discovery" refers to two different phenomena: *new detections* and *new explanations*. Explanation as purposeful practice is crucial for science and faces different kinds of challenges during each of Kuhn's three phases. During the phase of pre-normal science, there is no established paradigm that the explanation could draw upon. For this reason, scientists need to come up with their own groundbreaking approaches. This leads to competition between various attempts. In the phase of normal science, when paradigms have been established for the vast majority of scientists, explanation consists in the application of such established paradigms. During the phase of revolutionary science, however, a standard paradigm is challenged by a new and presumably superior way of explanation that can, for example, account for anomalies that were not explicable by means of the former.

Unlike the development of most explanations, detection of something new can be the result of both purposeful action and lucky coincidence. Here again, the nature of each of these two types of detection differs during the three phases of pre-normal, normal, and revolutionary science. Matching Altshuller's three types of discovery with Kuhn's three phases allows us to set up a 3 by 3 matrix (see Table 1). It illustrates nine different types of discoveries with examples from the history of science. While all of these matter for development in science, we will limit our focus in this paper to the last row, which covers explanation.

In the next chapter, we will give an example of how explanations can be viewed as *explanatory systems* and thereafter apply ARIZ to reconstruct in hindsight the respective paradigm shift from a problem-solving perspective. Discoveries that are new detections can be viewed similarly by studying them as *experimental systems*. This, however, goes beyond the scope of our paper.

Table 1. Altshuller's three types of discoveries—accidental detections, purposeful detections, and purposeful explanations—are viewed in Kuhn's pre-normal, normal, and revolutionary phase.

Types of discovery	Pre-normal phase (no established paradigm)	Normal phase (established paradigm)	Revolutionary phase (established paradigm is challenged)
Detections by accident	A phenomenon is accidentally detected during research in a field for which no dominant paradigm has yet been established	While doing research in the tradition of an established paradigm, anomalies are detected that cannot be explained	The established paradigm is already challenged, while an unexpected phenomenon is unintentionally detected
	Example: While conducting experiments with a dissected frog nearby an electrical machine, Luigi Galvani's assistant accidentally touched an inner nerve with a scalpel so that the frog's limbs twitched. A debate with at least three competing schools arose [13]	Example: Experimenting with air, Lord Rayleigh and Sir William Ramsay found out that the nitrogen extracted from the air was by 0.5% heavier than the chemically produced element. Looking for the cause, they discovered Argon [14]	Example: Heike Kamerlingh Onnes synthesized liquid Helium, then studied current flows at low temperatures, discovered super-conductivity and detected what has later been studied under the name super-fluidity [15]
Detections on purpose	There is no paradigm that can explain a phenomenon that was detected as the result of purposeful experimentation	Investigation of a phenomenon, for which the established paradigm suggests a certain outcome	The established paradigm is already challenged and based on a new paradigm a heretofore undetected phenomenon is detected on purpose
	Example: Michael Faraday experimented with electric currents and magnets in order to determine the laws of induction of currents, which resulted in the detection of phenomena of electro-magnetism [13]	Example: Based on his general theory of relativity, Albert Einstein predicted gravitational waves in 1916 (Einstein, 1916). When his theory became accepted, scientists started to look for these waves. In 2015, they were finally detected [16]	Example: In 1915, Albert Einstein predicted the bending of light by the gravity of the sun. Sir Arthur Eddington and his team took advantage of a total solar eclipse in 1919, detected the deviation and contributed to the acceptance of Einstein's General Theory of Relativity [17]

(continued)

Table 1. (*continued*)

Types of discovery	Pre-normal phase (no established paradigm)	Normal phase (established paradigm)	Revolutionary phase (established paradigm is challenged)
Explanations on purpose	In the absence of an existing paradigmatic way of explaining certain phenomena, attempts of explanation are undertaken	Phenomena are explained with the help of an established paradigm	The established paradigm is challenged by a new paradigm that claims to be superior
	Example: In the early days of studying phenomena of electricity, a group of theories existed that considered attraction and factional generation as fundamental electrical phenomena [4]	Example: The paradigm of covalent bonds allows for explanation of a compound's chemical properties even if this substance has not yet been synthesized	Example: Nikolas Copernicus challenged the well established geocentric model of planetary motion by suggesting his heliocentric model [4]

When it comes to studying creative problem solving in science, the focus of attention is to be put on the creation of new kinds of explanations that either yield a shift from the pre-normal phase to the normal phase or successfully end a revolutionary phase.

5   Scientific Explanation as System

Equipped with the above definition of *system* and the brief excursion into the history of science, the difference between technological objects and scientific explanations can be outlined on a common ground. Technical objects can be viewed as *artificial systems* (a) insofar as they are designed for certain purposes, and (b) insofar as they can be decomposed into functional parts. (c) If one of these parts was missing, actual or potential undesirable effects would arise within the system or its context (at least if the part's function was not somehow compensated or made irrelevant). Scientific explanations or theories, in return, can also be viewed as *artificial systems* [18, 19]—at least (a) insofar as they are designed for explaining something in certain contexts (explanatory purpose), and (b) insofar as they can be decomposed into functional parts. (c) As mentioned before, parts are *functional* if taking one of them out results in effects that are undesirable in some context. In the case of scientific explanation, these effects most often turn out to be epistemic in nature. Potential *sub-system—system—super-system* relations can be found in both the technological and the epistemic context.

5.1   Explanatory Sub-systems

We can analyze the system structure of technical objects by singling out their components and functional relations. These components might themselves be systems and appear from the perspective of the analyzing subject as *sub-systems*. Something similar happens in explanations, which are based on the use of concepts in judgements and inferences. Most of the time, we need additional concepts, judgements and inferences in order to explain the ones that we are using in our explanations. Moreover, digging deeper into the *system structure* of explanations (the concepts, judgements, and inferences) leads us to the epistemic practices and the experimental technologies that provide referential data.

Take for example the Ptolemaic geo-centric model that was used for predicting the position of vagabonds at a given time. An astronomer from the Ptolemaic tradition would approach this task with the help of her explanatory model. When asked for the exact reasons why this and not another position was predicted, she would have to refer to the system structure of her explanatory model. Her simplified answer might look like this: The vagabond revolves with speed S_1 around a point P_1, while P_1 revolves with speed S_2 around a point P_2 that is close to the Earth (see Fig. 1).

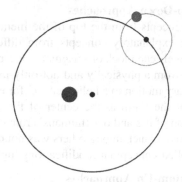

Fig. 1. Simplified version of an elementary explanatory unit in the Ptolemaic model: A planet revolves in epi-cycles (smaller circle) around the Earth, which is close to the centre of the planet's revolution.

This formulation alone already refers to at least eight explanatory concepts: (1) speed S_1, (2) point P_1, (3) speed S_2, (4) point P_2, (5) revolution around P_1, (6) revolution around P_2, (7) the vagabond in question and (8) the Earth. Given each of these concepts, we could ask for further explanation, for example: *What is speed?*— and at the time of the creation of the Ptolemaic system we might have received an answer like: The speed of a moving object tells us how far the object gets in a certain amount of time (see for example [20]). In other words, the explanatory concept *speed* appears to be an *explanatory sub-system* in the Ptolemaic *explanatory system* of the vagabonds' motion. The same holds for the other explanatory concepts listed above.

5.2   Explanatory Super-Systems

From the above definition of system, we also derived the concept of a super-system. Technological systems, for example, can merge and build such super-systems: Multiple computers connected as a network build, for instance, the internet. Likewise, we can join explanatory concepts in order to explain a phenomenon that is more complex: Among others, the concept of movement, for example, could be applied to (i) a body and a straight line or (ii) a body and a circular line. The first might result in the concept of a body moving straight forward and the latter in the concept of a body revolving around something.

5.3   Hierarchy and Complexity

It follows from the definition of *system* that each system might be built from multiple sub-systems and that likewise, each super-system consists of more than one system. This means that complexity increases no matter where we start to explain a phenomenon. Let us distinguish two perspectives on hierarchies of explanatory concepts— (i) *top down* and (ii) *bottom up*. (i) When explaining from a top-down perspective, we start with the help of an explanatory concept from the top of the hierarchical order and (ii) when explaining from a bottom-up perspective, we start with one from the bottom.

Potential Problems of Top-Down Approaches

Starting with explanatory concepts from the top of the hierarchy allows us to see the whole picture and to unite explanatory concepts from different domains. However, misconceptions on higher levels can block or misguide conceptual developments on the lower levels. The transition from a physically and not-only-mathematically-understood geo-centric model of planetary motion to a helio-centric, for example, was complicated by the Christian doctrine of the Earth as the center of the universe. This belief was imbedded in an overall vision of life and our (humans') role in a world created by God. Conceiving of the Earth as one planet among others was not only radical in the domain of astronomy, but also implied conceptual modifications higher up the hierarchy.

Potential Problems of Bottom-Up Approaches

Starting with a concept from the bottom in order to explain a phenomenon is a feature of reductionist strategies: A concept seems to have so much explanatory power that its scope is to be extended either to other phenomena or to other aspects. The Ptolemaic system, for example, uses a circle to model the revolution of vagabonds around the Earth. Seen from a geo-centric perspective, year by year the sun takes about 365 days for one whole cycle, Venus about 225 days, and Mars about 687 days. These regularities can be perfectly explained in terms of revolution and geometrically modeled with the help of a circle.

However, from the perspective of our Earth, it seems that both Venus and Mars move backward from time to time. The Ptolemaic model accounted for these phenomena by using the same explanatory concept again. Instead of the vagabonds themselves, the center of much smaller circles—so-called epi-cycles—revolved around the Earth. The vagabonds, in return, were revolving around the center of their epi-cycles.

Thanks to this analogous usage of the explanatory concept of *revolution around something*, the model could explain, not only the occasional backward movement, but also its periodicity and the changes in speed that the vagabonds seem to undergo during these periods. In order to improve the model's accuracy even further, additional epi-cycles where added and the Earth was slightly moved out of the center of the epi-cycles' revolutions. Although the system's predictive power increased, it became increasingly complicated (see Fig. 2).

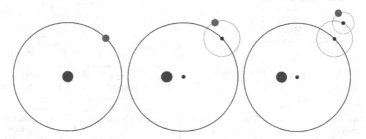

Fig. 2. The model for explaining the periodic movement of vagabonds was further extended to explain the backward movement as well.

Primary and Secondary Explanatory Concepts
Note that there is not only a historical but also a functional priority behind the use of circles in the Ptolemaic model. From a functional perspective, the role of the larger circle was to explain the periodic revolution of vagabonds around the Earth, while epi-cycles were introduced in order to explain details of this overall motion. Let us call the larger circle a *primary explanatory concept* of the model and the epi-cycle a *secondary explanatory concept*. The first has historical and, more importantly, functional priority, since the whole model would break down if the concept of the *revolution of planets around the Earth* was eliminated. It is of *primary* importance, since it directly affects the realization of the model's primary function. The concept of epi-cycles, in contrast, could be eliminated without causing the model's collapse. It is true that without epi-cycles, the model could no longer account for the vagabonds' backward movement, but it would still get the periodicity of their overall revolutions right. In this sense, the explanatory role of the epi-cycles is only of *secondary* importance.

6   Applying ARIZ-85C to the Shift from the Ptolemaic to the Copernican Explanatory System

We now possess all the distinctions needed for applying ARIZ-85C to explanatory systems in science (following the ARIZ version in [2]). For the sake of brevity, we slightly simplified the algorithm without compromising on the overall logical structure (see Fig. 3). The way we are counting the steps does not fully match the original version of ARIZ-85C. We abbreviate the series of steps, since we neither go through the full analysis of the Ptolemaic system nor discuss all intra-systemic problems. Moreover, if not explicitly highlighted, we refer to ARIZ-85C simply by *ARIZ*.

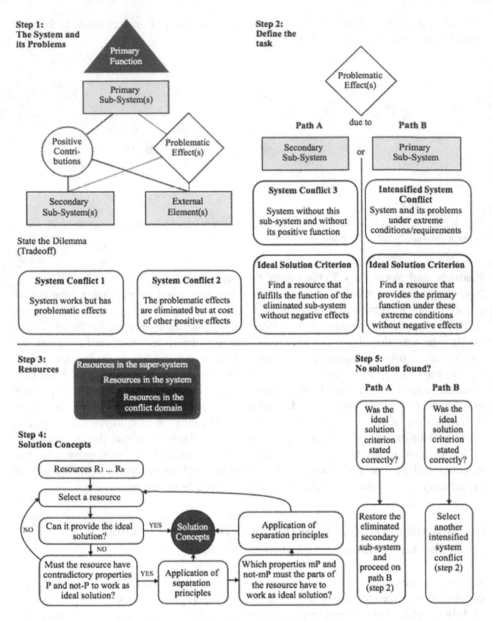

Fig. 3. General structure of ARIZ-85C

6.1   Step 1—Towards an Understanding of the System Conflict

Step 1.1: According to ARIZ, the guiding thread for the development of a system is its primary function (or its primary functions). In case of the Ptolemaic system, the primary function consists in explaining the vagabonds' movement.

Step 1.2: Since ARIZ views its subject as a system with a primary function, it can be further decomposed into interacting parts or (if they are further decomposable) sub-systems. Altogether, these sub-systems have to achieve the system's primary aim—which is the original reason why it exists at all. Moreover, sub-systems often have to achieve secondary aims. A functional analysis of the Ptolemaic explanatory system reveals that the backward motion of some of the vagabonds could not be explained without the help of epi-cycles. The explanation of this backward movement, for example, is such a secondary aim.

Step 1.3: Both primary and secondary problems turn into systemic conflicts when the solution to them yields a tradeoff. As we have seen, dealing with epi-cycles yields the tradeoff between the system's accuracy and its simplicity.

6.2   Step 2—Stating the Task to Be Solved

Step 2.1: After having identified the system-conflict, ARIZ asks whether or not the conflict is due to a secondary sub-system. If so, its elimination is suggested. Since the epi-cycles are responsible for the tradeoff between *simplicity* and *accuracy*, and since they are secondary sub-systems, their elimination is suggested. Seen from a historical perspective, this decision implies that the ongoing search for solutions starts from a problem situation prior to the introduction of the malfunctioning sub-system. If, in contrast, the analysis in step 1 had concluded that the problem to be solved was due to a primary sub-system, ARIZ would not suggest its elimination because, given such an elimination, the primary aim could no longer be achieved, which would amount to an elimination of the entire system. Rather, ARIZ suggests here an extreme intensification of the requirements and conditions for the system's performance.

Step 2.2: The elimination of the malfunctioning secondary sub-system leads to a new system conflict: The malfunctioning of the eliminated sub-system disappears, but the secondary problem that had been solved before reemerges. When eliminating the epi-cycles from the Ptolemaic system the conflict arises: *The system is simple but it cannot explain the backward movement of the vagabonds.*

Step 2.3: As soon as the system conflict is clearly understood, the task to be solved can be stated in an abstract but precise way (see Fig. 3): *Find a resource (within the system itself or in its environment) that—when slightly modified—helps to explain the backward movement of the vagabonds without complicating the system.*

6.3   Step 3—Looking for Potential Resources that Might Help to Solve the Task

Step 3: In order to facilitate the creation of a solution concept, ARIZ recommends to list potential problem-solving resources within the system and its·

environment. In the case of the Ptolemaic system, the system's center, the Earth, the Sun and the Moon (these two vagabonds never move backward) appear to be particularly interesting.

6.4   Step 4—Creation of Solution Concepts

Step 4.1: Each resource that can be selected form the list might contribute to the potential solution. Selecting the Earth, for example, yields the question: How can the Earth help to explain the vagabonds' temporary backward motion without complicating things? The answer to this question is far from obvious.

Step 4.2: However, when asking which contradicting properties P and not-P the Earth might need to have in order to help explain the backward movement of the vagabonds, we put ourselves on the right track. We know, for example, that the Earth must be in the center of the vagabonds' movement, because that is how we observe the phenomena we want to explain. *Being in the center* is thus a property of the Earth within our explanatory system. But could it be the case that the Earth must *not be in the center* such that the backward movement of the vagabonds can be explained? Following this line of reasoning, we force ourselves to imagine the Earth as *being in the center of the vagabonds movement* (in order to explain the observations) and *not being in the center of their movement* (in order to explain their backward movement).

Step 4.3: When facing this type of contradiction—something needs to have both property P and not-P—ARIZ recommends the application of three separation principles. The goal of their application is to resolve the contradiction by finding a way in which the selected resource can have both properties in two different regards:

- (1) *Separation in time*: At time T_1, the Earth is in the center of the vagabonds' movement and at time T_2, the Earth is not in their center.
- (2) *Separation in space*: Within the spacial part P_1, the Earth is in the center of the vagabonds' movement, but within the spacial part P_2, the Earth is not in their center.
- (3) *Separation between the system and its sub-systems*: From the sub-system perspective, the Earth is in the center of the vagabonds' movement; from the system perspective, the Earth is not in their center.

While the first two separation principles do not articulate concepts that could explain the backward movement, the third gives a surprisingly clear description of what the Copernican shift is about: The Earth is only in the center of the appearances of the vagabonds' movement. We observe the overall system from the perspective of Earth (as sub-system)—in this sense the Earth is in the system's center. However, as a sub-system among others (the system perspective), the Earth itself is not in the center of the system. As soon as a sub-system (a vagabond) overtakes another, it looks from the respective vagabond's perspective as if the other would turn into the opposite direction. Only when viewed from the real center of the system, no vagabond appears to change direction.

This raises the question as to which sub-system is to be placed in the center. Here the Sun and the Moon come into play. Neither shows any backward motion, which makes them promising candidates. Putting the Moon into the center would imply that the Sun moved back and forth from time to time. Moreover, it would be impossible to make sense of the observations of any of the vagabonds' movements. In contrast, placing the Sun in the center of the vagabonds' revolutions matches the observations quite well. However, it raises the question why the Moon never changes its direction. Copernicus' answer was straight forward: While all vagabonds—the Earth included— were revolving around the Sun, the Moon was revolving around the Earth.

6.5   Step 5—What if no Solution Was Found?

In case that no solution could be found, ARIZ recommends to check whether the solution criterion in step 2 was correctly stated. If so, the restoration of the previously eliminated sub-system in step 2 is recommended; ARIZ then continues at step 2— without the elimination of any sub-system (see Fig. 3, step 2 and step 5). On this track, ARIZ recommends intensifying the conditions and requirements for the system's performance. This was Johannes Kepler's path. He had been working for Tycho Brahe, Europe's leading astronomer at the time. Brahe had been working on the improvement of tools for observing the sky and had perfected the geo-centric Ptolemaic system to an extent that outclassed the Copernican predictions. In contrast to Brahe, Kepler preferred the Copernican model for its simplicity. It's predictions, however, were not sufficiently accurate. Seen from the perspective of ARIZ, the inaccuracies were due to one of Copernicus' primary explanatory sub-systems: circular revolutions. Kepler was thus dealing with the intensified task (see step 2.1) of having to develop a fully accurate model by sticking to the Copernican paradigm. In order to do so, he had to rethink Copernicus' primary sub-system of circular revolutions. As a result, he turned them into ellipses.

7   Conclusion

We have shown that ARIZ-85C—originally designed for solving problems in technology—can be expressed in a more general vocabulary of systemic thinking. This allows for its application outside of the technological domain without relying on crutches such as metaphorical analogies. The application of this generalized version of ARIZ was tested on one of the most famous paradigm shifts in the history of science— the shift from the Ptolemaic geo-centric system to Copernicus' helio-centric one. Many more such tests are needed to evaluate whether or not the study of Kuhnian paradigm shifts can shed light upon the nature of creative problem solving in science. It seems, however, to be a promising path. Before Genrich Altshuller and Raphael Shapiro started to systematically examine the nature of paradigm shifting solutions in technology, not much knowledge about this type of problem solving was available. Kuhn's position [21] is a quintessential example of a widely shared pessimism on this topic:

What the nature of that final stage is—how an individual invents (or finds he has invented) a new way of giving order to data now all assembled—must here remain inscrutable and may be permanently so.

Considering the abundance of examples of such shifts in the history of science and technology, this pessimism is surprising. It seems that Altshuller and Shapiro were the first who systematically studied these transformations in technology in order to gain insight into the logical operations necessary for bringing about paradigm shifts. In this way, they became the founders of the *Theory of Inventive Problem Solving* (TRIZ), which aims at making invention on purpose possible. With this paper, we want to suggest that something similar is possible in science. The goal of the resulting theory could be called *discovery on purpose*.

References

1. Altshuller, G.S.: Creativity as an Exact Science: The Theory of the Solution of Inventive Problems. Gordon and Breach Science Publishers, New York (1984)
2. Fey, V., Rivin, E.I.: Innovation on Demand, pp. 82–111. Cambridge University Press, Cambridge (2005)
3. Altshuller, G., Shapiro, R.: About technical creativity. Quest. Psychol. **6**, 37–49 (1956). (In Russian)
4. Kuhn, T.S.: The Structure of Scientific Revolutions, 2, Enlarged edn. The University of Chicago Press, Chicago (1970)
5. Altshuller, G.S.: How to discover? Thoughts on the methodology of scientific work (1960/1979). (in Russian). http://www.altshuller.ru/triz/investigations1.asp. Accessed 31 Jan
6. Bukhman, I.: TRIZ: Technology for Innovation. Cubic Creativity Company, pp. 240–259 (2012)
7. Hubka, V.: Theory of Technical Systems. Springer, Heidelberg (1984). https://doi.org/10.1007/978-3-642-52121-8. (in German)
8. Cummins, R.: Functional analysis. J. Philos. **72**, 741–765 (1975)
9. Machamer, P., Darden, L., Craver, C.F.: Thinking about mechanisms. Philos. Sci. **67**, 1–25 (2000)
10. Wright, L.: Functions. Philos. Rev. **82**, 139–168 (1973)
11. Neander, K.: The teleological notion of 'function'. Austr. J. Philos. **69**, 454–468 (1991)
12. Gayon, J.: Do biologist need the concept of function? Philosophical perspectives. Comptes Rendus Palevol **5**, 479–487 (2006). (in French)
13. Whittaker, E.: A History of the Theories of Aether & Electricity: Two Volumes Bound as One. Dover Publications Inc., New York (1989)
14. Rayleigh, L., Ramsay, W.: Argon, a new constituent of the atmosphere. In: Proceedings of the Royal Society of London, vol. 57, pp. 265–287 (1895)
15. APS News: This month in physics history - January 1938: discovery of superfluidity. APS News **15**(1), 90 (2006). Accessed 31 July 2018
16. Collins, H.: Gravity's Kiss: The Detection of Gravitational Waves. The MIT Press, Cambridge (2017)
17. Dyson, F.W., Eddington, A.S., Davidson, C.: A determination of the deflection of light by the sun's gravitational field, from observations made at the total eclipse of May 29, 1919. Philos. Trans. R. Soc. Lond. **220**, 291–333 (1920)

18. Chang, H.: Beyond case-studies: history as philosophy. In: Mauskopf, S., Schmaltz, T. (eds.) Integrating History and Philosophy of Science, vol. 263, pp. 109–124. Springer, Dordrecht (2011). https://doi.org/10.1007/978-94-007-1745-9_8

19. Hoyningen-Huene, P.: Systematicity: the Nature of Science. Oxford University Press, New York (2013)

20. Aristotle, B.J.: The Complete Works of Aristotle: The Revised Oxford Translation. Princeton University Press, Princeton (1984)

21. Kuhn, T.S.: The Structure of Scientific Revolutions, 2, Enlarged edn, p. 90. The University of Chicago Press, Chicago (1970)

TRIZ and Functions

Study on Establishing Functional Periodicity of New Products Based on TRIZ

Ya-Fan Dong[1,2(✉)], Peng Zhang[1,2], Run-Hua Tan[1,2], Wei Liu[1,2], Rui-Qin Wang[3], and Jian-Guang Sun[1,2]

[1] National Engineering Research Center for Technological Innovation Method and Tool, Tianjin 300130, China
dyafan@foxmail.com
[2] Hebei University of Technology, Tianjin 300130, China
[3] Tianjin University, Tianjin 057750, China

Abstract. Functional periodicity plays an important role in the process of product automatic innovation for ensuring stable systems. But there is no method of establishing Functional Periodicity. In order to establish the functional periodicity of a new product, an existed product called the goal product is firstly chosen, if it is similar to the new product on aspects of function, effect or structure. Subsequently, difference between the new product and the goal product is identified by establishing the mapping relationship between the functional requirements and design parameters. Using the tools from TRIZ, the function model of the new product is formulated based on the above-mentioned mapping relationship. Afterwards, the system functional periodicity of the new product is proposed in form of TRIZ function model by combining the results of proposed function model and the relationship among functions. Finally, the feasibility of the proposed method is verified with a specific design case.

Keywords: Functional periodicity · Automatic innovation · New products
Function model · TRIZ

1 Introduction

The function is the core of the concept design in the process of product automatic innovation, and it is also the foundation of establishing functional periodicity. Suh [1] put forward the concept of functional periodicity, which is an important way to reduce system complexity. Functional periodicity plays an important role in the process of product automatic innovation for ensuring stable systems. The product function analysis mainly includes the function structure and the function model based on TRIZ [2]. The problems existing in the system can be found out by these two methods. However, they can't help the designers to build the system functional periodicity. The literature [3–7] verified that the function model is an important way to solve problems for the innovation. However, most of the studies improved the present products, not a new product. The literature [8] emphasizes that functional periodicity is the foundation for a system operating stability. The literature [9] verified that functional periodicity is the most important way to reduce the system complexity and introduced several functional

D. Cavallucci et al. (Eds.): TFC 2018, IFIP AICT 541, pp. 113–125, 2018.
https://doi.org/10.1007/978-3-030-02456-7_10

periodicity determination methods based on TRIZ. However, they did not put forward a method of a new product functional periodicity established.

The traditional function model based on TRIZ is applied to improve the existing system, not to develop a new product, not to establish functional periodicity. In this paper, according to function, effect or structure, a product is found out similar to the new product function, the structure or the effect. Namely, it is regarded as the goal product. Subsequently, difference between the new product and the goal product is identified by establishing the mapping relationship between the functional requirements and design parameters. Using the tools from TRIZ, the function model of the new product is formulated based on the above-mentioned mapping relationship. According to the improved function model and the relationship between each function, the system functional periodicity is determined. The process model of functional periodicity assisted by function model is set up for the new product development.

2 Time Independent Complexity and Functional Analysis

2.1 Time Independent Complexities

The complexity concept in axiomatic design theory is defined as a measure of uncertainty in achieving the desired set of functional requirements [10] (see Fig. 1). The size of the complexity is directly determined by the relationship between the design scope and system range. It may be a constant, and also may be changing over time. There are four different types of complexity, namely, time-dependent combinatorial complexity, time-dependent periodic complexity, time-independent real complexity and time-independent imaginary complexity [10].

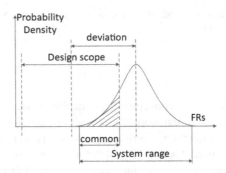

Fig. 1. The schematic diagram of the design scope and system range [10]

Time-independent real complexity is that the system range is not fully in the design scope. Namely, the area of the shaded part is uncertain in Fig. 1. It is real and does not change with time. Because the designer is not fully familiar with the product design, the system produces the uncertainty. Time-independent imaginary complexity isn't really system complexity.

2.2   Function Analysis

The carrier of the function is the product. The manifestation of the product is the function. In the 1940s American engineer Myers [2] put forward the concept of the function at first and put it on the core problems of value engineering research.

The main advantages of the function analysis are as follows: (a) Through the function analysis, unnecessary parts can be found out and be eliminated completely; (b) Through the function analysis, a cheaper alternative material can be found to instead of some parts, and even the total product; (c) Through the function analysis, the original design can be improved; (d) Through the function analysis, some parts which manufacturing tolerance is too high often can be found.

Function analysis is mainly from the total function and then divided into two directions: the function structure and the function model based on TRIZ.

(a) The function structure

The basis of the function structure is regarding product design as the conversion of substance, energy and signal. Starting from the total function to decomposition for each sub-function, the function structure is comprised of system sub-function, as shown in Fig. 2 [2]. The function structure is widely used in new product innovation and design.

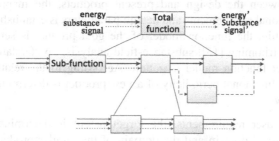

Fig. 2. Product function structure

(b) The function model

According to a total function, the function model is from the total system to subsystems, until the typical components. Then a verb is used in each element, with the different linear representative of the interaction between components, such as harmful effects or shortage effect. The function model is set up. Function model which includes super systems, systems and products mainly improves the existing product or system. But there isn't a method of function model for a new product or system.

2.3   Functional Periodicity

Based on the complexity of the axiomatic design theory, functional periodicity is defined as a set of functional requirements [10]. Function mentioned is a functional periodicity, but it is repeating a set of the same function, not only a time period.

Namely, that has a fixed time period. In Axiomatic Design Complexity Theory, functional periodicity types include time periodicity, geometric periodicity, biological periodicity, chemical periodicity [11–13], thermal cycle, power cycle and material cycle [7] etc.

Functional periodicity is a kind of characteristic of the natural system and the technical system. This is an essential characteristic of the stable system. It is the premise and foundation of the stable operation of the system [8].

To ensure systems operating stability, it is very important to establish the functional periodicity. Suh [1] shows that functional periodicity is defined as the period set by repeating a set of function requirements. It is very important to establish the functional periodicity of the new product in the process of new product development. But there isn't a method of function model for a new product or system.

3   Determining Process Model of Functional Periodicity of a New Product

According to the product functional requirements (FRs), the similar products are determined in the market at present; the mapping relationship [14] between the functional requirements (FRs) and design parameters (DPs) is established; then considering the difference between the design and present products, the mapping relationship between the functional requirements and design parameters is established. Based on the mapping relationship, the function model of the goal product is set up using TRIZ tools, such as the trimming [15], substance-field analysis, 76 standard solutions, etc., and a new product function model is gotten; According to the relationship between each function, the functional periodicity of a new product is determined. The concrete steps are as follows:

I. According to user requirements, the target patent is determined. Through the analysis functional domain and the domain of the similar products, the mapping relationship between the functional requirements (FRs) and design parameters (DPs) is established.

According to the product design requirements and market studies, the product to be designed is still blank in currently. The function model of the new product can't be established directly. Therefore, the existing products similar to the designed product are found out. Namely, starting from the function, the effect and the structure, a product similar to the new product function, the structure or the effect is found, namely, it is regarded as the goal product. The function model of the target product is set up. According to similarity principle [16, 17], the similarity between the products has different forms, mainly including the following several aspects:

(a) Similar to the new product function: it refers to the similarity between the product or system function.
(b) Similar to the new product working principle: it refers to the similarity between the product or system working principle.

(c) Similar to the new product structure: it refers to the similarity between the product or system structure.

(d) Similar to the new product function and structure: it refers to the similarity between the product or system function and structure.

(e) Similar to the new product function and working principle: it refers to the similarity between the product or system function and working principle.

(f) Similar to the new product function, working principle and structure: it refers to the similarity between the product or system function, working principle and structure.

As long as a product meets the above anyone, it can be regarded as a similar product to the new product. Through the analysis functional domain and the domain of the similar products, the mapping relationship between the functional requirements (FRs) and design parameters (DPs) is established (see Fig. 3 [9]).

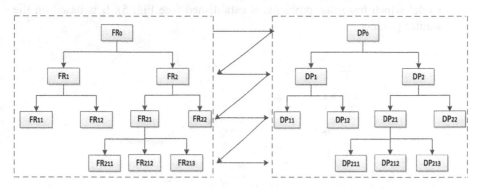

Fig. 3. The mapping relationship between the FRs and DPs [9]

II. Compared to the new product functional requirements and design parameters, the problem parameters are determined in the mapping principle. The mapping principle applied to the new product design requirements between the FR's and DP's is established.

Relative to the original design, the mapping relationship of the similar product is right. However, in order to apply to the design requirements of new products, some of the original design parameters may be changed. Therefore, the system will have some problems, such as a big bulk, complexity, missing some functions and so on. And then, the DPs would change into DP's (see Fig. 4). Compared to the new product functional requirements and design parameters and based on the mapping relationship of the similar product, the mapping principle applied to the new product design requirements between the FR's and DP's is established (see Fig. 4).

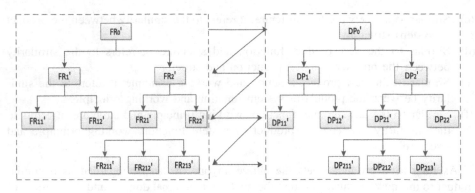

Fig. 4. The mapping relationship between the FR's and DP's

III. According to the mapping relationship between the FR's and DP's, the function model which has some problems is established (see Fig. 5). It is based on the similar product.

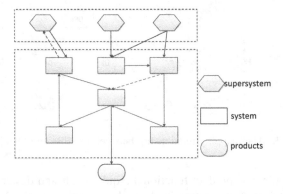

Fig. 5. The function model based on the similar product

IV. Introducing TRIZ tools, the improved function model of the new product is set up.

Analysis of problem function model established, designers introduce TRIZ tools, such as the trimming, substance-field analysis, 76 standard solutions, etc., and get a new product function model.

V. According to each function of the new product and the order of each function under working, the functional periodicity is determined.

According to the improved function model and the work order, the functional periodicity can be determined (see Fig. 6). Therefore, the design requirements and the stability of the system can be ensured.

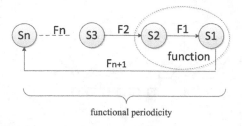

Fig. 6. Functional periodicity determined by function model

4   Case Study

Nowadays since the German government put forward the strategy of "Industry 4.0", countries gradually raised a global upsurge of "Internet+", including China. Our country also puts forward "made in China 2025". Under the background of a more and more rapid pace of life today, People prefer to nutrition improvement of a healthy diet. But now most of the people are doing all kinds of porridge according to their own subjective consciousness.

Therefore, the auto-mixed system of porridge needs to develop urgently to substitute manual work. The product should be simple and convenient, meet the gradually rapid pace of the life and work, and satisfy people the different preferences of porridge. What's more, according to the special groups of customers (such as diabetes, etc.) requirements, it can provide the correctly kind of porridge. At the same time, application of "Internet+" concept, it can realize the remote control, and realize the customer to make an appointment. The auto-mixed system of porridge is rare at present. There are more vast development space and a broad market.

I. According to the calculation method of similar products, the ore automatic batching system in the patent CN202656318U [18] is similar to the auto-mixed system of porridge in function. Through the analysis of the similar products, the mapping relationship between the functional requirements (FRs) and design parameters (DPs) of the ore automatic batching system in the patent CN202656318U [18] is established.

Currently existing batching system is composed of storage hopper, weighing hopper, weighing sensor, unloading conveyor belt, devices, etc. such as ore automatic batching system (see Fig. 7 [18]), having a large volume and high precision requirements. At the same time, technology is not very mature and less finished products in the food industry.

Through the analysis of the similar products, the mapping relationship between the functional requirements (FRs) and design parameters (DPs) of the ore automatic batching system in the patent CN202656318U [18] is established (see Fig. 8).

II. Compared to the new product function requirements and the mapping principle of the ore automatic batching system, the control systems are complex and the size of device is too large. Therefore, the DPs of controls are changed into DP's.

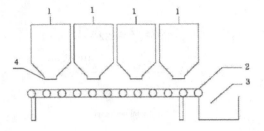

1---Weighing and blanking mechanism; 2--- Burden delivery mechanism;

3--- Material mixing mechanism; 4--- Valve

Fig. 7. The ore automatic batching system schematic diagram

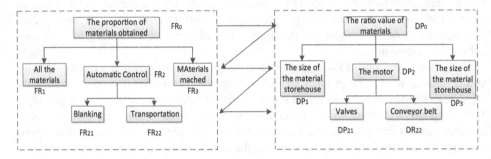

Fig. 8. The mapping relationship of the ore automatic batching system

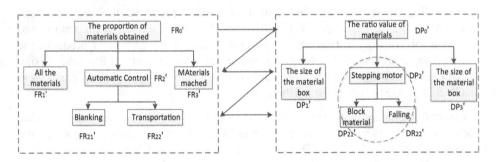

Fig. 9. The mapping relationship of the auto-mixed system of porridge

The mapping principle applied to the auto-mixed system of porridge design requirements is established (see Fig. 9).

III. According to the mapping relationship of the auto-mixed system of porridge, the function model is established. It is based on the ore automatic batching system.

Through the analysis of system function model (see Fig. 10), a Material Storehouse needs a set of control systems, namely two Material Storehouses need two sets of control systems, so the equipment is complex, big volume and complicated operation.

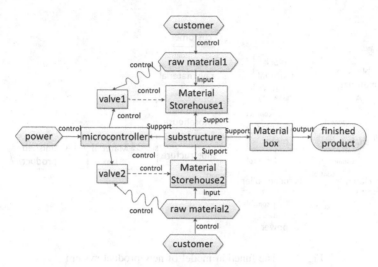

Fig. 10. The function model (two Material Storehouses)

IV. Introducing TRIZ tools, such as the trimming, substance-field analysis, 76 standard solutions, etc., the improved function model of the new product is set up.

The valve 1 is similar to the valve 2 and so on (see Fig. 10). Therefore, considering the principle of trimming, the control valves are regarded as trimming objects [19, 20] (see Fig. 11).

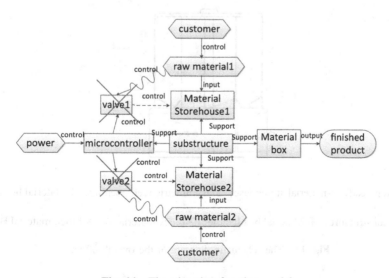

Fig. 11. The trimming function model

A clutch is referenced. Therefore, a set of control systems is applied to complete control of multiple storage bins. The function model of the new product system is shown in Fig. 12.

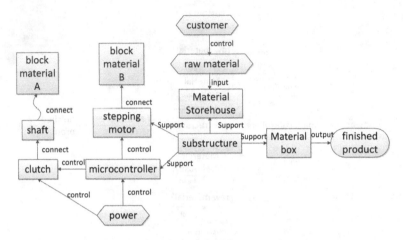

Fig. 12. The function model of new product system

Using substance-field analysis and 76 standard solutions, a convex flange is introduced, with the shaft directly, and then meets the block material A to eliminate the harmful effect. At the same time, it can strengthen the block material A rotational stability. The overall effect is as shown in Fig. 13.

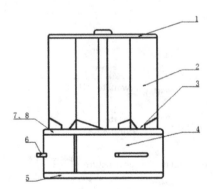

1-top head; 2-material storehouse; 3-asymmetric feed opening; 4-Material box;

5-substructure; 6- Material box handle; 7-block material A; 8-block material B

Fig. 13. The schematic diagram of the overall effect

V. According to the relationship between each function, the new product functional periodicity is determined.

In working condition, the stepping motor and the clutch are electrified at the same time. Block material A and B rotate simultaneously. When they arrive at the asymmetric feed opening of the material storehouse, electromagnetic clutch with power off, block material A stops rotating and block material B continues. When the aperture of block material A is obscured completely, the stepping motor stops running. Now blanking, materials are directly into the material box. When the expected regulation is achieved, stepping motor controls block material B inversion until keeping out the blanking round hole of block material A. At this point, the first time the material is completed. As repeating operation, the automatic batching of porridge is completed (see Fig. 14).

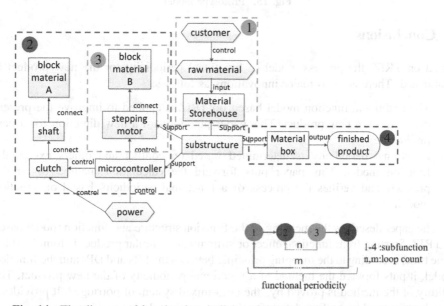

Fig. 14. The diagram of functional periodicity of the auto-mixed system of porridge

Therefore, according to the order of each function under working, functional periodicity is determined (see Fig. 14). The cylindrical structure of the new product can be designed according to the function model shown as Fig. 14. A new product is innovated. The prototype model is shown as Fig. 15.

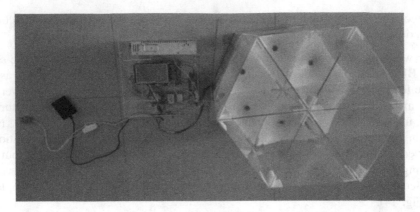

Fig. 15. Prototype model

5 Conclusions

Based on TRIZ, the process model of functional periodicity for the new product is established. There are two major innovations as follows:

(1) The traditional function model based on TRIZ is applied to improve the present product, not a new product. This paper puts forward a new direction for a new product design.

(2) Functional periodicity is determined based on conflict and others except the function model. This paper puts forward the calculation method of similar products and verifies the process of a functional periodicity based on function model.

The paper describes the meaning of the function structure and function model based on TRIZ. Starting from function, effect or structure, the similar product is found. At the same time, according to the mapping principle between the FRs and DPs and the function model, it puts forward the method of a functional periodicity of the new product. The validity of the method is proved by "the auto-mixed system of porridge". It provides a new direction and lays a foundation for the new product design and innovation.

Acknowledgement. Supported by National Natural Science Foundation of China (Grant No. 51675159), National Natural Science Foundation of China (Grant No. 51305123), the National Science and Technology Basic Project (Grant No. 2017IM040100) and the Central Government Guides Local Science and Technology Development Projects (No. 18241837G).

References

1. Suh, N.P.: On functional periodicity as the basis for long-term stability of engineered and natural systems and its relationship to physical laws. Res. Eng. Des. **15**(1), 72–75 (2004)
2. Tan, R.H.: Innovation Design-TRIZ: Theory of Innovation Problem Solving. China Machine Press, Beijing (2002)

3. Altshuller, G.S.: Creativity As an Exact Science: The Theory of the Solution of Inventive Problems. Gordon & Breach Science Publishing, New York (1984)
4. Cao, G., Guo, H., Zhang, C., et al.: Function evolution and forecasting for product innovation. In: 2010 IEEE International Conference on Management of Innovation and Technology (ICMIT), Singapore, pp. 40–44. IEEE (2010)
5. Orloff, M.: Inventive thinking through TRIZ: a practical guide. TQM Mag. **18**(3), 312–314 (2006)
6. Tan, R.H., Yuan, C.Y., Cao, G.Z., et al.: Function model for products existed using reverse fishbone. J. Eng. Des. **8**, 197–201 (2003)
7. Lu, X.M., Zhang, F.Y., Zhang, Q.Q.: Product innovation design based on the theory of TRIZ and functional analysis. Mech. Des. Manuf. **12**, 255–257 (2010)
8. Lee, T.-S.: Complexity Theory in Axiomatic Design. Massachusetts Institute of Technology, Massachusetts (2003)
9. Zhang, P., Tan, R.H.: Design model for the combinatorial complexity elimination process. Trans. Chin. Soc. Agric. Mach. **41**(3), 182–188 (2010)
10. Suh, N.P.: Complexity: Theory and Applications. Oxford University Press on Demand, England (2005)
11. Prokoph, A., Bilali, H.E., Ernst, R.: Periodicities in the emplacement of large igneous provinces through the phanerozoic: relations to ocean chemistry and marine biodiversity evolution. Geosci. Front. **4**(3), 263–276 (2013)
12. Zhang, P., Tan, R.H.: Rapid acquirement method for ideal result of system complexity. Comput. Integr. Manuf. Syst. **16**(4), 746–754 (2010)
13. Suh, N.P.: Complexity in engineering. CIRP Ann.-Manuf. Technol. **54**(2), 46–63 (2005)
14. Matt, D.T.: Achieving operational excellence through systematic complexity reduction in manufacturing system design. Key Eng. Mater. **344**, 865–872 (2007)
15. Yu, F., Tan, R.H., Cao, G.Z., et al.: Study on trimming priority based on system functional model study. Comput. Integr. Manuf. Syst. **19**(2), 338–347 (2013)
16. Gitlow, H.S.: Innovation on demand. Qual. Eng. **11**(1), 79–89 (1998)
17. Qi, G.N., Gu, X.J., Yang, Q.H., et al.: Principles and key technologies of mass customization. Comput. Integr. Manuf. Syst. **9**(9), 776–783 (2003)
18. Yunnan Chengjiang Panhu Chemical Co. Ltd.: Ore automatic batching system. CN PATENT 202656318U, 09 January 2013
19. Bariani, P.F., Berti, G.A., Lucchetta, G.: A combined DFMA and TRIZ approach to the simplification of product structure. Proc. Inst. Mech. Eng. Part B: J. Eng. Manuf. **218**(8), 1023–1027 (2004)
20. Wang, B., Xu, G., Song, Q., et al.: Design of multi-function blade clean-polishing machine based on TRIZ theory. In: 6th International Forum on Strategic Technology (IFOST), pp. 361–365. IEEE (2011)

On the Efficiency of TRIZ Application for Process Intensification in Process Engineering

Pavel Livotov[✉], Mas'udah, and Arun Prasad Chandra Sekaran

Offenburg University of Applied Sciences, Badstr. 24,
77652 Offenburg, Germany
pavel.livotov@hs-offenburg.de

Abstract. In recent years, the application of TRIZ methodology in the process engineering has been found promising to develop comprehensive inventive solution concepts for process intensification (PI). However, the effectiveness of TRIZ for PI is not measured or estimated. The paper describes an approach to evaluate the efficiency of TRIZ application in process intensification by comparing six case studies in the field of chemical, pharmaceutical, ceramic, and mineral industries. In each case study, TRIZ workshops with the teams of researchers and engineers has been performed to analyze initial complex problem situation, to identify problems, to generate new ideas, and to create solution concepts. The analysis of the workshop outcomes estimates fulfilment of the PI-goals, impact of secondary problems, variety and efficiency of ideas and solution concepts. In addition to the observed positive effect of TRIZ application, the most effective inventive principles for process engineering have been identified.

Keywords: TRIZ efficiency · Process engineering · Process intensification

1 Introduction

Innovation in process engineering is becoming more challenging in developing new processes or in transforming conventional chemical processes into more economical, productive, and environmental friendly. Process Intensification (PI) is a knowledge-based innovation methodology evolved over the last three decades mainly for gas-liquid systems, is focusing now on processes involving solids handling [1]. Besides its basic concept of equipment miniaturization, the new PI equipment and methods enable to substitute common batch processes into faster and safer continuous processes with higher efficiency, productivity, and reduced costs [1].

PI is expected not only to improve processes and resulting products, but also able to bring a high value profit through innovation. However, due to the secondary problems, the implementation of the novel PI apparatus and methods is not as simple as perceived. The use of systematic creativity approaches for PI seems to be an opportunity to faster overcome the secondary problems. Therefore, in the last few years the analytical and inventive tools of the theory of inventive problem solving TRIZ [2] have been

© IFIP International Federation for Information Processing 2018
Published by Springer Nature Switzerland AG 2018. All Rights Reserved
D. Cavallucci et al. (Eds.): TFC 2018, IFIP AICT 541, pp. 126–140, 2018.
https://doi.org/10.1007/978-3-030-02456-7_11

applied for intensification of various processes to ensure PI goals are achieved. As outlined in [3], TRIZ helps to identify secondary problems of PI and limits these negative side effects. The benefits of TRIZ approach above conventional creativity methods in practice are reported in several interdisciplinary domains [4–6], as well as in the field of process engineering [7, 8] and in particular of chemical processes [10]. The authors of [8] adapt TRIZ contradiction matrix to resolve contradictions related to process engineering problems. Their research proposes new characteristics and inventive principles for TRIZ contradiction matrix to counter problems in chemical process industries. Another work introduces TRIZ methodology and framework for problem solving and forecasting of product development in chemical engineering [11]. Furthermore, the authors of [12] demonstrate that TRIZ-based approach is well-suited for accelerating innovation in chemical engineering. Additionally, TRIZ application has been modified and enhanced to the design of inherently safer chemical processes [13]. The coupling of TRIZ with the Case-Based Reasoning in chemical engineering is proposed in [14], and the advantages of linking TRIZ and Process Intensification are disclosed in [17]. Evidently, TRIZ helps engineers to create inventive solutions and to deliver radical improvements, but it still shows lower application level in industrial practice, ranking for example with 14% in fifth place of the top five creativity methods supporting innovation process in German companies [15]. Therefore, the objective evaluation of the TRIZ effectiveness for process engineering remains a significant research issue.

This paper presents an effort to evaluate the efficiency of TRIZ application in process intensification involving solids handling through six case studies assessment in the field of chemical, pharmaceutical, ceramic, and mineral industries as shown in Table 1.

Table 1. Six case studies of intensification of processes involving solid handling.

Case study (CS)	Process description
CS1	Separation of ceramic-metal powders
CS2	Dry granulation of ceramic powders
CS3	Metal ore beneficiation
CS4	Granulation of pharmaceutical powders
CS5	Drying of pharmaceutical powders
CS6	Mixing of chemical reagents

To reach the research objectives, in each case study a one or two-days TRIZ workshop was prepared, carried-out and evaluated with the team of researchers and engineers. Each TRIZ workshop emphases on improving abilities in systematic problem definition and ideation. It starts with the comprehensive analysis of the initial problem situation and ends with the creation of alternative or complimentary solution concepts for the PI case studies. The objective measures of ideation effectiveness defined in [16] such as variety, quantity and quality of proposed novel ideas and solution concepts are documented and evaluated. The corresponding most effective

TRIZ inventive principles and sub-principles frequently used in creation of PI solution concepts are identified. Additionally, a few months later review is conducted for each case study to observe and evaluate the positive effect of TRIZ application in the practice.

2   Case Study Overview

2.1   CS1 - Separation of Ceramic-Metal Powders

The case study CS1 aims to intensify the powder classification system for separation of ceramic-metal powders produced by high energy ball milling. The system should be able to divide the input powder by mass or size without disposable parts, in continuous and without human intervention for powder handling. Even though the existing system of air classification and sieving system is simple and flexible for powders classification, it still has disadvantages on discontinuous process, generation of fine phase in milling process and generation of environmental contaminant particles.

2.2   CS2 - Dry Granulation of Ceramic Powders

High shear mixer granulator (HSMG) is an established technology for dry route of ceramic powders granulation with lower energy and water consumption which is not shown in wet route processing. However, dry granulation contains many constraints regarding final granulated product such as higher moisture content, bimodal size distribution and low productivity. Therefore, the main challenge of case study is to produce granulated powders with adequate physical and chemical properties through the dry route with the same properties as the ones obtained through the wet route.

2.3   CS3 - Metal Ore Beneficiation

In mineral beneficiation processes, on-line mineral analysis based on Raman spectroscopy monitors mineral concentrations at selected locations along the process line. Routine operation of the system is easy and can be carried out by persons who have no in-depth knowledge about the fundamentals of Raman spectroscopy. Nevertheless, undesired measurement deviations caused by the presence of dark and different minerals, varying particle size of incoming ore, varying solids content and poor representability of the sampling have to be minimized.

2.4   CS4 - Wet Granulation of Pharmaceutical Powders

The objective for this case study is to perform wet granulation of pharmaceutical powders in a single shift which is currently carried out in four shifts. This method would reduce the number of granulations per batch, and in consequence, decrease the process time per batch. The main task of the new process is to obtain stable homogeneous granules in a wet high-speed mixer, with set dissolution and other analytical specifications achievable in the current process.

2.5   CS5 - Drying of Pharmaceutical Powders

Drying is one of the heart processes in granulation of pharmaceutical powders. Spiral Flash Dryer (SFD) is a swirling fluidized bed reactor [1] and can be considered as an alternative to conventional flash dryers and other fluid bed applications. The SFD is designed to dry granules with a minimal amount of drying air and providing intrinsic separation of dry particles from wet particles, which are recirculated and dried further. In addition, the operating principle is similar with an expanded fluid bed, with a very short residence time, maintaining a fast-drying effect due to the high-induced turbulence. The intensification goal of this case study is preventing undesired properties of SFD such as moisture deviation, generation of fine dry powders and sticky product over the equipment (fouling of solids).

2.6   CS6 - Mixing of Chemical Reagents

The CoFlore® Agitated Tube Reactor is a general purpose dynamically agitated chemical reactor, and therefore offers a range of applications as broad as that of existing batch reactor technology [1]. It can handle a large variety of reaction schemes, sequences, processes, and phase combinations over a wide range of reaction and residence times. Additionally, it also gives high level of mixing, reduces the required maintenance, and improves operational life of the reactor, allowing for easy disassembly and cleaning. However, the system should be enhanced to give the best possible mixing characteristics, to increase uniformity of solid distribution, to enable scalability of reactor, and to avoid fouling of solids.

3   Research Approach

Concerning inventive problem solving for process intensification, TRIZ offers a systematic direction to figure out ideas and solutions for developing new technology or improving the existing one. Even though TRIZ does not give directly an applicable solution, it helps to generate novel ideas faster and provides a basis for selecting the best ideas [14]. According to the Advanced Innovation Design Approach (AIDA) for process engineering [7], the application of TRIZ follows a process with a series of phases:

   I. Identification, analysis and ranking of partial problems.
  II. Systematic idea generation with TRIZ inventive principles.
 III. Creation of the solution concepts.
  IV. Concepts optimization with elimination of the negative side effects.

In this research work, the first 3 process phases (I, II and III) were performed during TRIZ workshops in each of six case studies, with the process engineers and academia researchers, currently involved in the corresponding PI projects. Each workshop was carried out under the guidance of one TRIZ specialist as moderator within 1 or 2 days with 6...9 participants working in smaller teams of 2...3 persons. The relative duration of the single workshop phases was I - 25%, II - 50%, III - 25% of the total time. The ideation phase II comprised one ideation session in the one-day workshops (CS1, CS3), and two ideation sessions in the two days workshops (CS2, CS4, CS5, CS6). The presented research assesses the efficiency of TRIZ application for problem solving, idea generation and concepts creation. Due to the time limit attached to the workshop duration, the process phase IV "Concepts optimization" was not a part of the workshops.

3.1   Phase I: Problems Identification, Analysis and Ranking

The approach starts with analyzing initial situation of process intensification using innovation situation questionnaire, followed by the comprehensive problem analysis including understanding primary function of equipment, operation, environment and working conditions for each case study. Function analysis and process mapping techniques [7] break down the complete production process into unit operations which results in identification of useful functions and undesired properties of unit operations. Finally, identification of the key negative effects or disadvantage of the analyzed system in accordance to the principles of Cause Effect Chain Analysis and Root-Conflict Analysis RCA+ [2], helps workshop participants to identify the root causes of problems and to rank them accordingly the objectives of process intensification in each case study, as presented in Table 2. The problems were formulated in detail as (a) enhancement of insufficient positive function, (b) elimination of negative effect or (c) engineering or physical contradiction.

Table 2. List of partial problems with higher ranking in case studies.

Case study	PI technology	Partial problems (Pp)
CS1 - Separation of ceramic-metal powders	Elbow-Jet Air Classifier (EJAC)	1. Avoid discontinuity in classification of powders 2. Avoid fine phase powders while milling
CS2 - Dry granulation of ceramic powders	High Shear Mixer Granulator (HSMG)	1. Reduce moisture content of granules 2. Avoid bimodal size distribution of granules 3. Increase productivity
CS3 - Metal ore beneficiation	Flash Flotation Cell - Raman spectroscopy	1. Avoid dark and different minerals 2. Reduce variability in size and solids content of incoming ore
CS4 - Granulation of pharmaceutical powders	Wet High-Speed Mixer	1. Achieve stability of product 2. Achieve target dissolution of product
CS5 - Drying of pharmaceutical powders	Spiral Flash Dryer (SFD)	1. Achieve desired final moisture content of granules 2. Avoid fine powder generation 3. Avoid sticky product over equipment
CS6 - Mixing of chemical reagents	CoFlore® Agitated Tubular Reactor (CATR)	1. Increase uniformity of solid distribution 2. Scalability of reactor 3. Connectors optimization

3.2   Phase II: Systematic Idea Generation with TRIZ

As a majority of workshop participants were not skilled in the TRIZ methodology, this phase of the workshop required a 45 min introduction to the TRIZ basics with a short training in application of 40 inventive principles. The enhanced version of 40 inventive principles with in total 160 sub-principles [17] was applied in the workshops as a universal ideation tool convenient both for process engineers and researchers. The idea generation was also supported by solutions examples in chemical and process engineering known in TRIZ literature [18, 19]. The application of the principles was performed for each partial problem separately in the order proposed in Table 3, whereby each idea generation phase was started with statistically strongest principles (group 1), optionally followed by the group 2 in case of design problems or group 3 for process optimization problems. All generated ideas were documented with a description and mandatory drawing and assigned to the inventive principles they were based on.

As a rule, different partial problems presented in the Table 2, were operated by different working teams. If more than one team worked on same partial problem, each team applied different TRIZ inventive principles to avoid similar ideas.

Table 3. Recommended order for application of 40 inventive principles.

Group 1: Statistically strongest principles [9]	(35) Transform physical and chemical properties, (10) Prior useful action, (1) Segmentation, (28) Replace mechanical working principle, (2) Leaving out/Trimming, (15) Dynamism and adaptability, (19) Periodic action, (3) Local quality, (17) Shift to another dimension, (13) Inversion, (18) Mechanical vibration, (26) Copying
Group 2: Principles for solving design problems	(6) Universality, (5) Combining, (29) Pneumatic or hydraulic constructions, (30) Flexible shells or thin films, (7) Nesting/Integration, (8) Anti-weight, (4) Asymmetry, (40) Composite materials, (24) Mediator, (14) Spheroidality and Rotation, (23) Feedback and automation, (31) Porous materials, (25) Self-service
Group 3: Principles for specific problems in Process Engineering	(16) Partial or excessive action, (27) Disposability/Cheap short living objects, (20) Continuity of useful action, (32) Change colour, (21) Skipping/Rushing through, (11) Preventive measure/Cushion in advance, (33) Homogeneity, (22) Converting harm into benefit, (39) Inert environment, (37) Thermal expansion, (36) Phase transitions, (38) Strong oxidants, (34) Rejecting and regenerating parts, (12) Equipotentiality, (9) Prior counteraction of harm

The Fig. 1 shows statistics of inventive principles of three groups applied by the participants during TRIZ workshops for idea generation. The lowest amount of the inventive principles was used in one-day workshops with one ideation session (CS1 – 8 principles; CS3 – 11 principles).

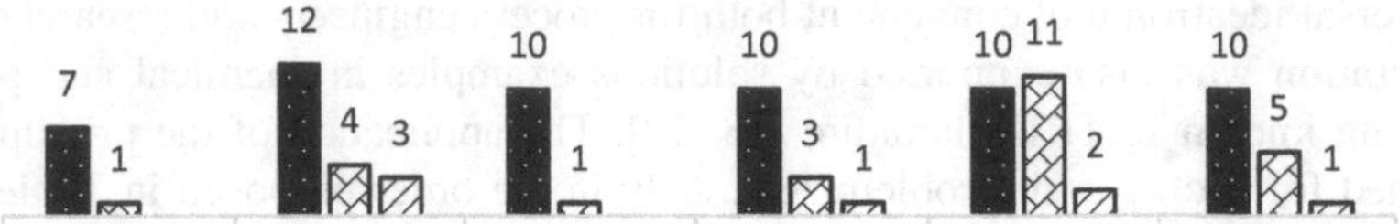

	Case study 1	Case study 2	Case study 3	Case study 4	Case study 5	Case study 6
■ Group 1	7	12	10	10	10	10
▨ Group 2	1	4	1	3	11	5
▨ Group 3	0	3	0	1	2	1

Fig. 1. Amount of inventive principles in corresponding groups applied in the case studies.

The number of principles used in two-days workshops with accordingly two ideation session (CS2, CS4, CS5, CS6) varies between 14 and 23. The ideation session duration was on average 3 h including idea generation (1.5 h) and idea presentation and discussion (1.5 h). The identification of the most effective inventive principles and corresponding sub-principles applied by the participants for idea generation was one of the tasks in presented research.

3.3   Phase III: Concepts Creation

Idea generation phase provides solution ideas for the partial problems with different stages of concretization. To develop a new solution concept at least one solution idea must be selected for each partial problem. Thus, a robust solution concept delivers solutions for all partial problems. Workshop participants with their specific knowledge on processes, existing and new technologies are in position to select most promising ideas overcoming the partial problems and to combine complementary partial solutions into solution concepts. Due to the multi-objective aspect of the concept creation and optimization, more than one solution concept can be designed in this phase, including "best performance", "minimum cost" or "optimal performance to cost ratio" conceptual alternatives. Therefore, the creation of solution concepts in a situation comprising several problems remains one of the challenging phases in the workshops. For example, Table 4 compares briefly six solution concepts developed in case study 5 (CS5) from in total 52 ideas. As one can see, the concepts C1 - C5 contain solutions for all three partial problems, and the concept C6 offers solutions for the problems 1 and 3 only.

Table 4. Amount of ideas selected for use in 6 solution concepts of the case study CS5.

Partial problems (Pp)	Solution ideas	Ideas selected for solution concepts C1–C6					
		C1	C2	C3	C4	C5	C6
Pp1	31	3	3	1	1	2	4
Pp2	9	2	1	1	1	1	-
Pp3	12	2	1	3	1	3	1
Total	52 ideas	7 ideas	5 ideas	5 ideas	3 ideas	6 ideas	5 ideas

4 Discussion of Results

4.1 TRIZ Impact on Quantity and Novelty of Proposed Ideas

The quantitative analysis of the case studies undoubtedly shows that TRIZ methodology can effectively support the process intensification tasks in the industry and with 234 novel ideas and 28 solution concepts for 15 partial problems consistently yields good results in the variety and novelty of ideas and solution concepts. It is important to note that in each case study all problem-solving attempts and ideas known prior to the workshops were documented in the initial situation questionnaire. Thus, the discussed ideation outcome of the workshops includes different ideas only, new to the initial situation. In other words, all 234 solution ideas can be considered as dissimilar and novel. Furthermore, the combination and adaptation of the selected novel ideas to the solution concepts leads to the patentable inventions and creation of new intellectual property.

As presented in Table 5, each case study (CS) can be served with several ideas and solution concepts: for instance, 17 ideas and 3 concepts in the CS1, 58 ideas and 8 concepts in the CS2, etc. The mean number of solution ideas proposed for each partial problem is 15.6. The average number of ideas generated in one ideation session (IS) by a team is 9.17 (SD = 1.51). The mean value of dissimilar new ideas proposed by each workshop participant in one ideation session along all case studies is 3.12 (SD = 0.52). However, a missing direct comparison with a control group of engineers working without TRIZ belongs to the limitation factors of the present analysis.

Table 5. Number of ideas, solution concepts, ideation sessions and teams in the case studies.

Case study	Partial problems	Solution ideas	Solution concepts	Ideation sessions (IS)	Number of teams (persons)	Ideas in one IS per team (person)
CS1	3	17	3	1	2 (6)	8.5 (2.8)
CS2	3	58	8	2	3 (9)	9.7 (3.2)
CS3	2	24	4	1	2 (6)	12.0 (4.0)
CS4	2	28	3	2	2 (6)	7.0 (2.3)
CS5	3	52	6	2	3 (9)	8.7 (2.9)
CS6	3	55	4	2	3 (8)	9.2 (3.4)
Total	15 partial problems	234 ideas	28 concepts	10 sessions	15 teams (44 persons)	Mean 9.2 (3.1)

4.2   TRIZ Impact on Variety of Proposed Ideas

In order to assess the variety of the ideas proposed in the workshops, every idea was assigned to the most appropriate knowledge domain. For this purpose, both problems and generated ideas were related to the eight engineering MATCEMIB fields and their interactions [20] applied in TRIZ: Mechanical, Acoustic, Thermal, Chemical, Electric, Magnetic, Intermolecular, Biological. For example, a uniformity problem caused by the surface effects of solid particles can be assigned to the intermolecular field, and a corresponding solution idea based on ultrasound treatment - to the acoustic field.

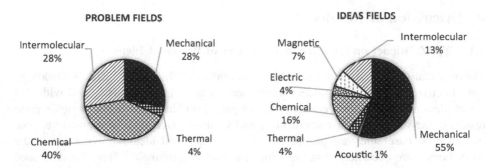

Fig. 2. Distribution of problems and ideas over the eight fields of MATCEMIB in all case studies.

As shown in Fig. 2, the 15 partial problems presented in all case studies belong to following engineering fields: chemical problems 40%, mechanical problems 28%, intermolecular problems 28%, and thermal problems 4%. At the same time, the 234 ideas from all case studies can be assigned to all fields excepting biological. As a result, the majority of the problems could be solved within mechanical (55%), chemical (16%) and intermolecular (13%) knowledge domains in the process engineering.

The variety of solution ideas in relationship between the engineering domains of problems and proposed ideas is illustrated in Table 6. Thanks to the TRIZ inventive principles engineers were able to find solution ideas in 7 engineering domains for mechanical, chemical, and intermolecular problems. However, no ideas based on acoustic, electric, or magnetic fields were proposed for thermal problems.

Table 6. Relationship between engineering domains of partial problems and ideas.

Engineering domains of 234 ideas	Engineering domains of 15 problems			
	Mechanical	Thermal	Chemical	Inter- molecular
Mechanical	x	x	x	x
Acoustic	x		x	x
Thermal	x	x	x	x
Chemical	x	x	x	x
Electric	x		x	x
Magnetic	x		x	x
Intermolecular	x	x	x	x

4.3 Quality of Proposed Ideas and Ideation Efficiency

Despite of high quantity and variety of the novel ideas proposed with TRIZ inventive principles, the industrial companies require technically feasible, economically afford-able, and safe solutions. On that reason, only a smaller number of high quality ideas has been selected by the engineers for further *implementation* in the solution concepts taking into account the following criteria: idea value (how a partial problem is solved), implementation efforts, costs and technical risks. The number of such *implementation* ideas Id divided by the total number of the ideas Id_t generated in one case study (see Table 5) can characterize the efficiency of an ideation technique. These efficiency values are presented for each case study in Fig. 3. For example, in the case study CS1 ($Id = 6$; $Id_t = 17$) only 35% of all generated ideas were considered as mature for further implementation and were applied for concepts creation. The mean value of TRIZ efficiency for all Process Intensification case studies can be calculated with the formula (1) and is equal 33.8%.

Thus, roughly only one third of the proposed ideas is estimated by the engineers as especially promising for process intensification. However, in the opinion of researchers many of ideas, which were not selected by engineers for implementation, possess a substantial potential for significant technological innovation in future.

$$E_{Id} = \frac{1}{n}\sum_{i=1}^{n} \frac{Id_i}{Id_{ti}} \tag{1}$$

E_{Id} – mean efficiency of ideation estimated on the base of all case studies
Id_i – number of implementation ideas in one case study used for concepts creation
Id_{ti} – total number of ideas generated in one case study
n – number of case studies

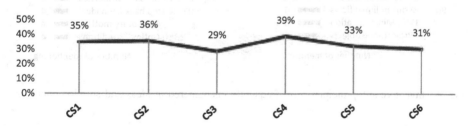

Fig. 3. Ideation efficiency with TRIZ inventive principles in the case studies CS1–CS6, defined as the ratio of implementation ideas and total number of ideas in a case study.

4.4 Identification of Most Efficient Inventive Sub-principles

The analysis of the solution ideas and concepts created in six case studies has also resulted in identification of the most frequently used top 10 inventive sub-principles, as presented in Fig. 4. These top 10 sub-principles can be generally considered as most efficient and recommended for the new development or optimization of PI equipment or methods in the field of processes involving solids handling. The identified sets of strongest sub-principles differ from the recommended group of statistically strongest inventive principles, presented in Table 3.

To the most often applied sub-principles belong *Change concentration* (35b), followed by *Use electromagnetism* (28a), and *Reversed sequence* (13b). It is also interesting to notice that top 10 sub-principles used in idea generation such as *Periodic action* (19a), *Optimal performance* (15a), *Gaseous or liquid flows* (29a), *Miniaturization* (17b) and *Pre-arrange objects* (10b) don't appear in top 10 sub-principles applied in solution concepts. Vice versa, the top 10 sub-principles *Utilize harm* (22a), *Spheres and cylinders* (14b), *Different functions* (3c), *One step back from ideal* (16a) and *Rotary motion* (14c) found in the solution concepts don't belong to the top 10 sub-principles in idea generation phase.

The TRIZ sub-principles mentioned above belong to the updated version of 40 inventive principles with in total 160 sub-principles presented in the previous research [17]. The study [17] analyses 155 Process Intensification technologies and 150 patent documents in the field of solid handling in the ceramic and pharmaceutical industries. It partially restructures and enhances the classical 40 inventive principles and extends them with additional 70 inventive sub-principles for the problems frequently encountered in process engineering.

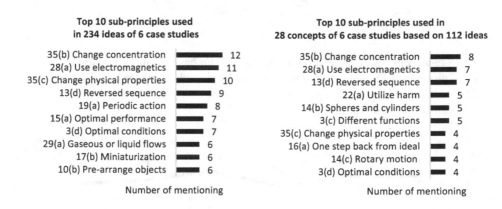

Fig. 4. Inventive sub-principles most frequently encountered in ideas and solution concepts.

The identified sets of top 10 TRIZ inventive principles and sub-principles in the analyzed case studies show clear differences to the corresponding top 10 sets of frequently used TRIZ principles and sub-principles extracted from the 155 PI technologies show some differences and from 150 patents for intensification ceramic and pharmaceutical operations with solids in previous investigation [17]. As illustrated in Fig. 5, there are 9 inventive principles (No 1, 5, 6, 14, 18, 24, 28, 29 and 35) most frequently used in all three sources of analysis: (I) Case studies, (II) PI technologies, (III) Patents.

The comparison on the level of sub-principles delivers a higher resolution and depicts only 5 frequently used sub-principles: *Spheres and cylinders* (14b), *Rotary motion* (14c), *Use electromagnetism* (28a), *Change concentration* (35b) and *Change temperature* (35d). In general, the identified selection of principles and sub-principles in Fig. 5 can be recommended for problem solving in processes involving solids handling.

The top 10 inventive principles and sub-principles applied in the case studies as well as top 10 inventive principles identified in the PI technologies and patents in [17] belong to the different groups of TRIZ principles recommended for ideation in Table 3. This statement is illustrated in the Fig. 6. Understandably, that 9 of 10 top principles (left diagram) and sub-principles (right diagram) applied in 234 case studies (CS) ideas come from the group 1 of statistically strongest principles as group 1 was primarily recommended for ideation in each workshop. However, the solution concepts in the case studies are based on principles from all three groups. More uniform distribution of top 10 principles over the groups 1, 2 and 3 can be observed for PI technologies and patents.

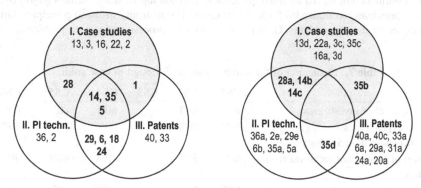

Fig. 5. Top 10 most frequently used TRIZ inventive principles (left) and sub-principles (right) in solution concepts of 6 case studies (I), 155 PI technologies (II) and 150 patent documents (III).

4.5   Efficiency of TRIZ Application for Process Intensification

A series of reviews has been conducted several months after the workshops to observe and assess the positive effect of TRIZ application in the case studies. The industrial teams of engineers or researchers who participated in the TRIZ workshops, evaluated the current state of their PI projects with different criteria, such costs, time expenditures, technical risks, innovation impact and TRIZ support, as presented in Table 7.

For each criterion the following scale has been used: 100% - very high, 80% - high, 60% - middle, 40% - low, 20% - very low. The estimated supportive impact of TRIZ workshops in the case studies was with on average 80% high. The evaluation results of the case study 3 could not be made available to the public.

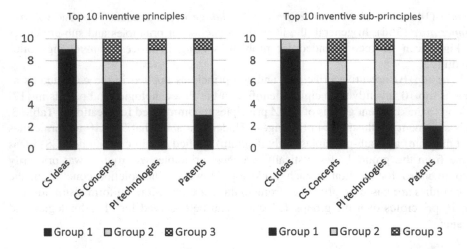

Fig. 6. Distribution of top 10 inventive principles (left) and top 10 sub-principles (right) over 3 groups of principles recommended for ideation: Group 1: statistically strongest principles; Group 2: principles for design problems; Group 3: Principles for process engineering problems.

Table 7. Evaluation of the current state of PI design in case studies.

	CS1	CS2	CS3	CS4	CS5	CS6
1. Costs, level of investments	40%	60%	-	80%	80%	60%
2. Time expenditures for implementation of technology	60%	80%	-	60%	-	80%
3. Level of anticipated technical risks in future	60%	80%	-	40%	80%	40%
4. Innovation impact of new technology in terms of PI-goals	80%	80%	-	100%	100%	100%
5. Supportive impact of TRIZ	80%	60%	-	100%	80%	-

5   Conclusion and Outlook

The presented research assesses the efficiency of TRIZ support for process intensification (PI) applied to solids handling in six industrial case studies in the field of chemical, pharmaceutical, ceramic, and mineral processes. The positive experience with combination of TRIZ and PI gives us confidence to extend the findings regarding TRIZ efficiency to the other fields of process engineering.

The application of TRIZ as a systematic problem-solving method demonstrates a positive impact on faster achieving PI goals. Moreover, TRIZ allows to identify and solve secondary PI problems comprehensively with numerous and interdisciplinary solution concepts. TRIZ inventive principles improve the outcomes of idea generation regarding novelty, quality, quantity, and variety of ideas.

Furthermore, it is worth to mention the identified sets and application order of the strongest inventive principles (14, 35, 5, 28, 1, 29, 6, 18, 24, 13, …) and inventive sub-principles (35b, 28a, 14b, 14c, 35d, 13d, 22a, 36a, 3c, 40a, …) which can be recommended for systematic and creative problem solving in processes involving solids handling.

The later review of the case studies progress shows that most engineers and researchers positively judge the TRIZ application in the PI practice. However, the research is still required to optimize and formalize the phase of concept creation as wells as to better identify inventive solution principles and sub-principles for other PI domains.

Acknowledgments. The authors thank the European Commission for supporting their work as part of the research project "Intensified by Design® platform for the intensification of processes involving solids handling" under H2020 SPIRE programme.

References

1. Wang, H., et al.: A review of process intensification applied to solids handling. Chem. Eng. Process. **118**, 78–107 (2017)
2. VDI Standard 4521: Inventive Problem Solving with TRIZ. Fundamentals and Definitions. Beuth Publishers, Berlin (2016)
3. Casner, D., Livotov, P., Masudah, Kely Da Silva, P.: TRIZ-based approach for process intensification and problem solving in process engineering: concepts and research agenda. In: Koziołek, S., Chechurin, L., Collan, M. (eds.) Advances and Impacts of the Theory of Inventive Problem Solving. The TRIZ Methodology, Tools and Case Studies. Springer, Cham (2018)
4. Hua, Z., Yang, J., Coulibaly, S., Zhang, B.: Integration TRIZ with problem-solving tools: a literature review from 1995 to 2006. Int. J. Bus. Innov. Res. **1**, 111–128 (2010)
5. Ilevbare, I.M., Probert, D., Phaal, R.: A review of TRIZ, and its benefits and challenges in practice. Technovation **33**(2), 30–37 (2013)
6. Chechurin, L., Borgianni, Y.: Understanding TRIZ through the review of top cited publications. Comput. Ind. **82**, 119–134 (2016)
7. Casner, D., Livotov, P.: Advanced innovation design approach for process engineering. In: Proceedings of the 21st International Conference on Engineering Design (ICED 17), vol 4: Design Methods and Tools, Vancouver, pp. 653–662 (2017)
8. Pokhrel, C., Cruz, C., Ramirez, Y., Kraslawski, A.: Adaptation of TRIZ contradiction matrix for solving problems in process engineering. Chem. Eng. Res. Des. **103**, 3–10 (2015)
9. Livotov, P., Petrov, V.: TRIZ Innovation Technology. Product Development and Inventive Problem Solving. Handbook, 284 p. (2013). Innovator (06) 01/2013, ISSN 1866–4180
10. Kim, J., Kim, J., Lee, Y., Lim, W., Moon, I.: Application of TRIZ creativity intensification approach to chemical process safety. J. Loss Prev. Process Ind. **22**(6), 1039–1043 (2009)
11. Rahim, Z.A., Sheng, I.L.S., Nooh, A.B.: TRIZ methodology for applied chemical engineering: a case study of new product development. Chem. Eng. Res. Des. **103**, 11–24 (2015)
12. Abramov, O., Kogan, S., Mitnik-Gankin, L., Sigalovsky, I., Smirnov, A.: TRIZ-based approach for accelerating innovation in chemical engineering. Chem. Eng. Res. Des. **103**, 25–31 (2015)

13. Srinivasan, R., Kraslawski, A.: Application of the TRIZ creativity enhancement approach to design of inherently safer chemical processes. Chem. Eng. Process. **45**(6), 507–514 (2006)
14. Cortes Robles, G., Negny, S., Le Lann, J.M.: Case-based reasoning and TRIZ: a coupling for innovative conception in chemical engineering. Chem. Eng. Process. **48**, 239–249 (2009)
15. Livotov, P.: Advanced innovation design approach: towards integration of TRIZ methodology into innovation design process. J. Eur. TRIZ Assoc. – INNOVATOR **02-2017**(04), 1–3 (2017). ISSN 1866-4180
16. Shah, J.J., Vargas-Hernandez, N., Smith, S.M.: Metrics for measuring ideation effectiveness. Des. Stud. **24**(2), 111–134 (2003). https://doi.org/10.1016/S0142-694X(02)00034-0
17. Livotov, P., Chandra Sekaran, A.P., Law, R., Mas'udah, Reay, D.: Systematic innovation in process engineering: linking TRIZ and process intensification. In: Chechurin, L., Collan, M. (eds.) Advances in Systematic Creativity. Springer, Cham (2018). ISBN 978-3-319-78074-0
18. Grierson, B., Fraser, I., Morrison, A., Chisholm, G.: 40 Principles – Chemical Illustrations. Triz J. (2003). https://triz-journal.com/40-principles-chemical-illustrations/. Accessed 29 Mar 2018
19. Hipple, J.: 40 inventive principles with examples for chemical engineering. TRIZ J. (2005). www.triz-journal.com/archives/2005/06/06.pdf. Accessed 29 Mar 2018
20. Belski, I., Livotov, P., Mayer, O.: Eight fields of MATCEMIB help students to generate more ideas. Proc. CIRP **39**, 85–90 (2016). https://doi.org/10.1016/j.procir.2016.01.170

Convergence and Contradiction Between Lean and Industry 4.0 for Inventive Design of Smart Production Systems

Rabih Slim[✉], Houssin Rémy, and Coulibaly Amadou

CSIP-ICube – INSA Strasbourg, 24 bd de la Victoire, 67084 Strasbourg, France
rabih.slim@insa-strasbourg.fr

Abstract. Due to the globalization, we have witnessed the emergence of new challenges, driven by a sharp drop in industrial production costs and a great ability to produce high quality products at competitive prices. To cope with these growing challenges, Industry 4.0 were launched in 2011. This concept represents the digitalization of the industry, integrating resources into production: people, machines and processes. These networked resources can interact with each other. Industry 4.0 optimizes the production system. The plant becomes agile, with flexible production methods, reconfigurable tools, and more efficient.

Considering the Lean requirements during the early stages of production system design could facilitate the development of Industry 4.0.

This paper mainly focuses on both Lean and Industry 4.0 by considering their requirements during the early stages of production system design. In this study, we analyze the convergence and contradictions for the implementation of these two concepts.

Keywords: Industry 4.0 · Lean · Design process · Production systems Contradiction

1 Introduction

Industry 4.0 will be able to produce a customized product more quickly, while limiting costs, better use of resources and with new solutions to reduce the difficulty of work and increase human ability to operate there [1].

Recent studies on both the Lean and Industry 4.0 concepts have proven the possibility of linking these two approaches [27–30]. In addition, concrete examples of the combination of these two concepts have been mentioned in literatures.

Our study makes an analysis of convergences and contradictions for the implementation of these two concepts.

After the introduction, we present a state of the art on industry 4.0 and Lean, their definitions, their evolution, their principles and their appropriate technologies. The third section deals with previous studies related to their combination and the next section outlines our study. In the two last sections we discuss our proposition and make a conclusion.

© IFIP International Federation for Information Processing 2018
Published by Springer Nature Switzerland AG 2018. All Rights Reserved
D. Cavallucci et al. (Eds.): TFC 2018, IFIP AICT 541, pp. 141–153, 2018.
https://doi.org/10.1007/978-3-030-02456-7_12

2 Literature Review

2.1 Industry 4.0

A production system represents all the resources (users, machines, methods and processes) whose synergy is organized to transform the raw material (or components) in order to create a product or a service [2]. One of the driving forces of the evolution of production is the evolution of customer demand over time.

To meet the challenges, the history of the industry has three major changes.

The evolution of technology is accelerated and recent technologies are emerging in all areas. It then became necessary to be used more and more in factories. A good integration of recent technology into industries can increase industry performance in terms of productivity and customer satisfaction. We talk about industry 4.0.

Under "Industry 4.0" we mean the beginning of the fourth industrial revolution after mechanization, industrialization and automation.

Innovation should be promoted in order to overcome future challenges in meeting market requirements. A production system should be efficient, flexible, reactive reconfigurable [3], that can quickly change its structure, and agile in terms of volume of production.

Therefore, flexibility is a basis of production systems in Industry 4.0 to realize individualization of products [4]. Industry 4.0 focuses on improving competitiveness by reducing costs and increasing the flexibility of decentralized production systems to deliver customized products, which is an advantage to satisfy customer markets [5]. Which implies a small lot sizes and a large number of varieties.

According to Yin [6], Industry 4.0 is grouped into three dimensions according to the customer demand:

1. Variety: Companies can introduce multiple models for each product.
2. Time: The delivery time requested by customer must be short.
3. Volume: Standard product and platform volumes can be high or medium.

Industry 4.0 meets all these requirements; it is a term that was invented at the Hanover Fair in Germany in 2011 to describe how these technologies will revolutionize organizations. The Fourth Industrial Revolution creates a world in which virtual and physical manufacturing systems cooperate globally with each other in a flexible way. This allows for absolute product customization and the creation of new business models [7].

Industry 4.0 describes the integration of modern ICT information and communication technologies into production [8].

This is the vision of automated "intelligent" factories, in which operators, production system, products and customers are connected in physical cyber systems [9]. In these technical systems networked computers and robots interact with the real world to connect physical objects.

Sung [10] claims that the digitalization of the manufacturing sector is driven by four disturbances:

1. The huge increase in data.
2. The power of calculation and connectivity.
3. The emergence of analytic and intelligence capabilities and new forms of human-machine interaction such as tactile interfaces and augmented reality systems.
4. The improvements in the transfer of digital instructions to the physical world.

The current work allows to emerge several concepts and need to define the relations between them (see Fig. 1).

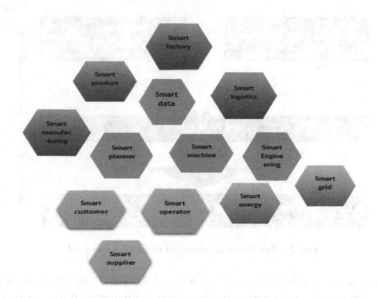

Fig. 1. Concepts of Industry 4.0 [11]

In the literature, the main components of Industry 4.0 are Cyber-Physical system (CPS), Internet of Things (IoT), Internet of Services (IoS) and Smart factory.

Through the Cyber-Physical systems (CPS), Industry 4.0 can react in an autonomous way, it is self-adaptable and agile. The use of such systems in production is then often described as Cyber Physical Production Systems (CPPS).

The Internet of Things (IoT) is an information network of physical objects (sensors, machines, …) that allows devices to communicate and interact both and connect using standard technologies with centralized controllers [12]. The (IoT) involves the integration of both (CPS), which connect the physical and the virtual worlds, and the (IoT) into industrial processes. It also decentralizes analytics and decision making, enabling real-time responses [13].

In this environment, (CPS)s communicate and cooperate with each other and with humans in real-time and via the Internet of Services (IoS), that allows' service providers to offer their services via the Internet.

Based on (CPS) and (IoT), Smart Factory can be defined as a factory where (CPS) communicate over the (IoT) and assist users and machines in the execution of their tasks [14].

Hoffmann [15] illustrates that the smart factory is defined as follows:

- Products and services are flexibly connected via the internet.
- The digital connectivity enables an automated and self-optimized production of services.
- The value networks are decentralized.

Therefore, a Smart Factory contains technologies that provide the optimum methods and techniques for production system [16] (see Fig. 2).

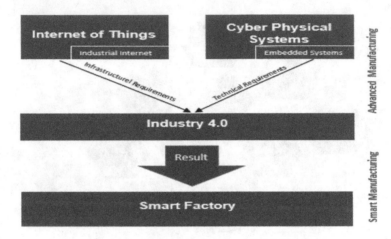

Fig. 2. Key terms in advanced manufacturing [16]

In order to make this Smart Factory, industry 4.0 builds on six main principles. Moreover, these design principles make the factory autonomous, flexible and adaptable to a changing of the production system (see Fig. 3).

Fig. 3. Industry 4.0 design principles

Interoperability is a characteristic of a production system in which its components are able to exchange information among themselves [17]. Smart Factory is virtualized in order to be able to simulate and follow in 3D products and production process. Decisions are decentralized via cyber-physical systems that can make decisions autonomous and in real time.

Recent advances in service-oriented computing and cloud computing including computational power, storage, and networking offer exciting opportunities for solving complex problems [18]. The Modularity lies in the plant's ability to adapt quickly to a changing demand, which increases the flexibility of production system.

In this environment, smart Factories need new technologies to enhance productive processes and to aim for value-adds to the concept of Industry 4.0.

To this moment, there are nine appropriate technologies and considering as the pillars of this concept. These technologies are integrated along these three dimensions:

1. The technical system: processes and tools.
2. The management system: organization, IT, performance management.
3. The people system: capabilities and behaviors.

To support the data needs in these smart factories, a Big data is necessary to integrate several layers and components for the collection, storage, processing, analysis and distribution of data [19]. With the use of cloud computing that enables to store Big Data, company will be more agile and flexible [20]. Virtual models of manufactured products are essential to bridge the gap between design and manufacturing [21], enabling simulation, testing and optimization in a virtual environment. Integration and agility in industrial automation need to improve to connect the company with the outside (suppliers and customers). Augmented Reality (AR) allows to give a virtual image in real time on all the information necessary for the operator, to help him perform these tasks in an optimal way. Thanks to mobiles and tablets, 3D glasses, other (AR) devices…, flow information, production monitoring, breakdowns, etc… are in the hands of operators in real time; enabling them to improve decision making, self-maintenance and quality. (AR) connects operators with each other and with their managers, quality teams, maintenance teams… The future of manufacturing with 3D printing, which allows real objects to be created using a computer-aided design (CAD) tool are in the integration automation of the production processes with Additive Manufacturing technologies [22]. In order to enhance factory automation, sensors and software capabilities will make the new manufacturing equipment smarter [23].

In order to increase productivity, the new generation of robots are becoming autonomous, flexible and cooperative. They work side by side with humans do it for him the complex tasks, or by automating repetitive tasks in an ergonomic, user-friendly environment, while simultaneously ensuring the highest possible levels of security and safety.

2.2   Lean Production System

The Toyota Production System (TPS) is a concept developed by Toyota engineers to eliminate waste of the entire industrial process from design to distribution.

They have identified a seven forms of waste (Muda) [24]: by overproduction, waiting time, transport. Processing, storage, through movement and producing bad parts.

Lean's goal is customer satisfaction in terms of cost, quality and delivery time; which requires the optimization of production systems in its three dimensions (technical, management and users). In order to achieve the goals laid down, lean is based on five principles (see Fig. 4).

The first principle is to link the value principle to the customer. In principle, it means that everything that brings value to the customer is essential, but anything else is waste and must be eliminated. The second principle introduces the notion of flow. This notion is crucial because it brings the visualization of the process, this makes it possible to visualize flows of materials and information and will facilitate waste identifications. Value Stream Mapping (VSM) provides an overview of activities, inputs, outputs and connections to detect wastes and plan their elimination. The elimination of waste allows for a continuous flow in a process where the operations are linked without disturbances and without interruptions. The Pull system is the technique of planning the production according to the customer's request, which makes it possible to reduce the stock. It is also about offering the customer a product whose added value is aligned according to their needs. The fifth and final fundamental principle is perfection, by examining and improving processes continuously. It is a process of permanent progress to bring new ideas and eliminate new wastes.

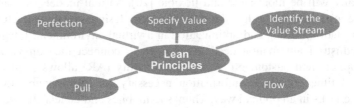

Fig. 4. Lean principles

Lean relies on tools developed over several decades and proven methods. Lean means the application of various lean tools or techniques including value stream mapping (VSM), 5S, visual management, for cost reduction.

The famous Lean house contains Lean tools (see Fig. 5) [25]. The House contains (Jidoka) that is one of the two pillars of the Toyota Production System with Just in Time (JIT). (Jidoka) is introducing a culture of adapted systems that automatically detect deviations from normal operation. Thus, the necessary measures can be taken immediately to avoid the propagation of errors or machine breakdowns. The second pillar is Just in Time (JIT), it is the synchronization of the production process by using (Kanban), which are a signboard for the management of production via a pull system under a production with zero defects.

The main tools that are related to (Jidoka) are:

- Man machine Separation which allows operator to work on several machines at the same time.
- (Poka-yoke) which serves to improve the visibility of operators and limit these choices to perform a task in a way that the right choice is the only possible.
- (Andon) to alert operators in case of breakdown.

And the main tools that are related to Just in Time are:

- (Heijunka) is the smoothing of production.

- (Takt) time which allows to rhythm the production according to customer's demand.
- Pull flow according to customer demand which guarantees the variety of production.
- (SMED) (Single-Minute Exchange of Dies) is to reduce the changeover times less than 10 min, which increases the flexibility of the system.

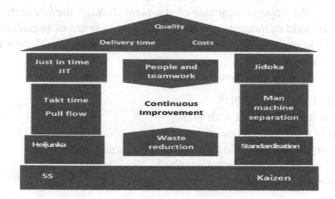

Fig. 5. Methods and tools proposed by Lean

In addition, to involve users in an orderly and organized environment, tools such as standardization serve to ensure the stability of the entire process and to facilitate the work of operators and reduce complexity. (5S) serves to increase the quality in the work area, based on lean thinking, all that is useless is to eliminate. Visual management is used to display information about the current status of production. Total Productive Maintenance (TPM) is used to achieve the highest possible plant performance the availability of production equipment in order to minimize maintenance costs.

The value stream serves to clarify and visualize the process including material flow and information flow for all the plant. In this way, the potential for improvement can be identified and the waste in the process can be reduced.

Therefore, lean's idea serves to create an organized environment in which the process is optimized, tasks are simplified and people are involved in order to reduce waste, increase performance and satisfy customer.

All these Lean tools could be integrated and taken into account from the early phases of the production systems design. This could lead to a more optimal production system from the beginning, which requires fewer improvements during the utilization.

Dekogel in [26] proposes a tool to integrate Lean philosophy into the design of new production systems. They consist of:

1. Describe the steps of the production systems design.
2. Illustrate the flow of different types of information during the design process.
3. Establish guidelines for taking Lean into account during design phase.

3   Convergence and Contradiction Between Lean and Industry 4.0

The elimination of waste requires new technologies. The combination of Lean and Industry 4.0 has already been mentioned in recent studies, and most of the Engineering Department of large international companies have developed a concrete solutions for a good implementation of Industry 4.0 in a manner consistent with principles and concepts of Lean on the improvement side of the plant through the integration of recent technology in the field of industry, and the consequent in terms of organization and the human machine interaction, in order to satisfy the requirements of customer and to enhance the performance.

In this context, many questions may be raised:

- Are Lean and I4.0 compatible?
- Lean should it be combined with I4.0?
- Is industry I4.0 a contradiction of lean?
- Lean tools are they applicable in the concept of smart factory?
- Will we go towards complete automation?
- Where is the role of human in this environment?

Dombrowski [27] tries to answer some of these questions by asking 260 German industry with the aim of making a detailed analysis of the interdependencies between Lean and Industry 4.0. His study shows that the application of modern information and communication technologies (ICT) in Lean Manufacturing, can improve the performance of production systems by obtaining more efficient production and logistics processes.

Many concrete examples of such convergence to link Lean tools with the Industry 4.0 technologies have been mentioned in literature. Via sensors that makes the product intelligent and connects operator to products and machines, operator can be alerted in case of failure or defects by detecting the anomaly (self-maintenance). In addition, an electronic Kanban can be added to product, it contains the necessary information for the production which allows to receive the requirements of customers or suppliers in real time [28]. Accompanied by robots that works in an autonomous way next to human, add to that the technology of augmented reality, operator will be smart, he can obtain all the information on the process and product in real time. It is connected to the production systems and to the outside (customers, supplier). Andon systems are integrated to alert human in real time in case of malfunction. Even though the lean's philosophy that put people at the center of these objectives is preserved. The risk is that human missions may be limited to surveillance.

The smart machine is reconfigurable, flexible, able to work autonomously via the (RFID) technology, it can warn operator in real time in case of failure (Poka-yoke), it is possible also to reduce the changeover times (set up times) less than 10 min by using the Plug'n Produce technology, which increases the flexibility and reduce the unexpected stop [29]. Wagner [30] proposes to develop a cyber-physic system, that replace the Kanban cards by a vertical integrated of machine to machine communication to link the all the flow information from the supplier between manufacturing order, machines to the customer, that guarantee the just in time delivery.

To more understand the convergence from examples in literatures, the table below is used to link lean tools combined with industry 4.0 technologies to obtain Smart concepts for successful implementation of both concepts in the of the new optimal production systems design. The ladder shows the possibility of linking these two concepts and that these can support each other (see Fig. 6). The connections were made according to concrete examples mentioned in the literature.

Lean \ I4.0	Poka-yoke	Andon	Heijunka	Man-Machine	Pull flow	SMED	VSM	5S	Standardisation	TPM	Visual Management	Kaizen
Smart Product		1	1		1		1					1
Smart Planner			1	1			1			1	1	1
Smart Machine	1					1		1		1		
Smart Operator	1	1	1	1		1	1	1			1	1

Fig. 6. Linking Lean to Industry 4.0

The table (see Fig. 7) illustrates the limits of the implementation of industry 4.0 and lean concepts, pointing out the convergences and contradictions according to different criteria, based on the three dimensions: human, process and organization. It derived from the views and examples mentioned in the literature, which was explicitly stated above in the state of the art.

The code "+" presents the effect of the implementation of Lean and Industry 4.0 on production systems according to criteria that influence the aspect of the production system and their ability to respond market requirements and the integration of recent technologies.

"+" shows that there can be a low positive effect.
"++" shows that there can be a high effect.
"+++" shows that there can be the highest effect.

		I4.0	Lean	Convergence	Contradiction
Technical System	Applicability	+++	+		I4.0 is applicable In production systems design, while Lean is a continuous improvement on existing system.
	Productivity	+++	++	The digital connectivity enables an automated and self-optimized production	
	Flexibility	+++	++	Both increase the flexibility of production system	
	Agility	+++	+		I4.0 make the plant more agile then Lean
	Reconfigurability	+++	+		Lean does not propose more configuration
	Adaptability	+++	++	Smart factory is self-adaptable	
	Complexity	+++	+		I4.0 increases the complexity and Lean simplifies it
	Automation	+++	+		Risk of a lot of automaticity and a reduction of the role of the man
	Autonomous	+++	+		I4.0 can make decisions autonomously via the RFID technology
	Machine to Machine Interaction	+++	+		I4.0 interconnected machine without Human interaction
Management System	Standardization	+++	+++	is fundamental to guarantee interoperability	
	Auto maintenance	+++	+++	can react in an autonomous way to resolve problem	
	Zero Defect	++	++	Both promote the elimination of defect	
	Elimination of waste	+	+++		I4.0 does not propose a structured method
People System	Team Work collaboration	+++	+++	Both require connecting operators with each other.	
	Decision Making	+++	+		Cloud availability makes decision making easier
	Man-Machine Interaction	+++	+++	New robots work side by side with humans to help him to do complex tasks	
	Tasks	+	+++		Lean requires more simple task. Artificial intelligence may eliminate human tasks and reduce its role in monitoring operations.
	Operator autonomous	+++	++	(AR) devices put all information that they needs in the hands of operators in real time	

Fig. 7. Convergence and contradiction between Lean and Industry 4.0

4   Discussion

From examples mentioned in recent studies, Lean and Industry 4.0 can combine together to design an optimal and modern production system in a way of satisfaction of market requirements. The concept of Industry 4.0 covers all phases of system life cycle. In order to design more efficient production systems, it seeks to make smart not only the use of systems but also their logistics, their maintenance and their end of life. Nor would it be in contradiction with Lean principles in terms of customer satisfaction, reducing costs and eliminating waste with a view to designing an optimal production system. But the risk which we think they could be quite real nowadays engendered from making the mistake of full automation that limit the role of human and almost can be completely cancelled, which is one of the basic elements of Lean philosophy and which is all about it. In this paper, we analyze to what extent the two concept can be corresponded or clashed with each other within the process of design of production systems, following a several criteria listed above in the table. We see that I4.0 is applicable in production systems design, while Lean is a continuous improvement on existing system. In addition, integrating I4.0 in the early design stage allows to develop a flexible production system, which can produce a variety of products without the need for major changes, more agile that adapts quickly to a changing demand, reconfigurable who can adjust quickly to adapt to new products. In contrast, Lean don't have a significant impact in regards to these criteria.

The complexity of system in I4.0 will be increased, accompanying by more automation that makes the system more autonomous. As we have previously stated, that's against the Lean principles which aims to simplify all tasks and procedures done by the system and its users. Lean is a set of methods and tools that can be applied on existing system, but I4.0 is a set of principles and objectives to consider in the design of new systems.

Despite these some contradictions, the combination of the two concepts remains possible; That analyses should enable us to how to overcome these contradictions in order to integrate the two concepts Lean and Industry 4.0 in the early design stage of production system.

5   Conclusion and Perspectives

Studying the convergences and contradictions of the implementation of Lean concepts and Industry 4.0 in production systems may strengthens the premise of considering the Lean and Industry 4.0 requirements during the early stages of production system design, which could facilitate the development of Industry 4.0. What is suggested was an overall approach aimed at a synergy between the two concepts Lean and Industry 4.0. And that could prove for future work to consider their requirements during the early stages of production system design.

References

1. Bidet-Mayer, T.: L'industrie du futur: une compétition mondiale. Presses des Mines, Paris (2016)
2. Benama, Y.: Formalisation de la démarche de conception d'un système de production mobile: intégration des concepts de mobilité et de reconfigurabilité (2016)
3. Long, F., Zeiler, P., Bertsche, B.: Modelling the flexibility of production systems in Industry 4.0 for analysing their productivity and availability with high-level Petri nets. IFAC-PapersOnLine **50**(1), 5680–5687 (2017)
4. Zawadzki, P., Żywicki, K.: Smart product design and production control for effective mass customization in the industry 4.0 concept. Manag. Prod. Eng. Rev. **7**(3), 105–112 (2016)
5. Meissner, H., Ilsen, R., Aurich, J.C.: Analysis of control architectures in the context of industry 4.0. Procedia CIRP **62**, 165–169 (2017)
6. Yin, Y., Stecke, K.E., Li, D.: The evolution of production systems from Industry 2.0 through Industry 4.0. Int. J. Prod. Res. **7543**, 1–14 (2017)
7. Schwab, K.: The Fourth Industrial Revolution. World Economic Forum, Cologny (2016)
8. Kagermann, H., Wahlster, W., Helbig, J.: Securing the future of German manufacturing industry: recommendations for implementing the strategic initiative INDUSTRIE 4.0. Final report of the Industrie 4.0 working group, Berlin (2013)
9. Karre, H., Hammer, M., Kleindienst, M., Ramsauer, C.: Transition towards an Industry 4.0 State of the LeanLab at Graz University of Technology. Procedia Manuf. **9**, 206–213 (2017)
10. Sung, T.K.: Industry 4.0: a Korea perspective. Technol. Forecast. Soc. Change **132**, 40–45 (2017)
11. Xu, J., Gen, M., Hajiyev, A., Cooke, F.L. (eds.): ICMSEM 2017. LNMIE. Springer, Cham (2018). https://doi.org/10.1007/978-3-319-59280-0
12. Kiel, D., Arnold, C., Voigt, K.I.: The influence of the industrial internet of things on business models of established manufacturing companies – a business level perspective. Technovation **68**, 4–19 (2017)
13. Rüßmann, M., et al.: Industry 4.0, p. 20. The Boston Consulting Group (2015)
14. Hermann, M., Pentek, T., Otto, B.: Working Paper, A Literature Review (2015)
15. Hofmann, E., Rüsch, M.: Industry 4.0 and the current status as well as future prospects on logistics. Comput. Ind. **89**, 23–34 (2017)
16. Jeschke, S., Brecher, C., Meisen, T., Özdemir, D., Eschert, T.: Industrial internet of things and cyber manufacturing systems. In: Jeschke, S., Brecher, C., Song, H., Rawat, D.B. (eds.) Industrial Internet of Things. SSWT, pp. 3–19. Springer, Cham (2017). https://doi.org/10.1007/978-3-319-42559-7_1
17. Liao, Y., Ramos, L.F.P., Saturno, M., Deschamps, F., de Freitas Rocha Loures, E., Szejka, A.L.: The role of interoperability in the fourth industrial revolution era. IFAC-PapersOnLine **50**(1), 12434–12439 (2017)
18. Bessis, N., Zhai, X., Sotiriadis, S.: Service-oriented system engineering. Future Gen. Comput. Syst. **80**, 211–214 (2018)
19. Santos, M.Y., et al.: A big data system supporting bosch braga industry 4.0 strategy. Int. J. Inf. Manag. **37**(6), 750–760 (2017)
20. Ooi, K.B., Lee, V.H., Tan, G.W.H., Hew, T.S., Hew, J.J.: Cloud computing in manufacturing: The next industrial revolution in Malaysia? Expert Syst. Appl. **93**, 376–394 (2018)
21. Schleich, B., Anwer, N., Mathieu, L., Wartzack, S.: Shaping the digital twin for design and production engineering. CIRP Ann. – Manuf. Technol. **66**(1), 141–144 (2017)

22. Chua, C.K., Wong, C.H., Yeong, W.Y.: Standards, Quality Control, and Measurement Sciences in 3D Printing and Additive Manufacturing (2017)
23. Witkowski, K.: Internet of things, big data, industry 4.0 - innovative solutions in logistics and supply chains management. Procedia Eng. **182**, 763–769 (2017)
24. Takeda, H.: The Synchronized Production System: Going Beyond Just-in-Time Through Kaizen. KoganPage, London (2006)
25. Dombrowski, U., Mielke, T.: Ganzheitliche Produktionssysteme: Aktueller Stand und zukünftige Entwicklungen, vol. 53. Springer, Heidelberg (2015). https://doi.org/10.1007/978-3-662-46164-8
26. De Kogel, W., Becker, J.M.J.: Development of design support tool for new lean production systems. Procedia CIRP **41**, 596–601 (2016)
27. Dombrowski, U., Richter, T., Krenkel, P.: Interdependencies of industrie 4.0 & lean production systems: a use cases analysis. Procedia Manuf. **11**(June), 1061–1068 (2017)
28. Kolberg, D., Zühlke, D.: Lean automation enabled by industry 4.0 technologies. IFAC-PapersOnLine **28**(3), 1870–1875 (2015)
29. Mrugalska, B., Wyrwicka, M.K.: Towards lean production in industry 4.0. Procedia Eng. **182**, 466–473 (2017)
30. Wagner, T., Herrmann, C., Thiede, S.: Industry 4.0 impacts on lean production systems. Procedia CIRP **63**, 125–131 (2017)

Multi-users of a Product: Emergence of Contradictions

Jean Renaud[1], Rémy Houssin[1(✉)], Mickaël Gardoni[2], and Mhamed Nour[2]

[1] ICube, UMR-7357, Strasbourg 67, France
{jean.renaud, remy.houssin}@insa-strasbourg.fr
[2] ÉTS, 1100, rue Notre-Dame Ouest, Montréal, QC, Canada

Abstract. The use of the product is randomly taken into account in the final phase of the design process, which leads to certain iterations and difficulty in use.

Generally, the designer has taken into account customer requirements without really knowing the end user, sometimes our end users.

By analyzing the different users, it is a question of measuring the functionality of the product for each of them. The various functional analyses must take into account the needs of all these users. Thus, it is necessary to identify: the expectations and cognitive barriers of each user in a competitive environment and to consider the evolution of the use and performance of the product and its interaction with its users.

In this article, it's about listing the product features for each user case. The different functional analyzes must present the expectations for each use case. Thus, in an order of the product use life cycle, it is necessary to identify the purposes and behaviors of users and the level of constraint of each feature. By comparing the functions between them, it is a question of identifying the contradictions or not that can have an effect on the design of the product. A concrete example (baby car seat), is proposed in this article in order to target the different users from the functions and to identify the contradictions that can be resolved by the TRIZ principle.

Keywords: Usage · User experience · Multi-user · Contradiction
Design · Functional analysis

1 Introduction

When a customer wishes to acquire a commercial product, tool or technology system, they choose it according to its ultimate intrinsic use, in a well-defined situation at a specific time. The customer does not care if the product may be perceived or used by other users at other times for different purposes or objectives.

These products, which have several users, will be called 'multi-user products'. The product is designed and manufactured generally for the main function, a purpose of the product for a need of the user. The designer designs a product through experience, out of habit, assuming how the product can be used or handled. The version or model of the

© IFIP International Federation for Information Processing 2018
Published by Springer Nature Switzerland AG 2018. All Rights Reserved
D. Cavallucci et al. (Eds.): TFC 2018, IFIP AICT 541, pp. 154–164, 2018.
https://doi.org/10.1007/978-3-030-02456-7_13

product is generally related to the designer's personality, character, choice criteria and design service.

In general, the designer does not specify how the user wishes to use the product [1–3] or how the user should use the product due to the critical lack of tools and methods of design help available for designers. The designer works by habit, persuaded that the product he designs will be suitable for the customer's use, that the product will seduce him in priority over its use.

Generally, the designer puts himself in the user's place, he considers that his design criteria are the best, without worrying about the real needs to integrate the conditions of use of the product [4, 5]. It is not uncommon to find that the product is designed to be used manipulated, or stowed by a single user considered to be the primary user without worrying about potential users at different times in the product life cycle. The designer proposes, generally a user's manual of the product [6]. In this manual, only one user is mentioned.

Many authors have focused on the anthropo-centered approach. This approach concerns the improvement of the design from an ergonomic point of view [7]. It is used for custom design because of its high cost and because it is only feasible for large projects and luxury goods [8–14]. The techno-centric approach, the technical system is at the center of the design problem. Designers have only the product standards at their disposal. These standards have the obligation of results without specifying how the designer could obtain these results.

Some authors have been interested in the needs of the client. Ulwick [15, 16] proposes the method of Outcome Driven Innovation (ODI). It focuses on the customer's "primary" need rather than the solution they use. The method focuses on the "what" and not on the "how". Other methods, such as the QFD [17] or the "Voice of the customer" are commonly used to identify the needs of the client.

It is known that the product can have multiple users. Users have different needs that can lead to contradictions of solutions to be solved early in the design phase. In the next section, we present the notion of the user experience. In Sect. 3, an application on a baby seat, a product that requires several users, is presented to illustrate our point.

2   User Experience

Analyzing a need means translating the product into "Customer specifications" or "User specifications". The "client user" reasons in solutions rather than needs [18]. When there are multiple users, we talk about multi-users. The functional analysis approach is a response to the search of the needs of the users.

In recent years, some authors have focused on the user experience, called "user experience (UX)". This refers to the experience of a person using a particular product, system or service. It's about making a product, a system easy to use, understandable (immediately, ergonomic, logical…) by integrating the user experience into product design based on ergonomics and human sciences, the goal of the user experience is to increase satisfaction with the use of functions by continuously improving the form, content and accessibility of the product [19–22].

UX stands out as a major marketing asset and becomes at the heart of business strategies. The user comes back to the center of all marketing concerns. The UX therefore contributes to increase the act of purchase. So it is proven that user satisfaction is as much related to the product/service marketing ability as to the perception of the brand by the user, the term refers to essential notions of communication, design and marketing. It is no longer based solely on ergonomic criteria.

In the continuity of the user's explanation, design studies must be able to identify or register different users according to the life cycle of the product. It is not uncommon to find that the product in its operation phase has several users. Designers must transform customer requirements into product performance. It should be noted that the requirements of the customer are not the same as those of the user (there is the first level of contradiction). Subsequently, the designer will have to prioritize these users, to better understand the functionality of the product according to the type of user. The functional analysis makes it possible to answer it.

Usually, the customer is the person who buys the product and uses it. It is never specified all of all users and how they are used. The customer takes note of the overall product function, cost, efficiency…, while the end user wants to pay more attention to product reliability, security, usability and operability. This means that designers must transform not only the customer's requirements, but also the user's requirements in product performance.

3   Case Study: Baby Car Seat

In our study, we chose to study the baby car seat. This product can potentially be unsafe. It presents several users at different level of use, not always identified (Fig. 1).

Fig. 1. Car seat model for baby or child <12 years old

The baby seat must fulfill two important conditions, be well installed on the car seat and be adapted to the weight and size of the child in case of an accident. Hence, a deadline for using the seat and the safety standards to be respected. Depending on the size of the child or baby, the seat is either facing backwards or forwards. It is mandatory up to 10 years in Canada for example. There are five groups of seats depending on the size and weight of the seat. There are "adaptable" seats depending on the size of the child and his weight.

The design of the seat and its use introduce many criteria or parameters very varied and very complementary. The client (parents) is not the privileged user, it is the baby but who cannot express himself. The parents are also users because they are the ones who install and fix the seat in the car. Hence the interest of taking into account the different types of users. In the following paragraphs, we detail the different phases of the product life cycle, in use.

3.1 Product-Study-Background

The usage context must be explained by the use that will guide the product design result. The context must be exhaustive (ease of assembly, use, maintenance, respect of security…).

3.2 Identification of the Study Phases of the Product Cycle

A product does not only have one main function to be used. It has several, depending on where we are in the phase of the product life cycle. Thus, it is proposed to detail the different stages of the product life cycle, such as:

- Study and design of the baby seat (seat, headrest, harness, the shape of the secure shell, mandatory standards…), The seat can be in one piece or detachable
- Unpacking the product and reading the instructions for assembly and use of the product,
- Installing the baby seat and checking it,
- Installing the baby seat on the car seat and securing the seat,
- Safe installation of the baby in the seat and its safety,
- Unlock the baby's seat belt.
- Remove the baby safely from the seat,
- Removing the baby seat from the car seat,
- Storing the baby seat in a storage place,
- Drafting and validation of the instructions for use.

Among all these steps, it is necessary to make apparent the various functions of the users which can be different.

We use functional analysis to better understand the product's functionalities according to the type of user and the phase of the product's lifecycle. Before identifying the product's functionalities according to the type of user, it is necessary to position the different users of the product's parts of use. Figure 2 describes the product and the different users.

In this example, we have identified four types of child seat uses for children less than 2 years of age and their function in using this seat (Table 1).

Table 1. The different users of the child seat

No.	Type of use	UX$_j$	Description or function of the user
1	Parent (1)	UX$_1$	The person who puts the child seat on the seat
2	Parent (2)	UX$_2$	The person who gets the child to cooperate
3	Child <2 years	UX$_3$	Securing the child in his seat
4	Parent (3)*	UX$_4$	The person storing the child seat in the storage area

In the case of Fig. 2, the aim is to identify the different links between the different types of users and the different main parts of the product. This link graph makes it possible to visualize the functional roles of the users. These functions can also be specified as: safety, fixing or tying, storage, confidence building... The links can also be contact, removable, manual...

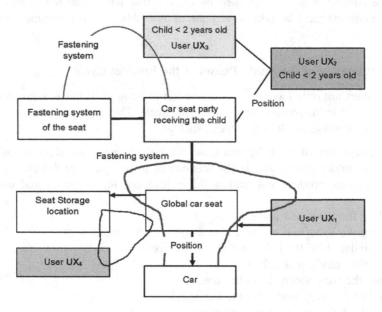

Fig. 2. Diagram of links between product parts and users

From Fig. 2, we report on Table 2, the types of users, the types of malfunction, the types of operation or tasks to be performed by the user and the type of phase of the product lifecycle. Each user thinks differently according to their missions or objectives in relation to the product.

Table 2. Comparison of potential malfunctions between the three users

Type UX$_i$	User	Types of operations or tasks	Type of malfunctions	Phase of the product cycle
UX$_1$	Father or Mother	Attaching the car seat to the seat of the car	Strap passage, locking system, seat position, secure fastening,	Functional Analysis 1 Phase 1 (fixing the seat on the bench)
UX$_2$	Father or Mother	Position of the child in the child seat and attachment of the seat belt	Baby attachment system, strength of the attachment, optimal position	Functional Analysis 2 Phase 2 (Child positioning and fixation)
UX$_3$	Child <2 years old	Be properly installed and able to move freely	Freedom of movement in complete safety	Functional Analysis 3 Phase 3 (Child in safe position)
UX$_4$	Father or Mother	Easy to handle and store	Weight too heavy, fastening systems too loose, volume	Functional Analysis 4 Phase 4 (Storage)

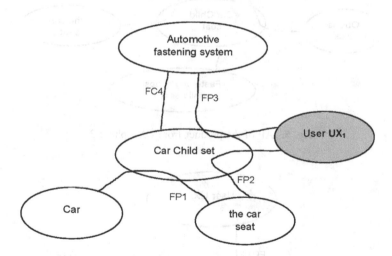

Fig. 3. AF of product from UX$_1$, phase 1

We propose for each phase of the life cycle of the product, to carry out the corresponding functional analyzes. Each functional analysis corresponds to a different user. These functional analyzes are a first reflection. These four functional analyzes focused on the missions of the different users according to the phases of the product life cycle (Figs. 3, 4, 5 and 6).

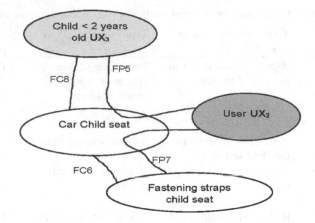

Fig. 4. AF of the product from UX₂ and UX₃, phase 2

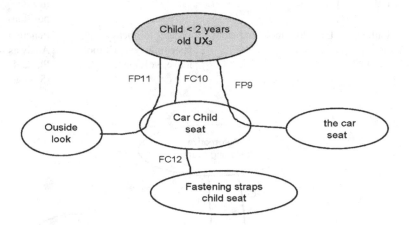

Fig. 5. AF of the product from UX₃, phase 3

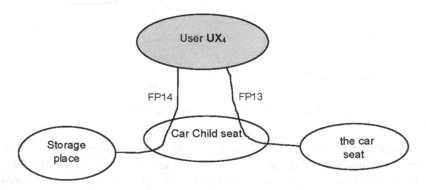

Fig. 6. AF of the product from UX₄, phase 4

4 Discussion

In our example, we can note the presence of four types of users who have four different profiles, four different objectives or missions.

The UX1 user has the concern to make solid the fixing of the child seat. That the fastening system (straps) of the car is efficient, practical and secure. The shape of the seat must marry at best the seat of the car. The shape of the seat for the baby is not the priority for the user UX1. The knowledge of the user UX1 is rather in the technicality and the practical sense. It usually refers to the manufacturer's instructions. Security is at stake in this phase.-

The UX2 user gives priority to the child, his well-being and his safety on the seat, but also the cleanliness of the seat and the ease of its maintenance. The technical knowledge of the UX2 is mainly practical sense, not requiring technical knowledge. Generally the UX2 user looks little or not the product designer's manual. The user UX2 combines the safety and comfort of the child in its implementation on the child seat.

The UX3 user, the baby, must be able to move without the risk of being detached or touching safety components of the car. The child's tether straps must resist the child's mobility force in the seat.

The UX4 user must be able to detach the child seat quickly and efficiently. It does not refer to the manual. His only concern is to untie it, carry it and put it away. The ergonomic shape of the seat must allow the UX4 user to carry it effectively. Reading the missions of the four users, we can observe that their level of technical knowledge, practical, safety, well-being… is totally different from one user to another and taking their needs into account could cause contradictions:

UX 4 needs the seat to be as light as possible, but for UX2 it must be as strong as possible and for UX2 the seat must be as soft as possible.

UX1 is interested in baby seat attachment systems in the car, UX2 is interested in baby seat attachment systems. Then there are two TRIZ point of view fastening systems. There should only be one system.

The UX1 needs the seat to have the simplest form, on the other hand, the UX3 needs the seat to take at most the shape of car seat on course (more complex).

UX2 needs the seat surface to be made of easy to clean material (plastic for example), whereas UX3 needs the seat surface to be made of cotton, for example, because it is more pleasant.

In Annex 1, we summarize all functions, criteria, levels and contradictions by different phases

5 Conclusion

In this research work, we wanted to show that products designed today no longer have a single user, but several who may have contradictory needs. Hence the importance of identifying the different users and their missions or functions, in order to better design the product under the angle of the "experienced user".

In our case study, we have broken down the life cycle of product use in stages. Then, we used the functional analysis to list all the features by user type and step. Each function is characterized according to different levels of importance and flexibility.

Then we identify the criteria that conflict or complement each other. Unlike other studies where we seek to better define the functionality of the product according to a single client, here we seek to better define the functionality of each user according to the study of use of the product. All for the purpose of better designing the products.

This work of identification of contradiction between the criteria or users makes it possible to propose recommendations for the designer of the product in order to eliminate or minimize the consequences of these contradictions on all the uses of the products.

Appendix

Annex 1

Fct.	Description	Cj	Criteria	Levels	Contradictions (Ct) Complementarity (Cp)		
PHASE 1						Ct	Cp
FP1	The child seat must fit into the shape of the seat and be attached to the car	C_1 C_2 C_3	Form of the bench Solidity Esthetic	Angle of the car backrest 300 daN pressure Design and *color*	C_{20} (Adult forme $\neq$ Child)	X	
FP2	The user UX1 quickly and efficiently positions the child seat on the bench	C_4 C_5	Duration Seat shape	<10 mn Low gap	C_1 (Gap between bench and seat	X	
FP3	The user UX1 fixes the seat in a flexible, efficient and strong way	C_6 C_7 C_8	Fixing type Duration of fixation Handling of bindings	By pressure <3mn Without notice			
FP4	The straps on the bench must adapt in an efficient and solid way to the child seat	C_9 C_{10}	Fixing type How to use	Ergonomic Simple Solution	C_{23} (robust and fast mounting)		
PHASE 2							
FP5	The user UX2 comfortably positions the child securely in the child seat	C_{11} C_{12}	Shape seat/child shape Comfort	Minimal gap Adapted form			
FC6	The child seat straps must fit the child seat in an efficient and secure manner	C_{13} C_{14}	Solidity Effective fastening system	According to regulations Ergonomic	C_{17} et C_{18} (Security and freedom of movement)	X	

(continued)

(continued)

Fct.	Description	Cj	Criteria	Levels	Contradictions (Ct) Complementarity (Cp)	
FP7	The user UX2 must handle the straps of the child seat without difficulty to fix the baby in an effective and practical way	C_{15} C_{16}	Simple technology Materials	A point of contact Armored fabric	C_{21} et C_{22} (Assembly and disassembly)	X
FC8	The child must adapt to the seat that can move freely	C_{17}	Degree of freedom	According to regulations	C13 et C18 (freedom of movement)	X
PHASE 3						
FP9	The user, UX3, child can move freely in the child seat fixed on the bench of the car	C_{18}	Degree of mobility	According to the regulations	C13 et C17 (freedom of movement)	X
FC10	The child is held in the seat safely, attached and free of movement	C_{19}	Pressure, safety	According to the regulations	C22 et C24 (locked and unlocked)	X
FP11	The position of the child in the seat must not challenge the external gaze	C_{20}	Seat shape	Rules in force	C1 (inner form of the seat)	X
FC12	The locking system (straps) of the child in the seat must adapt according to the movements of the child	C_{21} C_{22}	Adaptability Efficiency	3 anchor points Ergonomic	C17 (Tight and free straps) C17 (Inner seat shape)	X X
PHASE 4						
FP13	The user UX4 must be able to separate the child seat from the car seat	C_{23} C_{24}	Efficiency duration	Ergonomique Quelques secondes	C1 et C4 (Assembly and disassembly)	X
FP14	The child seat must be able to be stored easily in its place of storage by the user UX4	C_{25} C_{26}	Storage volume Accessibility	Same as the seat Handy		

References

1. Sun, H., Houssin, R., Gardoni, M., de Bauvrond, F.: Integration of user behaviour and product behaviour during the de sign phase: software for behavioural design approach. Int. J. Ind. Ergon. **43**(1), 100–114 (2013)
2. Sun, X., Houssin, R., Renaud, J., Gardoni, M.: Integrating user information into design process to solve contradictions in product usage. Procedia CIRP **39**(2016), 166–172 (2016)
3. Sun, X., Houssin, R., Renaud, J., Gardoni, M.: Towards a use information integration framework in the early product design phase function-task-behaviour. Int. J. Prod. Res. (2018). ISSN 1366-588X

4. Fadier, E.: L'intégration des facteurs humains à la conception. In: Phoebus, la Revue de la Sûreté, de Fonctionnement – Numéro Spécial, pp. 59–78 (1998)
5. Darses, F., Wolff, M.: How do designers represent to themselves the users' needs? Appl. Ergon. **37**(6), 757–764 (2006)
6. Renaud, J., Houssin, R., Gardoni, M., Armaghan, N., Hachali, H.: Aide à la rédaction d'une notice d'utilisation à partir de l'analyse fonctionnelle comportementale prenant en compte l'usage. In: Congrès CIGI les Innovations Numériques, Compiègne, du 3 au 5 Mai (2017)
7. Das, B., Sengupta, A.K.: Industrial workstation design: a systematic ergonomics approach. Appl. Ergon. **27**(3), 157–163 (1996)
8. Carballeda, G.: La contribution des ergonomes à l'analyse et à la transformation de l'organisation du travail: l'exemple d'une intervention dans une industrie de process continu. Thèse de doctorat d'Ergonomie, Laboratoire d'Ergonomie du CNAM, Paris (1997)
9. Belliès, L., Jourdan, M.: Le retour d'expérience: un outil pour aborder les questions organisationnelles. In: Recherche, Pratique, Formation en Ergonomie: Évolutions et Interactions dans le Contexte Social, Économique et Technique, Actes du XXXII Congrès de la Self, Lyon, pp. 159–170, septembre 1997
10. Jackson, M., Jamali, M., Roux, O.: Entre situations de gestion et situation de délibération: l'action de l'ergonome dans les projets industriels. Thèse de doctorat d'Ergonomie, Laboratoire d'Ergonomie du CNAM, Paris (1998)
11. Norman, D.A.: The Design of Everyday Things, pp. 190–191. Basic books, New York (2002)
12. Garrigou, G., Thibault, J.-F., et al.: Contributions et démarche de l'ergonomie dans les processus de conception. PISTES **3**(2), 16 (2001)
13. Folcher, V.: Appropriating artifacts as instruments: when design-for-use meets design-in-use. Interact. Comput. **15**(5), 647–663 (2003)
14. Obradovich, J.H., Woods, D.D.: Users as designers: how people cope with poor HCI design in computer-based medical devices. Hum. Factors: J. Hum. Factors Ergon. Soc. **38**(4), 574–592 (1996)
15. Ulwick, W.A.: What customers want. CEO. of Strategyn.inc (2005)
16. Ullman, D.: The Mechanical Design Process. Why Study the Design Process?, vol. 4, p. 2. McGraw-Hill, New York (2010)
17. Chang, C.H.: Quality function deployment (QFD) processes in an integrated quality information system. Comput. Ind. Eng. **17**(1–4), 311–316 (1989)
18. Marchat, H.: Gestion de projets par étapes, analyse des besoins, 2ème edition, Edition Organisation, 1ère étape. Groupe Eyrolles (2008)
19. Gero, J.S.: Design prototypes: a knowledge representation schema for design. AI Mag. **11**(4), 26–36 (1990)
20. Gero, J.S., Rosenman, M.A.: A conceptual framework for knowledge-based design research at Sydney University's Design Computing Unit. Artif. Intell. Eng. **5**(2), 65–77 (1990)
21. Gero, J.S., Kannengiesser, U.: The situated function-behaviour-structure framework. Des. Stud. **25**, 373–391 (2004)
22. Maguire, M.: Socio-technical systems and interaction design-21st century relevance. Appl. Ergon. **45**(2), 162–170 (2014)

TRIZ and Knowledge Management

A Creative Design Approach Based on TRIZ and Knowledge Fusion

Wei Liu[1,2(✉)], Run-Hua Tan[1,2], Ya-Fan Dong[1,2], Guozhong Cao[1,2], and Limeng Liu[1,2]

[1] Hebei University of Technology, Tianjin 300401, China
lwofhebut@126.com
[2] National Engineering Research Center for Technological Innovation Method and Tool, Tianjin 300401, China

Abstract. Knowledge is an important driving force for creative design. The knowledge fusion, which is formulated by knowledge from different backgrounds, is able to inspire novelty solutions to engineering design. In this paper, a design method is proposed to facilitate knowledge fusion in engineering design based on the theory of inventive problem solving (TRIZ). In order to formulate this method, the mechanism that fosters creative ideas through knowledge fusion is firstly explained, subsequently, approaches that transform the design problems in each of the above-mentioned design stages into TRIZ problems are discussed, since the standard problems in TRIZ can be solved by corresponding TRIZ methods. A design process is therefore formulated by integrating formerly discussed strategies. Moreover, its workability is verified by a case study. The advantages of the proposed method such as the expanding the searchable range of knowledge resource for TRIZ problem solving are discussed in the final section.

Keywords: TRIZ · Knowledge fusion · Creative design · Design method

1 Introduction

Innovation has been regarded as an imperative for the success of a company under the intensive competition in global market [1]. An obvious characteristic shared by current engineering design is the innovation originated from the information and knowledge of multi-disciplinary backgrounds [2]. Previous studies have claimed that the knowledge-based dynamic capabilities that refers to the ability to acquire, generate and combine internal and external knowledge resources to sense, explore and address environment dynamics [3] has a significant impact on companies' ability to innovate [4]. To facilitate the knowledge implementing in product innovation, study on knowledge management (KM) was carried out with regards to engineering design [5]. However, the KM is not well adopted to innovation in engineering design due to its lack of the mechanisms about how to apply knowledge in innovation from a systems thinking perspective [6]. Thus, one main objective of this study is to propose a framework to facilitate the systematical implementing of knowledge in innovation.

D. Cavallucci et al. (Eds.): TFC 2018, IFIP AICT 541, pp. 167–179, 2018.
https://doi.org/10.1007/978-3-030-02456-7_14

Knowledge accumulation is the prerequisite for knowledge-based innovation [7]. Current methods from KM are helpful for gathering the appropriate knowledge that meets requirements of design. In terms of KM methods, knowledge fusion works outstandingly by transforming the discrete, relevant knowledge source into a single knowledge unit that inherits the wisdoms from all its contributors [8]. On one hand, knowledge fusion focuses on the technological implementation of the knowledge other than its domain. Thus, the knowledge from multidisciplinary background is clustered through knowledge fusion for solving the defined design problems. There is a finding suggesting the out-domain knowledge is useful for increasing the novelty of design result [9], which supports the idea that knowledge fusion is promising for obtaining creative solutions to engineering design. However, the function of knowledge fusion has very limit workability in practice since the absence of a systematical method for innovation.

This paper proposes a creative design method based on the integration of knowledge fusion and TRIZ in which TRIZ wisely guides knowledge fusion in creative design and knowledge fusion provide inspirations for solving TRIZ problems. Moreover, the design for a new protective shell for isolator is used as a case study to verify the feasibility of proposed method.

The rest of this paper is organized as follow: Sect. 2 briefly reviews the relevant studies on knowledge fusion in innovation, integrations of TRIZ and knowledge-based innovation methods and knowledge fusion. Section 3 expresses the strategies and a step-by-step workflow to facilitate the innovation based on TRIZ and knowledge fusion. Section 4 uses a specific design case to stress the feasibility of the method proposed. Section 5 discusses and concludes the advantages and future developing trends of the method at the end.

2 Literature Review

2.1 Knowledge Fusion in Product Innovation

Knowledge fusion [10] is firstly proposed to represent knowledge combination from disparate sources in a highly dynamic way. Knowledge inflows from different domains enhances the chance of arising ideas that would not be considered by the designers in a single domain due to their psychological inertia [11]. As a result, cross-links that are initialized by the knowledge fusion often result in "creative leaps" in creative thinking [12]. Technological innovations usually emerge from complex fusion processes that integrate knowledge, technologies and other organizational resources. Therefore, knowledge fusion plays an important role in integrating all of the various knowledge sources for product innovation.

A typical knowledge fusion management system usually encompass at least four parts [13] to support technological innovation, to name them respectively: acquiring knowledge, fusion knowledge with resources, executing projects and assessing the performance of results. As a consequence, with an feasible management approach, knowledge fusion especially that is formulated by outside domain knowledge have potential for binging about "destructive technology" and propelling the innovation. In information era, the development of computer science and big data is reshaping the background of knowledge fusion. Nowadays, it is easy to accumulate a large amount of knowledge from various fields for technological innovations. However, the explosion of knowledge in turns can hinder the innovation results partially due to the lack of systematic approach for processing the huge amount of collected knowledge.

Regarding the development stage of management for knowledge fusion, the existing methods such as the repository for cross-domains knowledge, searching approaches are mainly belong to the section of "knowledge acquiring". A more sophisticated version of knowledge management still requires the sub-sections as "fusion knowledge with resources", "executing projects "and "assessing the performance of results". Therefore, a part of this research is to propose feasible strategies to provide the required parts in current knowledge fusion management.

2.2 TRIZ in Knowledge-Based Innovation

TRIZ, a Russian acronym, translated into English as "Theory of Inventive Problem Solving (TIPS)" was introduced by Altshuller in the mid-1940s [14]. The philosophy of TRIZ is built on five key elements: ideality, functionality, resources, contradiction, and evolution. With a well-established tools system, TRIZ provides designers with strategic and pattern-based guidelines to solve innovative problems.

Within TRIZ framework, knowledge for innovation can be expressed, preserved, accessed and exploited by its users from any perspectives. By holding a series of tools, TRIZ enables its integration with other methods such knowledge management and plays an increasingly important role in knowledge–based innovation. The tools of TRIZ such as invention principles are usually applied to find the appropriate knowledge for ideation [11]. There is a study proposed a modified TRIZ technical system ontology by linking TRIZ problem solving to knowledge retrieval process, in which a document processor helps knowledge-based innovation regardless of users' experience [15]. A previous study also revealed that the application of TRIZ in multidisciplinary teams can boost the problem solving by providing generic models to communicate the knowledge among team members [16].

From the discussion above, it is evident that TRIZ has potential to merge with the knowledge-based innovation. Moreover, interactions between TRIZ and knowledge-based innovation enhances their practical usability since knowledge-based innovation approaches bring about the inspiring for solving TRIZ problems, in turns TRIZ directs the technological implementation of knowledge.

2.3 TRIZ and Knowledge Fusion

Knowledge fusion is a process through which individual knowledge and group knowledge from many sources are fused and integrated with other knowledge sources to generate technological innovations [17]. Combination of knowledge from different sources has the potential to generate new kinds of technology, which can make a breakthrough in the technology development [18]. TRIZ has the potential to facilitate the innovations through knowledge fusion, since its systematic approach to solve the inventive problems. There are attempts [19, 20] to apply the TRIZ to process the patent data from different backgrounds to inspire innovations. Besides patent knowledge, biological knowledge is another issue that has attracted the interest from the domain to incorporate in TRIZ problem solving, such as Bio-TRIZ [21] and efforts to integrate TRIZ and biomimetics [22]. The study has a promising prospect when it provides a general approach to integrate TRIZ with the knowledge from different sources including patents and biology to generate creative ideas.

3 Methodology

This section explains the framework of the proposed method from two aspects: design strategies for the integration between TRIZ and knowledge fusion, the design workflow based on raised strategies.

3.1 Strategies to Facilitate TRIZ in Knowledge Fusion

Prototype Integrates TRIZ and Knowledge Fusion. The attempts to integrate TRIZ and knowledge fusion boost the innovative problems solving since knowledge fusion can enhance TRIZ by providing knowledge that meet the design requirements. A prototype in Fig. 1 illustrates a modified TRIZ problem solving process by incorporating knowledge fusion.

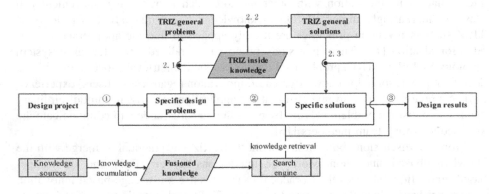

Fig. 1. A prototype for a modified TRIZ process integrated with knowledge fusion

Refers to Fig. 1, there are three phases in knowledge fusion driving innovation: ① design problem decomposing and analyzing; ② problem resolving; ③ solution evaluation. Besides these phases, knowledge accumulation and knowledge retrieval are indispensable for fostering innovation through knowledge fusion.

The prototype has incorporated TRIZ problem solving process in phase ② problem resolving with three specific steps:

2.1   transferring to standard TRIZ problems;
2.2   choosing the appropriate TRIZ methods to solve the defined TRIZ problems;
2.3   mapping from TRIZ standard solutions to specific solutions.

In the prototype, the step 2.3 is the most difficult part in TRIZ problem solving especially for TRIZ beginners since it largely depends on designers' professional knowledge and experience. With the integration of knowledge fusion, the proposed prototype improves the status quo by providing abundant knowledge for mapping the TRIZ standard solutions to specific solutions.

In order to gain the complete design process, there are four important problems should be solved beforehand, to name them respectively:

The first is "how to apply the knowledge fusion in decomposing and analyzing the design problems?"
The second is "how to transfer and resolve the specifically defined design problems by TRIZ?"
The third is "how to apply knowledge fusion to facilitate the mapping from TRIZ standard solutions to specific design solutions?"
The forth is "what is suitable evaluating strategy for combining the specific solutions to formulate a final design results?"

The answers to these four problems formulate the innovation strategies to facilitate the integration of TRIZ and knowledge fusion innovation.

A Fuzzy Front Analysis Based on Knowledge Fusion. The answer to the first problem lies in a fuzzy front analysis method for design project, since it clearly defines design problem at the beginning of design project.

In this paper, the fuzzy front analysis depends on the knowledge from both inside and outside TRIZ.

For inside TRIZ knowledge, theory of technological evolution can indicate the improving opportunities for the design project of interest by analyzing the current products and patents from relevant domains.

The design knowledge accumulation method such as Web-based patent search engine is able to provide the references from knowledge outside TRIZ about current design status. The knowledge outside TRIZ reveal the current technological solutions in related domains, which can be matched for their corresponding stages in certain evolution routes and laws.

As a result, several new ideas are put forward. However, not all of them are practicable enough for in-depth development. Among them, the most practical one is chosen as the start point to define design problem. Figure 2 illustrates how knowledge from both inside and outside TRIZ fused to work together in the fuzzy front analysis.

Defining, Transferring and Solving the Design Problems by TRIZ. After the design problem is defined, TRIZ methods such as the theory of contradiction and 76 standard solutions transfers these specific design problems into TRIZ standard problems as the step 2.1 shown in Fig. 1. Subsequently, in step 2.2 the corresponding methods are applied to attain the TRIZ general solutions. These specific methods and working steps are referred in classic TRIZ. Therefore, their detailed explanations are omitted in this paper even though they are necessary to the proposed method.

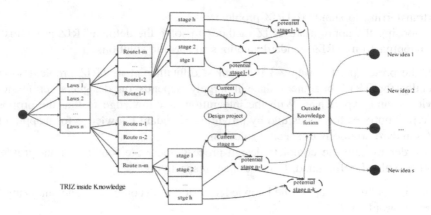

Fig. 2. Fuzzy front analysis of design projects based on knowledge fusion

Mapping from TRIZ General Solutions to Specific Solutions. In most cases, it is the bottleneck for solving TRIZ problem to map TRIZ general solutions to specific solutions. In general, resource is usually applied to extend the solutions space of TRIZ problems and provide knowledge to inspire solutions. In this study, resource is reinforced by knowledge fusion to enhance innovation resource searching with its searching strategy shown in Fig. 3. In the searching strategy, the knowledge resources are divided into three levels: the first is knowledge about the solutions that are similar to design problems from the same specific domain; the second level involves the principles from adjacent domains that are belonging to the same discipline as the design problem, knowledge on the third level of knowledge goes deeper to cover the physics and mathematics principles that are basis for the majority of disciplines, which enables a broad range for screening out the suitable principles for solving design problems.

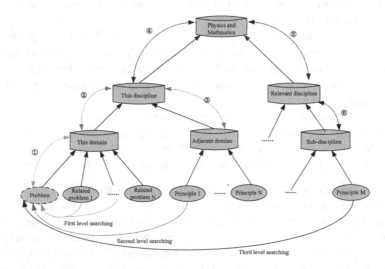

Fig. 3. An extended resource searching strategy to facilitate knowledge fusion

An Idea Evaluation Approach Based on Knowledge Fusion. The specific design solutions should meet all the design requirements. however, a design problem is usually divided into several sub-problems after the design problems definition. In order to formulate the complete design solution, all these subdivided specific solutions should be combined as one during which supplementing knowledge is needed to finish the system construction. In most cases, there is more than one solution that meets all design requirements, the theory of ideality is usually applied to assess all the candidate design solutions and screen out the most valuable one. It depends on the knowledge from various backgrounds to assess the parameters in the ideality formula. Both the benefits parameters including useful functions and harmful parameters containing cost and harmful effects need the reference to make reasonable comparisons among these solutions. In general, the knowledge for evaluating design ideas comes from the common senses and professional comments from the evaluators.

3.2   Workflow of the Proposed Design Method

Based on the aforementioned strategies, the complete workflow of the proposed method is shown in Fig. 4, which consists of nine specific steps:

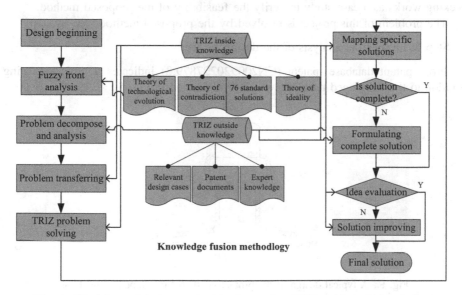

Fig. 4. Workflow of design method by integrating TRIZ and knowledge fusion

Step 1: Fuzzy front analysis of design projects based on abovementioned strategy for defining problem definition and confirming the potential improving directions.
Step 2: Problem decompose and analysis in which the specific design problems are defined before being transferred to TRIZ general problems.
Step 3: Problem transferring converts the specific design problems into standard TRIZ problems.

Step 4: TRIZ problem solving provides TRIZ standard solutions to the defined problems.

Step 5: Mapping TRIZ general solutions to specific solutions with knowledge fusion from different domains for formulating the appropriate specific solutions.

Step 6: Completeness evaluation. If the solution is complete the subsequent job goes to Ideality evaluation in Step 8, otherwise, the solution should be made complete at the first in Step 7.

Step 7: Formulating complete solution to make the design solution complete that may requiring knowledge both inside and outside TRIZ.

Step 8: Idea evaluation applies the theory of ideality to analyze whether there is the possibility to further improve the ideality of design solution.

Step 9: Solution improving stresses optimizing the solution to reach a ideality level that leads to an satisfying result.

4   Case Study

In this section, a new protective shell for protecting the composite insulator from bird's pecking works as a case study to verify the feasibility of the proposed method.

The problem of this project is resolved by the proposed method step by step:

Step 1: Fuzzy front analysis of the design project

From patent database, patent (CN200920227879.8) indicates a typical existing solution to the mentioned problem, which is illustrated in Fig. 5.

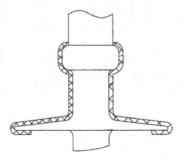

Fig. 5. A typical design of the protective shell for composite insulator

In specific, a layer of shell material covers and encases the insulator, which is tough enough to absorb the shock from bird's pecking and prevent the damage to the insulator. After the fuzzy front analysis based on technological evolution, there are four specific potential opportunities found in technological evolution routes for improving the current design by referring to the classic TRIZ [14]:

(1) Law 3 Dynamic: Route 3-1 Evolution to a continuous status system.
    Current stage is single status since it is a permanent protective shell and its next stage is a double status system which indicates a system has two different working modes.

(2) Law 4 Super system: Route 4.1 Evolution to multiple systems.
    Current stage is only a protective shell as the function operator, next stage is a double system main including other subsystems such as control system.

(3) Law 6 Completeness: Route 6.1 Evolution to system comprising subsystems of working unit, transmission, energy and control. Current stage only has a working unit, the next stage makes it complete with transmission, energy and control subsystems.

(4) Law 8 Controllability: Route 8.1 Evolution to increase the controllability. Current stage has no control section. The next step will incorporate the control system in the system.

Step 2: Design problem definition and decomposition

After a long term of observation, it is found that the bird pecking mostly occurred at the interval when the laying work has finished but still wait for powering on. Moreover, the use of protective shell may hinder the insulation capability of the composite insulators by change their surface material. In summary, the protective shell is needed for preventing the insulator from bird pecking during its waiting period for the powering on, on the other hand, the shell should be removable when the insulator work under normal condition after powering on. Based on the analysis of potential improvements and the background information, the function architecture of the new design is shown in Fig. 6.

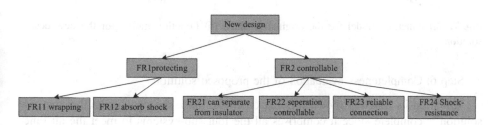

Fig. 6. Function architecture of the new design concept

Step 3: Design problems are transformed into TRIZ general problems

Evidently, the paradoxical requirement for protective shell is a physical contradiction since a protective shell is needed and not needed under different conditions. Besides this problem, the introducing of absent subsystems such as control system is possible to be properly solved by TRIZ tools such as 76 standard solutions.

Step 4: Solving the TRIZ problem by TRIZ methods

To resolve the defined physical contradiction, the time separation principle is chosen to inspire a design idea that is a new protective shell can cover the insulator during its waiting period and depart from insulator when the powering is on. The function model of the original product is in Fig. 7(a) which is built by substance-filed analysis. The product is not complete for lacking of other sub-systems, therefore, the No. 1.1.1 form the 76 standard solutions is used for building a complete system as the premise of the following design. As a result, several substances and fields are added to the product system.

Step 5: Formulating the specific design solution based on knowledge fusion

With the TRIZ general solution obtained at the previous step, a new specific design solution is proposed by implementing the knowledge to facilitate the functions such as the "remote control", "activate the separation" come from the design cases in relevant domains and fusing them with the original product. The function model of new design concept is shown in Fig. 7(b).

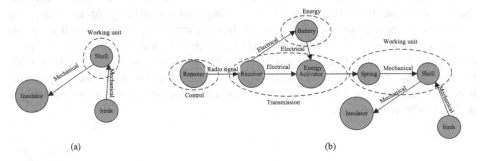

Fig. 7. (a) Function model for the original product; (b) Function model for the new design solution

Step 6: Completeness evaluation of the proposed solution

Based on its function mode, it is reasonable to make the conclusion that the new solution is complete since it comprises all the four sub-systems to meet the all functional requirements. Therefore, the step 7 is skipped over and the design goes directly to the Step 8 in the workflow of Fig. 4.

Step 7 (original step 8): Ideality evaluation of the proposed solution

The most ideal means to prevent the insulator bird pecking from root is driving the birds away from the insulators. Therefore, the ideality of new product can be improved if it able to drive the bird away with no obvious cost, in turns a longer services life will be premised for the shell since the chance of bird pecking has been cut down dramatically.

Step 8 (original step 9): Solution optimization

The optimization of design solution also depends on the knowledge outside TRIZ, in this case, the biological knowledge is used as imitating the eyes of eagle which are painted on the surfaces of shell to scare the birds away. As a result, the ideality level of design solution is improved by extending the lifespan of protective shell with trivial cost. The final solution is shown in both Fig. 8(a) and (b).

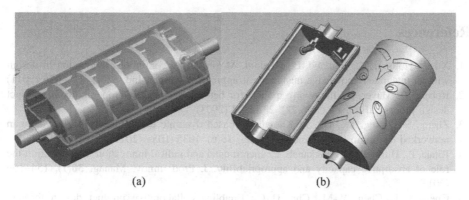

(a)   (b)

Fig. 8. Conceptual solution of the new design solution

5   Discussion and Conclusion

In this paper, a novel design method is put forward by incorporating TRIZ and knowledge fusion to solve design problem. In this method, TRIZ provides a bridge for fusing knowledge from patent or biology in creative design owing to its sophisticated methodology. On the other hand, knowledge fusion is able to bring about abundant resource for inspiring TRIZ problem solving. Generally speaking, TRIZ is a powerful problem solving methodology but it requires learners' knowledge and experience to formulate the well-built design solutions. From this viewpoint, with the suitable knowledge at hand, it is possible for all the TRIZ learners to become good TRIZ users, which in turns promotes the development of TRIZ. Knowledge fusion, an effective way for knowledge accumulation, is suitable to play the role of knowledge provider in TRIZ problem solving. The method that is represented by this paper stresses the feasibility of combing the TRIZ and knowledge fusion in creative design. With the proposed framework, it is practical to bring about promising solutions to design project, which has been proved by the case study in this paper.

To be honest, this paper is just a preliminary step for exploring the combination of TRIZ and knowledge fusion in product design. It is still a long way to go in the future, which requires continuous effort for developing a computer-aided tool for managing the knowledge fusion in TRIZ problem solving and a reasonable evaluation method to screen out the design solutions. With these effort in the future, an ideal design method can be formulate in which designers handle the manual tasks such as fuzzy analysis and making decision, while the computer doing the part that are more suitable for themselves, for examples knowledge accumulation and data processing.

Acknowledgement. This paper was sponsored by the National Natural Science Foundation of China (Grant No. 51675159), China Scholarship Council, Chinese Hebei Province High-level Talent Support Project (Grant No. A201500113). Chinese Central Government Guides Local Science and Technology Development Project (Grant No. 18241837G).We are grateful to all the anonymous reviewers for their positive comments and constructive suggestions.

References

1. Xu, J., Houssin, R., Caillaud, E., Gardoni, M.: Fostering continuous innovation in design with an integrated knowledge management approach. Comput. Ind. **62**(4), 423–436 (2011)
2. Robert, T., Mayer, F.: Improving models for better knowledge interoperability in product design process. IFAC Proc. **36**(22), 233–237 (2003)
3. Zheng, S., Zhang, W., Du, J.: Knowledge-based dynamic capabilities and innovation in networked environments. J. Knowl. Manag. **15**(6), 1035–1051 (2011)
4. Ritala, P., Hurmelinna-Laukkanen, P.: Incremental and radical innovation in coopetition-the role of absorptive capacity and appropriability. J. Prod. Innov. Manag. **30**(1), 154–169 (2013)
5. Chen, Y.-J., Chen, Y.-M., Chu, H.-C.: Enabling collaborative product design through distributed engineering knowledge management. Comput. Ind. **59**(4), 395–409 (2008)
6. Rubenstein-Montano, B., Liebowitz, J., Buchwalter, J., McCaw, D., Newman, B., Rebeck, K.: A systems thinking framework for knowledge management. Decis. Support Syst. **31**(1), 5–16 (2001)
7. Geng, J., Tian, X.: Knowledge-based computer aided process innovation method. In: World Conference: TRIZ FUTURE, TF 2011-2014, pp. 97–101 (2010)
8. Guo, B., Geng, J., Wang, G.: Knowledge fusion method of process contradiction units for process innovation. In: World Conference: TRIZ FUTURE, TF 2011-2014, pp. 816–822 (2015)
9. Delgado-Verde, M., Martín-De Castro, G., Amores-Salvadó, J.: Intellectual capital and radical innovation: exploring the quadratic effects in technology-based manufacturing firms. Technovation **54**, 35–47 (2016)
10. Preece, A., et al.: KRAFT architecture for knowledge fusion and transformation. Knowl.-Based Syst. **13**(2), 113–120 (2000)
11. Albers, A., Deigendesch, T., Schmalenbach, H.: TRIZ-box-improving creativity by connecting TRIZ and artifacts. In: TRIZ Future Conference 2009, pp. 214–221 (2011)
12. Chou, J.R.: An ideation method for generating new product ideas using TRIZ, concept mapping, and fuzzy linguistic evaluation techniques. Adv. Eng. Inf. **28**(4), 441–454 (2014)
13. Heffner, M., Sharif, N., Heffner, M., Sharif, N.: Knowledge fusion for technological innovation in organizations. J. Knowl. Manag. **12**(2), 79–93 (2008)
14. Altshuller, G.: Creativity as an Exact Science, pp. 1–5. Gorden and Breach, Luxembourg (1984)
15. Prickett, P., Aparicio, I.: The development of a modified TRIZ technical system ontology. Comput. Ind. **63**(3), 252–264 (2012)
16. Schöfer, M., Maranzana, N., Aoussat, A., Gazo, C., Bersano, G.: The value of TRIZ and its derivatives for interdisciplinary group problem solving. In: World Conference: TRIZ FUTURE, TF 2011-2014, pp. 672–681 (2015)

17. Heffner, M., Sharif, N.: Knowledge fusion for technological innovation in organizations. J. Knowl. Manag. **12**(2), 79–93 (2013)
18. Han, S.H., Kim, H.J., Cho, K.H., Kim, M.K., Kim, H., Park, S.H.: Research planning methodology for technology fusion in construction. In: 2006 Proceedings of the 23rd International Symposium on Automation and Robotics in Construction, ISARC 2006, pp. 15–18 (2006)
19. Cong, H., Tong, L.H.: Grouping of TRIZ inventive principles to facilitate automatic patent classification. Expert Syst. Appl. **34**(1), 788–795 (2008)
20. Park, H., Ree, J.J., Kim, K.: Identification of promising patents for technology transfers using TRIZ evolution trends. Expert Syst. Appl. **40**(2), 736–743 (2013)
21. Vincent, J.F.V., Bogatyreva, O.A., Bogatyrev, N.R., Bowyer, A., Pahl, A.-K.: Biomimetics: its practice and theory. J. R. Soc. Interface **3**(9), 471–482 (2006)
22. Baldussu, A., Cascini, G.: About integration opportunities between TRIZ and biomimetics for inventive design. Procedia Eng. **131**, 3–13 (2015)

Towards a Conceptual Design and Semantic Modeling Approach for Innovative Modular Products

Chérif Ahmed Tidiane Aidara[1(✉)], Bala Moussa Biaye[1],
Serigne Diagne[1], Khalifa Gaye[1], and Amadou Coulibaly[1,2]

[1] Laboratory of Computer Science and Engineering for Innovation (LI3),
Assane Seck University of Ziguinchor, BP 523 Diabir, Ziguinchor, Sénégal
{c.aidara3345,b.biaye3299}@zig.univ.sn,
{sdiagne,kgaye}@univ-zig.sn
[2] Laboratory of Sciences of the Engineer, Computer Science and Imaging
(Icube – UMR 7357), National Institute of Applied Sciences of Strasbourg,
University of Strasbourg, CNRS, Strasbourg, France
amadou.coulibaly@insa-strasbourg.fr

Abstract. To meet a demand more and more personalized for different users, the products must be innovative but also reliable, modular with good maintainability. Considering all these requirements in the design and modeling process would facilitate an evaluation of the behavioral performance of the future product. Most works deal with aspects related to functional criteria whereas behavior is rarely taken into account in the search for solutions. In this paper, we propose a design approach for innovative modular products, easily maintainable and adaptable to different user profiles. In order to evaluate the modularity, we propose a method of semantic modeling. The semantic model obtained makes it possible to identify innovative modular solution concepts by solving technical contradictions taking into account both the functional characteristics and the behavioral performances. As an illustration, a case study is outlined.

Keywords: Inventive design · Conceptual design · Semantic modeling
Modularity · Innovation

1 Introduction

From the Russian acronym, TRIZ is a theoretical approach for inventive problem solving. Indeed, several works have been done in this direction, from the ontology proposal of the main notions of the concepts associated with the acquisition of knowledge [1], to the formal definition of the contradiction and its potential manipulations in the inventive conception according to the basic principles of TRIZ [2], the application of TRIZ to real industry problems [3] or the proposal for an integrated framework for systems to support individual creativity [4].

D. Cavallucci et al. (Eds.): TFC 2018, IFIP AICT 541, pp. 180–190, 2018.
https://doi.org/10.1007/978-3-030-02456-7_15

However, setting up a product requires consideration of several factors that will reflect the product. The complexity of the design lies in the fact that the products must be innovative and more efficient, that is to say more reliable, resistant, easy to assemble and disassemble, etc. It is in this sense that it is said in [5] that the designer must opt for product solutions that are simple to manufacture, ergonomic, very reliable, safe, easy to maintain and have an overall cost over the entire life cycle that is attractive to the consumer.

Being more and more complex, the products imply an interaction between several actors [6, 7]. Managing all the factors in the design process requires taking into account the environment and evaluating the performance of the future product or system [8, 9]. Thus, we intend to conduct a scientific and technical study to propose innovative products through a semantic modeling method and the identification of innovative modular solutions concepts by the resolution of technical contradictions. In this article, we propose to implement a semantic design approach for modularity and to identify innovation paths, in terms of both modularity and other product-related behaviors.

2 Start of the Art

Following a literature review [10–12], it should be said that design methodologies have been continuously improved in recent years. Thus it has been proposed in [13], the combination of the systemic model and the V-model. On the one hand, they focus on design and modeling, and on the other hand, they help to improve the evaluation of products in the early stages of their design [10]. Others have done a lot of research on design and methodologies [14, 15]. While some have highlighted the steps of the conceptual design of mechatronic products [16]. In addition, there are several product design models among which, V design, spiral design, unified methods, agile methods, etc., [17]. Being the result of the decomposition of a product or system, the modularity makes it possible to solve several aspects of the product manufacture. Various works have been carried out in this sense [18, 19] and approaches have been developed to make the systems modular and to simplify their links. Let us note generative grammars for generating and classifying the components or the use of the concept of "holons" to model the connections between structure and functions [19]. Boothroyd et al. [20] propose a systematic methodology to assess the influence of Geometry, Material, Tolerance effects on Assembly. In this methodology, the emphasis was to relate Product design, Assembly operations, and Assembly Method to the single decision factor: the cost. Hitachi Assembly Evaluation Method is another approach based on very similar principals. The basic idea is the reduction of cost of a product through simplification of its design by:

- Reducing of number of components
- Ensuring that parts are easy to assemble
- Increasing the use of standardized parts across entire product range
- Designing with widest possible tolerances
- Material selection must consider manufacturing also, not just function.

Boothroyd-Dewhurst method includes:

- Preliminary (rough) design
- Selection of Assembly Method (manual, robotic, or high-speed automated)
- Design/Redesign of product for selected method
- The selection of assembly method must be done at an early stage in the product design process.

In most of these previous works, the authors highlight a structural and functional modularity of products or systems in order to obtain at a final product with a more flexible configuration. These different approaches were not intended to offer innovative and modular products in terms of new technological concepts. In this article we propose an approach of designing innovative and modular products based on the TRIZ method. Thus our design method allows to identify the problems, the solutions as well as the technical contradictions that result.

Our goal is to propose an innovative product design approach, modular, easily repairable and adaptable to different user profiles, we will in this article work on a semantic modeling method, in order to obtain modular solutions concepts innovative.

3   An Approach for Modularity Assessment

Starting from the conceptual design, the work in [6] defined a field of eligible solutions (instances, SS (Space of Solution), classes of solutions) respecting certain requirements and constraints as illustrated in the Fig. 1. We will consider a solution instance in the area of eligible solutions to highlight the modular aspect.

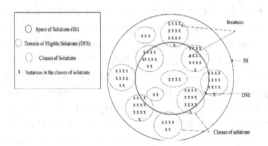

Fig. 1.   SS and DES

A solution instance will be represented by a graph G (C, L) with C the set of components and L the set of links. In this graph G (C, L), we have: C = {X1, X2, X3, X4} and L = {{X1, X2}, {X1, X3}, {X2, X4}, {X4, X2}} (Fig. 2).

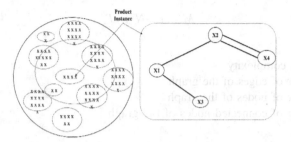

Fig. 2. Representation of a product instance by a graph G (C, L)

Moreover, to find the connected components, we will first build the adjacency matrix denoted M of the graph G and the matrix of the transitive closure of the same graph noted M *.

$$M = \begin{array}{c} \\ X1 \\ X2 \\ X3 \\ X4 \end{array} \begin{array}{cccc} X1 & X2 & X3 & X4 \\ \left[\begin{array}{cccc} 0 & 1 & 1 & 0 \\ 1 & 0 & 0 & 1 \\ 1 & 0 & 0 & 0 \\ 0 & 1 & 0 & 0 \end{array}\right] \end{array}$$

The adjacency matrix is obtained by noting:

✓ 1 if there is a relationship between two components
✓ 0 otherwise

Thus, we will be able to determine the matrix of the transitive closure denoted M *.

$$M^* = I + M^1 + M^2 + M^3 \tag{1}$$

I: matrix unit (put on the main diagonal of the 1 and the rest we put 0) M^{n-1}: adjacency matrix (n−1) we stop at 3, since n = 4 for this graph So:

$$M^* = \begin{array}{c} \\ X1 \\ X2 \\ X3 \\ X4 \end{array} \begin{array}{cccc} X1 & X2 & X3 & X4 \\ \left[\begin{array}{cccc} 1 & 1 & 1 & 0 \\ 1 & 1 & 0 & 1 \\ 1 & 0 & 1 & 0 \\ 0 & 1 & 0 & 1 \end{array}\right] \end{array}$$

From the matrix of the transitive closure, we deduce the following connected components: {X1}, {X2}, {X3} and {X4} because the lines are not alike, which is why each line is considered as a component related in itself. To calculate the modularity of an instance, we will use analogy based on the cyclomatic number to determine the complexity of a program (computer) by counting the number of paths. The cyclomatic number is defined by the following equation:

$$M = E - N + 2P \tag{2}$$

with

M: cyclomatic complexity
E: the number of edges of the graph
N: the number of nodes of the graph
P: the number of connected nodes of the graph

In software engineering, a simple code with a low cyclomatic number is theoretically considered as easier to read, test and maintain.

It is in this same logic that fits our approach to define a product modularity with the same equation:

$$M = E - N + 2P \tag{3}$$

where

M: Modularity of the product
E: the number of links between components of the product
N: the number of components of the product
P: the number of connected components of the product

For that we will take into account two graphs representing two instances of products, then will determine the most modular between these 2 products. If we consider a first graph G (C, L) in Fig. 3, the connected components of the graph G are: {X1}, {X2}, {X3}.

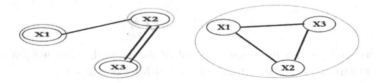

Fig. 3. Graphs (G (C, L)–G' (C', L'))

Then, consider a second graph G' = (C', L') whose connected components: {X1, X2, X3}.

$$\text{Graph G (C, L)} : \{X1\}, \{X2\}, \{X3\}$$
$$\text{Graph G' (C', L')} : \{X1, X2, X3\}$$

Modularity M

$$M = E - N + 2P \tag{4}$$

- For the graph G we will have:

$$\bullet \; M = 3 - 3 + 2*3$$
$$\boxed{M = 6}$$

- For the graph G' we will have:

$$\bullet \; M' = 3 - 3 + 2*1$$
$$\boxed{M' = 2}$$

M' < M so the solution M' is theoretically more modular

In the next section, we discuss about the influence of the different parameters involved in the modularity expression.

4 Discussion and Contradictions in Design for Modularity

To improve the modularity it is necessary that the value of **M** is the smallest possible. When is the best modularity for a product reached? If we take the example above, it should be said that M' of the graph G' is more modular since it is less than M of the graph G. However if we come to find that the value of M is equal to 1 (M = 1), but we will have a monobloc product. On the other hand, if we increase the value of M by acting on its parameters (e.g.: M = N), we will arrive at a product that is too fragmented. In addition to what should we tend to have an optimum value of M in terms of modularity and it is in this sense that we will talk about the notion of contradiction in the inventive design. The optimal value of M would be a solution that would optimize the modularity. So would be a way to look for a solution of a product not too compact or too exploded.

Thus we can act on the variables of the equation ($M = E - N + 2P$) to make a product more modular. We have three variables in our equation. Indeed, let's try to enlarge or minimize the modularity according to these parameters.

- For P: the number of related components
  - P is minimized if P = 1
  - P is maximized if P = N therefore P: the number of connected components is the largest possible,
  - We will have: $M = E - N + 2N$ so $M = E + N$
- For E: the number of links:
  - E is minimized if E = N-1 (allowing to traverse all the components of the product)
  - E is maximized if E > = N (E greater than or equal to N making it possible to cycle or even multi-instance links).
- For P = N and E = N
  - Then M = 2 N (aberration)
- For N: the number of components:

- N must be different from zero (0), N ≠ 0
- If N = 1 then M = 0-1 + 2 (1) => M = 1

5   Innovative Design for Modularity

Modularity remains one of the best ways to facilitate the maintainability of products once designed. The evaluation of the modularity in the above shows us that for n product we will be able to choose the most modular and therefore the most easily maintainable. However, the modularity must respect a certain threshold in order to reach a compromise with other behavior of the product. Because a product can be modular and less reliable or less ergonomic. It is in the sense that the resolution of technical contradictions takes into account all the functional characteristics and the behavioral performances. In our case, it would be important to act on the modularity by playing on the parameters of the equation of modularity.

Therefore, we will propose a case of illustration allowing implementing our solution of research of optimum modularity. For this, we will take the example of an electric wheelchair that allows people with reduced mobility to move.

6   Illustration Example

As an example, we will consider two wheelchairs (Instance I1 and Instance I2). Indeed these are manufactured with a mechatronic device to roll without help. The first chair Fig. 4. (Instance I1) comprises eight (8) components as illustrated in Fig. 5.

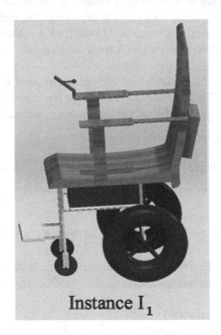

Fig. 4. Wheelchair (Instance I_1)

By applying the procedure proposed above to the instance I_1 of Fig. 4, we will evaluate its modular. Thus for the chair we will take into account the components shown in Fig. 5.

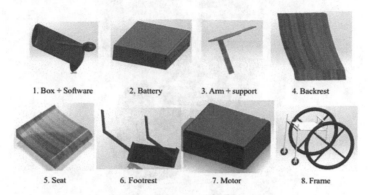

1. Box + Software   2. Battery   3. Arm + support   4. Backrest

5. Seat   6. Footrest   7. Motor   8. Frame

Fig. 5. Wheelchair components

If we consider the first instance I_1 in Fig. 4 the matrix of the following transitive closure is obtained:

$$M_1 = \begin{array}{c} \\ 1 \\ 2 \\ 3.a \\ 3.b \\ 4 \\ 5 \\ 6 \\ 7 \\ 8 \end{array} \begin{array}{c} 1\ 2\ 3.a\ 3.b\ 4\ 5\ 6\ 7\ 8 \\ \left(\begin{array}{ccccccccc} 1 & 1 & 1 & 0 & 0 & 0 & 1 & 0 & 0 \\ 1 & 1 & 0 & 1 & 0 & 0 & 1 & 0 & 0 \\ 1 & 0 & 1 & 1 & 1 & 0 & 0 & 0 & 0 \\ 0 & 1 & 1 & 1 & 1 & 0 & 0 & 0 & 1 \\ 0 & 0 & 1 & 1 & 1 & 1 & 1 & 1 & 1 \\ 0 & 0 & 0 & 0 & 1 & 1 & 0 & 0 & 0 \\ 1 & 1 & 0 & 0 & 1 & 0 & 1 & 1 & 0 \\ 0 & 0 & 0 & 0 & 1 & 0 & 1 & 1 & 0 \\ 0 & 0 & 0 & 1 & 1 & 0 & 0 & 0 & 1 \end{array}\right) \end{array}$$

The related components of I_1 are: {1}, {2}, {3.a}, {3.b}, {4}, {5}, {6}, {7}, {8}. Let's not forget that for instance I_1 component 3 (3. Arm + support) is multiplied by two (3.a, 3.b).

However, we will consider a second instance I_2 having almost the same characteristics as the first but with a detail, the grouping of the component 3 of Fig. 5. (3. Arm + support) in one module. In this sense, we will act on the parameters of equation M to arrive at a more modular product.

After evaluation of the second, instance I2 in Fig. 6 we will have the following related

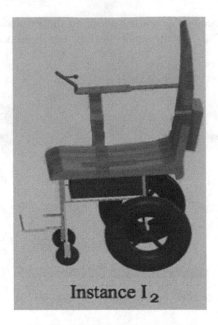

Fig. 6. Wheelchair (Instance I_2)

components: {1}, {2}, {3}, {4}, {5}, {6}, {7}, {8} as shown in the following matrix

$$
M_2 = \begin{array}{c} \\ 1 \\ 2 \\ 3 \\ 4 \\ 5 \\ 6 \\ 7 \\ 8 \end{array}
\begin{array}{cccccccc}
1 & 2 & 3 & 4 & 5 & 6 & 7 & 8 \\
1 & 1 & 0 & 0 & 0 & 1 & 0 \\
1 & 1 & 0 & 1 & 0 & 0 & 1 & 0 \\
1 & 0 & 1 & 1 & 1 & 0 & 0 & 0 \\
0 & 1 & 1 & 1 & 1 & 0 & 0 & 0 \\
0 & 0 & 1 & 1 & 1 & 1 & 1 & 1 \\
0 & 0 & 0 & 0 & 1 & 1 & 0 & 0 \\
1 & 1 & 0 & 0 & 1 & 0 & 1 & 1 \\
0 & 0 & 0 & 0 & 1 & 0 & 1 & 1
\end{array}
$$

- For instance, M_1 we have:

$$\bullet\ M_1 = 26 - 9 + 2*9$$

$$\boxed{M_1 = 35}$$

- For instance, the M_2 solution I_2 is more modular than I_1

$$\bullet\ M_2 = 24 - 8 + 2*8$$

$$\boxed{M_2 = 32}$$

Thus, we clearly see that Instance (I_2, M_2) is more modular than Instance (I_1, M_1), with fewer components because some are grouped into modules (3. Arm + support) and facilitate assembly and disassembly, hence the interest of maintainability.

7 Conclusions and Perspectives

The manufacture of innovative and modular products is a. good way to facilitate its maintainability, including the replacement of a defective part. Indeed, evaluating their behavior in the early stages of their design could help to improve the implementation of innovative products. Thus, these products will meet several requirements of the user before manufacture. This work will facilitate the use, maneuverability and especially the repair of future products. In our future work, we plan to carry out an ergonomic study of the products in order to alleviate the difficulty of use related to certain tools of work but also to solve the technical contradictions to get innovating products with respect to different behaviors.

References

1. Zanni-Merk, C., Cavallucci, D., Rousselot, F.: An ontological basis pour computer aided innovation. Comput. Ind. **60**, 563–574 (2009). www.elsevier.com/locate/compind
2. Rousselot, F., Zanni-Merk, C., Cavallucci, D.: Towards a formal definition of contradiction in inventive design. Comput. Ind. **63**, 231–242 (2012). www.elsevier.com/locate/compind
3. Sheu, D., Hou, C.T.: TRIZ-based trimming for process-machine improvements: slit-valve innovative redesign. Comput. Ind. Eng. **66**, 555–566 (2013). www.elsevier.com/locate/caie
4. Wang, K., Nickerson, J.V.: A literature review on individual creativity support systems. Comput. Hum. Behav. **74**, 139–151 (2017). www.elsevier.com/locate/comphumbeh
5. Menye, John the Baptist: Validation of maintainability and design availability of a multi-component system. Laval University (2009). http://www.exercicescorriges.com/i_107544. pdf
6. Diagne, S., Coulibaly, A., De Beuvron, F.: Towards a conceptual design for mechatronic product's family development, pp. 94–99. IEEE (2014). https://doi.org/10.1109/idam.2014. 6912677
7. Casner, D., Houssin, R., Knittel, D., Renaud, J.: An approach to design and optimization of mechatronic systems based on multidisciplinary optimization and based on the feedback of experiences. In: 21st French Mechanics Congress, 26–30 August 2013, Bordeaux, France (FR) (2013). http://documents.irevues.inist.fr/handle/2042/52520
8. Casner, D., Renaud, J., Knittel, D.: Design of mechatronic systems by topological optimization. In: 12th AIP-PRIMECA National Conference, AIP-Priméca (2011). https://hal. archives-ouvertes.fr/hal-00843025/
9. Coulibaly, A., De Beuvron, F.D.B., Renaud, J.: Maintainability assessment at early design internship using advanced CAD systems. In: Proceedings of IDMME-Virtual Concept, pp. 20–22 (2010)
10. Motte, D.: A review of fundamentals of systematic engineering design process models. In: International Design Conference - Design 2008, Dubrovnik, Croatia, 19–22 May 2008

11. Gausemeier, J., Mohringer, S.: Nes guideline VDI 2206 - a flexible procedure method for the design of mechatronic systems. In: Proceedings of the 14th International Conference on Engineering Design (ICED 2003), Stockholm (2003)
12. Ziemniak, P., Stania, M., Stetter, R.: Mechatronics engineering on the example of an innovative production vehicle. In: Proceedings of the 17th International Conference of Engineering Design (ICED 2009), 24–27 August 2009. Stanford University, Stanford (2009)
13. Rahman, R., Pulm, U., Stetter, R.: Systematic mechatronic design of a piezo-electric brake. In: Proceedings of the 16th International Conference of Engineering (ICED 2007), 28–31 August 2007. Design Society, Paris (2007)
14. Partto, M., Saariluoma, P.: Explaining failures in innovative throught processes in engineering design. Procedia - Soc. Behav. Sci. **41**, 442–449 (2012)
15. Chandrasegaran, S.K., et al.: The evolution challenges and future knowledge representation in product design systems. Comput.-Aided Des. **45**(2), 204–228 (2013)
16. Diagne, S., et al.: Towards a conceptual design for mechatronic products family development. In: 2014 International Conference on Innovative Design and Manufacturing, 13–15 August 2014, Montreal, Quebec, Canada (2014)
17. Diagne, S.: Conceptual semantic modeling for the behavioral performance engineering of complex products. University of Strasbourg, Graduate School of Mathematics Information and Engineering Sciences (MSII ED 269) UdS INSA Strasbourg Laboratory of Engineering Conception (LGeCo EA 3938). Doctor from the University of Strasbourg Discipline Engineering Sciences Specialty Computer Engineering Mechanical Engineering, July 2015
18. Baldwin, C., Clark, K.: Modularity in the design of complex engineering systems. In: Braha, D., Minai, A.A., Bar-Yam, Y. (eds.) Complex Engineered Systems, Science Meets Technology, pp. 175–205. Springer, Berlin (2006). https://doi.org/10.1007/3-540-32834-3_9
19. Homam_ISSA thesis dissertation: Contributions to the design of configurable products in advanced CAD systems, December 2015
20. Boothroyd, G., Dewhurst, P., Knight, W.: Product Design for Manufacture and Assembly. Marcel Dekker Inc., New York City (1994). ISBN 10: 0824791762, ISBN 13: 9780824791766

TRIZ and Patenting

TRIZ and Intellectual Property to Strengthen the Start-Up Spirit

Pascal Sire[1(✉)], Eric Prevost[2], Yves Guillou[3], Alain Riwan[4], and Pierre Saulais[5]

[1] Innoppie & VP TRIZ France, Strasbourg, France
`pascal.sire@innoppie.com`
[2] Oracle Corp & President TRIZ France, Paris, France
`president@trizfrance.org`
[3] Guilbert EXPRESS & Secretaire TRIZ France, Paris, France
`secretaire@trizfrance.org`
[4] CEA, LIST, Interactive Robotics Laboratory, Paris, France
`alain.riwan@cea.fr`
[5] Mines Telecom Institute, Paris, France
`pierre.saulais@telecom-em.eu`

Abstract. How can start-ups benefit from business innovation good practices while enforcing the link between invention, innovation and intellectual property (IP) to contribute to this vital discussion for the survival of our industries? Some experts of the TRIZ France association drawn from their practical experiences a path to illustrate the methodological and practical contributions of the Theory for inventive problem solving (TRIZ). This illustration highlights a specific focus on businesses where the "start-up spirit" facilitates ideation and accelerates the production of innovative products and services.

Keywords: Innovation design · Intellectual property · Start-up
TRIZ

1 Introduction: Inventive Design and Start-up Spirit

A start-up is "a human institution designed to create a new product or service under conditions of extreme uncertainty" [1], characterized by four conditions: high potential growth, use of a new technology, financial need and new market difficult to evaluate.

The start-up spirit is a mode of operation that stimulates innovation, creativity, perhaps even rebellion and strengthens team spirit, spontaneity, the risk of failure, agility and quick adaptation.

Important: "Start-up = disruption, growth and uncertainty and start-up spirit = pioneering spirit".

The purpose of this paper is therefore first to synthetize an approach able to solve technical problems blocking the functional evolution of a technical object, so as to advance the latter towards the ideality through successive optimizations in innovation trajectories that will be identified. The second purpose is to explore how to include this approach in stakeholder strategies (incubators and start-ups, innovative firm) in order to develop it in the start-up spirit as an application of innovation management.

© IFIP International Federation for Information Processing 2018
Published by Springer Nature Switzerland AG 2018. All Rights Reserved
D. Cavallucci et al. (Eds.): TFC 2018, IFIP AICT 541, pp. 193–203, 2018.
https://doi.org/10.1007/978-3-030-02456-7_16

This paper will begin by situating the problem-solving approach associated with TRIZ as a major phenomenon in the history of scientific methods (§ 2). Then, it will focus on highlighting the main elements constituting the basis of the mental progression of the methodology whose guiding thread is made of postulates of technical systems evolution leading to the principle of analogy used by TRIZ (§ 3). Paragraph 4 tries to link the TRIZ principles with stake holders strategy. The purpose of paragraph 5 is to illustrate the above considerations with case studies regarding an industrial group and start-up environment. The conclusion summarizes the lessons learned, limitations and perspectives of the paper.

2   TRIZ Historical Background

TRIZ, invented by Altshuller [2], is the Russian acronym for an expression ("Teoriya Res-heniya Izobreatatelskikh Zadatch") meaning "Theory of the resolution of inventive problems". It is a set of methods and tools, originally associated with the techniques of the years 1950–1960, whose objective is to help solve technical problems by systematizing the identification of models of solutions and of intellectual processes for inventive problem solving.

TRIZ tools are used particularly in the car industry and in aeronautics, but applications to other sectors are common [3]. They allow both to solve problems of inventiveness, to prepare patent filings but also to initiate the implementation of R & D strategies [4].

TRIZ is to innovation what Lean and SixSigma are to continuous improvement and, just as Toyota is the global reference Lean, Samsung has quickly become the world TRIZ reference. Its exceptional growth in innovation and in economic and commercial performance has allowed the South Korean conglomerate to become in a few years a leader in many fields (electronics, household appliances,...), largely through the systematic implementation of TRIZ since 2007 in all the layers of its organization, as main method of innovation of company, which allowed him to realize a strong growth of its turnover.

Other large groups are now massively using TRIZ to increase the efficiency of their innovation initiatives (Siemens, General Electric, etc.). The TRIZ process is wordly recognized as pragmatic and effective for the development of innovation in business and, like Lean and SixSigma, requires a rigorous and repetitive corporate approach to be effective.

The European TRIZ Association (ETRIA) set up a survey to measure the state of diffusion of TRIZ in the world. The results show that companies applying TRIZ observed a gain in the quantity but also in quality of new ideas. The study also shows that the inventive concepts originating from TRIZ are often subject to patenting. Likewise, most of the companies that have experimented with TRIZ want to set up their internal deployment [5].

3   TRIZ Basics

3.1   "Why" Rather Than "How"

The production of inventive ideas is the starting point of innovation, so much necessary in the current economic context. The performance requirement obligation imposes the implementation of a fruitful and rational process for the emergence of breakthrough ideas, able to better fix current and future problems.

In order to systematize the process of searching for concepts, patentable invention and value creation, it is necessary to understand WHY (there is a problem) rather than immediately looking for HOW (finding the solution). The How is a "reflex" question, whereas the Why is a "reflective" question [6].

TRIZ infers that the problems encountered during the design of a new business model, product or service present analogies with others and that similar solutions could be applied [2]. The result of the systematic analysis of patents allowed Altshuller to highlight three postulates, on which will be based the principle of analogy:

- The solutions are similar in most of industrial and scientific domains
- Models of technical evolution are repeated in most of industrial and scientific domains
- Innovations can use scientific effects coming from other technical fields

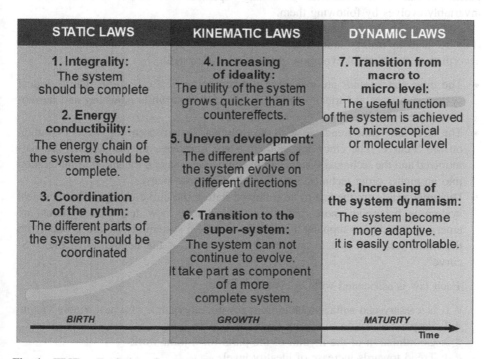

Fig. 1. TRIZ – Evolution characterized by S curve (grey curve in foreground) and general evolution laws [table in background] (Source: [9])

Thanks to these outcomes, Altshuller formalized his inventive problem solving approach by reformulating the problem to better solve it [7, 8], without any direct resolution of the initial problem, but through the transformation into a generic problem by abstraction.

3.2 Evolution Characterized by S Curve

According to Altshuller's postulates, the most of technical systems in our environment seem to evolve as shown by the curve in Fig. 1, where horizontal axis represents time and axis represents a vertical factor related to the performance of the technical system.

Figure 1 can decomposed into three main parts [10]:

- The first part represents the beginning of the technical system life, young and very perfectible and with fast improvements.
- The second part, almost linear, corresponds to the optimization of the technical system, which tends to lead to a synthesis, by successive simplifications.
- The third part corresponds to the end of the evolution of the technical system, arrived at maturity and stabilized at an optimum.

3.3 General Evolution Laws

The real discovery that emerges from these observations by the systematic analysis of patents is that these tendencies are highly repeated, that is, the technical system invariably evolves by following them.

Evolution trends characterizing the S curve are usually presented in three groups (Fig. 1, table in background). Each group has a very specific role and is applied according to the stage of evolution of the technical system:

- The three static trends are located at the beginning of the S curve. The technical system stammers and tries to fulfill its main function while adjusting and harmonizing the operation of its various components.
- The three kinematic trends go with the technical system according to its evolution on the S-curve. The efficiency of the system improves, the subsystems are harmonized and the technical system can in some cases make a transition to integration into an higher order technical system (called super-system).
- Dynamic trends are the last to be followed before the curve change. The technical system is becoming more and more controllable: new technical systems are emerging, tending to supplant the existing technical system. These are at odds with the initial technical system and are, for their part, at the beginning of their "S-curve".

Each law is associated with an evolution trend:

1: Necessary and sufficient conditions for the emergence of a new viable system
2: Proper circulation of energy flows
3: Coordination of the rhythm of the parts for a joint work
4: Trend towards increase of ideality level
5: No weak link in the different parts

6: Trend towards integration into a higher order system
7: Transition of each means from the macroscopic level to the microscopic level
8: Adaptation to external constraints.

3.4 Exploitation of Evolutionary Trends to Put the Principle of Analogy into Action

Evolutionary trends are a great tool for benchmarking products, functions, technical systems, based on the evaluation of the maturity of the technical system through evolution trends [11].

First, their use makes it possible to estimate the positioning of the technical system analyzed through criteria specific to each of the eight general trends, based on the notion of observation point, on a deeper analysis than a mere intuition. Thus, the analysis of the system according to the first general trend [# 1: Definition of the necessary and sufficient conditions for the appearance of a new viable system] makes it possible to check that nothing is missing to achieve the main function, then that the sixth general trend [# 6: Trend towards integration into a higher order system] makes it possible to ask in which super-system can the system migrate and under which conditions.

The technical system studied can therefore be examined by general trends, based on some references, among which:

- The previous technical system that we wish to change;
- Competitive products performing a similar function;
- The "ideal" system in view of the general trend examined;
- Technical systems from other technical fields, better satisfying certain general trends, potentially transposable;
- Nature (bio-mimicry)

Finally, once the various evaluation criteria have been established, it is interesting to be able to group these results graphically, while keeping in mind the system maturity:

- Synthesize the results obtained on a single schema;
- Follow the evolutions during the design;
- Predetermine product schemas;
- Manage the system evolution, over several generations, if needed.

4 TRIZ Seen as a Technique of Creativity

4.1 How Can TRIZ Be Defined?

TRIZ has been defined in many different ways [12]:

- A theory, which is established on objective trends of technology evolution; TRIZ describes the process of new technology creation by mankind [13]. ARIZ [acronym for the Russian phrase "Algorithm for Inventive Problem Solving"] had features of universality; it was also starting to be used by researchers for problem solving in science and arts [14]. Because of its uses in arts, sciences, nature, etc., many ideas and tools of TRIZ could be used to develop theories for non-technological problem solving [15].

- A science and an art [16]
- A science, which studies evolution of technological systems, and develops methodology for synthesis, development and prognosis of such systems [17]
- A set of concepts. These concepts do not create the whole unity, in contrast to many applied methodologies and theories. The knowledges and concepts, which are included in TRIZ, may be considered as art [18].

According to [19], TRIZ is above all the empirical approach of a technique of creativity applied to problem solving, based on a methodological formalization and instrumented by a set of tools. Fifty years after the initial work of Altshuller, the TRIZ approach has been theorized as part of the overall problem-solving procedure aimed at translating the logic of the transitions between contradictions [20], inspired from solutions from other technical fields. However, this principle of analogy is not itself theorized in the method [19].

4.2 Exploiting the Principle of Analogy

Associated with TRIZ, a methodology able to solve technical problems blocking the functional evolution of a technical object consists of a heuristic approach aimed at solving technical problems and based on the postulates of technical systems evolution, postulates resulting from the compilation of a large number of patents. TRIZ is therefore a systematic method of creative problem solving, intense in knowledge and exploiting the principle of analogy [3, 20, 21]. This principle suggests exploring generic solutions, borrowed from other domains, not yet applied to the particular problem. The importance of TRIZ in the sense of problem solving techniques comes from its nature of meta-methodology deployable in many fields of knowledge: indeed, TRIZ gathers reasoning orientations able to structure a mental process of problem solving [19]. TRIZ method is instrumented by ARIZ, which constitutes its operational instantiation in its proper methodological sense [19]. ARIZ stands for the acronym of the Russian expression "Algorithm for Inventive Problem Solving" [17, 22].

4.3 TRIZ Approach and Stakeholders Strategy

We have seen that the TRIZ approach came from the systematic analysis of patents of invention to tend towards a method to learn how to invent and that the strategy of problem solving must gradually reduce the area of research instead of increasing the number of variants according to a convergent approach which makes it possible to reformulate the problem to better solve it. It is necessary, in fact, to understand why (there is a problem) rather than immediately how (find the solution). Thus, by abstraction and in the form of contradictions, a problem is obtained which is independent of the technical field of the initial problem, which makes it possible to appeal for its resolution to scientific effects outside the initial technical field.

To build on the proven methods and practices of large groups, the authors wish to recall the following recommendations from their own experience:

- Start by "killing the myth" of the genius doing business by looking for the brilliant and inspired idea, but use a robust procedure of creativity to be ready to "jump on the next wave".
- Then put in place the right business environment, translate the strategic vision of the project leader into timing, adapt a different point of view by modeling the ideal, connect innovations with the strategy while being consistent with the customer experience and accelerate the "serial innovation" capability using the system's value chain model. By explaining to the young leader the notions of ideality and contradiction, allow him to keep in mind throughout his innovation process that the value chain of the start-up is closer to the "ideal final result" despite the necessities of everyday life. According to the experience of the authors, this pragmatic and effective support is done with the project leader or the management team in half a day, as soon as the start-up is ready to question and to revisit its model. [23]
- Finally, a regular reporting (face-to-face or remote) allowing considering and program the next steps in order to be medium-term efficient and to attract potential investors.

5 Case Studies

The object of the present paragraph is to illustrate the above considerations with case studies, extracted from an industrial group and start-up environment.

As seen in the first case study, by deconstructing a job into universal customer-centric steps from beginning to end, a big company gains a complete view of all the points at which an employee might desire more help from a product or service—namely, at each step in his/her job; with a job map in hand [24], the company can analyze the biggest drawbacks of the products and services customers currently use, and TRIZ can quickly help solve them.

In the context of advanced innovation design approach, the second case study shows that a small new start-up can compete with big companies it deals with, while combining several existing known business principles [25] (as TRIZ does for problem solving) like open business model (N° 32) and integrator (N° 23) to leverage customer data (N° 25). As detailed, the key issue for the start-up was to efficiently manage the IP.

With such methodological and business toolkits implementing inventive principles, knowing the past helps in creating the future. The proposed step-by-step process was detailed earlier [27] and got resonance with the start-ups using it.

5.1 Use of the Start-Up Spirit Within an Industrial Group

One company wanted the TRIZ France association to organize a two-hour workshop with a management and engineering school to innovate with students and employees of the company, on the theme of the computerization of tasks for operators with no-paper transmission of production orders and procedural instructions. To one of the mixed working groups (students, employees) led by an expert from the TRIZ France association, the expert asked to concentrate the group's reflection, not on the solution imagined by the client, but on the question expressed as: what is the best way to integrate software on PC or tablet provided to the operator?

With the first tool, "Day work Mapping", the participants described their vision of the operator's life in a typical day, after defining, with the help of the operator representative, the profile of the operator as observed in his daily work. Then, the group identified the most important questions: getting the right workbook for the right procedure, reading, understanding, memorizing and applying the instructions of the procedure, performing the self-check of the job, saving the job as done, and then go back to the first step for the next action.

Despite the explicit request of the large company to start immediately working on its own suggestions for solutions, this type of start-up approach has helped to "get out of the box" and redefine "in a bottom up" way the tasks of the operator to improve his work. Having not only automated some of his tasks with a tablet or a PC, the approach mostly reviewed the organization of his work by reordering tasks or eliminating unnecessary gestures to give back meaning to his daily work.

The challenge was then to understand the real problem to be solved and to identify the contradictions. With the second tool, "TRIZ Visualization", the group moved on to improving the lives of the operators by now actually searching for the "paperless" solution desired to support the manufacturing process. It turned out that the real problem to be solved was to get a heavy workbook with more than 200 pages, to bring it to your workstation and to flip through it for a long time before finding the right chapter and instructions to read.

Using some TRIZ methods (mainly the "Operation time" and the "Operation zone"), the question has been broken down into contradictions: the workbook must be heavy and light! As a matter of fact it should contain detailed information but easily accessible down to the right level and should not require too much effort yet without any detrimental simplification. Then the study of resources shown that the pictures and diagrams were the most effective support for instructions and that the screen of the standard PC was the most adapted media. The lesson learned from the second workshop is that visualization is a very powerful tool to help participants understand the underlying characteristics of an object or concept, in order to build their own mental representation of this object in real life.

With the conflict resolution guide to support the mental process, the team, heterogeneous, not previously trained in the TRIZ method, but guided "without his knowledge" by the expert (as "natural TRIZ thinkers" [26]), was able to effectively focus on solving the proposed problem. Formal implicit guidance helped the group not to diverge from the real problem to be solved and facilitated its concentration on its resolution. In addition, it helped demonstrate why the problem existed and how it was solved by allowing the reverse reading of the mental process.

As initially requested by the company, the problem was easily reformulated, better understood by the employees, and a solution was found with not trained participants in less than 2 h.

5.2   Start-Up and Need for Protection by Intellectual Property

For several years, the authors have been wondering about what TRIZ could do for young companies (validation of first ideas, improvement of concepts, strengthening of protection) and presented, in an international conference, the state of their experiments within a French incubator to train some start-ups in the TRIZ spirit [27].

TRIZ could bring this value differentiating them from incubators and their incubated start-ups, to help them understand what they do (systemic representation), give them a medium-term vision (trends of evolution) and thus guide them on the important aspects (resolution of contradictions) in terms of market, product or service innovation: this pragmatic way of pooling learning would give them a useful competitive advantage.

Guided by one of the co-authors for a year, the start-up adopted a strategy between the need for openness and the need for protection. This guidance went from the first successes to start-up competitions to funding difficulties (lack of seed funding), to industrial partnerships and to the INPI pre-diagnosis [28]; INPI is the French IP Office.

The purpose of the project is to develop and distribute an open-hardware connected object for the smart management of lighting and public infrastructure. It is a question of adapting the lighting to situations of use (road or city) in order to characterize a situation of danger or a zone of shade (preprogrammed or controlled light effects) to facilitate and secure the circulation of the vehicles and pedestrians (night path, light warning, tracking light or "white wave").

What are the Intellectual Property issues of this start-up emblematic of these entrepreneurs of the new economy, which combines elements existing on the market (industrial or public lighting managers, …) with an agile development mode and participatory (local and strategic partnerships) while keeping the "core of the system" secret [29]?

In its pre-diagnosis, the INPI has identified several IP needs/constraints for the start-up: relationships already established with major players, subcontractors or strategic partners, implementation of a demonstrator for public lighting of a municipality, "network intelligence" (heart of innovation and intellectual property), "big data" analysis and formatting of dashboards. The INPI has validated and recommended a combination of its intellectual capital protection tools: search (regular competitive searches via esp@cenet from the European IP Office), dating (regularly done for two years via a dedicated Facebook page), secrecy and confidentiality (particular contract via business lawyer), contractual practices (occasionally via a business lawyer), filing of trademarks (authorization in progress) and filing of patents (evaluation of the connected robot).

The inventive design approach can therefore help the start-up to establish a medium-term vision to subtly pace its innovations on the market according to the maturity of its offer, that of its competitors and the desire of its customers to buy their products or services.

Facing the "openness versus protection" dilemma, the start-up benefited from a free resource (INPI pre-diagnosis) which listed the usual "SME versus large group" constraints in terms of intellectual protection, and which transposed by analogy the most meaningful recommendations for the start-up in less than half a day.

6 Conclusion

The present paper has studied an approach able to solve technical problems blocking the functional evolution of a technical object. This TRIZ methodology was located as a phenomenon of technical thought born in the middle of the 20th century, still relevant two generations later, devoted to the methodological approach of technical invention as a method of creativity in the framework of inventive resolution of technical problems. The basis of the method consists of postulates of the evolution of technical systems, which is based on the principle of analogy used by TRIZ. It is put into action through the identification and analysis of evolution trends to give them a predictive sense in terms of the course of time considered as an element of functional and technical maturation. Case studies, in an industrial group or start-up environment, have illustrated the formal considerations previously developed, in particular for an in-depth analysis of the operational start-up of a start-up.

It was thus given to the reader the power of a formal logic of problem solving inscribed in the prism of evolution, participating in an approach looking for, on the one hand, by abstraction, a specific genericity able to generate other decontextualized applications by the principle of analogy and, on the other hand, an optimal implementation. These two fundamentals fully characterize the field of knowledge, and it is not surprising that the empirical construction of such a methodology, largely based on the founding principles of theories of knowledge as well as the usual considerations of general methods for problem solving, inspired later theorization. The success of the very broad deployment in the industry is therefore due, among other things, to the simplicity of the few logical reasoning, which hide from the user the formal depth of theories later formulated that justify them.

With the concrete cases solved within a few hours of the big company trying to think with the "start-up spirit" and of the open hardware start-up struggling to exist in the complex world around it, the reader will have noted that the formalism of problem solving can extend to many of the young entrepreneur's decision making and therefore this formalism of mental exploration is itself a state of mind, rigorous and oriented toward the search for progress, applicable by the same principle of analogy as that which is at the heart of the TRIZ method.

Engineers and practitioners, the co-authors are much more focused on the core of the methodology and its concrete applications than on the very theorization that this methodology inspired. They do not address the limitations brought to light by this theorization that they leave to researchers specialized in the subject.

Moreover, the format of the paper did not exhaust the subject of the potential contribution of the TRIZ method to start-up entrepreneurs, which of course means that the prospects it opens up concern of this field of potential for young start-ups.

References

1. Ries, E.: The Lean Startup. Pearson (2012)
2. Altshuller, G.: Creativity as An Exact Science: The Theory of the Solution of Inventive Problems. Gordon & Breach, New York (1988)

3. Leung, W.L., Yu, K.M.: Development of online game-based learning for TRIZ. In: Hui, K.-c., et al. (eds.) Edutainment 2007. LNCS, vol. 4469, pp. 925–935. Springer, Heidelberg (2007). https://doi.org/10.1007/978-3-540-73011-8_89
4. Dubois, S., Rasovska, I., De Guio, R.: Comparison of non solvable problem solving principles issued from CSP and TRIZ. In: Cascini, G. (ed.) CAI 2008. TIFIP, vol. 277, pp. 83–94. Springer, Boston, MA (2008). https://doi.org/10.1007/978-0-387-09697-1_7
5. Cavalucci, D.: Une théorie de l'invention en support des activités R & D: Outil et mise en œuvre par l'exemple. Techniques de l'Ingénieur (2012)
6. Guillou, Y.: Le comment et le pourquoi (2012). Consulté le 22 11 2016. http://triz-experience.blogspot.fr/2012/06/le-comment-et-le-pourquoi.html
7. Riwan, A.: TRIZ helps blind people to find their ways in subway stations. In: TRIZ Future Conference 2013, Paris, France (2013)
8. Riwan, A.: Enhanced experience and safety in interactive robots. In: Global TRIZ Conference 2014, Seoul, Korea (2014)
9. Seradinski, A., Jadaud, D.: TRIZ: les notions de base. Revue Technol. **172**, 2011 (2011)
10. Guillou, Y.: La courbe en S (2011). Consulté le 22 11 2016. http://triz-experience.blogspot.fr/2011/04/la-courbe-en-s.html
11. Guillou, Y.: L'évaluation au travers des lois d'évolution (2014). Consulté le 22 11 2016. http://triz-experience.blogspot.fr/2014/08/levaluation-au-travers-des-lois.htm
12. Zakharov, A.: Explore the future of TRIZ with the trends of evolution. TRIZ J. (2008). https://triz-journal.com/explore-the-future-of-triz-with-the-trends-of-evolution
13. Lenyashin, V., Kynin, A.: What is TRIZ? http://www.metodolog.ru/01008/01008.html
14. Altshuller, G.: History of ARIZ Development (1986). http://www.altshuller.ru/world/eng/
15. Altshuller, G.: Summary TRIZ 1988 (1988). http://www.altshuller.ru/world/eng/
16. Mitrofanov, V.: My TRIZ Understanding. http://www.metodolog.ru/01291/01291.html
17. Devoyno, I., Skuratovich, A.: In Short, What Is TRIZ? http://www.metodolog.ru/01296/01296.html
18. Minaker, V.: http://www.metodolog.ru/01296/01296.html
19. Saulais, P.: Application de la gestion des connaissances à la créativité des experts et à la planification de la R&T en milieu industriel de haute technologie. Thèse de doctorat, Telecom Ecole de Management (2013)
20. Louafa, T., Perret, F.-L.: Créativité et Innovation: L'intelligence collective au service du management de projet. Presses Polytechniques et Universitaires Romandes, Lausanne (2008)
21. Sue, N.: The Principles of Design. Oxford University Press, New York (1990)
22. Fey, V., Rivin, E.: The Science of Innovation: A Managerial Overview of the TRIZ Methodology. Southield, Michigan (1997)
23. Lepot, X., Neveux, A., Guillou, Y., Baudrux, S.: 2A2CI, an effective innovation methodology that makes TRIZ people & business compatible. In: Global TRIZ Conference 2014, Seoul, Korea (2014)
24. Bettencourt, L., Ulwick, A.: The customer-centered innovation map. Harv. Bus. Rev. **86**(5), 109–114 (2008)
25. Gassmann, O., Frankenberger, K. Csik, M.: The Business Model Navigator: 55 Models That Will Revolutionise Your Business (2014). ISBN 978 1 292 06581 6
26. Mann, D.: Case study: of David's and Goliath's. TRIZ J. (2008). https://triz-journal.com/case-study-of-davids-and-goliaths
27. Prevost, E., Bruno, G., Guillou, Y., Sire, P., Conrardy, C.: What roles can TRIZ play in start-up incubators? In: Global TRIZ Conference 2014, Seoul, Korea (2014)
28. Sire, P.: «Objets connectés pour systèmes d'éclairage intelligent - gestion proactive de la lumière». Forum Intelligence économique et stratégique IES 2016, Rouen (2016)
29. INPI: La Propriété Intellectuelle et la transformation numérique de l'économie (2016). Consulté le 22 11 2016. HTTPS://WWW.INPI.FR/FR/SERVICES-ET-PRESTATIONS/ETUDE-PI-ET-ECONOMIE-NUMERIQUE

Facilitating Engineers Abilities to Solve Inventive Problems Using CBR and Semantic Similarity

Pei Zhang[1,3](✉), Denis Cavallucci[3], Zhonghang Bai[4],
and Cecilia Zanni-Merk[2]

[1] CSIP @ ICube (UMR-CNRS 7357), 67084 Strasbourg Cedex, France
pei.zhang@insa-strasbourg.fr
[2] LITIS, Norm@Stic (FR CNRS 3638),
INSA Rouen Normandie, 76800 Rouen, France
[3] INSA de Strasbourg, 67084 Strasbourg Cedex, France
[4] Hebei University of Technology, Tianjin 300131, China

Abstract. Our industry currently undergoes a period of important changes. The era of computerization implies to companies to change not only through their organization, but also in automating as much as possible their internal processes. Our research focuses on the computerization of the problem-solution couple when facing inventive situations in R&D. The method used is based on Case-Based Reasoning (CBR) that has already been proven to be useful in routine design. On the other hand, CBR is hardly used in inventive situations because the latter require reasoning outside the circle of knowledge recorded in a database. Our proposal consists in coupling CBR with semantic similarity algorithms. The aim is to resolve a new problem based on its semantic similarity with the old problems. Then the old solution can be adapted to solve the new problem. We postulate that a multidisciplinary case base sufficiently populated of multidisciplinary problem-solution couples is likely to considerably improve the performance of R&D engineers to solve inventive problems. This being possible by bringing them alternative solutions based on the semantically similar problems, which are distant from their field of origin. In this way, we provide the possibility to enhance the inventiveness of solution. This type of reasoning, largely inspired by the TRIZ theory, is the subject of this paper. The methodology, the experiments and the conclusions that we develop here validate that this type of approach produces the claimed effects on designers although limited to the context where it has been conducted.

Keywords: TRIZ · Case-based reasoning (CBR) · Semantic similarity

1 Introduction

Our industry is moving through a period of important changes. The era of computerization pushes companies to change not only through their organization, but also through their internal physical functioning. Among the research performed around the notion of industry 4.0, a large part is dedicated to the computerization of workshops,

© IFIP International Federation for Information Processing 2018
Published by Springer Nature Switzerland AG 2018. All Rights Reserved
D. Cavallucci et al. (Eds.): TFC 2018, IFIP AICT 541, pp. 204–212, 2018.
https://doi.org/10.1007/978-3-030-02456-7_17

machines, controls and computer flow that optimizes and responds to customer demand by its physical functioning. However, there is a sector of the company, which is only little researched in industry 4.0, its R&D department. As the most important stage that leads to an inventive product, a methodology adopted by R&D departments is the theory of inventive problem solving (TRIZ) [1].

TRIZ offers various components for solving different types of inventive problems, such as the 40 Inventive Principles, the 76 Inventive Standards. According to the researches respectively carried by [2–4], the Contradiction Matrix with its 40 Inventive Principles and the Su-Field analysis with its 76 Inventive Standards are among the most popular tools used by the TRIZ community.

However, the "intellectual" cost for an enterprise to use a tool such as TRIZ, which is based on the users' experience, is exceptionally high. In addition, in the era of Industry 4.0, where the world is engaged in sharing data and automating the manufacturing technologies, R&D departments seem to be behind schedule in the way they automate problem solving.

Therefore, a legitimate axis of research is to find ways to facilitate the inventive problem solving process. Researches can be mainly categorized into two groups. One group addresses the problem solving model, and finding ways to ease the use of the models, while another group addresses on the knowledge sources used by TRIZ and attempts to facilitate the use of TRIZ by knowledge modelling.

The first group of researchers regard problem solving as an analogical process with the objective of finding inventive solutions to their problems [5]. This process is composed of two essential activities, with the help of TRIZ tools. One is the analogy reasoning between the problem and the problem model, the other is the analogy reasoning between the problem model and the solution model. To cope with the former problem, the work of [6] provided a way to systematically map design parameters with the Generic Engineering Parameters in axiomatic design. Moreover, to ease the use of the Contradiction Matrix, the authors in [7] matching considered the aspects regarding to the human factors issues of the Generic Engineering Parameters. To cope with the latter problem, ASIT [8] grouped 32 Inventive Principles into 5 thinking tools; the analysis conducted in [9] classified the Inventive Principles into clustered principles assuming the fact that there might be losses as compared to the use of TRIZ in a classical way.

The other direction of research addresses the aspect of taking advantage of the knowledge sources of TRIZ and knowledge modeling. The work of [10] proposed the TRIZ Technical System class ontology with its four sub-ontologies provided a framework that will enable the storage of knowledge found by other problem solving applications. The work of [11] connect the TRIZ knowledge sources with different abstract levels and designed rules to facilitate the problem solving process using ontology and its related rules.

Compared with the researches above, we propose an approach to collect and represent the problem-solution pairs from the problem solving know-how of experts (their professional life experience). In addition, we adopt Case-based reasoning to reuse available solution at hand in order to support the problem solving process. This paper is organized as follows: Sect. 2 discusses the importance of experience, Sect. 3 details the proposed approach, Sect. 4 validates the proposed approach by a case study and finally Sect. 5 gives the conclusion and the future perspectives.

2 Is Experience Important?

With the aim of finding out how experience influences the problem solving, we did an experiment about how it can influence the time used for problem solving. We asked 28 students of the same grade in an engineering department of our university, and separate them into two groups with respectively 14 students: the experimental group and the control group.

For the experimental group, we designed a set of online forms with 10 simple cases and assigned them to 14 students. Each form contains the problem description and multiple-choice questions to guide students to find a solution model for each given problem. Once a student solves a problem and submits an online form, his/her problem solving time is recorded. For the control group, we ask the students to use the rule-based problem solving prototype [12] to solve the same 10 problems. The time used by each student for finding the solution model is automatically recorded by the prototype. The data we gathered concerning the time spent for problem solving is presented in Fig. 1. The x-axis represents the average time used by the two groups using the assigned approach and the y-axis represents the ID of the problems.

As it can be observed in Fig. 1, the average time used by the experimental group (the green bars) is decreasing as the students are solving more problems while the control group (the blue bars) remains stable. This result indicates that experience is a crucial factor influencing the time used of inventive problem solving, the more problems the students solve; the faster they tend to be. Furthermore, the students of the control group who uses the rule based approach; the time they use for solving the first problem until the last problem stays stable. This is because when using the rule-based approach, the problem solving is facilitated by if-then rules and the needed knowledge for each step, which makes the problem finding process easier. Therefore, the students in the control group use less time than the students in the experimental group for solving problem No. 1. However, the problem with the rule-based approach is that every time the student solves a new problem, they have to go through the problem solving process from the beginning. In addition, this is why the problem solving time used by the control group stays balanced.

We can conclude that the collection and reuse of experience have the potential to improve problem solving, at least in terms of time. In addition, it is worth mentioning that in this experiment, we only ask the students to find the solution model in order to make the time used for problem solving comparable. In fact, the rule-based approach is not able to provide the knowledge about the solution in its knowledge base. Therefore, the user with no experience would have trouble to interpret the solution model into a solution. Consequently, our research is focusing on finding a proper way to collect and reuse experience in the previous problem solving with the aim of providing users with the knowledge needed for solution finding.

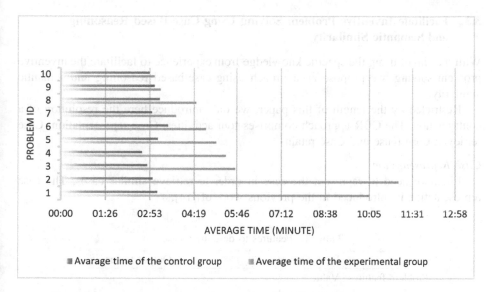

Fig. 1. Average time respectively used by the two groups (Color figure online)

3 Facilitating Inventive Problem Solving Using Case-Based Reasoning and Semantic Similarity

3.1 Case-Based Reasoning

Case-based reasoning (CBR) is a methodology that has been widely adopted for problem solving and learning. It can benefit from the specific knowledge of the previous experience rather than making associations between general problems and its general solutions. In this way, when a problem needs to be solved, it is able to retrieve similar cases in the past and solves the new problem by reusing it in the new problem [13]. Applying case-based reasoning consists in retrieving a similar past case, reusing the past case and retaining the new case.

3.2 Semantic Similarity

If we want to find a similar past problem to a new inventive problem, the problem is that they are expressed in terms of natural language. Depending on the way the problem is described, the words used can vary but the meanings are similar. For example, something that is big and small is similar to something that is large and tiny. This type of problems are semantically similar but do not share a single word. In order to solve this problem, we need some external knowledge that enables us to find the semantically similar problems.

3.3 Facilitate Inventive Problem Solving Using Case-Based Reasoning and Semantic Similarity

With the aim of using the specific knowledge from experience to facilitate the inventive problem solving, we propose an approach using case-based reasoning and semantic similarity.

Restricted by the length of this paper, we only introduce here the resolution of a contradiction. The CBR approach comprises four activities: Case representation; Case retrieval; Case reuse and Case retain.

Case Representation

First, we need to represent the case in order to retrieve similar cases. The case representation is introduced in the previous work of [14].

Table 1. Features to describe a case.

	Input features	Output features
Problem features	Value	
	Negative value	
	Action parameter	
	Evaluation parameter to improve Evaluation parameter to degrade	
Solution features		Inventive Principle Concept solution

Case Retrieval

In order to retrieve similar cases, we need to find semantically similar cases. Therefore, we adopted WordNet[1] as the knowledge base for calculating the semantic similarity between the new problem and the old problem. We apply the semantic similarity algorithm based on the short-text similarity proposed in [11].

To calculate the similarity consists in two steps: calculating the similarity between the new problem and the old problems and then calculating the weighted similarity between the new problem and the old problems. The former is composed of five sub-steps, which are:

1. Pre-processing: It includes a sequence of actions. Firstly, split the shot text into single words (for example "smoothing the surface" becomes "smoothing", "the" "surface"). Next, remove the stems of the words (for example, the words obtained in the previous step becomes "smooth", "the" and "surface"). Finally, eliminate stop words (words like the, of, or etc., are eliminated). The output of this step is a set of terms.
2. Sense search: For each term, we look for its corresponding senses using WordNet (e.g. the word "smooth" has eight different senses).

---

[1] https://wordnet.princeton.edu/

3. Sense similarity: We adopt Lin's method [15] to calculate the semantic similarity between two terms. Using this method, the higher rate of sharing information, the more the two terms are similar.
4. Term similarity: The maximum value of the sense similarity value between two terms is the term similarity.
5. Semantic similarity: Based on the obtained term similarity, we can calculate the semantic similarity. Let's assume that a new problem, P_1, includes a sequence of words $P_{11}, P_{12} \ldots P_{1n}$ and an old case P_2, includes a sequence of terms $P_{21}, P_{22} \ldots P_{2m}$. $s(P_{1i}, P_{2j})$ represents word similarity between P_{1i} and P_{2j}, $1 \leq i \leq n$, $1 \leq j \leq m$. We can build the matrix of similarity $M (P_1, P_2)$:

$$\begin{bmatrix} s(P_{11}, P_{21})s(P_{11}, P_{22}) & \cdots & s(P_{11}, P_{2m}) \\ \vdots & \ddots & \vdots \\ s(P_{1n}, P_{21})s(P_{1n}, P_{22}) & \cdots & s(P_{1n}, P_{2m}) \end{bmatrix}$$

In general, we select the most similar terms in P_2 for each term in P_1 and then we calculate the average value as defined in Eq. 1:

$$\frac{\sum_{i=1}^{n} \max_{1 \leq j \leq m} \left(s\left(P_{1i}, P_{2j} \right) \right)}{n} \tag{1}$$

Then, we apply the tf*idf method [16, 17] to assign weight to the obtained similarity. Applying the tf*idf method, we can obtain the word weight ww_{1i}, that is the ith word in P_1 and the word weight ww_{2i}, that is the ith word in P_2. In addition, to calculate the weighted similarity, we should apply the word weight to all possible situations. One is the most similar word in P_2 for P_1. The other is the most similar words in P_1 for P_2.

In both situations, $s(P_{1i}, P_{2j})$ represents the word similarity between new problem P_{1i} and the old problem $P_{2j} (1 \leq i \leq n, 1 \leq j \leq m)$.

$$S_{weighted}(P_1, P_2) = \frac{\sum_{i=1}^{n} ww_{1i} \max_{1 \leq j \leq m} \left(s\left(P_{1i}, P_{2j} \right) \right)}{n} + \frac{\sum_{i=1}^{m} ww_{2i} \max_{1 \leq j \leq m} \left(s\left(P_{2i}, P_{1j} \right) \right)}{m} \tag{2}$$

Case Reuse and Retention

When the similar cases are retrieved, the next step is to reuse the retrieved cases. If the user finds an identical case and reuse its solution without adaptation, the solved case will not be retained. However, if the user selects a similar case and reuse its solution with certain adaptations, the new case will be retained in the case base.

4 Case Study

Clothes hangers are used in our daily life to hang clothes vertically. Their design should make them versatile enough to fit for hanging clothes with different sizes. Therefore, length of the arm should be long enough to support the cloth, but short enough to ease their entering into the clothes without efforts. The traditional design of the cloth hanger is often in the shape of a triangle that has this type of fixed structure design has disadvantages. In this section, we apply the proposed approach to solve this problem.

First, we describe the problem in terms of a conflicting situation as the follows: *The length of the clothes hanger has to be both short to satisfy the ease of hanging and long to satisfy the clothes stability.* Then, we apply the semantic similarity calculating to find the similar problems in meaning. The retrieving results are illustrated in Table 1. We present in Table 1 the first 10 old cases similar to the new one. The similarity values are given in the first column in Table 1.

We can observe that the retrieved similar cases are similar in meaning rather than using the same words for describing the problem. For example, *large* is similar to *big*; *freedom of movement* is similar to *ease of hanging* and *length* is similar to *distance, and so on.* Among the similar cases we retrieved, suppose we want to reuse the solution of case 102, which is *making the arrangement of the shopping cart s-shaped*. Inspired by the solution, we can design the solution for the hanger problem as it can be seen from Fig. 2. The design of the s-shaped hanger, inspired by the S-shape of shopping carts case, is an interesting way of solving our new problem of cloth hanger. On the one

Table 2. Retrieval results

Case	Similarity	Action parameter	EP to degrade	EP to improve	Value	Negative value
Case10	0.816	Volume	Ease of handling	Hitting efficiency	Large	Small
Case2	0.752	Size	Vision	Protection from rain	Big	Small
Case7	0.752	Size	Freedom of movement	Comfort for cyclist	Wide	Narrow
Case9	0.739	Length	Precision	Efficiency	Long	Short
Case102	0.728	Distance	Clearance of driveway	Ease of storage	Long	Short
Case30	0.578	Connection	Cost	Need of gas cooker	Existing	Missing
Case21	0.528	Electrostatic	Painting adhesiveness	Less droplet rebound	Existing	Missing
Case1	0.509	Volume	Protection	Weight	Big	Small
Case8	0.508	Volume	Less plastic consumption	Storage volume	Big	Small

Fig. 2. The shopping cart problem

hand, if the cloth has a tight neck, we can first stick the hanger vertically by the long edge, and then rotate it to the horizontal position so that the short edge can be used to hang the cloth easily without damaging it. On the other hand, the long edge supports the cloth sufficiently so that it will not produce wrinkles (Fig. 3).

In this way, the application of the proposed approach facilitate problem solving by simply adapt the solution of the similar case that is retrieved (Table 2).

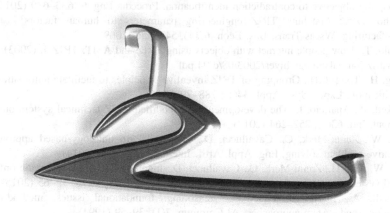

Fig. 3. The designed solution of the clothes hanger problem

5 Conclusion and Future Perspectives

In this paper, we explored an approach to combine case-based reasoning and semantic similarity to facilitate inventive problem solving. Compared with the rule-based approach [18], the proposed approach provides the users with the specific knowledge from past successful cases. In this way, the user can solve the new problem by only adapting the old solution of the old problem. Therefore, the proposed approach can ease the problem solving process by reusing experience. Moreover, since the case base stores cases from different domains, the proposed approach can benefit from finding similar cases from different domains and reuse its solution.

As it has been discussed in Sect. 2, a large case base has the potential to increase the efficiency of the problem solving process. However, we are limited to a small case base and the future work will be dedicated to enlarge the case base with more cases.

References

1. Altshuller, G.S., Shulyak, L., Rodman, S.: The Innovation Algorithm: TRIZ, Systematic Innovation and Technical Creativity. Technical Innovation Center, Inc., Worcester (1999)
2. Cavallucci, D.: World Wide status of TRIZ perceptions and uses a survey of results. Report of TRIZ Future (2009)

3. Ilevbare, I.M., Probert, D., Phaal, R.: A review of TRIZ, and its benefits and challenges in practice. Technovation **33**(2), 30–37 (2013)
4. Spreafico, C., Russo, D.: TRIZ industrial case studies: a critical survey. Procedia CIRP **39**, 51–56 (2016)
5. Slocum, M.S.: Analogies are the way of breakthrough innovation. Triz J. (2005). https://triz-journal.com/innovation-theories-strategies/innovation-general/analogies-way-breakthrough-innovation/
6. Duflou, J.R., Dewulf, W.: On the complementarity of TRIZ and axiomatic design: from decoupling objective to contradiction identification. Procedia Eng. **9**, 633–639 (2011)
7. Coelho, D.A.: Matching TRIZ engineering parameters to human factors issues in manufacturing. Wseas Trans. Bus. Econ. **6**(11), 547–556 (2009)
8. Toshio, T.: How people interact with objects using TRIZ and ASIT. TRIZ J. (2003). http://www.triz-journal.com/archives/2003/08/d/04.pdf
9. Cong, H., Tong, L.H.: Grouping of TRIZ inventive principles to facilitate automatic patent classification. Expert Syst. Appl. **34**(1), 788–795 (2008)
10. Prickett, P., Aparicio, I.: The development of a modified TRIZ technical system ontology. Comput. Ind. **63**(3), 252–264 (2012)
11. Yan, W., Zanni-Merk, C., Cavallucci, D., Collet, P.: An ontology-based approach for inventive problem solving. Eng. Appl. Artif. Intell. **27**, 175–190 (2014)
12. Yan, W., Liu, H., Zanni-Merk, C., Cavallucci, D.: IngeniousTRIZ: an automatic ontology-based system for solving inventive problems. Knowl.-Based Syst. **75**, 52–65 (2015)
13. Aamodt, A., Plaza, E.: Case-based reasoning: foundational issues, methodological variations, and system approaches. AI Commun. **7**(1), 39–59 (1994)
14. Zhang, P., Essaid, A., Zanni-Merk, C., Cavallucci, D.: Case-based reasoning for knowledge capitalization in inventive design using latent semantic analysis. Procedia Comput. Sci. **112**, 323–332 (2017)
15. Lin, D.: Extracting collocations from text corpora. In: First Workshop on Computational Terminology, pp. 57–63 (1998)
16. Salton, G., Lesk, M.E.: Computer evaluation of indexing and text processing. J. ACM JACM **15**(1), 8–36 (1968)
17. Sparck Jones, K.: A statistical interpretation of term specificity and its application in retrieval. J. Doc. **28**(1), 11–21 (1972)
18. Yan, W., Zanni-Merk, C., Rousselot, F., Cavallucci, D.: A method for facilitating inventive design based on semantic similarity and case-based reasoning. Procedia Eng. **131**, 194–203 (2015)

Automatic Extraction of IDM-Related Information in Scientific Articles and Online Science News Websites

Oriane Nédey[✉], Achille Souili, and Denis Cavallucci

Laboratoire CSIP: Conception, Système d'Information et Processus Inventifs,
24 Boulevard de La Victoire, 67000 Strasbourg, France
oriane.nedey@insa-strasbourg.fr

Abstract. Previous studies have made it possible to extract information related to IDM (Inventive Design Method) out of patents. IDM is an ontology-defined method derived from TRIZ. As its mother theory, IDM is primarily based on patent's observation and aims at finding inventive solutions on the basis of contradictions. In this paper, we present a new approach for extracting knowledge, this time out of other types of science-related documents: scientific papers and science news articles. This approach is based on sets of linguistics features which have been selected and evaluated semi-automatically with techniques of Natural Language Processing as well as Machine Learning.

Keywords: TRIZ · IDM · Inventive Design · Machine learning
Knowledge extraction · Text mining · NLP

1 Introduction

The World Intellectual Property Organization claims that more than 3 million patents were published worldwide in 2016, that is 8.3% more than in 2015 [1]. Next to this massive source of technical knowledge, scientific articles also carry weight in expert scientific content with at least 2.5 million new scientific papers published each year since 2013 [2]. While patents are legal sources which provide technical information about the innovations they aim to protect, scientific articles provide theoretical as well as technical answers which help the scientific community understanding and gaining control of their environment through diverse applications. With such a huge number of publications and given that they are not always easily accessible, science news websites have developed on the Internet and share some important researches and innovative breakthroughs in a condensed and accessible form, making it possible for the scientific community to stay update and learn about advances in other science-related fields.

With innovation going very fast, engineers are facing a challenge to find creative ideas that may lead to innovation. To help them in their innovation process, researches have been made since the 1990s, developing and adapting Altshuller's theory of inventive problem solving (TRIZ) [3]. Yet, though patents seem the best way for engineers to find solutions [4], it doesn't mean that other science-related documents cannot also lead to innovation. In order to determine the significance of this kind of

D. Cavallucci et al. (Eds.): TFC 2018, IFIP AICT 541, pp. 213–224, 2018.
https://doi.org/10.1007/978-3-030-02456-7_18

documents on innovation, we need to find out whether these documents include enough content useful for TRIZ theory application. During the last few years, our team has been developing a tool for automated extraction of knowledge related to the Inventive Design Method (IDM) from English-language patents [5].

Following these researches, we want to adapt the information extraction from patents to the case of scientific papers and science news articles, i.e. automating the extraction of topics, problems, partial solutions, evaluation and action parameters, as well as values, inside these two alternative types of science-related documents.

This is a challenging project in that both scientific research articles and science news articles are unstructured data, with much more liberty regarding their structure and writing style. Therefore, we need to evaluate the structural, syntactic as well as semantic features implemented in the patent-knowledge extraction tool [5], and then to find new features that are specific to the new document types. This implies the use of machine learning and other methods for Natural Language Processing.

In this article, we will give you an overview of the literature on the Inventive Design Method (IDM) and its tool for patent-knowledge extraction, followed by the literature on scientific research papers and science news articles (Sect. 2), and then we will present our methodology along with the current advances on the project and an emphasis on our evaluation method (Sect. 3).

2 State of the Art

2.1 The Inventive Design Method

The Inventive Design Method (IDM) is an application method derived from TRIZ, the theory of inventive problem solving. It describes four steps for innovation [6]: during the first phase, the users must extract knowledge and organize it into a graph of problems and partial solutions. With this graph, they must then formulate a set of contradictions, which will be solved individually in phase 3, and finally, they must choose the most innovative Solution Concept before they can invest in it and set it up.

For the contradiction formulation, the Inventive Design Method offers a formal and practical definition of the broad TRIZ contradiction notion, which is very useful for industrial innovation and introduces other notions linked to IDM-ontology [7]. This contradiction "is characterized by a set of three parameters [...] where one of the parameters can take two possible opposite values Va and $\overline{Va}$" (Fig. 1). The first parameter is called *action parameter* (AP) and is defined with its characteristic to be able to "tend towards two opposite values" and to "have an impact on one or more other parameters". Moreover, "the designers have the possibility of modifying them". The two other parameters in a contradiction are called *evaluation parameters* (EP) and are defined with their capacity to "evolve under the influence of one or more action parameters", thus making it possible to "evaluate the positive aspect of a choice made by the designer".

$$AP \ \frac{Va}{\overline{Va}} \ \begin{matrix} EP_1 & EP_2 \\ \begin{pmatrix} -1 & 1 \\ 1 & -1 \end{pmatrix} \end{matrix}$$

Fig. 1. Possible representation model of contradictions [7]

Knowledge of how the contradiction must be formulated helps for the knowledge extraction part as well as the graph creation, because the elements that must be extracted from the documentation are in priority: problems, partial solutions, evaluation and action parameters as well as their possible values Va and $\overline{Va}$. As of problems and partial solutions, research on IDM contains clear definitions, both in their form (syntax and graphical representation) and in their content [8]. A problem (Fig. 2) "describes a situation where an obstacle prevents a progress, an advance or the achievement of what has to be done". A partial solution (Fig. 3) "expresses a result that is known in the domain and verified by experience." Cavallucci et al. give more precision about the concept of partial solution [8]:

> "It may materialize a tacit or explicit knowledge of one or more members of the design team upon their past experience, a patent filled by the company or a competitor or any partial solution known in the field of competence of the members of the design team. We wish also to remind that a partial solution is supposed to bring the least possible uncertainty about the assertions of its effects on the associated problem. Confusion can appear between a "solution concept" (which is the result of an assumption made by a member) and a "partial solution", which has been validated by experience, tests, calculations or results known and verified."

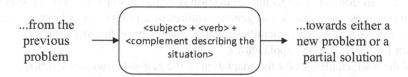

Fig. 2. Graphical representation of a problem

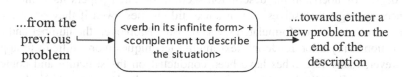

Fig. 3. Graphical representation of a partial solution

2.2   Patent-Knowledge Extraction

An important principle both for TRIZ and for IDM is that inventive solutions are generally found with analogy, and therefore thanks to solutions or tools which belong to another domain. Patents are documents with very rich technical content, which is generally not to be found elsewhere, like for instance in scientific papers [4]. In order to save engineers a lot of time and to help them getting to these analogies, a tool has been developed by Souili et al., which automatically creates a graph of problems, partial solutions and parameters out of English-language patents selected by a user in a large database [5] (Fig. 4). This corresponds to the first phase of the Inventive Design Method, which has been automated thanks to Natural Language Processing techniques.

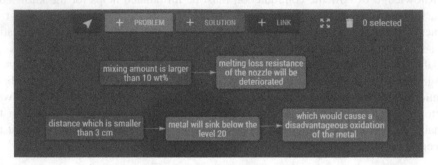

Fig. 4. An example of a problem-solution graph

2.3   Scientific Research Papers and Science News Articles

Scientific Research Papers. Many studies have been conducted on the automated information extraction from scientific research papers. While some of them are strongly related to their domain or a specific application (like biology) [9–13], other present, for general purposes, the extraction of general features of articles such as keywords or key phrases [13–16]. However, scientific research papers have not yet been the topic of research for TRIZ or IDM applications.

One of the main challenges for the adaptation of the patent-knowledge extraction tool is to understand and characterize the differences between the different types of documents: patents, scientific research papers and science news articles.

While all patents have a very similar structure with four sections and despite the higher degree of liberty in the description section, research papers have much more differences amongst themselves. For instance, title names, even if they often indicate the same concepts, are not formulated the same way. Moreover, the number and topics of the sections vary a lot, rendering text-mining techniques more difficult to apply.

However, many researches have been conducted on the structure and content of research papers. Pontille, based on a previous research by Bazerman [17], describes a generic structure format named IMRAD (Introduction, Materials and methods, Results And Discussion) [18] as a stabile tool for professional practice harmonization; "a particular form of proof expression"[1] and "a standardized argumentative matrix"[2]

---

[1] Our translation. The original sentence is: «Le format IMRAD constitue ainsi une forme particulière d'expression de la preuve» (p. 2)

[2] Our translation. The original phrase is: «une matrice argumentative standardisée» (p. 6)

which has become an official norm with the *Standard for the preparation of scientific papers for written or oral presentation* in 1979 in the USA.

According to Pontille, authors generally define a problem and propose hypotheses in the introduction. Therefore, it will be interesting for our research to study how the main problem is introduced in this section, in order ameliorate its extraction.

From the section about "Materials and methods", which explains "the way the study has been conducted"[3] and has become central for the argumentation in the last decades [18], we won't focus on intermediate problems and solutions for our research, since they are often criticized during the article. However, Pontille mentions the occasional presence of a subsection for the description of "variables", which we can link to the IDM-ontology concept of parameter. Therefore, it could be interesting to extract the main parameters and to find a way to know, with the help of their limited context, whether they are evaluation or action parameters, i.e. whether they have an impact on the final output and can be modified, or whether they are central to the evaluation of the output.

The discussion section, as described by Pontille, is also interesting for our extraction tool. By "identifying the practical and theoretical implications of their analysis"[4] and "opening perspectives for futures researches"[5] [18], we could find a repeated version of the main problem, hopefully the main partial solution of the article, and potential unresolved new problems. Moreover, since this section is the interpretation of the results evaluation, it will be interesting to look particularly for evaluation parameters here.

Considering the content, Gosden study on rhetorical themes and more specifically on contextualizing frames throughout research articles [19], with an analysis of their functions and even some links to problems and solutions, is very interesting for the extraction of features which will help us in our information extraction task.

The abstract is also a key part of a research article. According to a study conducted on articles in the field of linguistics and educational technology, three moves seem to be unavoidable in research articles: "Presenting the research", "Describing the methodology" and "Summarizing the findings" [20]. These moves are very close to actual sections of the IMRAD structure, and since it is a summary of the research, the presence of the major problem, partial solution and parameters seems very probable.

Science News Articles. Science news articles are not a famous research topic, but media coverage of science is [21–27]. An increasing amount of science-related content is published regularly on the internet, in very diverse forms: online versions of traditional print newspapers and magazines, science section of online newspapers, science blog articles from professional researchers, videos, specialized science news websites, etc. While traditional online sources are declining in terms of audience rates, nontraditional online sources such as blogs and "other online-only media sources for information about specific scientific issues" now get much more attraction for the public

---

[3] Our translation. The original phrase is: «explicitation de la manière dont l'étude a été conduite» (p. 6)

[4] Our translation. The original quote is: «ils identifient les implications pratiques et théoriques de leur analyse» (p. 7)

[5] Our translation. The original quote is: «ouvrir des perspectives de futures recherches» (p. 7)

[21]. Science news websites therefore seem to be interesting sources for condensed information, with regularly new publications in multiple research fields.

This kind of source is nevertheless contested in the literature because of the trustworthiness of its contents [22]. Since the targeted audience is interested in scientific innovation and breakthrough, but does not have a large scientific background, information is often summarized and the risk is that is diverts from the intention of the original author. In order to prevent engineers from using erroneous extracted data during the IDM process, we will have to compare the results of the extraction from the science news article on the one hand, and from the full original document on the other hand.

3   Methodology

The information extraction tool we aim to create is mainly an adaptation of the existing tool used with patents. This adaptation requires a certain number of steps, from building a corpus to the evaluation of the final program. As mentioned above, the major challenge for this project is to adapt the features needed to select the candidate sentences for problem or partial solution classification.

3.1   The Corpus Creation

Annotated Corpus. The first step for adapting the extraction tool is to build an annotated corpus that will be used for classification, in order to extract the main linguistic features (words or phrases) for each category – problems, partial solutions, evaluation parameters, action parameters, values.

Since research articles and science news articles have a very different structure, they should not be treated the same way, but preferably with two separated corpora. Moreover, there are multiple sources publishing articles in diverse fields, with differences in the global structure as well as the length and style of the articles. Therefore, each corpus must contain articles form different sources.

We chose to give the annotation task to 44 students enrolled in a course on Inventive Design. With this condition, we decided to build both corpora so that they correspond to the level and number of students who will annotate them.

For the annotation task, all articles have been cleaned and transformed into PDF when necessary for reading comfort and homogeneity of the annotation procedure, at least for the science news articles that were in HTML format in the beginning

The corpus of science news articles contains 44 articles from the 7 following sources:

- Machine Design [28] – 6 articles, about 1–2 pages long
- New Atlas [29] – 7 articles, about 1 full page long
- Phys.org [30] – 7 articles, about 1–2 pages long
- Research & Development [31] – 6 articles, about 1 page long
- Science Daily [32] – 6 articles, about 1 full page long
- Science News [33] – 6 articles, about 1–2 pages long
- Science News for Students [34] – 6 articles, about 2 pages long

The corpus of scientific research articles contains 44 articles from the 4 following sources:

- Accounts of chemical research [35] – 15 articles, about 8–10 pages long
- Annual Review of Condensed Matter Physics [36] – 8 articles, between 21–28 pages long
- Chemistry of Materials [37] – 11 articles, between 6–12 pages long
- Proceedings of the National Academy of Sciences of the USA (PNAS) [38] – 10 articles, about 6 pages long

The annotation procedure is done on the PDF-formatted files with the highlighting tool of Adobe Acrobat, following a given color legend for each element: problem, solution, evaluation parameter, action parameter, value. After collecting all annotations, evaluating and modifying them when necessary, we use Sumnotes, a web application [39], to extract a list for all sequences corresponding to each element.

Clean Corpus for the Extraction. For the extraction of the different elements related to IDM, we cleaned and transformed the articles into JSON format. Since most of the articles were available in HTML format, both for science news articles and scientific research papers, we used the BeautifulSoup library for Python 3 [40], which is a very efficient library for cleaning data from HTML and XML documents.

However, we are still looking for a way to efficiently clean PDF articles from PNAS, because the GROBID service [41] we used for transforming them into TEI-XML documents mixed up all the sections, therefore making our information extraction task impossible. In the meantime, we had to drop this source for the features extraction, implementation and evaluation steps.

3.2   The Extraction and Selection of Features

The adaptation of the linguistic features needed for the sentences, keywords or phrases selection and classification tasks involves three steps, and its goal is to create lists and dictionaries of words, phrases or n-grams that make the extraction efficient and specific to both scientific research articles and science news articles.

The three steps are:

- Patent features assessment
- Specific features extraction
- Features selection

Evaluation Method. The whole features adaptation process involves multiple evaluations which have to be undertaken with the same parameters. The main purpose for the extraction program is to get sufficient results for a further use in the inventive design process following IDM-TRIZ. All the evaluations have to be undertaken with the basis of a single Gold Standard for each element category (e.g. parameters or problems), built from the annotated corpora. The program has a two-step classification process for problems and partial solutions. The first step extracts candidate sentences and the second step confirms or rejects the first choice. The rejected sentences are then classified as "neutral". For a complete evaluation, we will also consider those sentences and add them to the "concepts" category (thus containing all extracted problems, solutions and neutrals). The evaluation criteria are:

- The number of concepts, parameters, partial solutions, neutrals and problems extracted in average per article
- The precision for each category, which is the ratio between the number of relevant elements found automatically in the category and the total number of elements automatically retrieved in the category.
- The recall for each category, which is the ratio between the number of relevant elements retrieved automatically in the category and those found manually in the Gold Standard for this category.
- The rate of misclassification, i.e. the proportion of sentences that should have been classified in another category but is considered useful. We consider as "useful" neutrals, sentences that are really interesting for the research or its future developments, but does not belong to the category of problems or partial solutions.

Patent Features Assessment. The first step is the assessment of the linguistic features from the original program that is made for patents. With a first minimal adaptation of the original program, keeping all the features intact, we assess the features globally, and then individually. The global assessment will be made by evaluating the whole program following the procedure described above. This assessment will serve as a comparison point for the individual assessments that follow, for which the program will run on a loop and evaluate its results, each time ignoring a different feature. This makes it possible to remove the features which don't have any positive impact on the final result. The removing task, however, considering the relatively small number of articles in our corpus, should be done manually in order to maintain the possibility of keeping some features for which we estimate a potential impact with a bigger corpus.

Specific Features Extraction. The second step is the extraction of new features. This task will involve several tools for Natural Language Processing (NLP):

- The feature selection tool included in the Weka software [42]
- Wordclouds created with the programming language Python
- Graphs of ranked token frequencies for a specific concept
- A graph created with the Bokeh library in Python which show the relative polarity of the most frequent tokens for partial solutions and problems
- A manual selection of feature candidates observed during the creation of the Gold Standard.

Features Selection. third task consists in selecting the final linguistic features from the remaining patent features and the previously extracted candidate features, then in implementing them into the main classification program, and again in making an assessment of these features with the same methodology as for the patent features assessment. Depending on the results, it could be necessary to make slight changes, and run a new evaluation again, in order to get the best performances as possible.

4 Results and Outlook

The annotation task taking more time than expected, we chose to focus on a corpus of 23 science news articles, from which we built a Gold Standard for each kind of elements related to IDM (Table 1).

Table 1. Gold Standard characteristics

Concept	Number of extracted concepts
Partial solutions	90
Problems	82
Action parameters	29
Evaluation parameters	134
Values	38

This Gold Standard was the basis of our evaluation during the project. The reference performances of the program (Table 2), established with the original features used for patents, show a precision of about 40% for topics and parameters. These results are not very satisfying, but they are far less concerning compared to the results for problems and partial solutions, where only 30 elements have been extracted, from which only one wrongly classified as a partial solution.

Table 2. Reference performances

	Problems	Partial solutions	Topics	Parameters
Extracted elements	29	1	115	128
Average per article	1.26	0.04	5	5.57
Useless elements	21	1	67	76
Correctly categorized elements	6	0	48	52
Precision	20.69%	0%	41.74%	40.62%
Recall	7.23%	0%	–	31.52%
Misclassified elements	2	0	–	–
Misclassification rate	6.90%	0%	–	–

With such initial results, we concentrated our efforts on improving the performances for the extraction of problems and partial solutions, especially the linguistic features assessment, extraction and selection tasks as presented in the methodology section.

The assessment task allowed us to remove the following linguistic features: "common", "high", "manufacturing", "complex", "espial", "field", "step", "might", "claim 1", "claim 2", "claim 3", "^-", "c higher than those for e-glass". Removing those linguistic features, combined to a few minor changes in the program, already improved the performances for problems, partial solutions and parameters.

The extraction and selection task allowed us to add 10 new linguistic features to the program. The following new linguistic features are useful for the extraction of partial solutions: "by", "discovered", "modeling", "resulting", "using", "through". The following linguistic features are useful for the extraction of problems: "because", "expensive", "how", "often".

The changes made in the program and in the linguistic features lists during this project have led to a significant increase of the performance indicators (Table 3).

Table 3. Performances after the changes in the program and features lists

	Problems	Partial solutions	Topics	Parameters
Extracted elements	64	25	115	121
Average per article	2.78	1.09	5.00	5.26
Useless elements	39	15	67	67
Correctly categorized elements	21	9	48	54
Precision	32.81%	36.00%	41.74%	44.63%
Recall	25.61%	10.00%	–	33.13%
Misclassified elements	4	1	–	–
Misclassification rate	6.25%	4.00%	–	–

5 Outlook and Summary

As a conclusion, this article relates about the project at CSIP to extend its automatic extraction techniques to research and science news articles in the field of the Inventive Design Method. Due to unexpected obstacles during the annotation phase of the project, we focused mainly on science news articles, for which we could evaluate and adjust the linguistic features, starting from another extraction program developed by our team and based on patents.

In spite of the increase of the program performance indicators, the results still need to be improved in order for engineers to be able to use the tool for their projects. A major point for its improvement is to create bigger corpora of annotated articles, which ally both quality and quantity.

Moreover, our program is able to extract information from research articles, but the number of extractions is too high (often nearly 70 extracted elements for one article). Therefore it seems even more important to separate completely the extraction processes for science news articles from research articles, and to find new sets of linguistic features as well as a system to interact differently depending on the article section for research papers.

A last angle to work on in order to improve the precision and recall is to cut the article contents more finely than only between sentences, making sure that a problem and a partial solution cannot be in the same meaning unit.

References

1. World Intellectual Property Organization: World Intellectual Property Indicators. WIPO, Geneva (2017)
2. Publish or perish? The rise of the fractional author…, Research Trends. https://www.researchtrends.com/issue-38-september-2014/publish-or-perish-the-rise-of-the-fractional-author/
3. Altshuller, G.: And Suddenly the Inventor Appeared: TRIZ, the Theory of Inventive Problem Solving. Technical Innovation Center, Inc., Worcester (1996)
4. Bonino, D., Ciaramella, A., Corno, F.: Review of the state-of-the-art in patent information and forthcoming evolutions in intelligent patent informatics. World Pat. Inf. **32**, 30–38 (2010). https://doi.org/10.1016/j.wpi.2009.05.008
5. Cavallucci, D.: The theory of inventive problem solving: current research and trends in French academic institutions. Springer, Heidelberg (2017). https://doi.org/10.1007/978-3-319-56593-4
6. Cavallucci, D., Strasbourg, I.: From TRIZ to Inventive Design Method (IDM): towards a formalization of Inventive Practices in R&D Departments, no. 2 (2012)
7. Rousselot, F., Zanni-Merk, C., Cavallucci, D.: Towards a formal definition of contradiction in inventive design. Comput. Ind. **63**, 231–242 (2012). https://doi.org/10.1016/j.compind.2012.01.001
8. Cavallucci, D., Rousselot, F., Zanni, C.: Initial situation analysis through problem graph. CIRP J. Manuf. Sci. Technol. **2**, 310–317 (2010). https://doi.org/10.1016/j.cirpj.2010.07.004
9. Andrade, M.A., Valencia, A.: Automatic extraction of keywords from scientific text: application to the knowledge domain of protein families. Bioinformatics **14**, 600–607 (1998). https://doi.org/10.1093/bioinformatics/14.7.600
10. Krallinger, M., Valencia, A., Hirschman, L.: Linking genes to literature: text mining, information extraction, and retrieval applications for biology. Genome Biol. **9**, S8 (2008). https://doi.org/10.1186/gb-2008-9-s2-s8
11. Müller, H.-M., Kenny, E.E., Sternberg, P.W.: Textpresso: an ontology-based information retrieval and extraction system for biological literature. PLoS Biol. **2**, e309 (2004). https://doi.org/10.1371/journal.pbio.0020309
12. Yakushiji, A., Tateisi, Y., Miyao, Y., Tsujii, J.: Event extraction from biomedical papers using a full parser. In: Biocomputing 2001, pp. 408 419. World Scientific (2000)
13. Gelbukh, A. (ed.): CICLing 2005. LNCS, vol. 3406. Springer, Heidelberg (2005). https://doi.org/10.1007/b105772
14. Lopez, P., Romary, L.: HUMB: automatic key term extraction from scientific articles in GROBID, p. 4 (2010)
15. Krapivin, M., Autaeu, A., Marchese, M.: Large dataset for keyphrases extraction. University of Trento (2009)
16. Kim, S.N., Medelyan, O., Kan, M.-Y., Baldwin, T.: SemEval-2010 task 5: automatic keyphrase extraction from scientific articles. 6 (2010)
17. Bazerman, C.: Shaping Written Knowledge: the Genre and Activity of the Experimental Article in Science. University of Wisconsin Press, Madison (1988)
18. Pontille, D.: Matérialité des écrits scientifiques et travail de frontières: le cas du format IMRAD. 16 (2007)
19. Gosden, H.: Discourse functions of marked theme in scientific research articles. Engl. Specif. Purp. **11**, 207–224 (1992). https://doi.org/10.1016/S0889-4906(05)80010-9

20. Pho, P.D.: Research article abstracts in applied linguistics and educational technology: a study of linguistic realizations of rhetorical structure and authorial stance. Discourse Stud. **10**, 231–250 (2008). https://doi.org/10.1177/1461445607087010

21. Brossard, D.: New media landscapes and the science information consumer. Proc. Natl. Acad. Sci. **110**, 14096–14101 (2013). https://doi.org/10.1073/pnas.1212744110

22. Brumfiel, G.: Supplanting the old media, (2009)

23. Puschmann, C.: (Micro)blogging science? notes on potentials and constraints of new forms of scholarly communication. In: Bartling, S., Friesike, S. (eds.) Opening Science, pp. 89–106. Springer, Cham (2014). https://doi.org/10.1007/978-3-319-00026-8_6

24. Allgaier, J., Dunwoody, S., Brossard, D., Lo, Y.-Y., Peters, H.P.: Journalism and social media as means of observing the contexts of science. Bioscience **63**, 284–287 (2013). https://doi.org/10.1525/bio.2013.63.4.8

25. Minol, K., Spelsberg, G., Schulte, E., Morris, N.: Portals, blogs and co.: the role of the Internet as a medium of science communication. Biotechnol. J. **2**, 1129–1140 (2007). https://doi.org/10.1002/biot.200700163

26. Mahrt, M., Puschmann, C.: Science blogging: an exploratory study of motives, styles, and audience reactions. J. Sci. Commun. **13**(3), A05 (2014). https://doi.org/10.22323/2.13030205

27. Brossard, D., Scheufele, D.A.: Science, new media, and the public. Science **339**, 40–41 (2013). https://doi.org/10.1126/science.1232329

28. Machine Design. http://www.machinedesign.com/

29. New Atlas. https://newatlas.com/

30. Phys.org: News and Articles on Science and Technology. https://phys.org/

31. Research & Development. https://www.rdmag.com/

32. ScienceDaily: Your source for the latest research news. https://www.sciencedaily.com

33. Science News. https://www.sciencenews.org/

34. Science News for Students: News and feature articles from all fields of science. https://www.sciencenewsforstudents.org/home

35. Accounts of Chemical Research. ACS Publications. https://pubs.acs.org/journal/achre4

36. Annual Review of Condensed Matter Physics. https://www.annualreviews.org/journal/conmatphys

37. Chemistry of Materials. ACS Publications. https://pubs.acs.org/journal/cmatex

38. PNAS. http://www.pnas.org/

39. FiftForce: Sumnotes - summarize PDF annotations. https://www.sumnotes.net/

40. Beautiful Soup Documentation—Beautiful Soup 4.4.0 documentation. https://www.crummy.com/software/BeautifulSoup/bs4/doc/

41. Lopez, P.: GROBID: a machine learning software for extracting information from scholarly documents (2018)

42. Frank, E., Hall, M.A., Witten, I.H., Pal, C.J.: The WEKA workbench. In: Online Appendix for Data Mining: Practical Machine Learning Tools and Techniques. Morgan Kaufmann (2016)

Text Simplification of Patent Documents

Jeongwoo Kang[✉], Achille Souili, and Denis Cavallucci

CSIP/INSA Strasbourg, 24 Boulevard de la Victoire,
67084 Strasbourg Cedex, France
{jeongwoo.kang,achille.souili,
denis.cavallucci}@insa-strasbourg.fr

Abstract. This paper represents an automatic text simplification system for patent documents. The simplification system is embedded in the broader context of an information retrieval system which extracts IDM related knowledge from patent documents. Extracting elements of IDM ontology from patents involves training machine-learning model. However, an accuracy of the model is compromised when the given text is too long, hence the need of simplifying the texts to improve machine learning. There have been precedent studies on automatic text simplification based on hand-written rules or statistical approach. However, few researches addressed simplifying patent documents. Patent document has its particularity in its lengthy sentences and multiword expression terminology, which often hinder accurate parsing. Therefore, in this research, we present our method to automatically simplify texts of patent documents and scientific papers by analyzing their syntactic and lexical patterns.

Keywords: Inventive Design Method · TRIZ · Information extraction
Text simplification · Syntactic analysis · Text mining

1 Introduction

This paper represents an automatic text simplification system for patent documents. The simplification system is embedded in the broader context of an information retrieval system which extracts IDM (Inventive Design Method) related knowledge from patent documents. Patent documents are important source of information which contains a history of the evolution of the artifacts [1]. By looking into patents, one can learn progress of technologies over the course of history, and more importantly, technological challenges and their solutions that were invented by specialists and engineers in the field. In the light of the importance of patents as information resource, there have been a number of academic researches and activities in patent mining in recent years.

The research of Souili [1], which inspired our work of research, applied text mining approach for information retrieval from patents. He analyzed patent documents and automated extraction of IDM related knowledge from patents. The Inventive Design Method presents a framework for inventive problem solving process. The IDM was created by Cavallucci and Khomenko [2] and it was inspired by the Theory of Solving Inventive Problem (TRIZ), a theory invented by Altshuller [3]. Therefore, it is worth looking into TRIZ before we discuss the IDM in further detail.

© IFIP International Federation for Information Processing 2018
Published by Springer Nature Switzerland AG 2018. All Rights Reserved
D. Cavallucci et al. (Eds.): TFC 2018, IFIP AICT 541, pp. 225–237, 2018.
https://doi.org/10.1007/978-3-030-02456-7_19

TRIZ is "a problem-solving, analysis and forecasting tool derived from the study of patterns of invention in the global patent literature" [4]. In the research of Altshuller [3], he suggested a systematic methodology to find inventive solutions to technological problems. According to Altshuller [3], there are generalizable patterns in the nature of inventive solutions and problems. These patterns can be applied across industries and sciences, therefore, by defining principles of technological challenges and inventive solutions, one can reuse this strategy to solve a similar problem in different context. Altshuller [3] also argued that a number of technical problems which necessitate inventive solutions stem from technical contradiction. Accordingly, defining these contradictory situations and the way to solve the contradiction are dealt as a key factor in TRIZ methodology.

IDM was created to complement the limits of TRIZ. Classical TRIZ methods are not easy to comprehend due to a lack of formalized ontology, nor simple to make a computation design model upon its concepts [5]. Therefore, IDM presented its formalized ontology to formulate relevant ideas and concepts for inventive design. IDM ontology mainly consists of three concepts: problem, partial solution, and parameter. Parameters consist of two sub-categories, which are evaluation parameters and action parameters. Problems often refer to a contradictory situation where two features conflict with one another, and therefore, ameliorating one feature deteriorates the other. Solution is a way to solve this contradiction without compromising any of the features. On the other hand, a partial solution is an incomplete solution and while it provides a solution to one problem, it may bring about another problem. Action parameter is what a designer can make a design choice on, and evaluation parameter represents a value with which one can evaluate the result of the choice of a designer [6].

PatExtractor is an information extraction system for patents, into which the simplification system presented in this paper is integrated. PatExtractor automatically retrieves IDM knowledge from patents with its machine learning algorithm. However, the accuracy of the system is compromised when the system analyses lengthy sentences, which are fairly common in patent documents. Overlong sentences in patents make it difficult for the machine learning algorithm to classify the texts accurately and extract relevant information from them. This is because the algorithm analyzes a sentence based on the words composing the sentence, and the algorithm can be distracted when there are too many words to analyze. It is even more so when the words in a sentence contain conflicting information. Moreover, a syntactically-complex sentence, which consists of more than one predicate, often has more than one piece of information to extract. For example, a sentence composed of a few predicates that are joined by concessive or contrastive conjunctions such as *yet*, *but*, *although*, *though* or an adverb *however* sometimes includes a problem and a partial solution at the same time in different predicates. Therefore, it is necessary to split this sentence into smaller pieces so that the classifier identifies each part of information and label them properly.

To handle the above-mentioned sentences and to improve accuracy of the classifier by doing so, this research contributes to making an automatic sentence simplification system. This simplification system detects complex sentences and simplify those sentences by splitting, dropping and modifying. This research addresses simplification on two levels: coarse simplification and fine simplification. The coarse simplification system is designed to improve the performance of the machine learning algorithm as mentioned above. The fine simplification system is, on the other hand, designed to improve the readability of the extracted data. PatExtractor not only extracts IDM knowledge from patents but also visualizes the results using an ontology-based graphic. As its name suggests, the fine simplification system simplifies given texts in more elaborate way after the coarse simplification. Further details on the two simplification systems will be discussed in methodology section. In the next section, we review precedent researches on automatic text simplification.

2 Literature Review

There have been a number of precedent researches on text simplification. Text simplification is a task that "aims to rewrite a sentence so as to reduce its complexity, while preserving its meaning and grammaticality" [7]. Complexity of sentences stem from either syntactic complexity or semantic complexity [8]. As its name suggests, syntactic complexity is derived from a syntactic structure of a sentence. Syntactically complex sentences consist of more than one predicate. These predicates are joined by conjunctions such as *but, and, for, until* or relative pronouns such as *who, which, that, whose* or relative adverbs such as *when* and *where*. Therefore, this syntactic complexity can be resolved by splitting a complex sentence into shorter phrases and then restructuring each phrase to complete it. Sentence 1 is an example of a syntactically complex sentence and Sentence 3 shows how its complexity is reduced by splitting. Semantic complexity, on the other hand, is derived from difficult vocabulary. Thus, this complexity can be reduced by paraphrasing, more particularly, replacing difficult words to understand with easier and more understandable ones. Sentence 4 is an example of semantically complex sentence and Sentence 5 shows how its complexity can be diminished by paraphrasing.

Sentence 1: I have a friend *whose* cat is annoying.
Sentence 2: I have a friend. Whose cat is annoying.
Sentence 3: I have a friend. *His* cat is annoying.
Sentence 4: The workers *acquiesced* to their boss' request.
Sentence 5: The workers *accepted* their boss' request.

Text simplification is mainly used in two contexts. First, it is used to help people with low-literacy or reading disability such as foreigners, kids or people suffering from dyslexia [8, 9]. In other context, it serves as a preprocessing tool for natural language processing (NLP) tasks [10]. Simplified texts are easier to parse or translate, thus text simplifications are often integrated into automatic text summarization [11] or machine translation system [12] as a preprocessing tool. Moreover, the desired results could vary depending on the context in which the simplification is used. For example, when text simplification is used as a supporting tool to aid people with low-literacy, both syntactic and semantic complexity should be reduced so that the texts are more readable and understandable for target readers. However, when text simplification is used to facilitate natural language processing, simple syntactic simplification could be enough to fulfil the objectives, depending on the context of its application.

There have been different approaches to achieve text simplification. At the early stage, most of researches were based on hand-crafted rules [10, 13, 14]. In most rule-based approaches, they use POS tagger or syntax parser to detect complex sentences, and then split these complex sentences into smaller pieces using predesigned rules [8, 12]. This step is often followed by phrase-reordering or restructuring. As shown above in Sentence 1 to 3, a syntactically complex sentence (Sentence 1) is firstly identified as a sentence to simplify by syntactic parsing, and then split into two or more phrases (Sentence 2) and finally, restructured (Sentence 3). To restructure the phrases, co-reference relations and grammar are taken into consideration and dependency parser is often used to achieve this. Dependency parser represents the words of a given sentence in its dependency relation with other words, so it enables to capture co-reference relations in a sentence, such as a relation between a relative noun (*whose* in Sentence 1) and its antecedent (*friend* in Sentence 1). However, this rule-based approach requires linguistic knowledge to craft the rules, and it is difficult to cover all the complex sentences of different structures with these rules.

To complement the limits of rule-based approaches, academic society shifted their focus to data driven approaches [7]. Some of these approaches use statistical machine translation system to achieve simplification [15, 16] and they are known to produce accurate results. This approach considers text simplification as a monolingual translation task. More particularly, they consider complex sentences as source texts and simplified sentences as target texts. These approaches use parallel corpus, which consists of original texts aligned with their simplified texts, to train their simplification model [17, 18]. This type of data is easily accessible on Simple English Wikipedia[1]. By aligning texts of Wikipedia and Simple English Wikipedia, one can obtain a parallel corpus needed to train their statistical text simplification model [15, 16]. To train this statistical simplification system, texts, syntactic parse trees or semantic parse trees [16] are often used as input data. This data driven method yields good results for lexical substitution and deletion, but is less effective for sentence splitting and sentence reordering [19, 20]. Moreover, parallel corpora to train this model are available for few languages.

Patents simplification has been studied in a few researches as a sub-category of general text simplification. Patent documents are known for its notoriously poor readability, and it is especially more so in the claims part. Poor legibility of patents stem from their abstract vocabulary, overlong sentences [17] and terminology. In patents, it is not uncommon to see a sentence with 200 words and there are even sentences with more than 500 words [1]. To make those documents more readable and comprehensible for readers, there have been a few, yet not many, researches on patent simplification [17, 18, 21]. In most researches on patents simplification, rule-based approaches are preferred to statistical approaches. This is not only because there are few parallel corpus on patent documents, but also because texts in patents have specific linguistic features such as long distance anaphoric references and repetitiveness [17]. Accordingly, hand-crafted rules which take these linguistic features of patents into consideration are often used for patent simplification tasks.

---

[1] It is an edition of Wikipedia geared towards students, children or adults with learning difficulties. It is therefore written in basic and easy English.

3 Our Methodology

3.1 PatExtractor and IDM Ontology

Our simplification system is integrated into an information extraction system, PatExtractor. PatExtractor takes patent documents (unstructured data) as input data, and extracts concepts of IDM ontology from the documents with NLP approach. As output, it creates a graphic (structured data), on which each node contains problem, partial solution or parameter.

In general contexts, ontology is an ensemble of relevant concepts in a specialized domain where each concept is interrelated to another. On the contrary, IDM ontology is a generic one and is not limited to a specialized domain, which makes it applicable across domains. IDM ontology is composed of concepts that are useful to formulate problematic situation and its solution during inventive design. Our simplification system is integrated to PatExtractor in order to aid the system with extracting main concepts of IDM ontology – problem, partial solution, action parameter and evaluation parameter – by simplifying the texts and thereby facilitating the information extraction process.

3.2 Text Simplification

Overall, our methodology for text simplification follows the precedent rule-based approaches. However, our method is distinguished from the previous methods in two aspects. First, we don't apply lexical simplification since our texts to simplify are patents and most of terminology in patent documents cannot be replaced with another lexicon. Moreover, our target readers are specialists who seek specialized knowledge from patents, thus we have to keep the precise information that is contained in the original terminology. Secondly, our simplification system consists of two different levels of simplification. Our system is integrated into PatExtractor, an information extraction system for patents, therefore, it should fit the objectives of PatExtractor. Integration of the simplification systems to PatExtractor is as shown in Fig. 1.

PatExtractor necessitates two levels of simplification for different goals. First simplification is to facilitate machine learning algorithm's identifying target concepts – concepts of IDM ontology – from texts. Thus, the objective of the simplification is to split sentences so that each phrase contains one idea, not several. Second simplification is designed to improve readability of the graph drawn with extracted information. PatExtractor identifies problems, partial solutions, and parameters, from a given text and then visualizes them as a graph[2]. Each node of the graph contains extracted knowledge. However, when the contents of each node are too wordy, it decreases readability of the graph, hence the necessity of simplifying texts. Desired outputs for each level of simplification will further be discussed in the following sections.

---

[2] The graph is displayed on Finder (https://finder.inventivedesign.unistra.fr), a web application which visualizes extracted information with a graph.

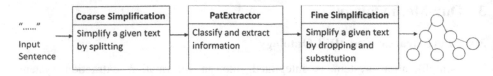

Fig. 1. Integration of the simplification systems to PatExtractor

Before we look into different methodologies for two levels of simplifications, we address a general approach and tools that were used throughout our experiment as well as a development environment for our system. First, we adopted a rule-based approach to simplify texts. Based on our analysis on patent documents, we determined that not every complex sentence is our target for simplification. Texts need to be split only when the splitting helps the classifier to label them correctly. Otherwise, it can hurt the performance of the classifier. Accordingly, a rule-based approach with which we could specify our own rules for simplification was adopted.

Furthermore, we used a syntactic parser to identify a subordinate phrase and split the subordinate off from a matrix phrase. Among several syntactic parsers, we adopted the BLLIP parser [22] given its high accuracy and fast speed[3]. The BLLIP parser is a statistical natural language parser which creates several candidate syntax parses of a given sentence and ranks n-best among them. Another advantage of using the BLLIP parser is that it supports NLTK module [23], so one can easily manipulate syntactic trees created by the BLLIP parser. Thus, in our research, the BLLIP parser and NLTK modules are mainly used tools for simplification task. Lastly, our system is written in Python 3.5 and operates on Linux.

Coarse Simplification System. Our goal at the coarse simplification level is basically to split subordinate phrases from a matrix phrase so that information extraction algorithm treats shorter phrases and yields more accurate results. More specifically, our coarse system splits subordinate phrases that begin with a subordinate conjunction such as *if, until, so that, because* or relative adverbs such as *as, when, where, why,* but it doesn't split relative clauses, which begin with a relative pronoun such as *who, that, which.* Relative clauses are handled at the fine simplification level, which is placed after classification task. Let's take an example of Sentence 1 to be clearer. When Sentence 1 is given as input, we expect to have two split phrases Sentence 2 and Sentence 3 as output after the coarse simplification.

Sentence 1: **If** there is any unmatched state, the signal A turns to H.
Sentence 2: If there is any unmatched state,
Sentence 3: the signal A turns to H.
Sentence 4: It is *advantageous* **if** all the permanent magnets are surrounded.

---

[3] According to the authors' experiment, compared to Standford Parser, which is one of the most commonly used parsers for syntactic analysis, BLLIPparser functions more accurately when analyzing sentences with multi-lexical terms, which are common in patents. As for parsing speed, BLLIPparser is slightly faster than Stanford Parser. NLTK syntax parser was not considered for our task since it requires users to write their own rules.

Sentence 5: A known *problem* with DC currents is that **when** opening a switch by separating the switch contacts a spark builds between the contacts.

To achieve this, our simplification system functions as shown in Table 1. First, for a given sentence, the system checks if the sentence contains a subordinate conjunction or a relative adverb with part of speech (POS) tagger. If the sentence contains these elements, it is analyzed by syntactic parser to create a syntax tree. The syntax tree is used not only to identify a scope of subordinate phrase, but also to double-check if it truly is our target structure. In this step, we filter out unwanted structures.

Table 1. Operation of coarse simplification system

Coarse simplification system
Identify complex sentences
If given text is a complex sentence
➔   Parse a complex sentence to obtain a syntactic tree
If given syntactic tree is our target structure
➔   Split off subordinates from a matrix phrase
➔   Clean the result sentence

Let us recall that the goal of our coarse simplification is to aid the classifier in identifying problems, partial solutions and parameters from a given text. In case of Sentence 4 and 5, a phrase located before *if* and *when* can be an indicator telling the class of the following phrase. For example, the phrase '*It is advantageous*'[4] in Sentence 4 indicates that the following phrase has a positive connotation, and therefore, can be a partial solution. Likewise, the phrase '*a known problem with DC currents is that*' in Sentence 5 gives information that the following phrase may contain a problem. Therefore, splitting these phrases from its subordinates can hurt the performance of the classifier. To avoid this, we rule out sentences containing some keywords such as *problem, solution, appreciated, advantageous* off the list of sentences to simplify. We use the same, but filtered, keywords list that is used to extract problems from patent documents.

Once the given structure is identified as our target structure after the filtering, we split subordinate phrases, which is represented as SBAR on a syntactic tree, from a matrix phrase. As a result, a sentence is divided into two or more phrases. As a last step, we clean the simplified sentence. During the syntax parsing, a sentence is tokenized, which means that words are segmented and then some punctuation and symbol

---

[4] This is a common sentence structure in patents and they indicate that the current sentence includes a solution (or a problem). This type of sentences has a structure of '*It is* **[adjective]** *if/when/that* **[subordinate phrase]**.' As for adjectives, there are certain adjectives or past participles that are commonly used, such as *beneficial, advantageous, recommended, appreciated, accepted*.

characters, such as quotation marks and parenthesis, are replaced with different signs. Moreover, there can be left-out phrases or words during the simplification. Therefore, the system normalizes the modification made during the syntax parsing and simplification, and joins the left-out part to an appropriate location of the split sentence.

Fine Simplification. The objective of fine simplification system is improving a readability of a graph drawn by a web application Finder, which enables a visual representation of extracted information from patents. This can be accomplished by dropping supplementary information such as conjunctions (such as *if, when, although*), connective adverbs (such as *then, therefore, however, by contrast, that is to say*) and supplementary subordinates. Let us take an example of Sentence 5 to clarify the desired result of the fine simplification. When a sentence 5 is given, it is firstly split into two phrases as Sentence 6 and 7 by the coarse simplification system. Then conjunction 'if' in Sentence 6 and 'then' in Sentence 7 are deleted to make each of them a complete sentence. Afterwards, relative pronoun phrase *'which could interrupt the system'* of Sentence 7 is deleted. The last two simplification steps – dropping a conjunction and connective adverb; deleting a relative subordinate – are done by the fine simplification system. As a final output of two simplification systems, we obtain two sentences, Sentence 8 and 9.

> Sentence 5: **If** this offset varies from test strip to test trip, **then** noise *which could interrupt the system* is added to the measurement.
> Sentence 6: **If** this offset varies from test strip to test trip,
> Sentence 7: **then** noise which could interrupt the system is added to the measurement.
> Sentence 8: This offset varies from test strip to test trip.
> Sentence 9: Noise is added to the measurement.

The general method of the fine simplification is similar to that of the coarse simplification in the way that it exploits syntactic tree to find subordinate phrases. In the fine simplification system, however, deletion is applied instead of simple split. Moreover, only certain types of relative subordinate clauses that are followed by *who, that, which, whose* are subject to be treated. Generally, relative pronoun subordinate carries supplementary information of its antecedent. This supplementary information does not affect a principle message of a sentence even when deleted. In Sentence 5, the relative clause *'which could interrupt the system'* carries additional information of its antecedent *'noise.'* However, even when it is deleted, it does not change the main idea, that is, a problematic situation to the stated system caused by added noise. Let us recall the final output of the entire system is a visual representation of extracted information, which, thus, should be concise and clear. Therefore, dropping additional information and conveying only principal ideas is the objective of the fine simplification system. Furthermore, original sentence before simplification is also provided to users on Finder, so that users can have access to the fuller information. This is to prevent information loss or distortion which could occur during the simplification process.

Table 2. Fine simplification system

Fine simplification system
Drop connective adverbs and conjunctions
Identify sentences containing a relative subordinate
If given text has a relative subordinate clause
➜ Parse the sentence to obtain a syntactic tree
If given syntactic tree is our target structure
➜ Delete subordinates from a matrix phrase
➜ Clean the result sentence

Table 2 shows how the fine simplification system functions. Overall, it roughly follows the same process as the coarse simplification. However, one difference is dropping connective adverbs and conjunctions at the beginning of the system. Let us recall the fine simplification system takes place after the coarse simplification. That is, some sentences are already split into more than two phrases such as in Sentence 6 and 7. In this case, we need to edit these sentences to make them complete. For example, in case of Sentence 6, it is grammatically not complete because of conjunction 'if.' Thus, we drop this conjunction to make it a complete sentence. Moreover, sentence 7 does not need its connective adverb 'then' anymore since it does not have the preceding phrase. Therefore, we drop this adverb.

Dropping connective adverbs (not conjunctions) are applied not only to complex sentences which were split by the coarse simplification system, but also to the simple sentences which were not treated by the coarse simplification system. Connective adverbs (or phrases) such as *however, by contrast, that is to say, in addition, moreover* present the semantic relation with its preceding sentence. However, our information extraction functions on a sentence unit, which means that each sentence extracted by the system is represented without its context – its preceding and following sentence. Thus, connective adverbs which show the links between a current phrase and its preceding or following sentence are dropped to keep the extracted information simple.

4   Discussion

The evaluation on our simplification systems is twofold given that each level of simplification has different objectives. We integrate the coarse simplification system to the information extraction system, PatExtractor. Afterwards, we evaluate the simplification system by evaluating the performance of classification algorithm. We compare the performance of the algorithm before and after the integration of the coarse simplification system. On the other hand, the fine simplification is evaluated by readability score of the result sentences since the fine simplification system is designed to improve legibility of a graph, on which extracted information is displayed.

Evaluation on the Coarse Simplification System. One of the most commonly used measures to evaluate a classification algorithm are precision and recall. Recall and precision score of PatExtractor V 2.0 for partial solution and problem is as shown in the Table 3. To evaluate the system, we randomly chose 250 patent documents with different topics and extracted information from them. During our experiment, however, we did not observe a significant improvement on precision score after the integration of the coarse simplification system. The precision remained roughly the same (its improvement rate was less than 0.1%) and recall was not measured because given the structure of the entire system, our simplification does not affect the recall of the algorithm. Nevertheless, more interesting observation could have been possible if more test data, especially annotated data were available. Given the fact that only a small number of phrases are selected to classify and simplify from one patent text, the phrases that were finally used for evaluation (from 250 corpora) were not large in number. Furthermore, for lack of annotated data, the evaluation was largely based on the author's judgement.

Table 3. Recall and precision of PatExtractor V 2.0

	Recall	Precision
Partial solution	47.87%	74.99%
Problem	43.83%	88.14%

Evaluation on the Fine Simplification System. To evaluate the fine simplification system, we used Flesch Reading Ease score [24]. It is one of the most commonly used scoring formula to evaluate readability of a text. The scale of the score is from 1 to 100 and the higher the score is, the more readable the text is. To evaluate the fine simplification system, we chose three sets of corpus: copurs1 consisting of 10 patent documents treating a topic in automatic transfer switch; corpus2 consisting of 10 documents covering a topic in automobile; corpus3 consisting of 10 documents addressing a topic of batteries. The score reflects not only the result of the fine simplification system but also that of the coarse simplification system. This is because the fine simplification takes place consecutively after the coarse simplification step where complex sentences are firstly split into shorter phrases. As shown in the Table 4, after applying the fine simplification system, we obtained higher readability score by 0.8 point with Corpus1, which is equal to 2.1% of improvement rate. With corpus 2, we obtained 1.6 higher readability score after the simplification, that is, 4.83% of the improvement rate. With corpus3, we obtained higher readability score by 1.3 point, which is equal to 3.5% of improvement rate. The average improvement rate is therefore 3.37%.

Table 4. Readability score before and after simplification

	Before simplification	After simplification	Improvement rate
Corpus1	37.1	37.9	2.1%
Corpus2	33.1	34.7	4.83%
Corpus3	36.7	38.0	3.5%
Average	35.6	36.8	3.37%

Let us take examples of sentences produced by PatExtractor v.3.0 to see the result in detail. Sentence 10 is produced by the previous version of PatExtractor, that is, version 2.0. which does not have the text simplification systems. The former part of the phrase *'if the water-absorbing ability exceeds over 800 g/g'* is a cause of a problem and the latter *'the paste may be gelled and become difficult to be uniformly coated on the conductive substrate'* is a resulted problem. Among these two ideas, only the latter is what our focus goes on since it concerns a problem, which is one of the IDM ontology elements we would like to extract. The previous version of PatExtractor extracts the full sentence and labeled the entire sentence as a problem. On the contrary, PatExtractor v.3.0 with the text simplification systems integrated extracts only the latter part and label it as a problem separately from its former phrase (Sentence 11). This is different from the previous version of PatExtractor which treats the entire sentence as a whole.

Sentence 12 is another example of extracted information by the previous version of PatExtracotr. Sentence 13 and 14 are extracted by the current PatExtractor v.3.0. Sentence 12 delivers two main ideas: *magnetic flux control means are controlled individually; the flow of the magnetic flux can be controlled more flexibly.* Both information contains important concepts which correspond to partial solution of an IDM ontology. The updated version of PatExtractor treats these two concepts separately (classifiy separately) and returns two results. This makes the final graph of extracted information more concise. However, as we discussed above, we observed that the integration of simplification systems does not improve the accuracy of the classification significantly. Sentence 12 corresponds to a partial solution but is labeled as a problem by PatExtractor v.2.0. This incorrect labeling remains unchanged in PatExtractort v.3.0 as seen in Sentence 13 and 14.

> Sentence 10: *If the water-absorbing ability exceeds over 800 g/g*, the paste may be gelled and become difficult to be uniformly coated on the conductive substrate. **[problem]**
> Sentence 11: The paste may be gelled and become difficult to be uniformly coated on the conductive substrate. **[problem]**
> Sentence 12: When the magnetic flux control means are controlled individually, the flow of the magnetic flux can be controlled more flexibly. **[problem]**
> Sentence 13: The magnetic flux control means are controlled individually. **[problem]**
> Sentence 14: The flow of the magnetic flux can be controlled more flexibly. **[problem]**

5 Conclusion and Future Work

Even though integration of the simplification systems did not lead to a significant improvement of the classification algorithm, it improved a readability of a graph created from extracted information to a certain degree. Furthermore, deleting supplementary information made it possible to extract information with focusing only on important part of information, which corresponds to elements of the IDM ontology. Moreover, simplification system enabled PatExtractor to treat different concepts and ideas in one sentence separately, contrary to the previous version which treated them as a whole. For the future work, phrase restructuring function could be added to the simplification system since, while splitting off sentences into several phrases, anaphoric relations between a pronoun and its antecedent could be lost. Moreover, it would be interesting to evaluate the precision of the upgraded version of PatExtractor with more corpus that are annotated by experts.

References

1. Souili, W.M.A.: Contribution à la méthode de conception inventive par l'extraction automatique de connaissances des textes de brevets d'invention (2015)
2. Cavallucci, D., Khomenko, N.: From TRIZ to OTSM-TRIZ: addressing complexity challenges in inventive design. Int. J. Prod. Dev. **4**, 4–21 (2006)
3. Altshuller, G.: And suddenly the inventor appeared: TRIZ, the theory of inventive problem solving. Technical Innovation Center, Inc. (1996)
4. Hua, Z., Yang, J., Coulibaly, S., Zhang, B.: Integration TRIZ with problem-solving tools: a literature review from 1995 to 2006. Int. J. Bus. Innov. Res. **1**, 111–128 (2006)
5. Souili, A., Cavallucci, D.: Toward an automatic extraction of IDM concepts from patents. In: Chakrabarti, A. (ed.) CIRP Design 2012, pp. 115–124. Springer, Heidelberg (2013). https://doi.org/10.1007/978-1-4471-4507-3_12
6. Cavallucci, D., Rousselot, F.: Structuring Knowledge Use in Inventive Design. Springer, New York (2007)
7. Lee, J., Don, J.B.K.P.: Splitting complex English sentences. In: Proceedings of the 15th International Conference on Parsing Technologies, pp. 50–55 (2017)
8. Carroll, J., Minnen, G., Pearce, D., Canning, Y., Devlin, S., Tait, J.: Simplifying text for language-impaired readers. In: Ninth Conference of the European Chapter of the Association for Computational Linguistics (1999)
9. Inui, K., Fujita, A., Takahashi, T., Iida, R., Iwakura, T.: Text simplification for reading assistance: a project note. In: Proceedings of the Second International Workshop on Paraphrasing, vol. 16, pp. 9–16. Association for Computational Linguistics (2003)
10. Chandrasekar, R., Doran, C., Srinivas, B.: Motivations and methods for text simplification. In: Proceedings of the 16th Conference on Computational Linguistics, vol. 2, pp. 1041–1044. Association for Computational Linguistics (1996)
11. Knight, K., Marcu, D.: Statistics-based summarization-step one: sentence compression. In: AAAI/IAAI, pp. 703–710 (2000)
12. Poornima, C., Dhanalakshmi, V., Anand, K.M., Soman, K.P.: Rule based sentence simplification for english to tamil machine translation system. Int. J. Comput. Appl. **25**, 38–42 (2011)

13. Siddharthan, A.: An architecture for a text simplification system. In: 2002 Proceedings of Language Engineering Conference, pp. 64–71. IEEE (2002)
14. Siddharthan, A.: Text simplification using typed dependencies: a comparison of the robustness of different generation strategies. In: Proceedings of the 13th European Workshop on Natural Language Generation, pp. 2–11. Association for Computational Linguistics (2011)
15. Zhu, Z., Bernhard, D., Gurevych, I.: A monolingual tree-based translation model for sentence simplification. In: Proceedings of the 23rd International Conference on Computational Linguistics, pp. 1353–1361. Association for Computational Linguistics (2010)
16. Narayan, S., Gardent, C.: Hybrid simplification using deep semantics and machine translation. In: Proceedings of the 52nd Annual Meeting of the Association for Computational Linguistics (vol. 1: Long Papers), pp. 435–445 (2014)
17. Mille, S., Wanner, L.: Making text resources accessible to the reader: the case of patent claims. In: LREC (2008)
18. Sheremetyeva, S.: Automatic text simplification for handling intellectual property (the case of multiple patent claims). In: Proceedings of the Workshop on Automatic Text Simplification-Methods and Applications in the Multilingual Society (ATS-MA 2014), pp. 41–52 (2014)
19. Bott, S., Saggion, H., Figueroa, D.: A hybrid system for spanish text simplification. In: Proceedings of the Third Workshop on Speech and Language Processing for Assistive Technologies, pp. 75–84. Association for Computational Linguistics (2012)
20. Siddharthan, A.: A survey of research on text simplification. ITL-Int. J. Appl. Linguist. **165**, 259–298 (2014)
21. Shinmori, A., Okumura, M., Marukawa, Y., Iwayama, M.: Patent claim processing for readability: structure analysis and term explanation. In: Proceedings of the ACL-2003 Workshop on Patent Corpus Processing, vol. 20, pp. 56–65. Association for Computational Linguistics (2003)
22. Charniak, E., Johnson, M.: Coarse-to-fine n-best parsing and MaxEnt discriminative reranking. In: Proceedings of the 43rd Annual Meeting on Association for Computational Linguistics, pp. 173–180. Association for Computational Linguistics (2005)
23. Bird, S., Loper, E.: NLTK: the natural language toolkit. In: Proceedings of the ACL 2004 on Interactive Poster and Demonstration Sessions, p. 31. Association for Computational Linguistics (2004)
24. Kincaid, J.P., Fishburne Jr., R.P., Rogers, R.L., Chissom, B.S.: Derivation of new readability formulas (automated readability index, fog count and flesch reading ease formula) for navy enlisted personnel (1975)

TRIZ Combined with other Approaches

Innovative Design Thinking Process with TRIZ

Kyeongwon Lee[✉]

Department of Mechanical Design Engineering, Korea Polytechnic University,
Siheung City, Gyeonggi-Do 429-793, Korea
lkw@kpu.ac.kr

Abstract. This paper describes an innovative design thinking process with simplified TRIZ that can be used to resolve contradictions in all domains with words such as "dilemma", "conflict", "contradiction" and "paradox". The design thinking process that have been used at d.school at Stanford and Potsdam University are popular as a human-centered innovation process with "Empathy" and "Define" stages for human-centered problem finding. However, many results may be not innovative because it uses mostly "Group brainstorming" at "Ideate" stage.

TRIZ users have complained that the Russian conventional TRIZ is so difficult to learn and apply. They consider that it is useful in manufacturing and mechanical fields mostly. This paper suggests an innovative design thinking process with simplified and generally usable the step-by-step TRIZ. Its effectiveness of the innovative design thinking process with the simplified and step-by-step general TRIZ is explained in the development case study, a smart wind free air conditioner.

Keywords: Innovative design thinking · Simplified TRIZ · Step-by-step TRIZ

1 Introduction

Among several conceptual design methodologies, Design thinking and TRIZ are popular in the world. Design thinking is a process of a human-centered innovation with collaboration of team members. TRIZ is technologically oriented methodology to resolve some contradictions using knowledge databases.

When it comes to TRIZ, newcomers are confronted with highly sophisticated tools and a very time-consuming learning process as explained in Claudia Hentschel and Alexander Czinki' paper [1]. They presented that Design Thinking as a door-opener for TRIZ is efficient for newcomers to understand and use TRIZ as a systematic innovation methodology.

There are several related papers by searching both "design thinking process and TRIZ" in scholar.google.com [2–4]. TRIZ is Russian acronym of "Theory of Inventive Problem Solving". There are so many problem-solving tools of TRIZ than tools for human-centered problem finding. It is very important to find and define the human-centered problem and project in highly competitive economics these days because of faster changes of customer's needs. TRIZ that has used mostly in mechanical and manufacturing fields gives just some conceptual ideas and sometimes looks like innovative, but still vague ideas so that TRIZ users do not confirm that the ideas are working well or not in short time.

© IFIP International Federation for Information Processing 2018
Published by Springer Nature Switzerland AG 2018. All Rights Reserved
D. Cavallucci et al. (Eds.): TFC 2018, IFIP AICT 541, pp. 241–252, 2018.
https://doi.org/10.1007/978-3-030-02456-7_20

The Design thinking process can compensate the weakness of TRIZ well. The "Empathize" and "Define" step of the Design thinking process are effective steps for compensating TRIZ for finding the human-centered problem as a "Pre-TRIZ".

The fast and cheap "Prototype" step of the Design Thinking process is serial step for communicating the TRIZ ideas much better with others and then, showing effective implementation of conceptual ideas by TRIZ as a "Post-TRIZ".

Vice versa, the Design thinking process has big shortage on generating innovative ideas in the "Ideate" step because it depends on group brainstorming method by all participants. Therefore, TRIZ and Design thinking process can compensate each other.

Design thinking process has strong points in problem finding with collaborative team play. Simplified TRIZ with interesting education samples are suitable to improve the creativity of even students at middle and high school better.

This paper describes a general-use innovative design thinking process with simplified and step-by-step TRIZ that can be used to resolve contradictions in all domains with words such as "dilemma", "conflict", "contradiction".

Its effectiveness is explained in a development case study, the smart wind free air conditioner at SAMSUNG Electronics.

2 Design Thinking Process

The design thinking process first defines human-centered problem carefully and then, implements the solutions, always with the needs of the user demographic at the core of concept development [5]. This process focuses on needs finding, understanding, creating, thinking, and doing. At the core of this process is a bias towards action and creation: by creating and testing something, you can continue to learn and improve upon your initial ideas. The design thinking process at d.school of Stanford University is most popular in the world. It consists of these 5 steps as shown in Fig. 1:

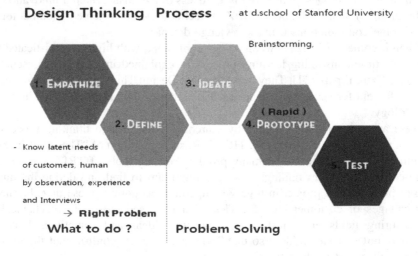

Fig. 1. 5 steps of design thinking process at d.school, Stanford University [5]

(1) "EMPATHIZE" step: Work to fully understand the experience of the user for whom you are designing. Do this through observation, interaction, and immersing yourself in their experiences

(2) "DEFINE' step: Process and synthesize the findings from your empathy work to form a user point of view that you will address with your design.

(3) "IDEATE" step: Explore a wide variety of possible solutions through generating a large quantity of diverse possible solutions, allowing you to step beyond the obvious and explore a range of ideas. In many cases, the methods to generate ideas almost depend on brainstorming of multidisciplinary team.

(4) "PROTOTYPE" step: Transform your ideas into a physical form rapid and cheaply so that you can experience and interact with them and, in the process, learn and develop more empathy.

(5) "TEST" step: Try out high-resolution products and use observations and feedback to refine prototypes, learn more about the user, and refine your original point of view.

The design thinking refers to the way designers solve problems, develop unique thought streams, visualize ideas quickly and then, start to modify the draft plans again after reviewing them as shown in Fig. 2.

It has been more popular in the world including Korea than TRIZ after big companies such as SAP, Google, Airbnb, IBM and Siemens have started to utilize it as collaborative working ways.

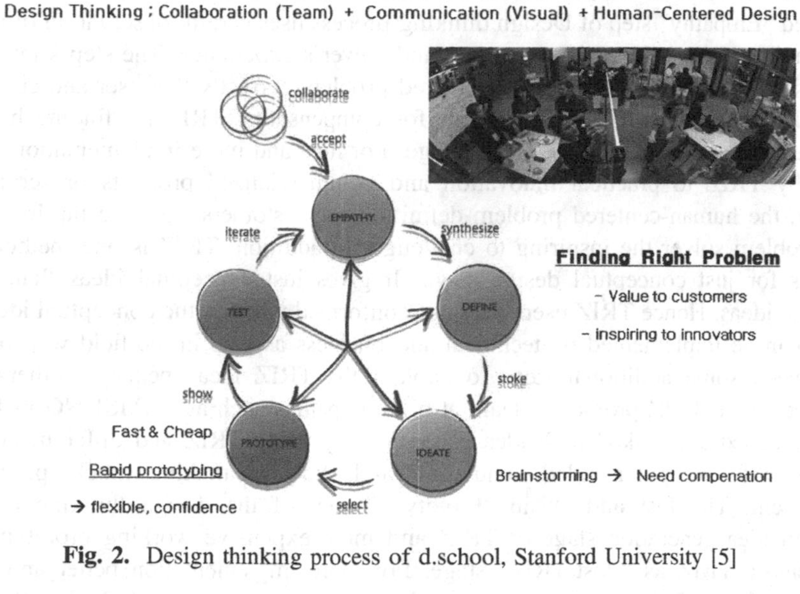

Design Thinking ; Collaboration (Team) + Communication (Visual) + Human-Centered Design

Fig. 2. Design thinking process of d.school, Stanford University [5]

It defines problems through the "Empathy" for real users, produces many possible ideas for problem solving through group brainstorming, and then produces an optimal number of ideas among them. It uses the several methods for empathy to identify potential user's latent needs using careful observation and deep interviews etc. with real users to identify problems on the viewpoint of users.

It forms a team of people from different fields to collect diverse ideas to solve problem with diverse viewpoints, knowledge and experiences.

For much better communication, it uses visual communication methods such as sharing the simple drawings on Post-its attaching to big panels and the fast prototype with low resolution with cheap materials, so that all participants can exchange diverse opinions, communicate freely and understand the ideas better and quickly.

However, the idea-generating phase (called by "IDEATE" step) is mainly based on the use of light idea-generating methods, such as group brainstorming and sometimes MINDMAP and SCAMPER as well. The quality and innovativeness of ideas are still poor in many applications.

Design thinking users have complained that design thinking looks like one of facilitating methods with funny ice braking and recreations without innovative results in Korea. Because design thinking experts have introduced and explained just mostly good innovation results and case studies from Stanford University and IDEO company. The design thinking or HCI (Human-computer interaction) promotion teams inside big companies in Korea such as SK groups have been disappeared by poor innovative business results for several years.

3   Innovative Design Thinking Process with Simplified TRIZ

TRIZ has no steps to include human-oriented latent and changing needs. The human-centered "Empathy" step of Design thinking process uses careful observation of user's vivid actions, user's intensive interview and solver's experience. The step knows and defines problem solvers the human-centered problem correctly that user and customer have latently. It is much effective steps for compensating TRIZ for finding human-centered problem well as "Pre-TRIZ" stage. For nice and more implementations from ideas by TRIZ to practical innovation and commercialized products or service in market, the human-centered problem definition for customers can give the innovator and problem solver the inspiring to challenge. In addition, TRIZ is one method and process for just conceptual design stage. It gives just conceptual ideas than more concrete ideas. Hence TRIZ users may not conformed whether the conceptual ideas by TRIZ can be implemented by technical and business aspects in the field well or not. They need some additional steps to explain the TRIZ ideas better to others. For instance, some TRIZ promotion team at big companies such as SAMSUNG in Korea have matched and linked both idea generators by using TRIZ and different domain experts with computer aided simulation and analysis, making mock-up, simple experiment. The fast and cheap "Prototype" step of the design thinking process between idea generation stage of TRIZ and more expensive working prototype can compensate TRIZ as "Post-TRIZ" stage. For more implementation better and time-reduction for R & D, the fast, cheap and low-level prototyping of Design thinking process is very important for TRIZ users who may not give strong confidence on their conceptual ideas. At early stage they can know technically feasibility before high-level and expensive prototyping product or service. Complementing innovative ideas to the

"IDEATE" stage of conventional design thinking by simplified and step-by-step TRIZ first and then, conventional complex TRIZ knowledges more as shown in Fig. 3.

Design Thinking ; Collaboration (Team) + Communication (Visual) + Human-Centered Design

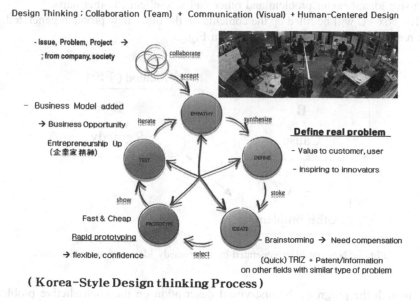

(**Korea-Style Design thinking Process**)

Fig. 3. Innovative design thinking process, "Korea-style design thinks process"

TRIZ is suitable method to resolve any kinds of contradictions, so-called dilemma in other fields besides Engineering problems. By the way, TRIZ beginners and general persons have some difficulty to model the right contradiction systematically. In addition, they have complained that the conventional TRIZ has so many tools such as 40 inventive principles, 76 standard and complex ARIZ process.

The simplified TRIZ, so-called the "Quick TRIZ" process with step-by-step conflict diagram in T.O.C (Theory of Constraints) was devised as follows [6]. As shown in the Fig. 4, it asks to describe the cause to remove the main cause of problem into box B and then, write down one first good idea (as the remedy) by users themselves or sometimes by group brainstorming in design thinking process, which can remove the cause in box B, into box D.

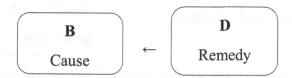

Fig. 4. Pair with one main cause and its remedy idea to remove the cause

Then, it asks a problem solver to describe the new problem generated by implementing the first idea (in many cases, the first idea generates the new other problem). In design thinking process, good ideas may generate a new other problem such as an expensive idea, heavier problem and other bad side-effect to other parts.

The box - C will be filled up the contents on the other new problem generated, that is to remove the new problem as shown in Fig. 5.

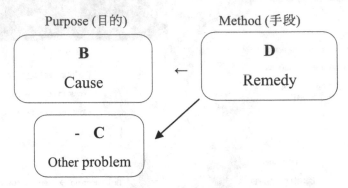

Fig. 5. New problem generated by the remedy idea to remove the cause

Through the progress, the first visual description on the contradictive problem is represented. In box D' shown in Fig. 6, the reverse (-) condition corresponds to the method to remove the cause should be described intentionally.

In other words, the minus or the reverse physical condition against the method in box D should be described in box D' as the physical contradiction of TRIZ.

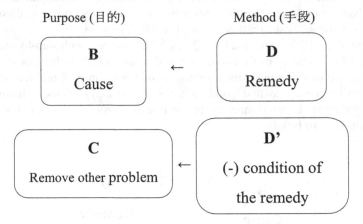

Fig. 6. Reverse condition of the remedy to remove new other problem

As the last step the box A will be filled with the Ideal Final Result (IFR) of TRIZ, that satisfies the two contradictive purposes in box B and C "at no cost concept" shown in Fig. 7.

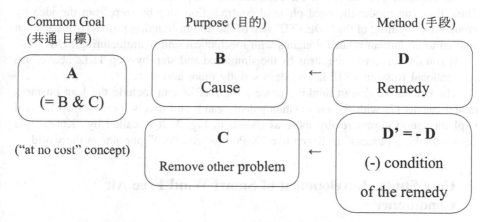

Fig. 7. Problem description in the Conflict Diagram in T.O.C.

TRIZ solvers can see the technical contradiction in box B and box C and the physical contradiction in box D and box D' corresponding the problem with the main cause, the method to remove the cause and the new problem generated by the method and the self-contradictory relation at the same time.

The author has realized through his over ten-year-experience in the field of TRIZ education and business that the terminology of the "contradiction" is what the TRIZ beginners find difficult. And it seems to be unfamiliar and hard to get the correct meanings of the physical contradiction or the technical contradictions and the differences between them as well.

That is why some Korean TRIZ experts call the contradiction the conflict for people working for non-technical field. In other words, they use the term, 'conflict' between two purposes (目的) instead of the technical contradiction in TRIZ and use the term, 'conflict' between two methods (手段) instead of the physical contradiction in TRIZ to make people more understandable.

And then, apply 3 separation principles and "Using other cheaper resources" simply as follows;

(1) Generate ideas by applying "separation in time"
(2) Generate ideas by applying "separation in space" including "separation in whole and parts"
(3) Generate ideas by applying "separation on conditions" with difference of level, standard and condition with "if" and "otherwise"
(4) Generate ideas by using other cheaper resources instead of 40 principles and standard solutions to escape from fixed and existing idea, means and method.

Notice that solvers intentionally describe the revere idea, means and method of D (-D) into the box D' to satisfy the contradictive purpose by removing the new other problem as shown in Fig. 7.

As common goal they add the contradictory purposes B and C into the box A. Thus, they can model the right physical contradiction step-by-step from the idea by group brainstorming of the "IDEATE" step of the design thinking process that has been applied to all human related domains with mechanical and manufacturing fields.

If you do not satisfy the ideas by the simplified and step-by-step TRIZ above, use conventional Russian TRIZ knowledges serially more and more.

The innovative design thinking process with TRIZ can include the lean business model canvas [7] with the information/patent search and user's journey map for real implementation commercially more as shown in Fig. 3. It is called by "Korea-style design thinking process" in Korea like "K-Pop (Korea Pop)" popular in the world.

4 Case Study: Development of Smart Wind Free Air Conditioner

Since the first commercial use of air conditioner by the company, CARRIER in the early 20th century, LG Electronics has led the global market these days. Many patents and core technologies of air conditioners have already been existed in the United States, Europe, Japan, and LG Electronics.

To enter this market and then, compete with the leading companies as a follower company, it is necessary to have consistent efforts to recognize and reflect the needs and demands of consumers on the product more in advance. Many users of air conditioner or purchasing customers surveyed are likely to require general complaints such as a lot of power consumption, loudness and expensive price. Are there any other potential complaints and demands?

Design thinking recommends to interview deeply the "Extreme users" in the "EMPATH" phase to gain new perspectives on users. The extreme user is a small number of people who live, think, and consume differently than most users. SAMSUNG Electronics can get unstructured perspectives and insights from them, skin-sensitive extreme users for cold strong wind of air conditioner.

The product developed by capturing different perspectives on air conditioners is the smart wind free air conditioner [8].

The development team members of SAMSUNG had observed carefully more than 600 large hotels, shopping centers, air conditioning system of an airplane and interviewed deeply the mechanics who install and fix the air conditioner up as well as users of home-use air conditioner. They had identified some latent needs of users and then, considered the new product considering the related technologies and patents.

They identified new target customers as extreme users who are very sensitive of cold strong wind to skins. Most ordinary users of air conditioner with the extreme users may remember the bad feelings from the cold strong wind of air conditioners to their skins.

Some users divert the direction of the wind of air conditioner from one side to the other by attaching extra wind-guiding wings not contacting it to their skin directly as shown as in Fig. 8.

Fig. 8. Wind guide plate to divert cold wind from air conditioner to other direction

However, it is likely to consume much more power due to poor cooling capabilities. The development team defined the problem with "How might we release the bad feeling of users who are very sensitive to cold strong wind from air conditioners while cooling the room down well simultaneously?"

They came up with an idea and then, have made a prototype for complete product based on the design thinking process. They had big difficulty that there is no wind preventing touching the skin by the cold strong wind from air conditioner while if there is no wind, the air conditioner does not cool the room down any more.

It is a situation of contradiction and dilemma that air conditioners must blow the "fast" and "not fast (=slow)" cold wind simultaneously. The ideas should satisfy both two opposing purposes of keeping cooling down and eliminating the bad feeling to skin by the strong cold wind resolving the physical contradiction of TRIZ with "fast cold wind" and "slow cold wind" as shown in Fig. 9.

It is not easy to resolve these conflicts and contradictions by brainstorming alone. It is much better to apply the separation principles of TRIZ for resolving the physical conditions. The consumer wants to cool down fast when he turns on the air conditioner. After several minutes using the air conditioner, he wants to turn it off for preventing the bad feeling by blowing the cold wind to his skins. It is possible to come up with the idea by the "separation in time" principle of TRIZ. For example, there are fast cold wind of the air conditioner for first 10 min. After the 10 min there is not fast (=too slow) cold wind.

Where in nature are places to satisfy these contradictory demands for cooling are accomplished? The answer is the cold "cave" in summer.

Human skin does not feel the badness against wind with the low velocity air conditioners. It feels like there's no wind. According to the scientific survey the wind speed from air conditioners is about 2 m/s. By careful measurement there is a weak wind in the cave with a wind speed of just 15 cm/s per second. It is not only the lack of fast wind in the cave, but also the breeze in the air conditioner's one-fifteenth wind that makes it cool. When you combine it with the idea of the separation in time principle, it

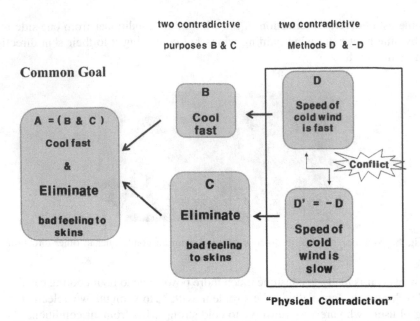

Fig. 9. Conflict diagram of physical contradiction with fast and slow cold winds

will satisfy users who want to feel cool like a traditional air conditioner and then, cool down like a cave after the 10 min. With this idea it develops detailed design and implementation with technical experts on air condition.

Since lowering the wind speed due to calm mode and extreme winds reduces the ability to cool the air conditioners down, it is important to ensure that the air conditioning capacity is maintained while lowering the wind speed significantly. Technically the cooling capacity is the multiplication of the discharge area with wind and wind speed.

In other words, if you want to achieve the same cooling capacity due to low wind speed you must make the air discharge area where air conditioners are produced very large.

To compensate for the wind speed that has decreased by 1/15, how can we expand the discharge area of air conditioners by 15 times? Whereas conventional air conditioners produce wind from a limited area of air vents, the idea is improved as if the entire body of air conditioners were made from air conditioner blast device like audio speakers as shown in Fig. 10. Engineering knowledges on air conditioner resolve the contradiction of low wind speed and cooling capacity with the concept of TRIZ.

Eventually about 100,000 very small holes in the entire body of the air conditioner were created, creating a new type of air conditioner that creates a sense of calm to humans. Samsung's home-use air conditioner was released to Korea domestic market in 2016. Despite of expensive price, it has become a hit product selling more than 200,000 units first year in Korea. It has been exported massively in the world market as smart innovative air conditioner recently.

Separation in Time - After strong & cold, weak wind

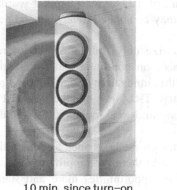

10 min. since turn-on   after 50 min. since turn-on

– Strong cold wind   – Sweet & weak wind

(as from whole body of audio speaker around)

Fig. 10. Air conditioner applied by "separation in time" principle

It introduced a new product and a new technology that can mark a new historic product and technology on over 100 years in the history of air conditioners by using the innovative design thinking process with TRIZ serially.

5   Conclusions

The design thinking process of d.school of Stanford University has strong point for collective intelligence through interesting and funny actions by team members, visual communication between all participants and human's (user's) latent needs found by careful observation and deep interview real users at the "Empathy" stage.

But many users to apply it have complained that the idea is not innovative as the ideas are based on the participants' group brainstorming. Even with innovative ideas, these innovative ideas become more expensive or heavier or have new other problems that make them less practical to apply. This new other problem situation will be a contradiction and a conflict. So TRIZ with the separation and invention principles can be used to resolve the contradictions, conflicts and dilemmas in any other domains.

By the way the conventional Russian style TRIZ is still quite difficult for ordinary people and beginners to learn and apply. Because there are so many complex problem tools of TRIZ. They are composed of many 40 invention principles that are suited to mostly mechanical field and manufacturing, 76 Standard Solutions with Substance Field Modeling and complex ARIZ process starting from defining the technical system. Especially it is difficult to define the conflicts and contradictions that are the real cause of the problem easily and step-by-step within several hours' TRIZ educations.

According to this innovative design thinking process with step-by-step TRIZ, ordinary people and beginners can learn only a few hours, but also model the conflicts systematically by using the conflict diagram of T.O.C. with familiar words.

This simplified and step-by-step TRIZ may be applied to any general domains with contradictions, conflicts and dilemmas.

Even young students can easily memorize only four principles to resolve contractions with "separation in time, in space, on condition and using other cheaper resources in any other contradictive. Thus, this innovative design thinking process with TRIZ, specially simplified and step-by-step TRIZ is good harmonized conceptual design methodology compensating the strong and weak points of Design thinking and TRIZ each other, respectively.

The results after applying conceptual design methods such as design thinking and TRIZ are often just conceptual ideas. If we add them by the prototyping and business modelling canvas for showing the business opportunities more and starting a little business with the lean start-up concept [7], you'll see far more practical business results from the just conceptual ideas.

In the innovative design thinking process with TRIZ, we will add how to choose the attractive, trendy, social and business issues to find good problems better and build innovation culture of organizations and heighten the enthusiasm and willingness of the participants to innovate more.

Acknowledgement. This work was partially supported by the Korea Foundation for the Advancement of Science and Creativity (KOFAC) and Korea Institute of Design Promotion (KIDP) grant funded by the Korea government, respectively.

References

1. Hentschel, C., Czinki, A.: Design thinking as a door-opener for TRIZ-paving the way towards systematic innovation. In: TRIZ Future Conference 2013, Paris, France (2013)
2. Thoring, K., Müller, R.M.: Understanding the creative mechanisms of design thinking: an evolutionary approach. In: Proceedings of the 2nd Conference on Creativity and Innovation in Design, Eindhoven, Netherlands, 19–21 October 2011, pp. 137–147 (2011)
3. Dabholkar, V.: Design thinking vs TRIZ: A panel discussion, on July, 5 as a part of Next Gear Workshop, Catalign Innovation Consulting (2012). www.catalign.com
4. Gray, C.M., et al.: What is the content of "design thinking"? Design heuristics as conceptual repertoire. Int. J. Eng. Educ. **32** (2016)
5. d.school of Stanford University. http://dschool.stanford.edu. Accessed 14 Apr 2018
6. Lee, K.: Simple TRIZ process "Quick TRIZ 2014" for non-technical fields with resolving the dilemma in business, service, government policy and social conflicts systematically. In: Proceedings of 14th ETRIA World Conference TRIZ Future 2014, Lausanne, 29–31 October (2014). J. Eur. TRIZ Assoc. INNOVATOR. ISSN 1866-4180, 01/2014 Volume 01, pp. 110–112 (2014)
7. Ries, E.: Lean startup, The lean startup: how today's entrepreneurs use continuous innovation to create radically success, 1st edn. Currency (2011)
8. Kim, J.-Y.: Thinking wind free air conditioner with Design Thinking, KOSCA (KOrea Society of Creativity Application, www.kosca.net) Domestic Fall Conference 2016, Seoul (2016)

Innovative Technical Creativity Methodology for Bio-Inspired Design

Pierre-Emmanuel Fayemi[1]([envelope]), Martin Gilles[2,3], and Claude Gazo[2]

[1] Active Innovation Management, 155 Rue Anatole France,
92300 Levallois-Perret, France
p.fayemi@aim-innovation.com
[2] Laboratoire Conception de Produits et Innovation, ENSAM,
151 bd de l'hôpital, 75013 Paris, France
[3] Ecole de Biologie Industrielle, 49 Avenue des Genottes, 95800 Cergy, France

Abstract. The present research primarily focuses on building an effective rationalization of the knowledge which can be extracted from biological experts. To achieve such results, a structural framework, allowing knowledge integration from different fields at specific phases of the creative process is proposed. The formalized methodology along with its associated frameworks relies on principles from C-K Theory, TRIZ, and their links with biologically inspired design.

To assess such design process methodology, an initial application within a case study has been implemented. This case study has been conducted through an industrial partnership with a Research & Development service department from a company working in the offshore oil production sector.

But more than the concepts themselves, this new approach of biologically inspired design has emphasized, within this study case, an interesting potential in its propensity to quickly guide designers in accessing the most relevant knowledge from the biological field.

Keywords: Bio-inspired design · TRIZ · CK · Methodology · Innovation

1 Introduction

Bio-Inspired Design (BID), supported by a growing number of works for the past 20 years, succeeds in attracting attention of more and more industrial R&D department.

Sometimes considered as a 3.8 billion years old R&D process [1], BID has been identified as one of the eight pillars to convey innovation during our century [2]. One major challenge when it comes to BID revolves around implementing it, in a robust way, within existing R&D processes [3]. In industrial structures, technical competences are usually mainly carried by a culture of general engineering. It is thus a tedious work for them to draw their inspiration from living systems [4]. The presented work aims therefore at clarifying both the interest and the feasibility of the implementation of such process, combined with a willingness to create an accessible method focusing on engineers with no biological background.

© IFIP International Federation for Information Processing 2018
Published by Springer Nature Switzerland AG 2018. All Rights Reserved
D. Cavallucci et al. (Eds.): TFC 2018, IFIP AICT 541, pp. 253–265, 2018.
https://doi.org/10.1007/978-3-030-02456-7_21

Presented methodology thus focuses on:

- Effectively integrating knowledge from Life Sciences experts by guiding engineering profiles towards the understanding of biological phenomena with a high degree of relevance.
- Identifying specific area of knowledge to tap into through a more precise the formalization of the function to perform.
- Generating a proper structure allowing to transpose a specific knowledge related language, used to understand the organization of potential systems (engineer vision) to a language dedicated to knowledge acquisition from living systems experts (or living systems literature).
- Providing a multilevel systemic dismantling, from macro to micro, targeting more and more precise expertise.

2 Towards a New Model to Strengthen Biological Research Efficiency Within a Problem-Driven BID Approach

2.1 Existing BID Approaches

Approaches

In general, BID practice can be carried out either as solution-based or as problem-driven [6–9]. Both the solution-based and problem-driven approaches have different starting points and different characteristics as design processes [10].

The solution-based approach describes the biomimetic development process in which the knowledge extracted from a biological system of interest is the starting point for the technical design. On the other hand, the problem-driven approach is the biomimetic development process that seeks to solve a practical problem with an identified problem as the starting point for the process [9, 10].

Our aim being to foster the usage of the biomimetics throughout the industry, the following presented work will focus on the problem-driven approach of biomimetics as this approach seems more appropriate to be initiated by industrial companies (i.e. the process starts within the technical field) while being less represented among commercially available biomimetic products [11].

Processes

Within the last decade the problem-driven approach of biomimetics has often been described in literature (e.g. [6, 10, 12]).

All the identified BID processes include a step of biological analogy research. This critical phase is tackled with great disparity as some work are only including it without any mention of how to perform it.

The following table attempts to classify some of the BID processes of reference according to the level of detail they provide to search for biological analogy (Table 1).

It is noticeable that among the listed processes, only the "what to search for" is clearly stated every time. Only two processes [18, 19] appears to clearly disclose their

Table 1. Level of details discloses by the BID processes of reference on the biological analogy search step.

Publication	Disclose how to search	Disclose what to search for	Disclose where to search	Prescribe a partnership with biological experts
[12]	X	✓	X	X
[13]	X	✓	X	X
[5]	X	✓	X	✓
[14]	X	✓	✓	X
[15]	X	✓	✓	✓
[10]	X	✓	✓	✓
[16]	✓	✓	X	X
[17]	✓	✓	X	X
[18]	✓	✓	✓	✓
[19]	✓	✓	✓	✓

entire strategy of analogical research. Furthermore, invoking a partnership with biologists is not a common recommendation, despite that it seems inevitably beneficial prima face: one could hardly consider initiating the construction of a plane without the supervision of an aerospace specialist. As a conclusion, even if it seems reasonable to rapidly be confronted to the diversity of the living world without attempting to create a dedicated research strategy, a proper description of the task seems of great importance.

Several tools have proven themselves to provide a relevant analysis of how living systems work in order to transpose their strategies to the technical world [3]. However, the identification of potentially relevant organisms shows methodological weaknesses:

- Their lack of recommendation during the search phase
- Their lack of organizational framework to classify the research results.
- Their lack of short iterative loops during the search phase

The presented work relies on the Unified Problem-Driven Process of Biomimetics on its process aspect [3]. This metaprocess is based on a representative set of 12 different presentations of the process aligned with the problem-solving process [20] to illustrate an holistic perspective on the state of the process models (Fig. 1).

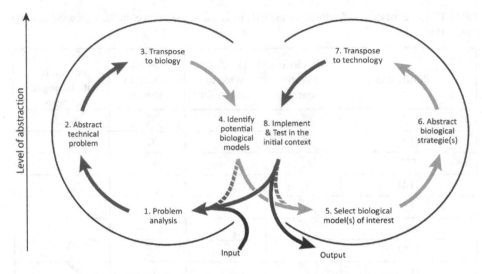

Fig. 1. The unified problem-driven process of biomimetics [3]

2.2   How Do Design Theories May Contribute to BID

TRIZ

TRIZ, the Russian acronym standing for theory of inventive problem solving, offers a theoretical frame to the evolution of technical systems. In addition to that, TRIZ provide a wide array of methods and tools in order to guide the cognitive process of designers towards innovative solutions. Based on the analysis of many patents, on the study of psychological behavior of inventors and on the scientific literature, Genrich S. Alshuller, inventor of the theory, formulated evolutions laws for technical systems, concepts, framework and tools allowing to better understand essential problematics to guide the creative process towards effective and usually innovative paths.

TRIZ originality resides both in its deterministic frame of reference, technical systems (regardless of their environmental context), follows a set of evolution laws [21], and in its ability to provide models of solutions (e.g. generic principles, separation principles and standards) [22] (Fig. 2).

During the modelling phase, resources from the working group are largely engaged to describe the technical system investigated by the project. TRIZ key concepts, such as evolution laws or ideality, provide a highly structural work frame to build a shared and innovative vision of both the technical problem to be solved and of the goal to reach to meet the established target [23]. Through the implementation of the TRIZ modelling tools, the level of understanding of the investigated system rapidly clarifies itself to create a shared area of knowledge, common to every participants.

The shared vision of a problem to be addressed as a matter of priority, combined with a strong convergence of perspective on the objectives to establish, condition the productivity of the models of solution required to be implemented from a performance standpoint: quantity, quality, level of details of the concepts of idea cards, comprehensiveness, convergence (especially through the concept of contradiction to overcome).

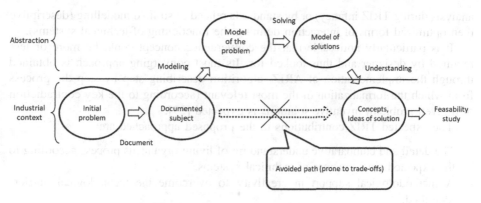

Fig. 2. General overview of TRIZ

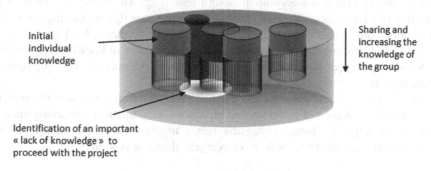

Fig. 3. Illustration of how the area of knowledge evolves during a TRIZ study

The modelling step is, by itself, a way for designer to acquire a creative posture through the creation of a skewed understanding, obtained by the definition of the Ideal Final Result (IFR) or the Multi-Screen Diagram (which provides a way to overcome mental inertia through the description of an ideal solution and the definition of the evolution of a system according to several systemic levels). This is reinforced through a deeper analysis of the technical scope (qualification and quantification of the physical phenomena involved).

While constituting a systematic approach in certain steps of the creative process (formalization of key contradictions), these methods induce significant adjustments within the problem space. It is thus quite common to observe brief iterations of the initial set of specifications in advance of a refocus on subtopics blocking the designers in a trade-off situation. According to Deguio and Cavallucci [24], formalizing a contradiction can be perceived as solution concept within the C space of the C-K theory [25, 26]. Solution space is also subjects to alterations: concepts are concentrated (channeling of the cognitive process by the problem models and prior expression of the IFR) and more precise, from a technical standpoint, through the implementation of generic principles of solution (initial tool resulting from the synthesis of the patents analysis during TRIZ infancy) or by standards related to su-field modelling (descriptive then optimized forms of interaction defining the functioning of technical systems).

It is particularly noticeable that the convergence concept could be more or less required by designer and thus looked for. Its most converging approach is obtained through the implementation of ARIZ, algorithm describing step by step the process from which the formalization of the most relevant (according to the key contradiction of a given problem) inventive solutions is expected [27].

The expected TRIZ contributions to the proposed approached are:

– The detail and comparative understanding of living organisms process according to the expected performances of technical systems.
– A methodological support in creativity to overcome the technological barriers identified.

C-K Theory

The C-K theory [25] is a theory upon design reasoning. The theory is rooted in the distinction of a Knowledge Space (K) from a Concept Space (C), structuring the mutual nurturing of both spaces through operators interconnecting them (See Fig. 3).

The K → C operator describes the addition or subtraction of knowledge chips from the Knowledge Space to the Concept Space. One example of K → C operator embodiment is the generation of alternatives.

The C → C operator involves the expansion of the Concept Space through the mathematical elaboration of partitions and inclusions, resulting in a tree arrangement of concepts. Concepts horizontal expansion refers to the divergent thinking process, where vertical expansion results from convergent thinking processes [26].

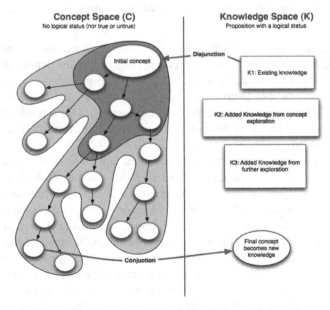

Fig. 4. Illustration of the concept space and the knowledge space as described by the C-K theory

The C $\rightarrow$ K operator describes activities usually involved during the detail design phases. This operator models actions such as concept validation or invalidation though the attribution of a logical status within the Knowledge Space.

The K $\rightarrow$ K operator refers to activities related to the Knowledge Space expansion. Such activities are induced by experimental deduction mechanisms. Activities related to knowledge creation may thus be modeled through this operator [26].

The main C-K Theory contribution to the presented approach is the creative posture induced by the constitution of two distinctive space (Concept and Knowledge) and the formalism through the process of building the tree to identify, in an exhaustive way, the physical process related to a given function.

2.3 Proposal of a New Model

The proposed approach aims at making it easy for industrial structures to be able to build their own solutions database which could be used on various problems. Autonomy is thus set as an important criterion, as no methodological prerequisites should be required. The proposed model is based on the work of APTE® [28] and their technological path tree. Similarly to a tree, the initial focus is set on the trunk, representing the main goal. The trunk is then subdivided in branches, representing the principles, themselves leading to a spray of solutions, the leaves. This model has notably been used in offshore oil projects [29].

In order to nurture the existing biomimetic toolset, the presented proposal is an hybridization of the technological path tree and the C-K theory. The APTE model contribution is its ability to decompose and to precisely describe functions to performs, while C-K theory is used for its formalism of relevant knowledge spaces.

In regards of the processes introduced in Sect. 2.1, the construction of the tree has been thought to occur between steps 2 and 3, when the initial problem is known and properly defined and when designers are able to depict an initial set of specification, in particular through the identification of contradictions (especially from a TRIZ perspective).

The tree, as illustrated in Fig. 4, has been made to be built in a team effort, allowing an immediate gathering of a larger knowledge base while generating dialogue upon its layout.

In its first cell, on the left, is stated the main objective, a concept, as induced by the C-K definition: a neither right or wrong proposition. This objective can be formalized from an expressed need by the working group thanks to the disjunction principle. Close to this initial concept, designers are invited to add a supplementary box to precise the different expected conditions to be realized through the concept (Fig. 5).

The implementation of the tree is then achieved from the left to the right, by adding proposals allowing to reach the stated objective from the box they are originating. To fulfill this model, designers are asked to answer the "How?". From a C-K point of view, the transition from the first box to the second is correlated to the K $\rightarrow$ C operator.

The early disconnection of "chemically" and "physically" within the fulfilling process seems interesting in the way that it allows, in addition of promoting creativity, the quick emergence of two sets of principles.

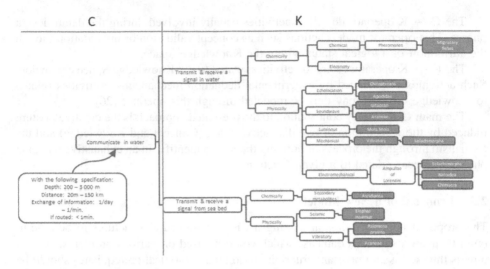

Fig. 5. Technological path tree applied to offshore oil [29]

The physicochemical principles search is a difficult task within the process, to ease it, designers may find assistance from thesaurus, literature or any other existing formalized resources.

Once the principles are identified, the work consists of connecting living organisms or even natural phenomena, in order to answer the "who?" question. For illustrative purposes, if one identifies the "transmission of a signal in an underwater environment" principle from a "physical" perspective, its personal knowledge may allow him to connect with the "cetacean" (e.g. dolphins) as a living organism embodying the principle. If the initial existing knowledge does not allow to create pathways to a living specie, tapping into formalized and accessible existing knowledge constitutes a good way to proceed. To be in line with the C-K theory, interconnection between identified principles and living species are Knowledge space extension: proposals made are ascertainable, waiting for the acquisition of the specific knowledge related to the implementation of the initial concept.

Following the implementation of the tree, a step to assemble documentation supporting the identified species, in particular the implementation in practice of the principles, is required.

3 Case Study

In order to assess the relevancy of the proposed tool, a case study followed-up with meetings and discussions has been implemented. This case study has been conducted through an industrial partnership with a Research & Development service department from a company working in the off-shore oil production sector. Its topic focuses on subsea filtration.

3.1   Hypothesis

The present work revolves around the following issue: "How to nurture the BID toolset to ease its adoption by an industrial structure with no prior biological background?"
Hypotheses are as follows:

- The creation of a double hybrid tree allows the increasing of the comprehensiveness of the potential bioinspired solutions. Thus, the use of an element to structure the techno-centered approach allows the exhaustiveness of the divergent thinking to be increased up. Combined with an analysis of the highlighted technological pathways, the approach will also increase the understanding of the phenomena which correlate technical and biological systems, by refocusing the problematic.
- The creation of a double hybrid tree facilitates the integration of biologists within the BID process. The depth of the tree, from macro to micro, allows to effectively point at areas of expertise to be questioned.

3.2   Methodology

Work with Student

As part of their final project of their penultimate year of engineering school, five students of the "École Nationale Supérieure des Arts et Métiers" agreed to work on a bio-inspired design product. In accordance to the case study, topic was set to tackle subsea filtration; purpose of their work was to design a "bio-inspired filtering system able to clean sea water". These students were mainly trained in mechanical engineering:

- Two of them where originating from preparatory classes for the grandes écoles.
- Two of them where orinigating from a DUT (University Technology Degree) in mechanical engineering.
- One of them initially studied medicine two year before its reorientation.

The hybrid tree has not been introduced to the student. Students where instead introduced to "classical" BID process, in order for them to better understand the challenges and issues of each step. They had access to every resources they were able to grasp (scientific literature, internet, experts, AskNature, etc.). The case study went on for approximately 12 h over 3 days.

Work with Biologists

In addition to the students' work, meetings with 2 fundamental biologists from the Pierre et Marie Curie University (Paris 5) has been performed. After an introduction to the industrial challenge, a debate on the methodological means to design creative biologically inspired solutions was initiated.

3.3   Results

The work done by the students has led to three bioinspired concepts:

- A set of variants from the sponges (phylum: Porifera)
- The use of mucus secreted by certain jellyfishes (subphylum: Medusozoa)
- The use of a principle of fluid mechanics from carpet sharks (order: Orectolobiformes)

Our goal here is not to delve into all the specificities of the developed concepts but rather to depict and discuss the relevancy of the methodology applied.

Consulted biologists were aware of the bio-inspired design approach as they were already supervising some pedagogical projects on the topic; they were aware of its actual customs and success stories. Focus was thus set on the context of the project and the company requirements.

The presentation of the proposed tool, the hybridized tree, was very much appreciated, as they were already projecting themselves in how they could be able to contribute to its fulfillment (in nurturing the branches extremities with both physicochemical principles and specific species). One constructive feedback was the outline of the definition of physicochemical strategies which seemed more suitable, according to them, for engineers than biologists. From their perspective, few biologists would be able to have the appropriate knowledge to contribute on how to "refine the problem" and the "functional analysis". Second, the discussion tackled the accessibility to resources and knowledge. On that specific topic, they stressed the importance of integrating biologists early in the design phases. An argument was that they were able to access researcher databases, allowing them to gather a large amount of information. This information could even be completed from their experiences and professional network which they can tap into with great ease. Finally, the subject of the competencies required to correctly interpret biological scientific publication was addressed. When considering the level of detail required by the BID process, possessing skill on that matter might be an important asset to decompose and understand biological strategies.

4 Discussion

The first observation with regard to implementation of the student's work is that species which they have found interest were already identified through the hybrid tree they did not have access to. This tree, compose of around twenty biological inputs, tends to show that it might be a good way to increase the exhaustiveness of the identification of the potential solutions to be investigated. On that aspect, the tree has the advantage to provide a clear methodology to guide the search process of biological strategies comparatively to the intuitive and disorganized research that is, for example, the keyword search.

One could also note that student focused on underwater species. If this may seem logical, considering the fact that the filtration system should, ultimately, operate in an underwater environment, it severely reduces the research scope.

On another note, interesting comments were made by students: they all agreed on the lack of resources they experienced in order to describe the identified phenomena. Being able to describe how the filtering system of the shark works, for example, were not an easy task for them. "Too much text, not enough figures", is one way to summarize their comments, which emphasize the preference of engineering students for schematics. In the following of the study of the variants of existing sponges in order to nurture their concept, students realized the heterogeneity of the filtration function embodiment according to the species considered. Somewhat like technical system, more or less complex, the use of TRIZ and its evolution laws could be used to learn more on the different biological strategies.

Meeting biological experts provided numerous answers. First, introducing an initially fulfilled hybrid tree to them, allowed them to directly contribute to it: they were able to nurture the branches from a biological perspective while being able to formalize some biological strategies.

The hybrid tree also allowed to exchange on the specific topic of filtration. Even with a background in biology, a comprehensive knowledge in macroscopic biology is difficult to possess. However, fulfilling the hybrid tree constitutes a relevant way to gather sufficient information to be able to discuss with experts.

At the end of the case study one question mark remains: should the tree be created with biologists or not? From the gathered experience, the answer slightly leans towards the no side. Working with biologists is interesting in order to obtain a direct competency or a knowledge input, but induces a non-synergetic effect. While the tree eases the interaction with the biologists and allows them to directly contribute to the work, their early involvement induces process counterparts, i.e. their identification, recruitment and engagement with few gathered knowledge on the topic. When it considering an optimal way for biologists to contribute, the pre-establishment of an initial tree comes to mind, as a way to both formalized a first batch of knowledge and to ease their involvement.

5 Conclusion

The presented work aims at developing a creative approach reinforced by the addition of biological knowledge while working on a design task or a problem resolution context. The paper introduces a hybrid tree including principles from both TRIZ and C-K theory.

During the case study, revolving around designing a new filtration system, new promising concepts has arisen. A concept of a self-cleaning vortex filtration system including a flow separation has notably drawn the industrial partner's attention. Initially, the storage function opposes itself to the flow function. Research is therefore naturally focused on living organisms implementing flow separation in fluid environment. The use of the tree initiated a change of view on the relation of current filters and impurities reservoir, to allow the consideration of an infinite flow capacity reservoir. While the part of serendipity within the process is hard to measure, the use of the presented hybrid tree has unequivocally contributed to the emergence of the new concepts.

Existing BID approaches ranges from methods based on intuition in which users have sufficient space to manoeuvre and automatic methods which use tools such as databases, seeking to disconnect users from the research process, i.e. tools operating as a black box from which a justification of the correlation between the input and the output is not clearly formalized. In our case, the presented approach provides all the reading grids to users performing a manual yet guided search without losing the "why" and the "how" of the considered research. The presented hybrid tree empowers designers in the sense that they remain in charge at any point of the accomplished work, which is not the case when considering automatic methods. The empowering of designers is achieved while their knowledge improvement is enhanced, both on the way to properly conduct the research but also on the underlying biological principles and their relation to their engineering counterparts, which is not covered by intuitive methods.

Future work should focus on the integration of the semantic approach and its considerable potential to populate the hybrid tree. This could be an effective way to reduce the time required to create a hybrid tree while raising its effectiveness to point at potential biological solutions in an exhaustive way.

References

1. Benyus, J.M.: Biomimicry: Innovation Inspired by Nature (1997)
2. Smith, M.H.: The Natural Advantage of Nations: Business Opportunities, Innovation and Governance in the 21st Century. Earthscan, London (2013)
3. Fayemi, P.-E.: Innovation par la conception bio-inspirée: proposition d'un modèle structurant les méthodes biomimétiques et formalisation d'un outil de transfert de connaissances. Dissertation, ENSAM, Paris (2016)
4. Wanieck, K., Fayemi, P.-E., Jacobs, S.: Biomimetics and its tools (2017)
5. Speck, T., Harder, D., Speck, O.: BIOKON centers in brief–Freiburg. In: BIOKON Bionik-Kompetenz-Netz–Creative Transfer of Biological Principles into Engineering, pp. 42–43 (2006)
6. Vattam, S., Helms, M.E., Goel, A.K.: Biologically-inspired innovation in engineering design: a cognitive study (2007)
7. Gebeshuber, I.C., Drack, M.: An attempt to reveal synergies between biology and mechanical engineering. Proc. Inst. Mech. Eng. Part C J. Mech. Eng. Sci. **222**, 1281–1287 (2008)
8. Baumeister, D., Tocke, R., Dwyer, J., Ritter, S.: Biomimicry Resource Handbook: A Seed Bank of Best Practices. Biomimicry 3.8, Missoula (2013)
9. ISO/TC266: Biomimetics - terminology, concepts and methodology, ISO 18458:2015. Beuth Verlag, Berlin (2015)
10. Goel, A.K., Vattam, S., Wiltgen, B., Helms, M.: Information-processing theories of biologically inspired design. In: Goel, A., McAdams, D., Stone, R. (eds.) Biologically Inspired Design, pp. 127–152. Springer, Heidelberg (2014). https://doi.org/10.1007/978-1-4471-5248-4_6
11. Jacobs, S.R., Nichol, E.C., Helms, M.E.: "Where are we now and where are we going?" The BioM innovation database. J. Mech. Des. **136**, 111101 (2014)
12. Helms, M., Vattam, S.S., Goel, A.K.: Biologically inspired design: process and products. Des. Stud. **30**, 606–622 (2009)
13. Bogatyrev, N.R., Vincent, J.F. Microfluidic actuation in living organisms: a biomimetic catalogue. In: Proceedings of the First European Conference on Microfluidics, Bologna, p. 175 (2008)
14. Vincent, J.F., Bogatyreva, O.A., Bogatyrev, N.R., Bowyer, A., Pahl, A.-K.: Biomimetics: its practice and theory. J. R. Soc. Interface **3**, 471–482 (2006)
15. Forniés, I.L., Muro, L.B.: A top-down biomimetic design process for product concept generation. Int. J. Des. Nat. Ecodynamics **7**(1), 27–48 (2012)

16. Gramann, J., Lindemann, U.: Engineering design using biological principles. In: International Design Conference. The Design Society, Dubrovnik (2004)
17. Sartori, J., Pal, U., Chakrabarti, A.: A methodology for supporting "transfer" in biomimetic design. AI EDAM **24**(4), 483–506 (2010)
18. Lenau, T.A.: Biomimetics as a design methodology-possibilities and challenges. In: DS 58-5: Proceedings of ICED 09, the 17th International Conference on Engineering Design, vol. 5, Design Methods and Tools (pt. 1), Palo Alto, CA, USA, 24–27 August 2009, pp. 121–132 (2009)
19. Schild, K., Herstatt, C., Lüthje, C.: How to use analogies for breakthrough innovations (No. 24). Working Papers/Technologie-und Innovations management. Technische Universität Hamburg-Harburg (2004)
20. Massey, A.P., Wallace, W.A.: Understanding and facilitating group problem structuring and formulation: Mental representations, interaction, and representation aids. Decis. Support Syst. **17**(4), 253–274 (1996)
21. Savransky, S.D.: Engineering of Creativity: Introduction to TRIZ Methodology of Inventive Problem Solving. CRC Press, Boca Raton (2000)
22. Altshuller, G., Al'tov, G., Altov, H.: And Suddenly the Inventor Appeared: TRIZ, the Theory of Inventive Problem Solving. Technical Innovation Center Inc., Worcester (1996)
23. Dupont, G.: TRIZ ou comment stimuler l'innovation en R&D. Société des Ingénieurs de l'Automobile (2002)
24. Rasovska, I., Dubois, S., De Guio, R.: Comparaison des modes de résolution de méthodes d'optimisation et d'invention (2009)
25. Hatchuel, A., Weil, B.: CK theory. In: Proceedings of the Herbert Simon International Conference on Design Sciences, vol. 15, p. 16, March 2002
26. Le Masson, P., Weil, B., Hatchuel, A.: Les processus d'innovation: Conception innovante et croissance des entreprises. Lavoisier, Paris (2006)
27. Altshuller, G.S., Victory, A.M.: Algorithm of inventive problem solving (ARIZ-85C). In: Methodological materials for trainees of the seminar "Methods of solving scientific and engineering problems"-L.: Leningrad Metal Works (1985)
28. de la Bretesche, B. (ed.): La méthode APTE: Analyse de la valeur, analyse fonctionnelle. Ed. Pétrelle, Paris (2000)
29. Chauvel, M.: Rapport de projet de recherche au LCPI. Short and Long Term Innovation Tools for Oil & Gas Offshore Challenges (2015)

Application of Standard Solution to Human-Machine-Environment Coupling Effect

Junlei Zhang[1,2(✉)], Run-Hua Tan[1,2], Guozhong Cao[1,2],
and Jian-Guang Sun[1,2]

[1] Hebei University of Technology, Tianjin 30013, China
1031186264sat@gmail.com
[2] National Engineering Research Center for Technological Innovation Method
and Tool, Tianjin 300130, China

Abstract. The reasonable design of human-machine-environment system is closely related to the automation and intelligence of industries. However, there is a lack of suitable analytical method and indicative solutions to the problems when the couplings of man, machine and environment fail to achieve the design. This paper compares the coupling as the Su-Field model, then the problems can be solved under the guidance of the standard solutions. Firstly, the set of constraint factors of the man, machine and environment are established respectively and the coupling between them are carried out. Secondly, the Su-Field model composed of people, machine and environment are established to analyze the problems in the coupling by analogy. Finally, under the guidance of the standard solutions, the problem are solved and the ideal coupling effects are realized. This method effectively solves the problem in the coupling of human, machine, environment and improves the rationality and effectiveness of the system design.

Keywords: Human-machine-environment system · Constrain · Coupling effect
Substance-field model · Standard solution

1 Introduction

Human-Machine-Environment system mainly researches the interdependent relations and laws between the three elements: H = human, M = machine and E = environment [1, 2]. In order to make the system more secure, efficient and economical for serving the human, we need to coordinate the relations among the three elements and optimize the system continuously.

The importance of ergonomics in modern engineering technology and product design has been recognized [3]. There has been a great deal of research and application on the design methods of the H-M-E system [4, 5].The design process of the H-M-E system (see Fig. 1). Generally includes the following steps:

Step 1: Establish the overall goal of H-M-E system design: operator attribute positioning, machine, working environment.
Step 2: Decompose the total target into multiple subsystems involving the H-M-E system: human-machine interaction, human-environment interaction, and machine-environment interaction.

D. Cavallucci et al. (Eds.): TFC 2018, IFIP AICT 541, pp. 266–275, 2018.
https://doi.org/10.1007/978-3-030-02456-7_22

Step 3: Analyze the relevant design constraints in the interaction process of each subsystem.

Step 4: Combine the above design requirements to design each subsystem.

Step 5: Perform the coupling of each subsystem to complete the system design.

Around this design process, the research content of human-machine system is mainly concentrated on the following aspects:

The geometric dimension design of products based on human body size measurement [6]; design for the comfort of the product based on human body working posture [7]; human-computer interaction design based on the research of user's vision, color attributes, human psychology etc. [8]; research on reliability of Human-Machine operating system [9].

The above research content mainly focuses on the establishment of the front-end design of the system–the adaptation constraints of the H-M-E system. But for the post-design–there is a lack of further analysis on the problems and solutions to the problems in the coupling process of three elements based on the adaptation constraints built in the front-end design. According the characteristics of the three elements in the H-M-E system, this paper proposes to analyze the problems in the coupling process of the H-M-E system through the Su-Field model in the TRIZ theory. And then solve the problem under the guidance of the Standard Solutions. The research expects some useful explorations in the design of the H-M-E system.

2 Establishment of the Set of Constraints for the H-M-E System

The process of product design is to weigh the various design constraints in order to achieve design goals. In this process, designers need to coordinate various design constraints. So the product design is a process of solving constraints essentially [10]. Human, machine and the environment are the three basic elements of the system design and each element has its own special characteristics. These characteristics constitute the constraints when the elements fit and interact with each other (see Fig. 2).

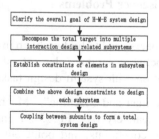

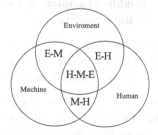

Fig. 1. H-M-E system decision process.

Fig. 2. A H-M-E system relationship.

For the establishment of the H-M-E system, designers and engineers must establish the design constraints of each of the three elements in conjunction with the design task at first. Then, do the coupling between the three elements of human, machine, and environment combined with the constraints. Discover problems that do not meet the constraints in the coupling process. The process is as follows:

2.1   The Set of Constraints for the Human, Denoted as H

According to human attributes and characteristics, human-related constraints in the H-M-E system mainly include two types, one is personal ability, that is, constraints related to physical strength and brain power; the other is limitation of personal experience.

Personal ability mainly includes age, gender, physical characteristics parameters, physical disability, work posture, etc. People's cognitive ability and psychological characteristics, etc.;

Personal experience mainly includes the mother tongue, cultural background, cultural level, professional skills and experience in using technical products [1, 2].

2.2   The Set of Constraints for the Machine, Denoted as M

Mainly include the Industry manufacturing standards, functional specifications, process constraints, physical size constraints, component connection methods, maintainability, error-proof design, costs and other requirements [1, 2].

2.3   The Set of Constraints for the Environment, Denoted as E

Environment constraints mainly refer to working conditions and external environmental conditions when the machine is running. Extreme conditions have a great influence on the human, operating processes and the run of the machine. This section mainly includes temperature, humidity, light, ventilation, color, and ideology under specific conditions [1, 2].

2.4   Establish Coupling Between Elements and Discover Problems in the Coupling

Applying the necessary constraints, designers and engineers need to find problem in the coupling process of the three elements. The coupling between the three elements of the H-M-E system is established in two steps in combination with system design tasks.

Step 1: Establish the coupling model between "Human and Machine", "Machine and Environment", "Human and Environment" separately (see Fig. 3). Identify whether the couplings between elements meet the constraints, and point out the problems that do not meet the constraints;

Step 2: Establish the coupling model between "Human, Machine, and Environment" (see Fig. 4). Identify whether the couplings between elements meet the constraints, and point out the problems that do not meet the constraints.

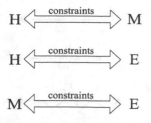

Fig. 3. The first step of the coupling.

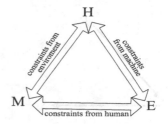

Fig. 4. The second step of the coupling.

3 Analysis of the Problems in the Coupling Process of the Elements

In the design of the H-M-E system, the establishment of the set of constraints is the front-end of the system design process. For the problems in the coupling of the three elements, we need to make further analysis and propose appropriate solutions to improve the design of the H-M-E system.

3.1 Su-Field Model

Translate complex system problems into simple models is a common problem analysis method. The Su-Field model is applied to describe the technology system and analyze system problems from the perspective of functional effects. Three elements(two substances and one field) are used to describe a technical system [11] (see Fig. 5). In the figure, F represents the field, S_1 and S_2 represent the substance. The significance of this model is that: S_2 has an action on S_1 in order to change S_1, through the role of field F [12].

The realization of the system functionality is a result of the interaction between multiple components in the system. Considering the results of the functionality, there are three types:

(1) Effective functionality with all three elements: the function of a technical system with all three elements(F, S_1 and S_2) are effective. Designers pursuit of this effect. The model is shown in Fig. 6(a).
(2) Non-effective functionality with all three elements: All three elements in a technical system exist, but the effects pursued by the designers have not been fully realized. E.g the generated force is not large enough and the temperature is not high enough. So the design of the system ought to be improved to meet the requirements. The model is shown in Fig. 6(b).
(3) Harmful functionality with all three elements: The three elements in a technical system are all present, but the effect of the system is conflict with the designer's pursuit. The harmful functionality model is shown in Fig. 6(c). In the process of product design, it is necessary to eliminate the harmful functions in the system.

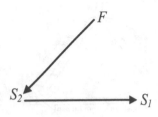

Fig. 5. Su-field model.

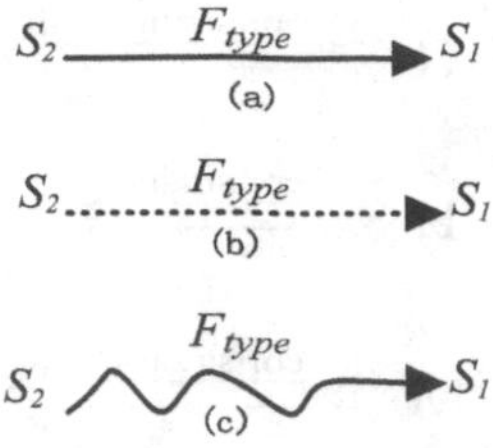

$$S_2 \xrightarrow{\quad F_{type} \quad} S_1$$
(a)

$$S_2 \cdots\cdots\xrightarrow{\quad F_{type} \quad} S_1$$
(b)

$$S_2 \xrightarrow[\quad(c)\quad]{\quad F_{type} \quad} S_1$$

Fig. 6. Effect of components.

The Su-Field model describes the specific problem in a system as a simple relationship between three elements. It can more intuitively analyze the functional relationships and effects between system elements. This is very important for designers to further analyze and solve problems improving the system design.

3.2   Establish the Su-Field Model for the Coupling of the H-M-E System Through Analogy

Human, machines and the environment are the three basic elements that make up the H-M-E technology system and implement the system design functions. The requirement of the machine from human is based on the specific environment in which the user work. So in the H-M-E system, human, machines and the environment are integral. The working mechanism of the system can be described simply as: human (H) operates the machine (M), under certain environment (E) to achieve the intended goal. In this process, the interaction between any two elements is under the "constraint" established by the third one, and the interaction and the effect of the interaction between any two elements must take place under the influence of the third one. The interaction models are shown in Figs. 3 and 4.

However, the current graphical description of the H-M-E system can only indicate that there is interaction between the three. For the interaction effect between the three elements, there is a lack of visual and effective graphic or symbolic description. Therefore, when designers describe the coupling effect between elements in the H-M-E system, they usually can not describe the problem effectively, which is not conducive for the designers to the further analysis and solution of the problem.

The Su-Field model describes the specific problem in a system as a simple relationship between three elements. It can more intuitively analyze the functional relationships and effects between system elements. This is very important for designers to further systematically analyze problems, apply invention principles and standard solutions to improve system design.

Therefore, in order to analyze the coupling effect of the H-M-E technology system, optimize the relationship between the three elements and improve the design effect of the H-M-E system, a method of solving problems by analogy has been developed. From three aspects: the basic meaning of the model expression, the form of the model, and the relationship between the components of the model, the Su-Field model and the H-M-E system model are compared, under the guidance of the analogy in the design

process. By analogy, the relationship between the three elements of the H-M-E technology system is further described as the following three cases:

(1) Under certain environmental conditions, human and machines can interact with
    each other. At this point, the role of the environment is seen as field F, denoted as
    F_E. Human and machine are regarded as substance S, and denoted as S_H and S_M
    respectively. The relationship between the three is represented in Fig. 7(A) and (a).
(2) Under the control and intervention of human, machine and environment can
    interact with each other. At this time, the role of the human is considered as field
    F, denoted as F_H. Environment and machine are considered as substance S,
    denoted as S_E and S_M respectively. The relationship between the three is shown in
    Fig. 7(B) and (b).
(3) Under the cooperation of the machine, human adapt to or change the environment.
    At this time, the role of the machine is considered as field F, denoted as F_M.
    Human and the environment are regarded as substance S, and are denoted as S_H
    and S_E. The relationship between the three is represented in Fig. 7(C) and (c).

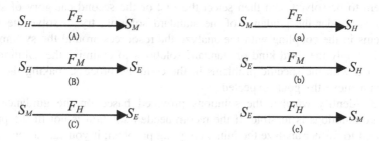

Fig. 7. Su-field model of the H-M-E system.

3.3 Analysis of the Problems in the Coupling Process

Process 1.4 describes the coupling process of the three elements of the H-M-E system
and find out the problems in the process. Combined with the description in 2.2.1,
establish the Su-Field model for the specific problems in the coupling process. The
specific operation is as follows:

Step 1: Establish the coupling between the three elements of the H-M-E system
combined the system design tasks.

Step 2: Apply the necessary constraints and then analyze whether there is a problem
in the coupling between the three elements. Do a further analysis of the specific
issues in the coupling, identifying the S1 and S2 (Human and Machine, Machine
and Environment, Human and Environment) and the F(Human, Machine, Environment)affecting the interacting components.

Step 3: Combined with the model in Fig. 7, establish the corresponding Su-Field
model of the problems above according to the types of functionality between
components (Effective functionality, Non-effective functionality, Harmful
functionality).

4   Solution to the Coupling Problem in the Design of the H-M-E System

The essence of the H-M-E system design is to solve the problems in the process of the coupling between three elements of human, machine and environment under the guidance of constraint factors, and constantly optimize the system design to make the system more secure, efficient and economical.

Through the above process, the specific problems in the process of coupling have been standardized and described—the Su-Field model. The standard solutions in the TRIZ theory, provide a variety of effective guidance for the specific issues which have established Su-Field model. The standard solutions can inspire designers to quickly find solutions to problems.

For this study, designers mainly uses the first, second, and third standard solutions to solve the problems in the coupling of the elements in H-M-E system, and uses the fifth standard solutions to improve the new. The specific process is as follows:

> Step 1: Identify the types of functionality according to the Su-Field model of the problem to be solved, and then select the first or the second category of standard solutions. Under the guidance of the standard solution, try to solve the specific problems in the coupling with the analyze the resources around the system;
> Step 2: Apply the third kind of standard solutions to optimize the solution above combined with the specific problems in the coupling process, making the H-M-E system achieve the goals expected;
> Step 3: Identify whether the solutions provided based on the guidance of the standard solutions is feasible. If the recommended solution is not fit the problem, you need to further analyze the initial coupling problem; if you can accept it, apply the category 5th solutions to simplify the recommended solutions so that the final solution of the problem is closer to the ideal state.

5   Case Study

X-ray detectors were used to check whether lollipop density is uniform and whether the lollipop is mixed with other matter in the production of lollipops. Figure 10(a) shows the working process of the X-ray detector. According to the design method proposed in this paper, the relevant constraints are established to analyze the problems in the existing system and the system is further optimized.

5.1   The Main Constraints of Each Element Are as Follows

H = {the physical parameters and age of the staff, the main operating position is standing, the machine should be easy to operate and the information should be easy to identify, work space and personal safety are required, etc.}

M = {meet functional and technical requirements, functional modules are built-in as required, buttons are easy to operate, efficiency (correlated with the speed of the belt in the production line), suitable for mass production, safety and reliability, and necessary weather resistance etc.}

E = {normal room temperature, weak electromagnetic interference, adequate lighting, certain humidity and noise, fixed test location, etc.}

5.2 Identification and Analysis of the Problems

Firstly, establish a coupled model of the three elements: the staff, X-ray detector, and working environment (see Fig. 8). Identify whether the coupling between elements satisfies the system constraints and point out the problems that do not meet the constraints step by step.

By the above analysis, it was found that X-rays emitted from the X-ray detector (M) can shine on staff (H) in the working environment (E), doing harm to the staff. Because, the curtain on the detector need to be opened when the lollipop enters the X-ray detector. However, the X-rays will shine on the workers around the X-ray detector. The process of the detection is shown in Fig. 10(a). In this system, X-ray detector (S_M) needs to check the quality of lollipops ($S_{lollipop}$), but the X-ray detector (S_M) has a detrimental effect on the staff (S_H) under the work environment (S_E). A Su-Field model of the problem is established, as shown in Fig. 9.

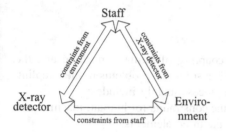

Fig. 8. The coupling between the elements.

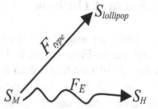

Fig. 9. The su-field model of the problem.

5.3 The Solution to the Problem

The harmful effects, for the safety of the staff (S_H), caused by X-ray detector (S_M) need to be eliminated. The standard solutions No. 9 and No. 10—add a substance or field to eliminate harmful effects provide solution to the problem.

With the same constraints and the system structure existed, the amount of change to the system is as small as possible, the cost is as low as possible, and it does not affect the operation of the staff. Under the guidance of the standard solutions, The improved scheme is shown in the Fig. 10(b):

Before the lollipops enter the X-ray detector with the conveyor belt, the straight conveyor belt is changed by the addition of guide rollers. The conveyor belt carries the lollipop, under the action of a guide roller, into the X-ray detector. As shown in Fig. 10 (b). The improved design avoids the X-rays doing harmful effect on the staff and meet the constraints of the system design.

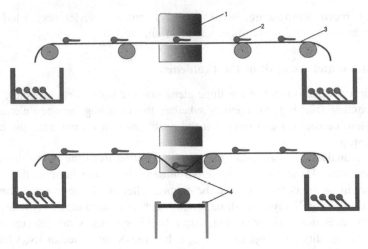

1.   X-ray detector, 2.Lollipop, 3.Conveyor belt, 4.Guide roller added

Fig. 10.   The lollipop detection system.

6   Conclusion and Outlook

This paper proposes an analogy between the coupling of human, machine and the environment and the Su-Field model in TRIZ. Then solve the problems in the coupling process with the aid of standard solutions. The process mainly includes:

In combination with design tasks, establish the constraints for human, machine and the environment, and make couplings between the three elements;

Establish Su-Field models consisting of three elements: human, machine, and the environment to analyze problems in the coupling;

According to analysis of the Su-Field models, the problems in the coupling process are solved under the guidance of standard solutions, and the ideal coupling effect is obtained.

This method can effectively solve the problems in the coupling of human, machine and environment in the H-M-E system; improve the system design process and make the H-M-E system design more reasonable and effective. The design of the H-M-E system requires a large number of experiments. Further research is needed in the establishment of database and systematic design method.

Acknowledgements. This paper is sponsored by Natural Science Foundation of China No. 51675159, No. 51305123 and the National Science and Technology Basic Project No. 2017IM040100, Special Project for Local Science and Technology Development under the Guidance of the Central Government No. 18241837G.

References

1. Wang, J.: Ergonomics in Product Design, 2nd edn. Chemical Industry Press, Beijing (2011)
2. Li, S.: Introduction to Interaction Design, 1st edn. Tsinghua University Press, Beijing (2009)
3. Liu, W.: Modern Human-Machine-Environment System Engineering, 1st edn. Beijing University of Aeronautics and Astronautics Press, Beijing (2009)
4. Yang, C., Chen, Y.: Research on integrated manufacturing system based on man-machine integration theory. Comput. Integr. Manuf. Syst. **6**(02), 51–54 (2000)
5. Tan, Y., Jun, W., Liu, Z., et al.: Research status and prospects of large complex man-machine system structure, process modeling and organization design method. Syst. Eng.-Theory Pract. **31**(S1), 73–81 (2011)
6. Gao, R., Guo, X., Xu, N.: Human factors and ergonomics in product design. Packag. Eng. **32**(22), 61–63 (2011)
7. Du, Y.: Research on modern office chair design based on human–machine–environment system engineering. In: Long, S., Dhillon, B.S. (eds.) Man-Machine-Environment System Engineering. LNEE, vol. 406, pp. 617–625. Springer, Singapore (2016). https://doi.org/10.1007/978-981-10-2323-1_69
8. Zhang, B., Ding, M., Li, Y.: Optimization design of human machine interaction interface based on visual perception. China Mech. Eng. **27**(16), 2196–2202 (2016)
9. Cheng, D., Hua, Y., Wang, Y., et al.: Research on active ergonomic design method for safety ergonomics. China Metalforming Equip. Manuf. Technol. **48**(06), 9–12 (2013)
10. Xiang, Z., Liang, G.: Product design method based on man-machine-environment constraints. Decoration **274**(02), 136–137 (2016)
11. Altshuller, G.: The innovation algorithm, TRIZ Systematic innovation and technical creativity. Technical Innovation Center Inc., Worcester (1999)
12. Runhua, T.: TRIZ and Applications–The Process and Methods of Technological Innovation, 1st edn. Higher Education Press, Beijing (2010)

Automatic Extraction and Ranking of Systems of Contradictions Out of a Design of Experiments

Hicham Chibane, Sébastien Dubois[✉], and Roland De Guio

CSIP, ICube Laboratory, INSA de Strasbourg,
24 bld de la Victoire, Strasbourg, France
sebastien.dubois@insa-strasbourg.fr

Abstract. This paper shows to what extent data used in design optimization process and TRIZ based models of contradictions can benefit from each other. New design often starts by optimizing existing systems by experimental and numerical means. This approach requires building a model linking on the one hand, a set of Action Parameters; and on the other hand, Evaluation Parameters measuring the quality of a solution. When none of the solutions satisfy the objectives, a redesign of the system is required. Our hypothesis in this paper is that the analysis of experimental or simulation data, can be used as input to automatically extract systems of contradictions, and moreover that it can help to make a ranking of these systems of contradictions.

In the article 3 ways to extract, out of Design of Experiments, and to prioritize Generalized Systems of Contradictions will be presented. These methods will be illustrated throughout a case study related to a cutting process.

Keywords: Generalized Systems of Contradictions · Design of Experiments Cross-fertilization optimization-invention

1 Introduction

The evolution of the design of products and manufacturing systems is leading to an increasing digitalization of design tools (big data analysis, simulation tools, computer-aided innovation, and s.o.). Many data related to this digitalization are gradually becoming available. We hypothesize that these tools contain a lot of information that artificial intelligence tools can use in the context of systems understanding and inventive design. Thus, for several years, we have addressed the development of contradiction identification tools based on experimental design data. This research forced us to clarify the concept of contradiction and propose the concept of generalized contradiction. Several methods for identifying contradictions are now available and we are moving into a phase of exploitation, improvement and validation of these tools in an inventive problem-solving context. The identification of contradiction systems has a dual purpose: (1) to thoroughly understand an invention or research problem; and (2) to be an input for problem-solving methods of invention such as TRIZ. This article proposes a feedback on the use of three methods of identifying contradictions from the

D. Cavallucci et al. (Eds.): TFC 2018, IFIP AICT 541, pp. 276–289, 2018.
https://doi.org/10.1007/978-3-030-02456-7_23

results of experimental design. In particular, we were curious to know if the strategies of reduction of the space of search of the contradictions of two of them are effective.

The paper is organized as follows. Section 2 below provides a brief review of the Design of Experiments (DoE) and of the work that led to the methods of identifying the contradictions that are employed in this study. Section 3 presents the case study and the results of the DoE; it is followed in Sect. 4 by the results of the identification of contradictions with the three studied methods. Finally Sect. 5 analyzes and discusses the results and concludes with the perspectives from this study.

2 Background

In this part will be presented, first a brief overview of Design of Experiments, then the classical TRIZ System of Contradictions, as well as some of its limits. Then the model of Generalized System of Contradictions, which enable to overcome these limits will be introduced, and also the first statements of the use of this generalized model.

2.1 Design of Experiments

Design of Experiments (DoE) is a powerful tool for analyzing, modeling and optimizing process. The term experiment is defined as the systematic procedure carried out under controlled conditions in order to discover an unknown effect, to test or to illustrate a known effect. When analyzing a process, experiments are often used to evaluate which process inputs have a significant impact on the process output, and what the target level of those inputs should be to achieve a desired result (evaluation parameters). Experiments can be designed in many different ways to collect this information.

Designed Experiments are also powerful tools to achieve manufacturing cost savings by minimizing process variation and reducing rework, scrap, and the need for inspection.

Appropriate data can be analyzed by statistical methods such as Response Surface Methodology (RSM) [1] and Linear Regression Methodology (LRM) [2]. Statistical validation of experimental design is necessary to draw meaningful conclusions from the data [3]. An effective alternative to the composite factorial design is the Central Composite Design (CCD), originally developed by Box and Wilson [4], and improved by Box and Hunter [5]. CCD gives as much information as a three levels factorial design, requiring a lower number of tests than the latter, and describes a majority of steady-state process responses.

In this study, the DoE was used to optimize the machining process of a composite material. The influences between several action and evaluation parameters were evaluated. The identification of contradictions from the DoE was developed. The resolution of these contradictions will allow to overcome the Pareto front (defined by the dominant points of the optimization space) of the solutions and to reach the targeted solution.

2.2 Classical TRIZ Systems of Contradictions Limits

The contradictions, in TRIZ, are recognized as being one powerful model to formulate the problems, as they well represent the limits of the considered system, and also because they are a strong cognitive tool to change the representation of the situation for human experts. Technical contradictions represent conflict at the system level, when two Evaluation Parameters (EP) of the specs cannot be satisfied together [6]. Physical Contradiction state the core of the problem, pointing out a design parameter which has to be in two different states to satisfy the previously identified conflicting Evaluation Parameters [7]. During the development of OTSM-TRIZ, Khomenko defined the System of Contradictions, linking the models of physical and technical contradictions and stating that "many Physical Contradictions may be linked to a given pair of Technical Contradictions" [8].

In [9] the authors have formulated the limit of this System of Contradictions, illustrating on a case example that a problem could occur for which it is impossible to formulate, formally, contradictions. Counter-examples were given that the presence of an OTSM-TRIZ System of Contradictions is not equivalent to the absence of solution. In such cases, human experts formulate problems but based on partial consideration of the model of the system, but considering the whole model, no such contradictions exist.

2.3 Generalized System of Contradictions (GSC)

To overcome the previously cited limitation, and to propose a model of contradictions that enable the equivalence between the absence of solution and the existence of contradictions, a generalization of the OTSM-TRIZ System of Contradictions was proposed in [9, 10]. This model is presented on Fig. 1, illustrating the difference between OTSM-TRIZ System of Contradictions and the generalized one, and how they can be recognized in table of experiments, where e_i are experiments, x_i are Action Parameters (AP) and y_i are Evaluation ones (EP). E_i and Y_i define sets of experiments or Action Parameters.

Furthermore, this model enables the automatic extraction of contradictions out of tables of experiments (which can, for example, be the result of Design of Experiments). In [11] the authors present an algorithm to identify the complete set of Generalized Technical Contradictions (GTC) from experiments. And in [12] the Generalized Physical Contradiction (GPC) is described through binary integer programming and an algorithm is proposed in order to identify and extract the complete set of Generalized Physical Contradictions. Thus this GSC generalized classical TRIZ system of contradictions, referring not only to pairs of EPs but to two sets of EPs, for the technical contradictions; and also to two different states of several APs for the physical one.

2.4 GSC Formulation and First Statements

The automatic extraction of the GSC have been performed throughout various examples and some ascertainments have been pointed out:

- In [11], the authors illustrated the big complexity in the search of technical and Generalized Technical Contradictions: there is a lot of GTC and the human expert is not able to deal with so many possibilities (more than 100 in the given example). Then the "best" set of GTC to solve the inventive problem have to be identified.

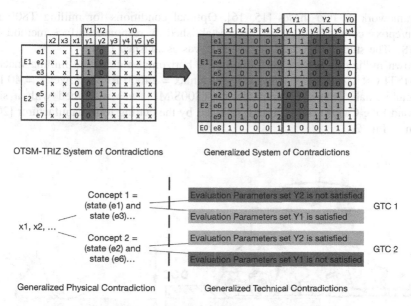

Fig. 1. OTSM-TRIZ and Generalized Systems of Contradictions

- In [12], the same kind of problem has been demonstrated, as for one selected GTC a huge number of GPC can be formulated (more than 3,000 in the given example).

Given these points, some questions have been formulated regarding the time to extract GSC, regarding the choice of the parameters to consider for building the problem model, and, finally, regarding the choice of the GSC to consider in priority to the others.

Another interesting result is the recognition that not all the GPC are equivalent in terms of resolution. If the formulated GPC can be very complex, the algorithm also enables the elicitation of "contextual" classical TRIZ physical contradictions, i.e., GPC were found with only one conflicting parameter. This means that they are equivalent to classical TRIZ contradiction but, under some conditions, which are defined by fixed values for the others action parameters [13].

In [14] a method was proposed to help in choosing the GTC to consider in priority and then the GSC that have the more weight on the chosen problem, based on the use of Feature Selection algorithm and based on the analysis of the Pareto frontier. In this article, 3 different ways to extract and choose the GSC to consider will be proposed and compared.

3 Case Study

3.1 Presentation of the Case

The experimental study was realized at the Center for Studies and Research on Cutting Tools (CEROC), Laboratory of Mechanics and Rheology (LMR), it was completed in the framework of two theses [15, 16]. Optimal conditions for milling T800 M21 carbon/epoxy composite material were established by response surface methodology [17, 18]. The study of the lead angle effect was established [19].

Down milling tests were performed on a horizontal high speed milling machine, PCI METEOR 10 HSK63A (spindle speed Nmax = 24000 RPM, Power P = 40 kW). The multi-axial composite carbon/epoxy T800S/M21 was machined with a single Diamond Like Carbon (DLC) insert provided by the cutting tool manufacturer [20] as shown in Fig. 2.

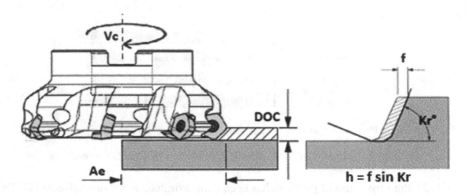

Fig. 2. Cutting tool and parameters

The axial depth of cut DOC was set at 1.04 mm, a thickness corresponding to four layers of carbon fabric, to avoid the effect of fiber orientation. The radial engagement ae was set at 50% of the tool diameter (ae = 36.4 mm). The cut length Lc is 55 mm.

The cutting conditions was tested with a depth of cut equals to four plies in order to minimize the influence of plies orientation. The orientation of the composite plies is described by [(45/90/135/0)16]s with ply thickness equal to 0.26 mm as illustrated in Fig. 3. Dry machining conditions were used during the experimental tests. The thickness h of the shaving depends on the feed rate f per tooth and the angle of attack Kr = 19° or 60°, and is given by equation: h = f × sin(Kr).

3.2 Design of Experiments and Action Parameters

To minimize the number of experiments, a central composite design (CCD) with 9 combinations was studied using two quantitative parameters, cutting speed (Vc) and chip thickness (h) as shown in Fig. 3. The same DOE has been doubled to take into account a qualitative parameter which is the lead angle Kr.

A diamond like carbon (DLC) with a thin film of 1 μm diamond coating has been tested through the experimental part. A 6% cobalt content cemented carbide has been chosen as a substrate. In Fig. 3, which shows the testing environment, an insert type PDKT0905DEFR11 with a Kr = 19° lead angle has been equipped on a penta high feed milling cutter from Safety manufacture. Another milling cutter called 'penta 60' has been used for Kr = 60° lead angle inserts.

Finally, the latter was repeated 3 times to take into account another qualitative parameter which is the coating of the cutting insert. Three diamond coatings were studied, a diamond like carbon (DB3), a micro-crystalline chemical vapor deposition (DSP3 N) and a nano-crystalline chemical vapor deposition (DB6).

The total number of experiments was 54.

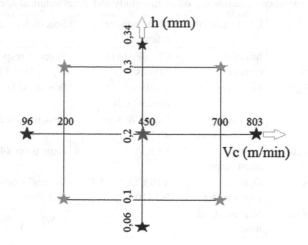

Fig. 3. Central composite design of experiment

Note that the central test was repeated 3 times.

The levels of machining parameters were chosen in accordance with the recommendations provided by the cutting tool manufacturer [21] as shown in Table 1.

Table 1. Machining parameters levels

Variables level	Quantitative parameters		Qualitative parameters	
Min (−1.21)	Cutting speed (m/min)	Chip thickness h (mm)	Lead angle Kr (°)	Coating of cutting insert
Min (−1)	96.5	0.06		
Mean (0)	200	0.1	19	DLC
Max (+1)	450	0.2		Micro-CVD
Max (+1.21)	700	0.3	60	Nano-CVD
	803.5	0.34		

3.3 Measuring Output Parameters (Evaluation Parameters)

In this study, several parameters related to the quality of machining parts were examined. Vibration levels (Arms), delamination length (DL), workpiece temperature

(T) and cutting force (Fmax), material removal rate (MRR), Surface roughness (Ra) and fiber flaking (FF), were measured for each test in one pass. The Table 2 summarizes the experimental methods used in this study and their technical specifications.

Table 2. Experimental methods used in this study and their technical specifications

Evaluation parameters	Used material	Manufacturer reference	Specificity
Workpiece temperature T (°)	Infrared camera	CEDIP, JADE MWIR	Spectral response 3 to 5 µm, fa = 176 Hz
Cutting forces F (N)	Force sensor	Kistler mod.9255B	fa = 10 kHz
Vibration levels Arms (m²/s).	Tri-axial accelerometer	(Brüel & Kjær 4520)	Sensitivities of 10 mV/g
Delamination length Ld (mm)	Stereo microscope	LEICA	Expansion x4
Surface roughness (µm)	Optical profilometer	VEECO, WYKO NT1100	Vertical resolution 0, 1 nm to 1 mm
Material removal rate (cm3/min)	Mathematical model		$MRR = \sqrt{\frac{ap \times f \times V_c \times a_e \times z}{\pi \times d}}$

3.4   Results of the Optimization

The purpose of this study was to find optimal configuration of machining process according to a defined situation. For example, an optimization situation that favors maximum production with a good surface roughness and without machining defects (flaking of the composite fibers, delamination of the composite folds and thermal degradation of the resin).

The choice of the values of the evaluation parameters targeted to was set according to the need sought, as shown in the Table 3.

The experiments were conducted and a part of this Design of Experiments is presented in Table 4.

Table 3. Targeted Evaluation Parameters

Evaluation parameters	Min	Max	Target
Workpiece temperature T (°)	0	80	Minimize
Cutting forces F (N)	0	200	Minimize
Vibration levels Arms (m²/s).	0	80	Minimize
Delamination length DL (mm)	0	0.1	Minimize
Fiber flaking FF (mm)	0	0.1	Minimize
Surface roughness Ra (um)	0	3	Minimize
Material removal rate MRR (cm3/min)	1200	2000	Maximize

Table 4. Design of Experiments

Test Number	Action Parameters (AP)				Evaluation Parameters (EP)						
	Coating of cutting insert	Lead angle Kr (°)	Cutting speed Vc (m/min)	Chip thickness h (mm)	Surface roughness Ra (μm)	Fiber flaking (mm)	Delamination length Ld (mm)	Workpiece temperature T (°)	Cutting forces F (N)	Material Removal Rate MRR (cm3/min)	Vibration levels Arms (m²/s)
test 1	DB3	19	96,5	0,2	11,26	3,30	0,00	56,41	164,4 1	754,56	61,94
test 2	DB3	19	200	0,1	4,20	2,10	0,00	95,00	302,7 8	1532,4 3	73,88
test 3	DB3	19	200	0,3	11,12	3,70	0,00	67,00	129,1 4	464,42	160,15
test 4	DB3	19	450	0,06	2,35	0,00	0,00	122,0 0	461,2 2	933,05	85,30
test 5	DB3	19	450	0,2	19,00	2,40	0,00	101,3 3	207,2 8	493,50	141,60
test 6	DB3	19	450	0,34	9,44	0,00	0,00	62,00	112,9 9	147,54	203,46
test 7	DB3	19	700	0,1	3,92	0,86	0,00	282,5 0	874,1 5	448,15	190,26
⋮	⋮		⋮					⋮			
test 50	DSP3 N	60	450	0,2	1,51	1,10	2,80	118,0 0	411,3 6	19,84	93,18
test 51	DSP3 N	60	450	0,34	2,59	2,00	6,10	98,00	285,2 8	12,86	113,78
test 52	DSP3 N	60	700	0,1	0,90	0,00	0,52	159,0 0	580,2 4	32,71	79,24
test 53	DSP3 N	60	700	0,3	1,68	0,00	3,67	121,0 0	314,6 6	12,35	124,50
test 54	DSP3 N	60	803,5	0,2	2,11	0,00	3,20	134,0 0	381,0 5	13,17	128,74

4   Contradictions Analysis

The previously presented case study and the results on Table 4 show the limits of the solutions that can be reached by optimization methods. In the table, no test was performed enabling to satisfy all the EP. This problem can then be recognized as an inventive problem, and the search of contradictions can be performed. In the next parts, three ways to extract and choose the contradictions will be presented.

4.1   Exhaustive Extraction of Contradictions

In [11, 12] algorithms to extract automatically Generalized Systems of Contradictions were presented. A first algorithm is applied on a table of experiments, a GTC is chosen, and for the chosen GTC, the GPC are extracted with the second algorithm. In [22] it was proposed to choose as priority contradiction, the dominant one.

If applying the exhaustive extraction of GTC on the previous table, with 54 tests, 201 GTC are proposed. But only one covering all the 7 EP, this one can thus be easily recognized as the dominant one. For this dominant GTC, 156 GPC are extracted by the application of the second algorithm. The only way to prioritize these GPC are the easiness of the use for resolution, the easiness for interpretation, but no objective ranking. And about this easiness some GPC are recognized more interesting as they are so-called "contextual classical-TRIZ Physical Contradictions", as, under some defined context (fixed values for some AP) Physical Contradiction on one AP can be formulated. In the previous case, two such contextual PC can be formulated, as the one represented on Fig. 4.

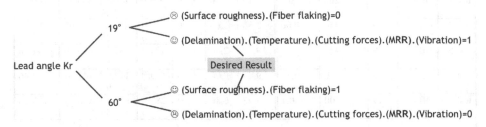

Fig. 4. Contextual classical-TRIZ General System of Contradiction

4.2   SVM Analysis of Data

The exhaustive extraction of GSC pointed out the huge amount of GSC than can exist for a given problem. Thus the choice of the one to consider priority is a real stake. In [14], the authors aimed at answering the questions: "How can the relevant contradictions be chosen or defined?" and "How can we extract the relevant contradictions without exhaustive research?". In the article a "SVM-based methodology was proposed to conduct data preprocessing to filter a large amount of irrelevant contradictions and reduce contradiction size". The Support Vector Machine (SVM) was proposed in [23]; SVM essentially performs linear classification by a non-linear mapping of the original space to a high-dimension space, which is called kernel trick.

Two ways to apply these SVM-based heuristics are proposed, the first enabling to weight, and thus to keep, the AP most influencing the EP, the second enabling to weight the values of the kept AP. The first result of this process was that all the AP are relevant candidates for the GTC identification. The second result was the set of relevant values and their relative weight, as illustrated in Table 5, were the most influent values have been highlighted in red for negative influences and in green for positive ones.

The analysis of the previous table leads the selection of a subset of 12 experiments, on which the extraction of GSC has been conducted. This reduces the number of GTC to 165, but it decreases dramatically the number of GPC, for one chosen GTC. Among them the contextual one illustrated on Fig. 4 is still present.

Table 5. Weights of values of AP on EP, after SVM analysis

		Ra (μm)	FF (mm)	Ld (mm)	T (°)	F (N)	MRR (cm3/min)	Arms (m²/s)
Coating of cutting insert	DB3	-0,32	0,30	-1,50	2,49	-1,10	0,00	-2,92
Coating of cutting insert	DB6	-0,32	-3,30	3,00	-1,59	1,88	0,00	2,40
Coating of cutting insert	DSP3N	0,65	3,00	-1,50	-0,90	-0,78	0,00	0,52
Lead angle Kr (°)	19,00	-0,47	-3,68	5,93	1,55	5,00	-5,72	-3,73
Lead angle Kr (°)	60,00	0,47	3,68	-5,93	-1,55	-5,00	5,72	3,73
Cutting speed Vc (m/min)	96,5	-0,10	-0,42	-1,59	4,73	1,42	-4,00	7,54
Cutting speed Vc (m/min)	200	-0,22	0,16	3,15	2,53	0,69	-1,34	4,80
Cutting speed Vc (m/min)	450	-0,30	1,61	0,82	-2,40	-0,31	0,85	-1,87
Cutting speed Vc (m/min)	700	0,73	-1,52	-2,36	-2,95	-1,21	2,66	-6,38
Cutting speed Vc (m/min)	803,5	-0,10	0,17	-0,02	-1,90	-0,58	1,83	-4,10
Chip thickness h (mm)	0,06	-0,10	9,95	2,16	-1,13	-2,56	-4,00	5,56
Chip thickness h (mm)	0,1	0,73	-1,95	1,08	-1,57	-3,56	-1,34	3,69
Chip thickness h (mm)	0,2	-0,30	-4,59	-2,01	0,50	-0,33	0,85	-1,25
Chip thickness h (mm)	0,3	-0,22	0,59	-0,29	1,15	3,04	2,66	-5,27
Chip thickness h (mm)	0,34	-0,10	-3,99	-0,94	1,04	3,42	1,83	-2,73

4.3 Pareto Analysis of Contradictions

A last method is illustrated in [24, 25] were the choice of contradictions to consider is based on the consideration and explanation of the concept of dominance, and thus, on the Pareto frontier of the experiments. This analysis revealed that 5 subsets of experiments are on the Pareto, but if combining this analysis with strategic weighting of EP defined by the experts, only two subsets (then one GTC) exist, which is represented on Table 6.

Table 6. Pareto and weighting analysis of the data

	Coating	KR	Vc	h	Ra (μm)	T (°)	MRR (cm3/min)	Ld (mm)	FF (mm)	F (N)	Arms (m²/s)
2	DB3	19	200	0,1	0	0	1	1	0	0	1
7	DB6	19	200	0,1	0	0	1	1	0	0	1
12	DSP3N	19	200	0,1	0	0	1	1	0	0	1
4	DB3	60	200	0,1	1	1	0	1	0	0	1

The analysis of this table, once more, pointed out, but as unique GPC, the one illustrated on Fig. 4, for different sets of EP.

4.4 Summarizing Results

Table 7 below summarizes results and contradiction search criteria of the 3 methods. The systems of contradictions of the 3 approaches overlap. Moreover, in our case, the same GSC, which seems afterwards to be the more relevant by experts, was found by the three methods. Thus it seems at least on our case that the three methods are effective for identifying the GSC. Comparison of the methods efficiency is provided in the next section.

Table 7. Comparison of the 3 methods

	Technical contradictions		Physical contradictions	
	Number of GTC	Selection criteria	Number of GPC	Selection criteria
Exhaustive extraction of contradictions	201	1. Dominance: Number of implied EP 2. Exhaustiveness: Number of implied experiments	156	Easiness to solve and interpret
SVM analysis of data	165	1. Dominance: Number of implied EP 2. Exhaustiveness: Number of implied experiments	6	Easiness to solve and interpret
Pareto analysis of contradictions	10	Expert ponderation of EP	1	N/A if one GSC; Weight of AP otherwise

5 Discussion and Perspectives

In this section we first comment on the results according to two points: comparison of the efficiency of the methods with each other, comparison of the methods in the context of analysis of the initial situation. Then we discuss their limitations and the research perspectives they generate.

5.1 Comparing Methods Efficiency

When comparing the number GTC and GPC for the chosen GTC, one can remark that some methods provide more contradictions than others. The purpose is then to know which contradictions are relevant or how to sort among them. In the first method (the exhaustive algorithm) many contradictions are proposed, but this methodology has not a real intrinsic capacity of generalization, but it provides several specific types of contradictions. That is the reason why the SVM method tries to reduce the area of search of the GPC by removing the variables that may provide "noise" in the interpretation of the DoE, that is to say by keeping only the AP that have a good discriminant influence on the objectives reaching/failing. The third method is more focusing on finding the relevant GTC, by selecting the candidates in the Pareto set of the binarized matrix of experiments (reducing the area of search of the GTC). Technical the computer time to provide the contradiction is small enough to be neglected. The difference is in the selection of the contradictions. The second and the third methods provide intrinsically a filter, which leads to reduce the noisy contradictions, thus the filtering activity of the human. To conclude this part we observed what was expected, which confirms that use of data analysis method brings promising benefits in the way to tackle big data complex problems, as it enables to decrease dramatically the number of GSC.

5.2   Impacts on the Analysis of the Initial Situation

The identification of contradictions from the DoE also has an impact on how one can perform the analysis of the initial situation. Indeed, one can have results of experiments established beforehand to a problem-solving study with the TRIZ. Thus, once the objectives are set, the contradiction identification is almost automatic and very fast compared to conventional methods requiring the use of experts. The contradiction is no longer the final phase of the analysis of the initial situation, but its starting point. The problem solver has not to bring out the contradiction anymore; he has to get it validated and/ or interpreted. This inversion of paradigm leads us to the questions: What we can learn from an identified contradiction? Does the contradiction bring a different understanding of the problem to the expert of the problem? Does the generalized contradiction bring a new qualitative vision to the understanding of the problem compared to the traditional TRIZ contradiction or traditional DoE analysis methods?

The feedback from the expert of the case study problem is the following. The expert participated in real time in the identification of contradiction by the third method. He had no difficulty in choosing the generalized technical contradiction among the five points of the binary Pareto. His comments are as follows: "The classical method analysis of the DoE makes it possible to understand the combined influence of APs on a EP while the system of generalized contradiction allows understanding the influence of a AP on all EP simultaneously. It provides a level of global understanding that traditional DoE analysis tools do not bring." We complete his commentary with ours. The analysis of pairwise conflicts of EPs (classical TRIZ) leads to the same limits of understanding of the problem as classical DoE analysis methods (i.e.: they do not allow having a global vision). Note that in our case there is no system of contradiction corresponding to the model of OTSM-TRIZ or classic TRIZ in the data of the DoE. Unfortunately we did not experiment in parallel in order to know what would have been the outputs when applying classical TRIZ approach for getting the contradictions.

The second lesson and feedback on the case study reported by the problem holder is that "the APs coating, Vc and h that influence the optimization process do not explain the EP values limitations". Our comment to this remark is that we hypotheses that the APs coating, Vc and h may also explain the limitation, but not in a parameter conflicting manner.

5.3   Limitations and Perspective

In the case study presented in this paper, we did not encounter any particular difficulty to identify the contradictions. Complementary cases have to be addressed to validate the methods. In [26] we have shown on an example of machining that some APs can act in harmony with the objectives in order to push the limits of a system. This information provides a complementary path of exploration and innovation to the contradiction. The highlighting of this property was made on a problem with 2 EPs. For the future, we want to develop an approach to identify this track systematically when the problem handles with more than two EPs. We could thus validate or invalidate the hypothesis made in the last paragraph of Sect. 5.2.

References

1. Box, G.E.P., Draper, N.R.: Response Surfaces, Mixtures, and Ridge Analyses: Probability and Statistics, 2nd edn. Wiley, Hoboken (2007)
2. Cohen, J., Cohen, P., West, S.G., et al.: Applied Multiple Regression/Correlation Analysis for the Behavioral Sciences, 3rd edn. Lawrence erlbaum Associates, Mahwah, London (2002)
3. Montgomery, D.C.: Design and Analysis of Experiments, 4th edn. Wiley, New York (1997)
4. Box, G.E.P., Wilson, K.B.: On the experimental attainment of optimum conditions. J. Roy. Stat. Soc.: Ser. B (Methodol.) 13(1), 1–45 (1951)
5. Box, G., Hunter, J.S.: MultiFactor experimental designs for exploring response surfaces. Ann. Math. Stat. 28, 195–242 (1957)
6. Altshuller, G.S.: Creativity as an Exact Science. Gordon and Breach, New York (1988)
7. Altshuller, G.S.: The Innovation Algorithm: TRIZ Systematic Innovation and Technical Creativity. Technical Innovation Center, Inc., Worcester (1999)
8. Khomenko, N., De Guio, R., Lelait, L., et al.: A framework for OTSM-TRIZ based computer support to be used in complex problem management. Int. J. Comput. Appl. Technology. 30(1), 88–104 (2007). (spécial issue Trends in computer aided innovation)
9. Dubois, S., Eltzer, T., De Guio, R.: A dialectical based model coherent with inventive and optimization problems. Comput. Ind. 60(8), 575–583 (2009)
10. Dubois, S., Rasovska, I., De Guio, R.: Interpretation of a general model for inventive problems, the generalized system of contradictions. In: Roy, R., Shehab, E. (eds.) Competitive Design. Proceedings of the 19th CIRP Design Conference, pp. 271–276. Cranfield University Press, Cranfield (2009)
11. Lin, L., Rasovska, I., De Guio, R., et al.: Algorithm for identifying generalized technical contradictions in experiments. J. Eur. Systèmes Autom. (JESA) 47(4–8), 563–588 (2013)
12. Lin, L., Dubois, S., De Guio, R., et al.: An exact algorithm to extract the generalized physical contradiction. Int. J. Interact. Des. Manuf. (IJIDeM) 9(3), 185–191 (2014)
13. Dubois, S., Lin, L., De Guio, R., Rasovska, I.: From simulation to invention, beyond the pareto-frontier. In: Husung, S., Weber, C., CantaMESsa, M., Cascini, G., Marjanovic, D., Graziosi, S. (eds.) 20th International Conference on Engineering Design (ICED) 2015, pp. 245–254. Design Society, Milano (2015)
14. Lin, L., Rasovska, I., De Guio, R., Dubois, S.: Optimization methods for inventive design. TRIZ – The Theory of Inventive Problem Solving, pp. 151–185. Springer, Cham (2017). https://doi.org/10.1007/978-3-319-56593-4_7

15. Chibane, H.: Contribution à l'optimisation multi-objectif des paramètres de coupe en usinage et apport de l 'analyse vibratoire: application aux matériaux métalliques et composites. In: Mécanique 2013. Centre-Val de Loire, Tours (2013)
16. Morandeau, A.: Méthodologie de caractérisation et de conception d'un outil coupant à plaquettes amovibles pour l'usinage de matériaux composites aéronautiques: application aux opérations de surfaçage. In : Mécanique 2012. Université François Rabelais, Tours (2012)
17. Chibane, H., Serra, R., Leroy, R.: Optimal milling conditions of aeronautical composite material under temperature, forces and vibration parameters. J. Compos. Mater. **51**(24), 3453–3463 (2017)
18. Chibane, H., Morandeau, A., Serra, R., et al.: Optimal milling conditions for carbon/epoxy composite material using damage and vibration analysis. Int. J. Adv. Manuf. Technology. **68**(5), 1111–1121 (2013)
19. Morandeau, A., Chibane, H., Bouchou, A., et al.: Machining carbon fibre reinforced plastics: lead angle effect. Int. J. Mach. Mach. Materials. **13**(2/3), 311–330 (2013)
20. Cochran, W.G., Cox, G.M.: Experimental Designs, 2nd edn. Wiley, Hoboken (1992)
21. Safety: Turning Catalog Safety 2007. TURN-CAT (2007)
22. Dubois, S., De Guio, R., Rasovska, I., et al.: From simulation to inventive problem resolution, a global method. In: Škec, S., et al. (eds.) 21st International Conference on Engineering Design (ICED 17) 2017, Vancouver, Canada, pp. 503–512 (2017)
23. Vapnik, V.: The Nature of Statistical Learning Theory. Information Science and Statistics. Springer, New York (1995). https://doi.org/10.1007/978-1-4757-3264-1
24. Bach, S., De Guio, R., Gartiser, N.: Combining discrete event simulation, data analysis, and TRIZ for fleet optimization. J. Eur. TRIZ Assoc. INNOVATOR **4**(2), 47–62 (2017)
25. Rasovska, I., De Guio, R., Dubois, S.: Using dominance relation to identify relevant generalized technical contradictions in innovative design. In: IESM 2017, Sarrebruck, Germany (2017)
26. Dubois, S., Chibane, H., De Guio, R., et al.: From simulation to contradictions, different ways to formulate innovation directions. In: ETRIA TRIZ Future Conference 2017, Lappeenranta, Finland (2017)

A Feedback on an Industrial Application of the FORMAT Methodology

Sebastien Dubois, Roland De Guio[✉], Aurélien Brouillon,
and Laetitia Angelo

CSIP, ICube Laboratory, INSA de Strasbourg,
24 bld de la Victoire, Strasbourg, France
{sebastien.dubois,roland.deguio}@insa-strasbourg.fr

Abstract. One of the main issues of industrial product evolution planning is the current state of the art, related to the product itself, its market competitors, and also the available resources that can become parts of the future product. Moreover, to plan evolution, it is required to well understand how the performance of the product will be evaluated, on a future market, and surely it won't be the same performance criteria as today habits.

This issue has been tackled and defined as Analysis of Initial Situation. A combination of TRIZ based approaches and Design of Experiments has been defined to clarify the problem to be solved. But all these approaches are dedicated to analyze today product and to choose the prior problem to be considered, but these methods have not been defined to analyze long-term evolution planning of products.

For this long-term planning, a method, FORMAT, has been developed and proposed. The purpose of this article is to describe the application of this methodology on an industrial case, to plan the evolution of kitchen hoods. The article will state the different methods to perform the Analysis of Initial Situation but also the benefits and the difficulties of FORMAT application.

Keywords: Analysis of initial situation · FORMAT method
Long-term prospective

1 Introduction

Solving problems has always been one of the main concerns for industrial engineers. And lot of methods to help them in this task have been developed, with different aims and ends [1, 2]. One can recognize various methods to:

- help in describing the design process at an operational level [3] or at a cognitive level [4],
- help in defining the problems to be tackled during design process in regard of the generated value [5],
- help in generating design concepts either algorithmically [6], either with humans [7],
- help in evaluating design concepts [8].

© IFIP International Federation for Information Processing 2018
Published by Springer Nature Switzerland AG 2018. All Rights Reserved
D. Cavallucci et al. (Eds.): TFC 2018, IFIP AICT 541, pp. 290–301, 2018.
https://doi.org/10.1007/978-3-030-02456-7_24

Among these different proposals, TRIZ has been widely recognized as increasing the inventive level of proposed concepts and as enabling engineers to propose new solutions' concepts. From the end of 50's till the end of 80's, TRIZ has been developed to help engineers to be more creative. This development has lead to the proposal of a general approach based on 5 steps:

1. The analysis of initial situation, which objective is to elicit the specific conditions under which problem appears, the inherent contradictions and also to choose the root cause of problem, the prior contradiction to be solved.   The definition of the problem. The objective of this step is to clarify the limits of the problem, i.e. the borders in which the solution can be found and thus to specify if the problem is a maxi or a mini problem.
2. The definition of the ideal solution aims to separate lower-level solution from higher-level ones by intensifying the constraints for solution concept synthesis.
3. The definition of the physical solution enables to select relevant information for concept solution synthesis, i.e. to identify inventive mechanisms enabling to satisfy the conditions of the ideal solution.
4. The definition of the technical solution reinforces the concept of the physical solution by defining which resources can be used and how these resources are used to fit the physical solution.

In border of this 4-steps general approach, several versions of ARIZ [9] have been defined, but the last one defined by Altshuller [10] does not fit with the first step. The analysis of initial situation has not been developed anymore and is still one key stake in problem solving process. The matter was the recognition that the proposed method for this step was not as developed as the methods inherent to the other steps [11].

In [12], the authors proposed to perform the Analysis of Initial Situation with sequential experimentation. This enabled to create a continuum between methods dedicated for optimization and the ones developed for invention. This continuum is still under development today [13, 14].

In parallel the consideration of Technical Systems' Laws of Evolution has also been considered as a way to state the level of maturity of a considered problem and thus enable the elicitation of the key problems to solve [15]. An European Project has been developed in this direction and lead to the proposal of the FORMAT method [16]. Thus an "innovative forecasting methodology" has been proposed "to support strategic decisions in industrial R&D activities, by managing the multi-disciplinary complexity of current systems and by anticipating the future characteristics of products and processes"[1].

In this paper, the authors will first introduce three known ways to perform the Analysis of Initial Situation: ARIZ-85A, the use of Design of Experiments, and the FORMAT method, then the general required steps will be elicited. The application of the FORMAT method will then be illustrated. And at last some discussion and conclusion will be proposed.

---

[1] http://www.format-project.eu/about.

2   Analysis of Initial Situation

In this part, three ways to perform the Analysis of Initial Situation will be presented: the one developed by Altshuller, ARIZ-85A, the proposal of the authors about the way to build a continuum between optimization methods and inventive ones, and, finally, the FORMAT project.

2.1   ARIZ-85A

Throughout the development of a method to tackle inventive problems, several versions of ARIZ (the Algorithm for Inventive Problem Solving) have been proposed as the results of seminars in which several problems have been tackled by groups of people, to identify the strong and weak points of the proposed method. By the end of the 50's the patterns of technological evolution have been included in the method. During the 60's the versions of ARIZ pointed out the importance of the problem statement, as ARIZ-64 introduced the section "Clarifying and verifying the problem statement", which has been decomposed in two different parts in 1968. In the 80's, starting with ARIZ-82, the method has been targeted specifically to solve difficult non-typical problems. And in 1985, "the former first chapter is no longer part of the algorithm as it is not rigorous enough compared to the other chapters" [17]. Thus the last version of this first chapter, that can be used to perform the Analysis of Initial Situation is ARIZ-85A [18].

ARIZ-85A is a set of 9 steps:

1. Definition of the final goal, which aims at defining the global objective of the problem, from technical and economical point of view
2. Investigate the bypass approach, to state how the problem occurs at different levels of the system
3. Choice of the considered problem, at which level it will be tackled
4. Determination of the required characteristics, to state the list of Evaluation Parameters
5. Intensification of the required characteristics, the intensification being one the TRIZ mean to propose more robust concept solution.
6. Definition of the constraints
7. Application of the inventive standards, to state if the problem is inventive or not
8. Analysis of the patents, also a mean to clarify if an existing solution, even coming from another domain can be applied. But this step raises the question of the non application of the laws of technical systems evolution.
9. Application of the STC operator, another mean to apply intensification.

In these 9 steps, one can formulate 4 main questions to be tackled: What is the scope of the problem? What is the system to consider? What is the strategic context? What is the problem? These 4 main questions, which will be used to represent the complementary aspects of the different methods, and the related questions of ARIZ-85A are represented on Fig. 1.

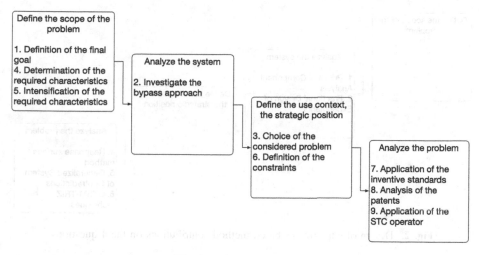

Fig. 1. ARIZ-85A process

2.2 Design of Experiments Based Methods

In [12] the authors proposed a 6 steps approach to merge optimization and invention methods. The use of sequential experimentation, a well-known sequence of different mathematical tools, aimed at fulfilling Analysis of Initial Situation and to identify the contradiction to consider for problem resolution. The 6 steps are:

1. Principal component and factor analysis to identify how many action parameters (AP) influence the evaluation parameters (EP)
2. Fractional design of experiments to identify which AP influence each EP
3. Factorial design of experiments with center-points to identify the direction which will allow to move towards an optimum
4. Response surface method to locate the optimum solution
5. Generalized System of Contradictions if the optimum does not satisfy the objective
6. OTSM-TRIZ techniques to solve the contradiction

These steps mainly participate to the questions of the system to be considered and to the analysis of the problem, as illustrated on Fig. 2.

It is thus already obvious that the methods based on optimization approaches could bring benefits to the Analysis of Initial Situation, and that they way the Design of Experiments should be defined would also benefits from TRIZ-based methods [19]. But one aspect that is still missing with these two methods is the consideration of the maturity level of the considered system and more generally the evolution of this system.

2.3 Format

FORMAT method focuses on making long-term prospective, and thus is mainly built on the crossed use of logistic and substitution curves [15] and qualitative elements to interpret them. These project FORMAT aimed at answering "the need to introduce

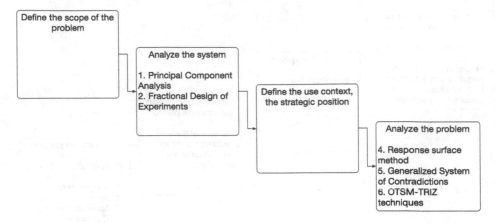

Fig. 2. Design of experiments based method contributions on the 4 questions

Table 1. Format stages [16]

Stage	Main functions	Questions and duties
FOR: Diagnose questions and plan project	Prepare and make decisions about forecasting project Define boundaries/resources of forecasting project	WHY do we need to know the future? WHAT do we need to know about the future? HOW do we plan to learn about future?
M: Define the system for forecast and study contexts	Review existing knowledge about system	WHAT the System To Forecast (STF) is for? (WHY we need the STF?) WHICH systems allow to get the same results? HOW to measure the performances and the expenses of the STF and its alternatives? WHAT the STF and its main alternative(s) are, were and are expected to be?
A: Develop forecast for defined system and context	Identify a system of problems that drives evolution of system Recognize evolutionary trends for identified system Identify changes of performance characteristic in time Aggregate and validate results of qualitative and quantitative studies into forecast	Extract limiting resources from problems of STF Define set of solutions addressing limiting resources Fit data-series about parameters measuring performance & expenses Build conclusions about future traits for STF
T: Prepare report and present results	Transfer results of study to decision makers	Transfer the forecasting results to beneficiaries/decision makers

structured methods and tools capable to support strategic decisions in industrial R&D activities, by managing the multi-disciplinary complexity of current systems and by anticipating the future characteristics of products and processes." (see Table 1)

All these steps also aim at identifying the general trends of evolution of technical systems, and thus, at formulating which problems are to be considered for resolution. Then, the method also enables to perform an Analysis of Initial Situation, and the benefits of each stage in regard of the 4 generic questions is presented in Fig. 3.

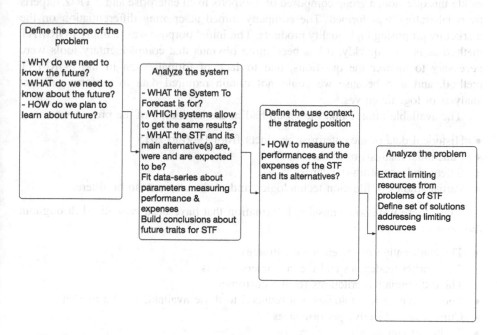

Fig. 3. Questions and duties of FORMAT methods' contributions on the 4 questions

2.4   Comparison of the Presented Methods

The three presented methods, ARIZ-85A, Design of Experiments based method to hierarchize contradictions, and FORMAT, could be recognized at three ways to perform the Analysis of Initial Situation. Each being more complete, or at least different, in the way to answer to each of the 4 mains questions. It seems thus quite obvious that complementary aspects could be built based on these differences.

In this article, the authors will present their application of the FORMAT method, on a case study, and will show the benefits they recognize in this application, but also, the difficulty they met.

3 Case Study

3.1 Presentation of the Case

The presented article is the application of the FORMAT method on an industrial case to investigate the long-term evolution of the kitchen hoods. The objective was to make a state-of-art of the current technologies, their advantages, their limitations, and to understand which of these technologies will be the leading technology in the future. To tackle this question, a group composed of 3 experts from enterprise and 2 TRIZ experts from laboratory was formed. The company aimed at creating differentiation on the market by proposing high quality products. The initial purpose was to apply FORMAT method as is, but, quickly, it has been quite obvious that complementary tools were necessary to answer the questions, due to lack of formalization in the FORMAT method, and also because we could not obtain required data to perform relevant analysis of logistic curves.

The available information the group had at the beginning of the project was:

- Historical data of the enterprise products from 1966 to 2015
- Functional analysis of kitchen hood
- Safety and operating standards
- Partial studies of filtration technologies and of the elements to be filtered

Thus, there were some missing information that have been capitalized throughout the project:

- The clarification of the enterprise strategy
- The market tendencies and the customers' needs
- The differentiation criterions for the customer
- The alternative technologies, not reduced to those available on the market
- Current and objective performances
- Technical constraints
- Pareto front and trade-off of current existing systems

Based on this missing information and trying to fulfill the first steps of FORMAT method, some ascertainments were made and some limitations of the direct applicability of the method were pointed out.

3.2 Ascertainments About FORMAT Method

Performing the FOR step of the method tackled some strategic questions, which enabled to clarify the previously cited missing information and to well clarify what the project aimed at. It also clarified the necessity to better investigate current systems, the market and technological competitors and a clear formulation of what performance means for the system. In fact, some elements of the M step were required to well answer FOR step.

The starting point of the method of the M step is to define the Main Useful Function of the observed system, thus the limits of this system and also its operating principle. One first conclusion about the analysis of the system was that the experts of the company were mainly oriented by the Evaluation Parameters defined in border of the standards. And one of the conclusion of the group was that the standards are proposed to evaluate existing systems, in regard of safety purposes, but not appropriate to evaluate future, not yet existing systems, in regard of performances.

In the method it is proposed to complete a multi-screen analysis of the system and to use the Element-Name-Value (ENV) model to formulate the criteria to measure the performances and expenses [20]. Only analyzing system through the TRIZ based models gives a partial understanding of this system, mainly functional. It was thus decided to complete this TRIZ system description with an analysis of the system also based on activities, using an IDEF0[2] and SADT[3] analysis, as proposed in the method.

It was also decided to have a global understanding of who is the customer, and this customer has been analyzed throughout a systemic perspective, then 4 kinds of potential future users were interviewed to point out their main concerns:

- The demanding customers for their high demand on functionalities
- The private users, as they will be the end-users of the product
- The kitchen furniture dealers to understand the constraints linked with the assembly constraints, transportability, and so on of the future system
- The professionals, renowned chefs for their high understanding of the current systems' limits and main functional advantages of future systems

Moreover, to better state the current limits of known working principles, the analysis of the market has been completed by kitchen hoods modeling and simulation.

At last, the use of logistic curves in order to plan substitution of technologies has led the group to the difficulty in having robust long-term data of past systems enabling to fit with accuracy the curves. It has then been difficult to have reliable conclusions on the analysis of logistic curves.

3.3 Realized Process and Main Results

The Fig. 4 details the process as it has finally been conducted, which starts at the top left of the figure. After a first realization of the stage "FOR" we could have access to a further marketing study and were able to question the participants of the whole value chain of the kitchen hoods. The first pass provided a first family of assessment criteria that were adjusted in the second study. Let us notice that it is not a linear process; lot of backtrackings were necessary to validate answers to initial questions, and the benefits of adding model and simulation to poor descriptions provided by the state of the art have been well appreciated to demonstrate the potential and limits of current working principles.

The available data about the sales on the market enabled to propose logistic curves, but not on technological information, only on the kind of settlement of the system. The analysis was performed with data from the world sale volume from 2004 to 2014. The collected data were then transposed, with dedicated tools (*Logistic Substitution Model*

---

[2] http://www.idef.com.

[3] http://www.lsis.org/dea/M6optionD/Exp-GL41-SADT.pdf.

II^4 and *Loglet Lab*[5]), into logistic curves, which are a graphical representation of the innovations' diffusion in the technologies' life cycle [21]. However, this analysis, presented on Fig. 5, remains superficial, as the amount of analyzed data is not sufficient enough to guarantee the robustness of the results. Nevertheless the global qualitative substitution that can be seen on Fig. 5 confirms the feeling of the marketing about the market. But as we explained at the beginning of this paragraph, these data represents settlement of the system substitution and not technology substitution.

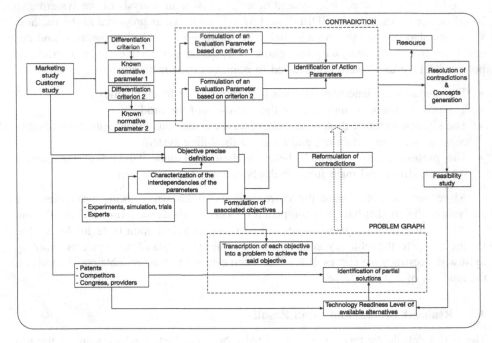

Fig. 4. Detailed process of analysis of initial situation in the case study

Another interesting result, based on the systemic description of the customers is the elicitation of more relevant set of Evaluation Parameters (EP). The customers study and other participants to the value chain pointed out five families of parameters but the standards only provided three measurable EP shared among two of them. The final set was composed of seventeen EP, as illustrated on Fig. 6. Some parameters like acoustical comfort have been added due to the evolution noise analysis in other domains. Others like uptake measurable parameters have been defined by the working group. The new set of assessment parameters allowed a better understanding of the state of the art and TRL of potential solutions related to PE families. We did not seek, through lack of resources, to carry out a quantitative analysis of the evolution, i.e.

---

[4] http://www.iiasa.ac.at.

[5] https://logletlab.com.

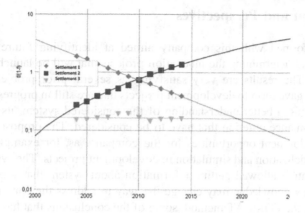

Fig. 5. Substitution curves for 3 different settlements of system

logistic curves of the new EPs. Nevertheless we did evaluate the actual performance of each component either with data from literature or from simulations and experiments. We have also established, through this technical and scientific state of the art, to what extent some performance tradeoffs observed on current systems can be potentially removed. It was proposed to address the remaining performance dilemma with TRIZ. The motivation for using TRIZ was to complete the state of the art and see whether it was possible with available knowledge to overcome the remaining contradiction or at least get a better understanding of the problem.

The decision how to go further was done by the stake holders based on the produced knowledge.

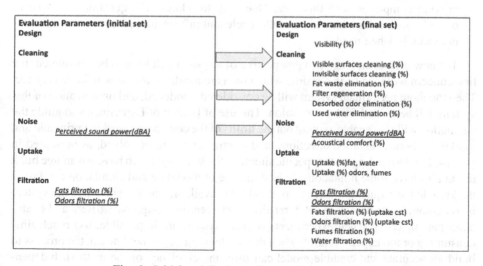

Fig. 6. Initial and final set of evaluation parameters

4 Discussion and Perspectives

The study performed with this company aimed at identifying future technological trends but also at determining the innovation projects that will be launched in the next coming years. The results are very satisfying as several prior problems have been formulated and gave birth to development projects that are still in progress. Moreover it helped in building a better understanding of the considered system, its evolution and the main performance criterion that have to be considered. The proposed method also gave new development opportunities for the company, as, for example, the systematization of modelization and simulation in development projects. The system modeling and later validating allowed getting information about system that was not available before. This new knowledge may change the way to address the competition.

Concerning the FORMAT method, some of the conclusions that have been pointed out during the application are:

- All the proposed steps in FORMAT are necessary to be performed, but it cannot be complied as a linear process, and some answers of further steps are required to well assess the answers of first steps, especially between FOR and M steps. Perhaps should FOR, M, A, T sequence be considered as a functional model, and consistencies checking between the sequences be added.
- TRIZ based models have to be completed with other systems' description models to have a more global understanding of the system
- One of the main benefits, but also one of the main difficulties in FORMAT method is the use of logistic and substitution curves. It gives very interesting information about the remaining years to improve an existing system, and the necessity to develop new generation one. But the collect of reliable data is really hard, and these data are not necessarily available. There is still research work to do in order to provide companies with this data. One way to address the question could be to provide companies with ways to collect relevant information progressively so that it is available when needed.

If a new project on long-term prospective of a system will have to be considered, the first concern will then be to consider which data are available and how reliable they are. Then the more performant system will be considered, modelled, and optimization of this system will be looked for by simulation. The use of Design of Experiments to guide the simulation will also enable to point out the limits of the considered working principle and to identify both innovation directions, and contradictions to be solved, as presented in [13, 14, 22]. Depending on the specific situation the latest approach have advantage but it might also have some limitations. Indeed the use of modeling and simulation can fasten the knowledge acquisition when a good model is available quickly and when the system is too complex for human to catch relations between the design parameters and evaluation parameters or when experiments on real system are impossible, too much time consuming or too expensive. But, when the model accuracy is not known, the process to build an accurate and credible model can limit the efficiency of the method. Independently from the resource consuming of this process the efficacy of the use of simulation might be improved by finding a way to evaluate beforehand the relevant degrees of accuracy and credibility that will allow the stake holders to use the results when deciding.

References

1. Carmichael, D.G.: Problem Solving for Engineers, 432 p. CRC Press (2013)
2. Horvath, L., Rudas, I.J.: Modeling and Problem Solving Techniques for Engineers. Elsevier Academic Press (2004)
3. Pahl, G., Beitz, W.: Engineering Design: A Systematic Approach. Springer Verlag, New York (1988)
4. Le Masson, P., Weil, B., Hatchuel, A.: Design Theory: Methods and Organization for Innovation. Springer, Heidelberg (2017). https://doi.org/10.1007/978-3-319-50277-9
5. NORmalisation AFd: Analyse de la Valeur, Caractéristiques Fondamentales (1990)
6. Haupt, R.L., Haupt, S.E.: Practical Genetic Algorithms with CD-ROM. Wiley-Interscience (2004)
7. Altshuller, G.S.: Creativity as an Exact Science. Gordon and Breach, New York (1988)
8. Suh, N.P.: Axiomatic Design: Advances and Applications. Oxford University Press, New York (2001)
9. Altshuller, G.S.: The Innovation Algorithm: TRIZ, Systematic Innovation and Technical Creativity. Technical Innovation Center, Inc., Worcester (1999)
10. Altshuller, G.S.: Algorithm of Inventive Problem Solving (ARIZ-85C), p. 32. OTSM-TRIZ Technologies Center, Minsk (1985)
11. Zlotin, B., Zusman, A.: ARIZ on the move. TRIZ J. **13**, 145–159 (1999)
12. Burgard, L., Dubois, S., De Guio, R., et al.: Sequential experimentation to perform the analysis of initial situation. In: Cascini, G., Vaneker, T. (eds.) TRIZ Future Conference 2011, pp. 35–45. Institute of Technology Tallaght, Dublin (2011)
13. Lin, L., Rasovska, I., De Guio, R., Dubois, S.: Optimization methods for inventive design. TRIZ – The Theory of Inventive Problem Solving, pp. 151–185. Springer, Cham (2017). https://doi.org/10.1007/978-3-319-56593-4_7
14. Dubois, S., Chibane, H., De Guio, R., et al.: From simulation to contradictions, different ways to formulate innovation directions. In: ETRIA TRIZ Future Conference 2017, Lappeenranta, Finland (2017)
15. Kucharavy, D., Schenk, E., De Guio, R.: Long-run forecasting of emerging technologies with logistic models and growth of knowledge. In: 19th CIRP Design Conference – Competitive Design, p. 277. Cranfield University (2009)
16. FORMAT Project (Forecast and Roadmapping for Manufacturing Technologies). Handbook of the FORMAT project (2014). http://handbook.format-project.eu/
17. Kucharavy, D.: Theory and practice of ARIZ. In: Materials for Master of Innovative Design, Module 6, INSA de Strasbourg (2005)
18. Altshuller, G.S., Zlotin, B., Philatov, V.I.: Analysis of the initial situation. In: Profession: to search for new, pp. 181–182. Kartya Moldovenyaske Publishing House, Kishinev (1985)
19. Dubois, S., De Guio, R., Rasovska, I., et al.: From simulation to inventive problem resolution, a global method. In: Maier, A., et al. (eds.) 21st International Conference on Engineering Design (ICED 2017), Vancouver, Canada, pp. 503–512 (2017)
20. Nikulin Chandia, C.N.: A method for forecasting design requirements based on experts' knowledge and logistic growth model. Dipartimento di Meccanica, Politecnico di Milano (2015)
21. Kucharavy, D., De Guio, R.: Logistic substitution model and technological forecasting. In: TRIZ Future 2008 - Synthesis in Innovation, Enschede, Netherlands, pp. 65–73 (2008)
22. Rasovska, I., De Guio, R., Dubois, S.: Using dominance relation to identify relevant generalized technical contradictions in innovative design. In: IESM 2017, Sarrebruck, Germany (2017)

Modelling CECA Diagram as a State Machine

Jerzy Chrząszcz[1,2(✉)]

[1] Institute of Computer Science, Warsaw University of Technology,
Warsaw 00-665, Poland
jch@ii.pw.edu.pl
[2] Pentacomp Systemy Informatyczne S.A., Warsaw 02-222, Poland

Abstract. Cause-Effect Chains Analysis (CECA) is one of the main TRIZ methods used for identification of system disadvantages. The analysis results in a diagram documenting these disadvantages and causal relations between them. Although the nature of causality implies that any effect must follow its cause, the original CECA concept does not address time explicitly. This drawback has been indicated by Yoon, who proposed *Occasion Axis* to describe changes of system state upon meeting particular conditions specified using values of parameters. Such an axis illustrates a sequence in time and an additional requirement is to interleave nodes referring to parameters with those referring to functions, originally dubbed as *Parameter-Function Pair Nexus*.

The method of transforming a CECA diagram into a logical model presented during TFC 2016 conference relies on decomposing the diagram into a context-dependent layer (specific content) and a context-independent layer, representing the structure of connections. The logical model describes the structure with a set of Boolean functions, which may be minimized and analyzed in a systematic way.

This paper explores the idea of Occasion Axis and examines the possibility of converting a CECA model into a state machine with transitions between the states described by conditions referring to parameters of objects in the analyzed system or its super-system. The expected benefits of such transformation range from better understanding of the time-domain interrelations of the causes up to describing the causality using standard notation, such as UML. The paper presents rules proposed for systematic conversion of CECA diagram into state machine representation and discusses required extensions to formal state machine definition.

Keywords: Cause-Effect Chains Analysis · Logical model · Boolean algebra
State machine · Harmful process

1 Basic CECA Model

Cause-Effect Chains Analysis (CECA) is an iterative method for revealing causal relations in the analyzed system [1, 2]. It starts with indicating drawbacks to be removed, which are called *target disadvantages*. Then their causes (*intermediate disadvantages*) are investigated subsequently, until finding primary causes (*root causes*) that reflect laws of nature or specific constraints of the project, remaining beyond control. Because root causes cannot be literally eliminated, CECA procedure aims at

© IFIP International Federation for Information Processing 2018
Published by Springer Nature Switzerland AG 2018. All Rights Reserved
D. Cavallucci et al. (Eds.): TFC 2018, IFIP AICT 541, pp. 302–314, 2018.
https://doi.org/10.1007/978-3-030-02456-7_25

identification of the *key disadvantages* instead, removal of which should remove target disadvantages.

The analysis results in a diagram with boxes containing descriptions of disadvantages, arrows denoting causality flow and – possibly – logical AND/OR operators, reflecting how the causes contribute to a given effect. Although the nature of causality seems simple at the level of intuition and common sense, it is not equally straightforward for systematic modelling and analyzing, as may be seen in [3, 4] and the accompanying discussions.

Several doubts regarding the original method have been indicated in [5], addressing possible approaches to in-depth and in-width growth of causality diagrams, as well as identifying proper stop conditions, which jointly affect completeness of the diagram. Significant improvements to the method employ using cause-effect patterns identified in real projects [6, 7], adding information about advantages (positive effects) in addition to disadvantages [8], observing specific structure of the causal chains to support their correctness and completeness [2, 9] or using additional criteria [8, 10].

2 Logical CECA Model

Systematic approach to conversion of CECA diagram into a set of logical functions is presented in [11]. It starts with decomposition of the diagram into two separate layers: contents and structure. The contents (box descriptions) are specific to a particular problem situation, while structure of the interconnections is context-independent. Proposed logical model uses binary logic with 0 representing inactive disadvantage and 1 representing active disadvantage. Logical operators are modelled with respective gates. AND gate outputs 1 only for 1s on all its inputs, while OR gate outputs 0 only for 0s on all inputs, and the truth tables of 2-input gates are as follows:

AND

x	y	xy
0	0	0
0	1	0
1	0	0
1	1	1

OR

x	y	$x+y$
0	0	0
0	1	1
1	0	1
1	1	1

Target disadvantages are outputs of the network and the inputs may reflect root causes or any intermediate causes – in particular, the key disadvantages. Such approach allows for describing structure of the CECA diagram with a set of combinatorial logical functions – one for each of the target disadvantages. These functions may be transformed using rules of Boolean algebra and minimized in order to obtain most concise representation of the logical relations between selected input causes and target disadvantages. This paves the way to answering important questions regarding the structure of the model of causality, ranging from *which inputs influence particular output?* up to *what minimal set of inputs must be acted upon in order to deactivate all the outputs?*

Some enhancements to the logical model were introduced in [12], including provisions for removal of intermediate disadvantages and criteria for verification of model completeness. Proposed representation was developed as a solution to a physical contradiction describing disadvantages in linear CECA chains (excluding the root causes):

- each disadvantage should have *exactly one control* to retain coherence between the model and the diagram (as we only draw one arrow between the boxes), BUT
- each disadvantage should have *more than one control* to retain coherence between the model and the concept (as we may remove a disadvantage without removing its predecessor).

Using *separation in relation* principle [13] the active/inactive status of the intermediate disadvantage was split between the input (independent of deeper causes) and the output (dependent on deeper causes). The logical model of a linear chain of disadvantages comprises of cascaded AND gates, with one input connected to the output of previous gate and the other input controlled by an independent variable, as shown in Fig. 1. The first input is used for passing information about deeper causes in the chain and the second input controls given disadvantage directly. If any of the inputs is disabled (i.e. set to 0), the output is disabled as well, simulating *indirect* and *direct* removal of the given disadvantage, respectively.

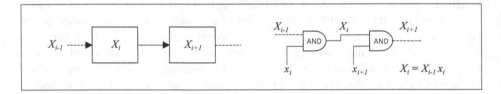

Fig. 1. Chain of AND gates modelling linear branch of a CECA diagram [12].

3 Time Axis and Occasion Axis

Although the nature of causality implies that any effect must follow its cause, the original CECA concept does not address time explicitly and the only notion of time precedence comes from arrows pointing from causes to effects. Such representation clearly defines a sequence of disadvantages in a given linear chain, but it tells nothing about the time relations between disadvantages located in different branches of a diagram.

This also holds true for the logical model considered so far, consisting of combinatorial functions i.e. with outputs depending solely on inputs. When a change is applied to an input of a combinatorial network, it propagates through subsequent gates until it reaches a particular output or disappears on the way due to a specific logical function. For an AND gate 0 on any input switches output to 0 independently of other inputs, so that AND output will reflect changes of a particular input if and only if all remaining inputs are 1s. Similarly, for an OR gate 1 on any input switches output to 1, hence the change of a particular input will propagate to OR output if and only if all other inputs are 0s. In the digital design area this approach is called *path sensitization* and it is used in testing to assure that changes of a given signal will propagate to an observable output.

The time axis is explicitly used in [14] for modelling causal chain as a sequence of events, which is similar to extending a single row of screens in the System Operator into the past (to identify the causes) and into the future (towards a solution). An obvious limitation of this method is the inability to model multiple connected chains of causes.

The lack of a strict notion of time in CECA method was extensively explored by Yoon [9], who pointed out that disadvantages occur due to changes of particular parameters of a system (or super-system), not just because of the time flow. The proposed approach uses concept of *occasion*, being a moment in time when a particular parameter pertinent to the analyzed problem situation has a certain value. And the *Occasion Axis* is a sequence of occasions in time that describes the development of a target disadvantage.

Points on this axis are determined by the nature and intensity of the interactions e.g. the moment of thermal shutdown of a computer is determined by a preset temperature limit and operating conditions, and so its location in time may vary. Depending on the amount of generated heat and the heat dissipation efficiency, the shutdown may be performed sooner or later, but it follows one scenario. And lack of the shutdown during a long operation also fits within the same scenario, yet unfinished. Therefore Occasion Axis may be considered discrete time axis defined by moments when some threshold values of pertinent parameters are achieved (i.e. specific events happen).

Furthermore, Yoon argues that a properly modelled chain of causes should consist of interleaved nodes of two types, defining conditions and actions. Conditions should refer to particular values of parameters, while actions should describe interactions between objects. The resulting chain was dubbed *Parameter-Function Pair Nexus*.

The justification for this interleaved structure is that a state of an object may only be changed as a result of interactions between the objects. Therefore neither two states nor two actions may appear in the diagram one after another and subsequent nodes of the same type indicate a missing node of the opposite type, which should be inserted in between. Recommended forms of descriptions are as follows [9]:

- state (condition): *entity + its parameter + value of the parameter,*
  e.g. : temperature of processor is higher than Ts,
- action (function): *tool + action + object,*
  e.g. : processor heats computer case (excessively).

Such structured approach to construction of the cause-effect chains allows for detection of other types of omissions, including overlooked parameter-function or function-parameter pairs. This results in additional support for ensuring completeness of the CECA diagram. Nevertheless, all information regarding the causes still comes from the contents of boxes and the arrows only indicate the flow of causality.

Time is also referred to in Root Conflict Analysis (RCA+) developed by Souchkov. The method is focused on both disadvantages and advantages, possibly brought by some of the causes identified during analysis [8]. This allows for indicating physical contradictions with conflicting requirements to be fulfilled "at the same time". Time references are used at the stage of selecting root conflicts, but they reflect conditions rather than specific moments in time (e.g. "during strong wind"), which seems similar to the concept of occasion. Another similarity between RCA+ and Yoon's approach comes from the recommendations for describing identified causes, which also distinguish conditions and functions.

4 Merging Occasion Axis with Logical Model

The question usually asked when building CECA diagram is *why* which seems adequate and correct in this context. But adding another box and arrow to a cause-effect chain is like answering only one part of this question, namely *what* causes a particular effect, while we are also interested in *when* and *how* does this "causing" happen.

A renowned approach capable of modelling conditional changes of a system in time is *state machine* representation. Therefore it seems interesting to attempt a conversion of a CECA diagram into a state machine (automaton) with finite number of states and deterministic transitions between the states, i.e. *Deterministic Finite State Machine* (DFSM). State machines and other abstract machines are covered by Automata theory, and an introduction to this topic pertinent to the scope of our paper is given in [15].

DFSM is formally defined as a 5-tuple $<Q, \Sigma, \delta, q_0, F>$, where:

- Q is a finite set of states,
- Σ is a finite set of input symbols,
- δ is the transition function (δ: $Q \times \Sigma \rightarrow Q$),
- q_0 is the initial state of the automaton ($q_0 \in Q$),
- F is a set of states called accept states ($F \subseteq Q$).

Informally, we need some *states* to be defined as well as conditional *transitions* between the states, which depend on inputs. Combinations of inputs form *input symbols* and the *initial state* is the predefined start state, in which the automaton awaits the first input symbol. Outputs of an automaton depend on its state and – in particular – may differentiate the *accept states* and the other states. Automata are usually depicted as graphs with nodes representing states and directed edges (arcs) representing transitions.

The simplest state machine implementation used in digital circuits is the D-type flip-flop with two states {zero, one} and two input symbols {0, 1}. Transition function makes the flip-flop state to follow the input, i.e. 0 on input causes transition to state zero with output 0 and 1 on input causes transition to state one with output 1. In other words, such flip-flop remembers the latest input symbol and so it may be considered a 1-bit memory element. To complete the definition, we select zero as the initial state and one as the accept state.

Respective transition graph is shown in Fig. 2 using generic notation and basic UML notation for state machine modelling. The "E" prefixes in the UML model denote that respective actions are performed upon entering given states (as this notation also allows for describing actions executed upon exiting the states).

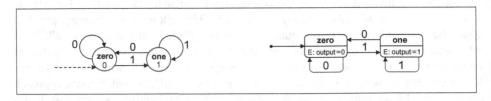

Fig. 2. State diagram (left) and basic UML model (right) of D-type flip-flop.

An example of an automaton with 4 states, 2 binary inputs and 1 output is shown in Fig. 3. The set of input symbols contains 4 elements {00, 01, 10, 11} and edge labels describe input symbols. The required operation is to detect the sequence 11-00-11. The initial state is denoted as A and the accept state is denoted as D. The successful detection is indicated with 1 on the output and all other states outputs 0. Response of the state machine to a test sequence 00-01-11-00-11-00-11-10 is presented below.

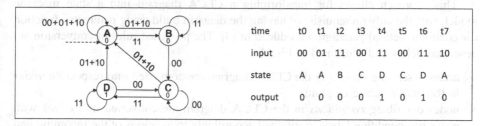

time	t0	t1	t2	t3	t4	t5	t6	t7
input	00	01	11	00	11	00	11	10
state	A	A	B	C	D	C	D	A
output	0	0	0	0	1	0	1	0

Fig. 3. Sample state machine and description of its operation. Plus sign denotes logical OR.

In taxonomy of the logical circuits state machines are categorized as sequential circuits. Outputs of a sequential circuit depend both on its inputs and its current state [15]. That is why a state machine (contrary to combinatorial logic) may produce different responses to the same input signals, and in the above example the first 11 symbol in the sequence (t2) could be distinguished from the second (t4). It is worth noticing that the third occurrence (t6) also matches the pattern, so that state D is traversed twice.

5 Converting CECA Diagram into State Machine Diagram

An apparent similarity between the state machine diagram and the CECA diagram is both promising and misleading. The former suggests an ability to reflect a structure of causal interrelations between disadvantages as states and transitions, while the latter comes from significant semantic differences between the respective elements:

- nodes in a CECA graph describe disadvantages, while nodes in a state machine graph describe states of the automaton,
- edges in a CECA graph only indicate direction of the causality flow (and so they do not need any labels), while edges in a state machine diagram describe transitions (and they are labeled with respective input symbols or logical conditions),
- logical operators in a CECA diagram reflect how the input causes combine to trigger the resulting disadvantages, with no direct counterpart in the state machine diagram.

Regardless of these differences, it should be noticed that:

- linear chain of disadvantages in a CECA diagram may be perceived as a model of the process of development of the last disadvantage in that chain,
- logical OR indicates that any of the input causes is sufficient to trigger the effect,
- logical AND indicates that all of the input causes are necessary to trigger the effect,
- state machine approach may be used for modelling processes.

From such perspective, we may interpret a CECA diagram as a model of the development of all target disadvantages included in that diagram. And this resembles the idea of a *harmful system* described in [16], being a conceptual source of the harmful functions resulting in the observed disadvantages of the analyzed system. By analogy, CECA diagram may be interpreted as a model of interconnected *harmful processes*, which – in spite of being unintended – "produce" unwanted effects in an organized and repeatable way.

This approach allows for transforming a CECA diagram into a state machine model, with the only prerequisite of having the diagram build using parameter-function (or condition-action) paradigm introduced in [9]. The proposed rules of conversion are described below and illustrated in Fig. 4.

- nodes describing *actions* in the CECA diagram are converted into respective *nodes* in the state machine diagram,
- nodes describing *conditions* in the CECA diagram are converted into *edges* with respective condition labels, positioned accordingly to locations of the incoming and outgoing edges in the CECA diagram,
- common causes, i.e. causes forking through edges to several nodes in the CECA diagram, are reflected in the state machine diagram as *groups of edges* modelling transitions to respective states (labelled with the same condition),
- OR operators appearing in the CECA diagram are converted into *groups of edges* in the state machine diagram (one edge for each input), modelling *alternative* of conditions required for transitions to the respective output states; in practice ORs are often omitted and modelled as multiple edges, which do not need conversion,
- AND operators appearing in the CECA diagram are converted into *additional nodes and edges* in the state machine diagram, modelling *coincidence* of conditions required for transitions to the respective output states,
- an additional *loopback edge* is created for each of the nodes in the state machine diagram, with a condition complementary to conditions of all other outgoing edges of this node to model waiting in the same state; such transition is default when none of the exit condition are met and it is usually not shown in diagrams.

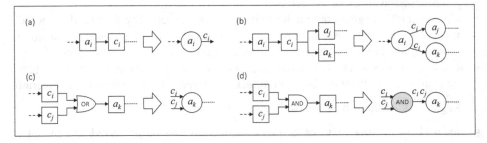

Fig. 4. Building blocks of a CECA diagram and their counterparts in state machine model: regular action-condition segment (a), action-condition segment with common cause (b), OR operator (c) and AND operator (d). Concatenation of symbols denotes logical AND. Loopback edges have been omitted for clarity.

A sample CECA diagram and the result of its conversion into state machine diagram is presented in Fig. 5, with root causes $a_1 \div a_5$ and target disadvantages $t_1 \div t_3$. As may be seen, the number of states is reduced compared to the initial number of nodes in the CECA diagram (14 vs. 24), because the nodes representing conditions are transformed into conditional transitions between the states.

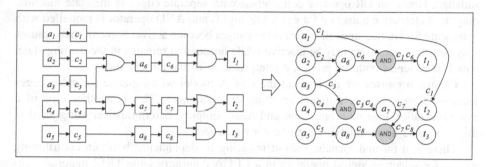

Fig. 5. A sample CECA diagram and an equivalent state machine diagram created using proposed conversion rules. Loopback edges have been omitted for clarity.

6 Analyzing Sequential CECA Model

Let us discuss the results of the conversion and the implications of the proposed rules.

Linear Chain of Causes. Described procedure properly transforms a linear chain of causes into a DFSM-like graph. The differences come from the specific interpretation of the states. For a regular automaton exactly one state is *current* and *active* at any given moment. In the transformed CECA model the states are related to functions performed in particular stages of a harmful process which "produces" a given disadvantage. Therefore the *current* state reflects the most advanced stage of the process reached within a chain (after a specific sequence of transitions), while some other states in this chain may be *active* i.e. their functions may still be performed.

Accept state of the automaton models the final product of the respective harmful process and therefore one accept (final) state should be generated during the conversion for each of the target disadvantages included in the CECA diagram.

Initial state of the automaton reflects the initial stage of the respective harmful process, which conforms to the criteria of identifying CECA root causes. Indeed, laws of nature or project constraints act continuously and thus qualify for the initial stages, when "production" of disadvantages has not started yet. And just like for the final states, we also need one initial state for each of the root causes included in the CECA diagram.

Input symbols are combinations of states of inputs and they are used for evaluating the transition function i.e. determining the next state of the automaton. Because transitions in the resulting state machine reflect conditions inherited from the CECA model, they should refer to particular objects, parameters and values. The inputs may be seen as logical signals evaluating to true or false – one for each of the conditions used in the state machine diagram, e.g. condition *temperature is higher than Ts* evaluates to true if $T > Ts$ and it evaluates to false otherwise.

Logical operators in the CECA diagram may be perceived as synchronization gates of the harmful processes. OR operator implies that the resulting transition will be triggered when the *first* of the involved conditions is satisfied, while AND operator implies that the transition will be triggered when the *last* of the involved conditions is satisfied. Hence an OR operator is modelled with separate edges in the state machine diagram (alternative transition for every OR input) and AND operator is modelled with extra state for waiting until all contributing causes become active. Some of these causes may be active and some may be inactive while automaton remains in the waiting state, which is coherent with the proposed interpretation of the current state.

Common causes are depicted in the CECA model with separate (or split) edges leading to two or more different resulting disadvantages. This is another type of a synchronization gate with one input and many outputs, deterministically triggered at the same time upon satisfying a particular condition.

There is a misunderstanding about referring to dependence between contributing causes for selecting logical operators in a CECA diagram. Some TRIZ materials recommend using OR operator "if underlying causes are independent of each other", while dependence (resulting, for instance, from a *common cause* of the input disadvantages) is not related to logical functions describing the influence on the output disadvantages. In other words dependence relates to causes and logical operators relate to effects, so that both OR and AND may be used for dependent as well as independent causes.

Concurrency and Hierarchy. Because a CECA diagram models a set of interconnected harmful processes, the resulting state machine is in fact a structured collection of automata running concurrently. The bottom level of the hierarchy is formed by linear chains, containing initial states, final states and – perhaps – some intermediate states, connected by respective conditional transitions. Such chains may contain root causes or target disadvantages and may connect on inputs (with common causes) or outputs (due to logical operators in the CECA diagram). And they may be treated as single *super-states* at the higher levels of the hierarchy. Taking the above into consideration, we should adjust the DFSM definition $<Q, \Sigma, \delta, q_0, F>$ presented before.

- set of states Q includes all stages of all processes modelled with linear chains in the CECA diagram and additional states resulting from conversion of AND operators,
- set of input symbols Σ is determined by all conditions inherited from the CECA diagram, so that all required transition criteria may be evaluated,
- transition function δ is determined by the locations and directions of the edges and OR operators in the CECA diagram; concurrent operation of automata is synchronized on transitions labelled with the same input symbol,
- instead of a single initial state $q_0 \in Q$ we need a set of initial states $Q_0 \subseteq Q$, which includes all root causes identified in the CECA diagram (each root cause determines the first stage of the respective harmful process),
- set of final states $F \subseteq Q$ includes all terminal stages of all linear chains in the CECA diagram – in particular, all target disadvantages.

The extended definition is close to *Hierarchical Concurrent Finite State Machine*, which may be systematically described using Unified Modeling Language, Place-Transition notation (Petri nets), state charts or other notations supported by modelling tools.

7 Example

As an example, we will consider computer overheating, which was briefly mentioned in Sect. 3. Target disadvantage is that *computer stops because of overheating* and a simplified CECA diagram is shown in Fig. 6, together with a state machine diagram obtained using proposed conversion rules. The model covers two scenarios of creating excessive amount of heat and two variants of stopping the computer, depending on the operation of the thermal protection: properly configured (and operable) vs. disabled (or misconfigured, or inoperable). For clarity, the descriptions are shortened and the alternative causes in the CECA diagram are depicted with multiple edges instead of the explicit OR gates. As can be seen, interleaving of actions and conditions is crucial.

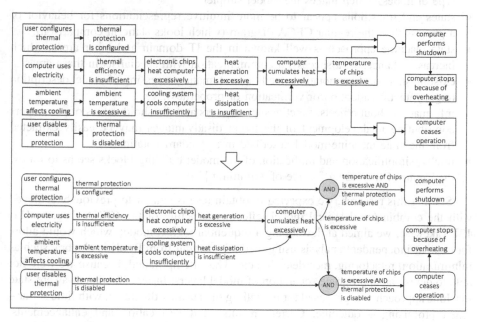

Fig. 6. An example CECA diagram (top) and the respective state machine diagram (bottom).

8 Summary and Conclusions

We have briefly presented original CECA method and some improvements proposed in order to produce correct and complete models of causality. The Yoon's idea of the Occasion Axis and structuring the diagrams using condition-action segments provides proper perspective for modelling the development of target disadvantages as sequences of events. On the other hand, it touches upon the natural limitation of regular CECA diagram by modelling essentially different aspects (conditions and actions) with same type of objects and asserting additional constraints regarding structure of the cause-effect chains to counterbalance that drawback. This construction looks artificial, compared to the original method, where all boxes are meant as disadvantages.

This paper reframes Yoon's approach by pointing out that cause-effect analysis actually identifies harmful processes responsible for "producing" target disadvantages, which may be represented using the state machine model. We have proposed rules for converting a CECA diagram into a state machine diagram and indicated required extensions to basic state machine definition. The resulting model employs heterogenic information about actions, conditions, logical operators and their interconnections inherited from the input cause-effect diagram. Such representation offers several benefits:

- stages of the process and transitions between stages are clearly distinguished, which makes the model more comprehensible,
- logical operators are converted into states or transitions and disappear as a separate type of nodes, which makes the model simpler,
- states and transitions appear to be more intuitive representations for behavior of a process than the regular CECA diagram (which looks static in comparison),
- state machine approach is well known in the IT domain and other areas, which increases chances of a successful communication with specialists in these areas,
- existing state machine notations facilitate automatic processing of model description (e.g. syntactic validation or verification of properties),
- information about objects, functions, parameters and threshold values of parameters contributing to development of the target disadvantages may be easily extracted from the state machine model described in a standard notation,
- finally, simplification and unification of the model building blocks seems to follow the Trend of Increasing Degree of Trimming [13].

Starting this research, we expected to obtain results similar to previously achieved with the combinatorial logical model reflecting structure of the CECA diagram [11, 12]. Likewise, we aimed at developing a sequential logical model, which would allow for content-independent analysis using methods coming from Boolean algebra, such as minimization, refactoring, race detection etc. This attempt failed, because we were not able to devise an appropriate separation of model layers. Instead, a content-aware state machine approach was proposed for modelling of causality diagrams, with little so far – albeit promising – outcome. Current results need verification and enhancements, because some elements seem rough, such as different approaches to modelling OR and AND operators and counterintuitive concept of many active states, to name a few.

Further work could address transformations (e.g. reduction) of the resulting diagram. It is also known, that every state machine defines a formal grammar describing rules of creating input expressions (sequences of input symbols) capable of causing transitions to final states. This duality indicates an interesting direction of research:

analyzing causal relations using linguistic approach. Another area of further work is identifying and exploring possible connections or fusions with other methods of cause-effect analysis, with Interaction Causality Scheme [17] and vulnerability-based approach [18] in the first places.

Acknowledgments. Author gratefully acknowledges Dr. Oleg Abramov for valuable materials and explanations regarding the CECA method, Mr. Piotr Salata for inspiring discussions and Mr. Dariusz Burzyński for helping to make the paper comprehensible.

References

1. Litvin, S.S., Akselrod, B.M.: Cause-Effects Chains of Undesired Effects, Methodical theses (in Russian). CPB, 1995/12/18–1996/01/03
2. Abramov, O., Kislov, A.: Cause-Effect Analysis of Engineering System's Disadvantages, Handbook on Methodology (in Russian), Algorithm, Ltd. (2000)
3. Falkov, D.S., Misyuchenko, I.L.: Analysis of typical errors made when choosing logical functions (in Russian) (2013). http://www.metodolog.ru/node/1643. Accessed 10 July 2018
4. Falkov, D.S., Misyuchenko, I.L.: Characteristics of building fragments of Cause-Effect Chains with serial connection of Disadvantages (in Russian) (2013). http://www.metodolog. ru/node/1654. Accessed 10 July 2018
5. Efimov, A.V.: Identification of Key Disadvantages and Key Problems using Cause-Effect Chains of Undesired Effects (in Russian) (2011). http://www.metodolog.ru/node/993. Accessed 10 July 2018
6. Pinyayev, A.M.: A Method for Inventive Problem Analysis and Solution Based On Why-Why Analysis and Functional Clues. TRIZ Master thesis (2007)
7. Medvedev, A.V.: Algorithm for Automated Building of Cause-Effect Chains of Disadvantages (in Russian). TRIZ Master thesis (2013)
8. Souchkov, V.V.: A Guide to Root Conflict Analysis (RCA+). ICG Training & Consulting. http://www.xtriz.com/publications/RCA_Plus_July2011.pdf. Accessed 10 July 2018
9. Yoon, H.: Occasion axis and parameter-function pair nexus for effective building of cause effect chains. In: Souchkov, V., Kässi, T. (eds.) Proceedings of the TRIZfest-2014 International Conference, Prague, Czech Republic, pp. 184–194. MATRIZ (2014)
10. Lok, A.: A simple way to perform CECA and generate ideas in practice. In: Souchkov, V. (ed.) Proceedings of the TRIZfest-2017 International Conference, Krakow, Poland, pp. 23–30. MATRIZ (2017)
11. Chrząszcz, J., Salata, P.: Cause-effect chains analysis using boolean algebra. TRIZ Future 2016 Conference, Wroclaw, Poland (2016). In: Koziołek, S., Chechurin, L., Collan, M. (eds.) Advances and Impacts of the Theory of Inventive Problem Solving. The TRIZ Methodology, Tools and Case Studies. Springer (2018). https://doi.org/10.1007/978-3-319-96532-1
12. Chrząszcz, J.: Quantitative approach to cause-effect chains analysis. In: Souchkov, V. (ed.) Proceedings of the TRIZfest-2017 International Conference, Krakow, Poland, pp. 341–352. MATRIZ (2017)
13. Ikovenko, S.: Level 1 Certification TRIZ Workshop, pp. 171–193. MATRIZ (2016)
14. Russo, D., Duci, S.: How to exploit standard solutions in problem definition. Procedia Eng. **131**, 951–962 (2015). https://doi.org/10.1016/j.proeng.2015.12.407
15. Wagner, F., Wolstenholme, P.: Misunderstandings about state machines. Comput. Control Eng. J. **15**(4), 40–45 (2004)

16. Lenyashin, V., Kim, H.J.: "Harmful System" – using this concept in modern TRIZ (in Russian) (2006). http://www.metodolog.ru/00859/00859.html. Accessed 10 July 2018
17. Axelrod, B.: Systems approach: modeling engineering systems using interactions causality scheme. In: Grundlach, K. (ed.) Proceedings of TRIZ Future 2007 Conference, Frankfurt, Germany, pp. 131–138 (2007)
18. Chrząszcz, J.: Indicating system vulnerabilities within CECA model. In: Mayer, O. (ed.) Proceedings of the TRIZfest-2018 International Conference, Lisbon, Portugal, pp. 31–37. MATRIZ (2018)

Parameter Deployment and Separation for Solving Physical Contradictions

D. Daniel Sheu$^{(\boxtimes)}$ and Rachel Yeh

Department of Industrial Engineering,
National Tsing Hua University, Hsinchu 300, Taiwan
dsheu@ie.nthu.edu.tw

Abstract. Physical contradiction is at the heart of TRIZ contradiction problem solving. The essence of a physical contradiction is that for two objectives, we have two contradictory demands on the same parameter of the same system. As part one of the two-part Parameter Manipulation approach to solve physical contradiction, this paper proposes a systematic new method to solve physical contradictions using the parameter deployment and separation.

By defining the local system to include the components directly at the immediate relevant components of the physical contradiction, the proposed parameter deployment systematically deploys the two objectives and the contradictory parameter into their respective causing constituent parameters. The essence of parameter separation is to assign the two contradictory requirements, either at the objective level or at the contradictory parameter level, to be satisfied by separate constituent parameters or distinct value ranges of a constituent parameter. Out of the 25 initial cases, with parameter deployment and separation, it was found that on average the number of solution ideas generated increased from 5.08 by all existing separation methods to 12.28 by parameter domination and parameter separation proposed by this paper - a net increase of 149%. Solutions conceivable by existing methods are all included in this set of problem solving strategies. With the addition of parameter transfer, the average number of solution ideas increased about 10 times compare to the number of ideas generated by all existing methods. In addition, all existing problem solving strategies constitute only 3 categories of strategies out of the 17-plus problem solving strategies proposed by this integrated set of parameter manipulation.

Keywords: Physical contradiction · Parameter deployment
Parameter separation · Parameter transfer · TRIZ · Systematic innovation

1 Introduction

1.1 Research Background and Objectives

Physical contradiction (PC) is at the heart of all problematic contradictions. At present, all methods to solve physical contradictions are based on either separation principles, by-passing contradictions, or satisfying contradictions. The majority of them at the end converted to inventive principles to solve the problems [1–3]. The deficiencies of the existing methods to solve physical contradictions include:

© IFIP International Federation for Information Processing 2018
Published by Springer Nature Switzerland AG 2018. All Rights Reserved
D. Cavallucci et al. (Eds.): TFC 2018, IFIP AICT 541, pp. 315–329, 2018.
https://doi.org/10.1007/978-3-030-02456-7_26

(1) Various existing methods appear to be independent and are lack of synergy among them.
(2) Most of existing methods at the end converted to the inventive principles. That means that the problem solver need only to examine the selected inventive principles. Many times, the 40 inventive principles are not enough to inspire good specific solutions.
(3) There is no detail thinking process which can lead the problem solver to reach solutions systematically and algorithmically.
(4) All the existing separating principles focus on the solving problem at the contradictory parameter level. Solving physical contradictions at the objective level has not been considered for problem solving. Even though solving problem at the objective level implies solving the corresponding technical contradiction, the methods proposed for solving at the objective level is completely different from the traditional way of contradiction matrix and inventive principles to solve technical contradictions. Note that technical contradictions and their corresponding physical contradictions are at different abstractions of the same problem. Solving at objective level is problem solving using the elements of physical contradiction. When the corresponding physical contradiction is solved, its corresponding technical contradiction is also resolved.

This research established a systematic thinking process which generates 17-plus strategies to solving physical contradictions of which all the existing methods constitute only 3 of the 17-plus strategies identified by this research. Furthermore, all the 17-plus problem solving strategies are under the same set of theory based on parameter manipulation. Due to space limitations, this paper focuses on the first part of the full strategies as parameter deployment and parameter domination/separation which contains 6-plus strategies [4]. A sequel will focus on parameter transfer which contains 11-plus strategies [5–7].

2   Foundations of Physical Contradiction and Parameter Manipulation

2.1   Formulation of Physical Contradiction

A physical contradiction occurs when one parameter cannot satisfy two incompatible demands in order to achieve two objectives at the same time. Model of physical contradiction can be expressed as:

- To O1, P should be +P. But, (Statement 1)
- To O2, P should be −P.

Where "O1" and "O2" are two disparate objectives, "P" is the contradictory parameter which causes the problem. "+P" and "−P" represent the two incompatible demands which need to be satisfied at P in order to achieve O1 and O2. Taking desk area as an example, the below statements express the physical contradiction.

- To accommodate more stuffs on the desk, the area of the desk should be big. But,
- To occupy less space in a room, the area of the desk should be small.

This paper proposes the systematic methods of:

(1) Parameter deployment: to assist users to identify all relevant parameters which contribute directly to the physical contradiction, and
(2) Parameter separation/domination: To separate the contradictory demands either at the objective level or the contradictory parameter level to solve the physical contradiction, or, to enhance a compatible parameter so that the O1 and O2 can be satisfied simultaneous as explained in Sect. 2.3.

To solve physical contradiction, the relevant parameters influencing, or affecting, the two objectives O1 and O2 or the contradictory parameter P need to be investigated. By deploying the O1, O2, and P into their corresponding causing constituent parameters, all the parameter separation or domination strategies to solve the physical contradiction can be systematically and so far most comprehensively identified thus ideas to solve the physical contradiction can be generated. The acts of identifying all immediate causes for achieving O1, O2, or P relies on deploying the O1, O2, P into their causing constituent parameters as explained below.

2.2 Definition of Systems

In order to define the scope of parameter deployment, the concept of "center components" and "local system" are defined.

The center components of a physical contradiction are the components whose attribute defines or owns the O1, O2, or P as in Sect. 2.1 Statement 1. For example, the physical contradiction "To improve the effectiveness of nail penetration, the hammer should be heavy; To carry the hammer easily, the weight of the hammer should be light". O1: effectiveness of nail penetration, center component is nail; O2: Carrying the hammer easily. The object/tool of the function is hammer/hand. In this case, we can pick either the object (hammer) or the tool (hand) of the function as the center component as it does not affect the identification of the Local System described in the next paragraph. For most disadvantages, the object owns the constituent parameter. Hammer should be heavy/light, center component for the hammer's weight is the hammer. The set of center components carries the parameters of core issues (O1/O2, P).

The local system (LS) of a physical contradiction consists of all center components and the components which directly contact with the center components. In this case, it will include the nail, the hammer, the hand holding the hammer, and the wood that the nail is going to penetrate. In a sense, the local system is the operating zone in traditional TRIZ with the condition that this operating zone is defined at the minimum system/components which DIRECTLY affect the problem. The local system defines the immediate problem area from where all immediate causes of the physical contradiction can be identified and the immediate scope from which the problem solving resources can be drawn. It is then the scope of parameter deployment. Note that the influence of any external factors affecting the problem must be transmitted via some local system parameters/component(s) to the problem point which is at the center components. The definition of the local system allows us to have a definitive scope for identifying ALL immediate causing factors of the problem on which we can separate the satisfactions of the contradictory demands at either O1/O2 or P level.

2.3   Parameter Deployment

The Generic Form of Parameter Deployment

The two objectives can be shown in the following generic forms:

$$O1 = fn(P_j, \ldots; E_i^1, \ldots; Z_k, \ldots) \tag{1.1}$$

$$O2 = fn(Pj, \ldots; E_i^2, \ldots; Zk, \ldots) \tag{1.2}$$

The contradictory parameters can be shown in the following generic form:

$$P_j = fn(X_{j1}, X_{j2}, X_{j3}, \ldots, X_{jm}) \quad Where\, j = 1, 2, \ldots, J \tag{2}$$

Where notation, $fn(\ldots)$, represents function of $(\ldots)$. The first semi-column, ;, denotes the delimitation between the contradictory constituent parameters and exclusive parameters. The second semi-column delimits the exclusive parameters and the compatible parameters.

In the generic forms above, "P" represents "contradictory parameter" of the two objectives, O1 and O2. "E" represents "exclusive parameter" of each objective, and "Z" represents "compatible parameters of the same direction" of the two objectives. More detail symbol definitions are shown in Table 1.

2.4   The Essence of Problem Solving Strategies with Parameter Manipulation

Two aspects for parameter manipulations are discerned: manipulation targets and manipulation modes. In terms of manipulation target, it is observed that previous solutions by parameter separations to solve physical contradictions were mainly about separating demands on the contradictory parameter with different value range of its certain Constituent Parameter, X_m. For example, when X_m assumes space, it is the Separation by space; when X_m assumes Time, it is the separation by time; When X_m assumes system level, it is the separation by system level, etc. In this sense, all existing parameter separation methods fall into one category of "within parameter separation (designated as IPV strategy later) of the proposed strategy by this research. Separating parameters to satisfy the two contradictory objectives was not taken into consideration by traditional separation principles. Therefore, this paper proposes two hierarchies of parameter manipulation targets to achieve: separation of parameter for two contradictory demands on the same contradictory parameter (P) and separation of parameters to satisfy two contradictory objectives (O1 and O2).

Three distinct modes of parameter manipulation are defined in Fig. 1. They are: Parameter Domination, Parameter Separation, and Parameter Transfer.

Table 1. Definitions and descriptions of each parameter categories

Symbol	Definition	Description
C_b^a	Constituent parameter for O1/O2	• C_b^a represents the b-th causing constituent parameter within the local system influencing the corresponding objective O1 when a = 1, or objective O2 when a = 2 • C_b^a can assume any role such as P (for O1/O2), E (as exclusive parameter), or Z (Compatible parameter)
P_j	j-th Contradictory parameter	• P_j represents the j-th common but contradictory parameter of the two objectives. To achieve O1, P must be +P; But, to achieve O2, P must be –P. +P and –P are two incompatible demands on P • It is possible to uncover additional contradictory parameter, P_j, as a results of parameter deployment. If there is only one P, $P_1 \equiv P$ is the explicit original contradictory parameter • Each additional P_j will provide 4 more strategies for problem solving via separation and 6 more strategies for problem solving via parameter transfer. Explained later
E_c^a	Exclusive parameter(s)	• Constituent parameters that are exclusive to either O1 or O2 but not both • E_c^a represents the c-th exclusive constituent parameter of objective O1 (a = 1) or O2 (a = 2)
Z_k	Compatible parameter(s)	• Z_k represents the k-th common constituent parameter of the two objectives having demands on Z_k toward same direction to achieve O1 and O2. For example, both O1 and O2 desire Z_k to be the larger the better
X_{jm}	Constituent parameter for P_j	• The m-th constituent parameter(s) of the contradictory parameter, P_j. When $j = 1$, $X_{1m} \equiv X_m$

With combinations of different **Manipulation Modes** and different **Target Levels of Satisfaction**, 17-plus strategies of solving physical contradiction can be conceived. Figure 1 defines the Strategy Symbols for Parameter Separation and Transfer. The first letter of the strategies indicates the mode of manipulation (I: separation withIn parameter, C: separation aCross parameters, T: parameter Transfer). The second letter indicates the target of manipulation (P: contradictory parameter as the target to resolve problem, O: two objectives as the targets to resolve problem). The third (and the fourth) letters indicate manipulation methods. (V: by using different Value ranges of a parameter, S: by Splitting one contradictory parameter into two so as to satisfy two incompatible demands separately, P: using contradictory parameters to satisfy one demand, E: using exclusive parameters to satisfy one demand, A: using non-constituent external Additional parameters which are not any of the constituent parameters from the local system. They are parameters from external components seemingly irrelevant to the problem but can be used as some resources for problem solving. Figure 2 shows the 17-plus strategies thus developed.

Acronyms of the strategies are summarized in Table 2.

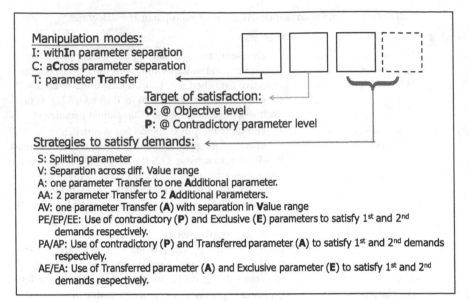

Fig. 1. Strategy symbols for parameter separation and transfer

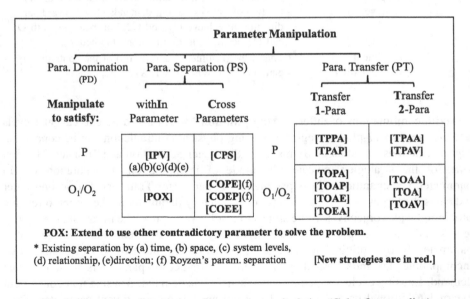

Fig. 2. Overview of strategies of parameter manipulation (Color figure online)

Table 2. List of the various strategies

PD	**P**arameter **D**omination. By enhancing one or multiple compatible constituent parameters (Z_k) greatly to the extent that the influence by Z_k dominate the influence of P_j thus O1 and O2 can be achieved simultaneously
IPV	With**I**n **P**arameter separation by **V**alue range. This includes all existing separation principles and more as indicated by separation at different value range of X_{jm} in Eq. 2
CPS	**C**ross **P**arameter separation by **S**plitting parameter. Splitting a contradictory parameter into two
COPE/ COPE	**C**ross **P**arameter separation. PE: Use +P to satisfy O1 and Exclusive parameter of O2 to satisfy O2. EP: Use −P to satisfy O2 and Exclusive parameter of O1 to satisfy O1
COEE	**C**ross parameter separation to satisfy at **O**bjective level. EE: Using **E**xclusive parameter of O1 to satisfy O1, EE: Using **E**xclusive parameter of O2 to satisfy O2
TPPA/TPAP	**T**ransfer a parameter to satisfy a contradictory parameter **P**. **PA**: Let P = + P and use an Additional (external) parameter to satisfy −P. AP: Let P = −P and use an Additional (external) parameter to satisfy +P
TPAA/TPAV	TRAA: **T**ransfer two contradictory demands at **P** level to <u>two</u> additional parameters (**AA**) separately TPAV: **T**ransfer two contradictory demands at **P** level to one **A**dditional parameter but at two separate **V**alue ranges
TOPA/TOAP	TOPA: **T**ransfer satisfaction of O2 to an **A**dditional parameter while letting **P** = + P to satisfy O1 TOAP: **T**ransfer satisfaction of O1 to an **A**dditional parameter while letting **P** = −P to satisfy O2
TOAE/TOEA	TOAE: Using **E**xclusive parameter of **O**2 to satisfy O2 and **T**ransfer satisfaction of O1 to an **A**dditional parameter TOEA: Using **E**xclusive parameter of **O**1 to satisfy O1 and **T**ransfer satisfaction of O2 to an **A**dditional parameter
TOAA/TOA/TOAV	Transfer satisfaction of O1/O2 (TO) to: (1) two distinct Additional parameters (AA), (2) one Additional parameter on which the contradiction disappear or become non-effectual, (3) one Additional parameter but separate them by **V**alue range (AV)
POX	Refer to Fig. 2 and Sect. 2.5. Satisfaction of contradictory demands at **P** or **O** level strategy e**X**tension by using P_j's as the contradictory parameter when j is greater than or equal to 2. For each additional P_j, or P', identified there are 3 additional separation strategies (IP'V, COP'E, COEP') and 6 additional transfer strategies (TP'PA/TP'AP/TP'AA/TP'AV/TOP'A/TOAP')

2.5   Three Basic Modes of Parameter Manipulation

Refer to Fig. 2. The three basic modes of Parameter Manipulations for problem solving are explained below:

(1) Parameter Domination (PD): By enforcing a compatible parameter Z_k to the extent that the impact of the contradictory parameter become much less influential and Z_k dominates the results, the two objectives can still be simultaneously satisfied.

Take eyeglasses as an example.

For glasses [O1] not slip off, nose-pad normal force [P] should be large [+P]. But, to avoid nose discomfort [O2], nose-pad normal force[P] should be small [−P].

Parameter Deployment:

[O1] For glasses not slip off = fn(nose-pad friction force↑, nose-pad friction coefficient↑; nose grease ↓; eyeglasses weight ↓, nose-pad area ↑)

[O2] To avoid nose discomfort = fn(nose-pad friction force↓, nose-pad friction coefficient → ; nose-pad softness ↑, air humidity → ; eyeglasses weight ↓, nose-pad area ↑)

Where:

↑/↓: Indicates that within the scope of observation in the practical range, the higher/lower the value is the better to satisfy the dependent O or P.

→: Indicates that within the scope of observation in the practical range, there exists certain optimal value to satisfy the dependent O or P.

PD Solution: The compatible constituent parameters for this case are "eyeglasses weight" and "nose-pad area". In the parameter observation range and other things being the same, we can lower the weight of the eyeglass frame and/or increase the contact area of nose-pad to achieve O1 and O2 simultaneous. Whether or not a compatible parameter Z_k *is* able to dominate the influence on O1/O2 can be easily tested by enhancing the Z_k *in* the desirable direction and check if the O1/O2 can be achieved simultaneously with certain P value.

(2) Parameter Separation (PS):

    (2a) Solution strategy IPV: Use 2 distinct value ranges of a constituent parameter of the contradictory parameter to satisfy the two contradictory demands. This includes all existing traditional separations by time, space, system levels, relationship, directions, etc. It is possible to have more constituent parameters thus more opportunities for problem solving using other parameters with IPV strategy.

    For example, to make a pencil comfortable to hold (O1), the pencil shaft should have no angles (+P: round shape). To keep the pencil from rolling (O2), the pencil shaft should have angles (−P: say, hexagonal cross-section). With [IPV] strategy, using space as the constituent parameter to solve the problem. We can make the pencil shaft to have no angles (+P) on the part where people hold it, and have angles (−P) at the end of the pencil shaft to avoid rolling.

    (2b) Solution strategy CPS: Split the contradictory parameter P into two parameters so that one P can satisfy +P and the other P can satisfy −P demand thus solving the problem.

    Taking outdoor public display panel as an example. Refer to Fig. 3. The cover plate for the display is a frame structure covering the glass display on its circumference. The formulation of physical contradiction follows:

- To prevent the panel from rain leakage in (O1), the holes of cover plate should not exist (+P).
- To allow good heat dissipation by ventilation of the hot air (O2), the holes of the cover place should exist (−P).

The CPS strategy suggested splitting the cover plate into two cover plates with a gap between them. The outer plate has no hole to prevent water coming in and opens at the bottom so that the water can not come up into the in-between gap while leaving space for air to vent from below. Make the inner cover plate contains holes so that the hot air can come out of the holes of inner layer and going through the gap down and out. See CPS in Fig. 3.

(2c) Solution strategy COPE/COEP, COEE: Use 2 distinct constituent parameters of O1/O2 to satisfy O1 and O2 separately. Royzen's Separation by parameter [2] falls into COPE and COPE. But, there is no methods proposed to identify the constituent parameters in Royzen's approach. This paper proposed the parameter deployment to systematically identify all constituent parameters for O1, O2, and P for comprehensive considerations.

With the same outdoor display panel mentioned above, the parameter deployment results in the below constituent parameters.

- Prevent rain leakage (O1) = fn(Holes on cover plateØ, cover plate thickness ↑, sealedness↑; cover plate water resistance↑, water amount↓;)
- Good heat dissipate (O2) = fn(Holes on cover plate∃, cover plate thickness↓, sealedness↓; Cover plate heat dissipation rate↑;)
- Holes on cover plate (P_1) = fn(.., heat generation rate, cover plate specification)
- Cover plate thickness (P_2) = fn(.., heat generation rate, cover plate specification)
- Sealedness (P_3) = fn(.., water amount, sealant specification)

Where Ø means non-existent, ∃ means existent. The "..," signifies the first default set of constituent parameters for traditional separation constituent parameters for the P_j's. They are space, time, system level, relationship, direction, etc.

Refer to Fig. 3 for partial solutions generated by parameter separation.

COPE suggest a solution of {no holes on cover plate, cover plate with high heat dissipation rate material/design}

COEP suggests solution of {holes on cover plate, high water resistance (design the hole downward out)}

Note that when there are more than one contradictory parameters, the P_1 in COPE/COEP above refers to the original contradictory parameter, holes on cover plate.

COEE suggest a combination of E_c^1 and E_c^2: such as {water resistant cover plate (hole or no hole), high heat dissipation cover plate}. There are multiple combinatory ways to substantiate the solution model by taking any one from E_c^1 to combine any one from E_c^2 to form a possible solution.

(3) Parameter Transfer (PT): Transfer one or both of the two contradictory demands to one or two parameter(s) of seemingly unrelated external component/system not

in the local system so that the two demands do not crash on the same parameter. This include as TPPA, TPAP, TOPA, TOAP, TOAE, TOEA, TPAA, TPAV, TOAA, TOA, TOAV in Fig. 2. As an example, one TOAA solution is to delegate the task of preventing water leakage to an external rain shield and/or the task of heat dissipation to a heat pipe both of which are external resources, not belonging to the local system, capable of satisfying O1 and O2 respectively.

Due to space limitation, the category of Parameter Transfer and how to systematically identify those external resources will be explained in a subsequent paper. This paper focuses on parameter domination and separation only.

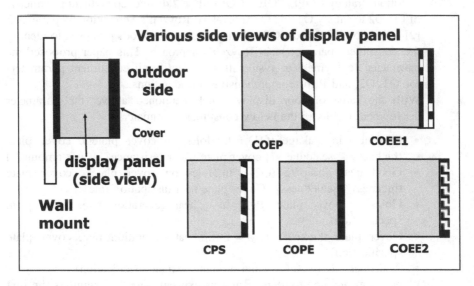

Fig. 3. Partial solutions of display panel

2.6   The POX Extension Strategy

Refer to Fig. 4. The strategy of POX is applicable when after parameter deployment, we found additional contradictory parameters P_j exist, $j = 2, 3, ..., J$. With each additional P_j, we can replace the original P_1 in the strategies of IPV/CPS/COPE/COEP or any of the parameter transfer strategies which involve using a contradictory parameter P such as TPPA/TPAP/TOPA/TOAP/TPAA/TPAV strategies for problem solving. With each additional identified $P' = P_j$, $j = 2, 3, ..., J$, to replace the original P_1, 10 more strategies can be used which 6 of them belong to Parameter Transfer category and 4 of them from the part of Parameter Separation. Therefore, a total of $5 + 4 (J - 1)$ strategies can be used to solve the problem using parameter separation. Together with Parameter Domination and Parameter Transfer categories, a total of $17 + 10 (J - 1)$ strategies can be used. Where J is the number of contradictory parameters identified by the parameter deployment.

For example (Fig. 4), if we use the Cover plate thickness (P2) as the subject contradictory parameter, apply the various strategies may generate ideas such as:

- IP_2V strategy: Let the frontal cover plate to be thick (no hole) to protect against rains. Let the lower side of the cover plate to be so thin with high heat dissipation so that the heat can dissipate from below the display.
- CP_2S: split cover plate thickness into 2 partitions. Partition 1 contains upper and side frames. Partition 2 contains lower frame. Make the partition 1 cover thick to prevent rain leakage and the partition 2 thin for heat dissipation.
- COP_2E: To prevent panel from rain leakage, make the cover plate thick (and no hole). However, use high heat conductivity materials for the cover plate to allow good heat dissipation.
- $COEP_2$: Make cover plate thickness thin (P_2) to dissipate heat better, but with water resistant design (E1) to prevent water leakage.

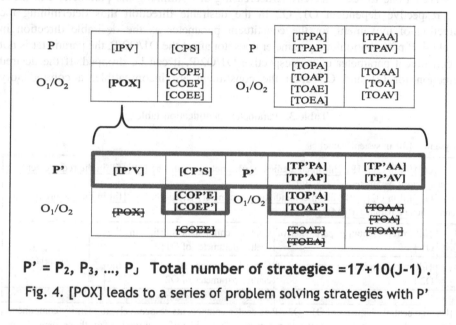

$P' = P_2, P_3, ..., P_J$ Total number of strategies $=17+10(J-1)$.

Fig. 4. [POX] leads to a series of problem solving strategies with P'

Fig. 4.   Cover plate thickness various strategies summary

3 Method of Parameter Deployment

3.1 Component Identification and Parameter Deployment

In order to identify all immediate causal parameters contributing to the physical contradiction for parameter deployment, a set of forms are designed. By filling out the designed tables step-by-step, the user is prompted to consider all necessary aspects of the parameter deployment procedurally and systematically. Table 3 is the Parameter Identification Table in which the users identify the center components, the representative parameters of O1, O2, and P. Then, and all the contacting components of the center components are identified. The set of center components and contacting components constitute the local system of the contradiction. All immediate causal factors must be coming from the parameters of the local system components.

To identify constituent parameters as complete as possible, two steps were taken:

(1) On each component of the local system, we ask Thought Provoking Question: What attributes/parameters of this component can cause or influence O1/O2/P? Those are the causing constituent parameters for deployment.

(2) Then, we quickly go through a list of some 83 collected parameters as a secondary check list to see if any of the parameters on the list of this component can cause/influence the O1/O2/P.

In Table 4, Parameter Deployment Table, users can determine the category of each parameters by perturbing each potentially relevant parameter around the current observed value to see if increasing/decreasing or optimizing the parameter can move the respective dependent O1, O2 in the desirable direction thus determining the direction of movement for the constituent parameter as the desirable direction in Table 4. If perturbation of a parameter does not affect the O1/O2/P, the parameter is not a constituent parameter of the respective O1/O2/P, it can be dropped. If the desired direction for O1 and O2 upon the constituent are incompatible, a contradictory

Table 3. Parameter identification table

System : {fill in system name}

For [O₁]{fill in O1}, [P] {fill in contradictory parameter} should be [+P]{fill in the requirement for contradictory parameter of O1}. But, For [O₂]{fill in O2}, [P] {fill in contradictory parameter} should be [-P]{fill in the requirement for contradictory parameter of O2}.			
O₁	{fill in representative parameter of O1 }	Central component : {fill in the central parameter of O1}	P {fill in Central component of P}
O₂	{fill in representative parameter of O2 }	Central component : {fill in the central parameter of O2}	

Component Contact Diagram
{Use the central elements of O1 / O2 / P as center components respectively, to identify components that directly contact those center components. Then, identify parameters of those central and contacting components for possible causing factors of the problem. Lines connecting cells below indicate the contact status.}

parameter P is identified. Using this method, it is possible to identify more than one contradictory parameter for O1/O2, as P_i. If both O1 and O2 require the constituent parameter to move the same direction, the constituent parameter is a compatible parameter, Z_k. If the constituent parameter only affect either O1 or O2, it is an exclusive parameter E_c^a. In this way, preliminary formula of the deployment can be obtained. In case there is some known scientific formula for O1/O2/P, the constituent factors of the scientific parameter can be added to its corresponding set of constituent parameters. This concludes the parameter deployment.

Table 4. Parameter deployment table

System : { fill in system name}						+P	{fill in +P state}	-P	{fill in −P state}
O_1	{fill in O1}					O_2	{fill in O2}		
Center/Contact components									
{Fill in component A}			{Fill in component B}			{Fill in component C}		{Fill in component D}	
Param.	O_1	O_2	Param.	O_1	O_2	Param.	O_1	O_2	Param.	O_1	O_2
{parameter name of component A}	{fill in required direction}	{fill in required direction}									
Parameter Deployment	[O1] {fill in the O1} = fn (P, ...; E, ...; Z, ...) {construct the deployment parameters of O1} [O2] {fill in the O2} = fn (P, ...; E, ...; Z, ...) {construct the deployment parameters of O2} [Pi] {the conflict parameter i} = fn(.., X1, X2, ...) {construct the deployment parameters of Pi} ...										

4 Test Results

25 cases of physical contradictions (PC) were tested with the parameter manipulation strategies. The results are given in Table 5 in which columns are explained below.

PD: number of solution ideas generated by Parameter Domination;
PS: Parameter Separation;
Para.: Parameter
Total net incr.: Total net increase of the number of solution ideas generated.

With the combination of various parameter manipulations, the number of net increase in solution ideas is 149% from an average of 5.08 ideas by all existing methods of PC problem solving to 12.28 ideas by the proposed 6-plus PD + PS strategies. With the additions of parameter transfer strategies, the number of solution ideas can be as many as 10 times more than the ideas generated from all existing methods.

Table 5. Comparison of numbers of solutions generated

Problem title	PD	Existing separation principles	COPE/COEP	All existing methods	PD + PS	Net incr. PD + PS	# of solutions by para. transfer	Total # of sol.
Public display	0	2	6	8	26	225%	161	187
Projector	1	0	4	4	14	250%	117	131
Smart phone	0	2	2	4	5	25%	70	75
PCB welding	0	3	4	7	11	57%	21	32
Bike glove	1	3	4	7	20	186%	166	186
Needle hole	1	2	5	7	16	129%	122	138
Ball valve	0	1	3	4	12	200%	41	53
Glasses	2	0	3	3	10	233%	52	62
Bike brake	4	1	2	3	10	233%	18	28
Probe stain	0	3	5	8	24	200%	48	72
Car tire	1	0	3	3	13	333%	32	45
Pcb flux cleaning	0	1	2	3	7	133%	38	45
Pencil	0	2	1	3	8	167%	20	28
Metal plating	1	2	1	3	5	67%	23	28
Probe stuck	0	1	3	4	6	50%	14	20
Bicycle seat	0	1	2	3	5	67%	31	36
Mold Preheating	1	2	5	7	15	114%	42	57
Mold injection curing	0	1	4	5	14	180%	9	23
Mold ejection	0	2	4	6	10	67%	20	30
Test tube machine	1	4	3	7	19	171%	16	35
Wind Turbines	0	2	5	7	13	86%	18	31
Bottle valve	3	1	2	3	12	300%	9	21
Bus wheel differential	0	0	4	4	8	100%	17	25
CMP Conditioner	0	3	4	7	10	43%	26	36
F-Connector	0	2	5	7	14	100%	11	25
Average	0.64	1.64	3.44	5.08	12.28	149%	45.68	57.96

5   Conclusion and Contributions

This paper established methods of parameter deployment and parameter separation/domination as part one of the full set of parameter manipulation for solving physical contradictions. The main contributions of this paper include:

(1) Proposing a systematic parameter identification, deployment, domination, separation, and transfer methods under a unified set of theory of parameter manipulation. Problem solving can be achieved by manipulating all the parameters for systematic problem solving at either contradictory parameter level or objective level.

(2) Proposing 6-plus problem solving strategies within a unified theory of parameter separation to achieve many more solutions beyond current approaches. All current solution methods fall only within three out of the 6-plus strategies developed thus capable of generating many more solution ideas which includes all solution ideas that can be generated by existing methods. As such, the quality of solutions using the proposed methods will be better or at least the same compared to using existing methods. In all the cases we have tested, the proposed strategies identified many good solutions which otherwise are not identified by existing methods.

(3) Providing a set of operational forms to facilitate convenient systematic problem solving.

Acknowledgment. This research is funded by Ministry of Science and Technology of the Republic of China under Project number: 103-2221-E-007-052-MY3.

References

1. Mann, D.: Hands on Systematic Innovation. IFR Press (2007). ISBN 90-77071-02-4
2. Royzen, Z.: Solving Problems Using TOP-TRIZ, TRIZCON2010 (2008)
3. Benjaboonyazit, T.: Solving the problem of ARIZ using ARIZ: case study on pipeline maintenance system design. Int. J. Syst. Innov. 4(2), 1–16 (2016)
4. Sheu, D.D., Yeh, R.: Parameter deployment and separation: a new way of solving physical contradictions. In: 2015 the 7th Systematic Innovation Conference and Annual Meeting of the Society of Systematic Innovation, Taipei, Taiwan (2015). (in Chinese)
5. Sheu, D.D.: Mastering TRIZ Innovation Tools: Part I, 4th edn. Agitek International Consulting, Inc. (2015). ISBN 978-986-85795-2-1 (in Chinese)
6. Li, H.C.: An integrated algorithm for TRIZ inventive problem solving (Master's thesis). National Tsing Hua University, Hsinchu, Taiwan (2013). (in Chinese)
7. Yeh, R., Sheu, D.D.: Parameter transfer for solving physical contradictions. In: The 6th International Conference on Systematic Innovation, Hong Kong, 15–17 July 2015 (2015)

Integrating the Theory of Inventive Problem Solving with Discrete Event Simulation in Supply Chain Management

Fatima Zahra BenMoussa[1]([✉]), Sébastien Dubois[2], Roland De Guio[2],
Ivana Rasovska[3], and Rachid Benmoussa[1]

[1] SyLPRO/ENSA Marrakech, University of Cadi Ayyad, Marrakech, Morocco
benmoussafatimazahra@gmail.com
[2] LGECO, INSA Strasbourg, Strasbourg, France
[3] ICUBE, University of Strasbourg, Strasbourg, France

Abstract. Supply chain challenges require not only effective management, but also a new innovative strategy to reduce costs and maximize its efficiency. Traditional problem-solving methodologies specific to the areas of supply chain management (SCM) find their limits when confronted with an inventive problem or a problem containing a contradiction. TRIZ (theory of inventive problem solving) is an effective theory for systematizing innovation and solving complex problems containing contradictions. Thus, the use of the theory TRIZ can be considered as a way to meet future challenges in SCM fields and get innovative solutions. This paper presents a method for solving supply chain problems and achieving a low-cost, based on complementarities between TRIZ and discrete event simulation and specific methods for solving supply chain problems. In the proposed model, a witness simulation model of the initial problem is developed to optimize the problem and find the system limits. Then, specific problem solving methods are applied to change the original description of problem and move towards a space in which a solution can be found. The discrete event simulation allows for experiments on the system to be created and analyzed. Thus, an experimental design was developed to establish the cause-and-effect relationships between the parameters of the system in order to formulate a generalized system of contradictions. And finally, ARIZ 85C, the most mature meta-methods of TRIZ, is used to address related contradictions for searching for an innovative solution, which must be subsequently implemented and evaluated in the discrete event simulation. The suitability of this new approach is finally proven through an industrial case study conducted in a company specialized in the manufacture of electronic devices for automobiles.

Keywords: Theory of inventive problem solving (TRIZ)
Algorithm for inventive problem solving (ARIZ) · Supply chain
Discrete event simulation · Design of experiments
Generalized system of contradictions

D. Cavallucci et al. (Eds.): TFC 2018, IFIP AICT 541, pp. 330–347, 2018.
https://doi.org/10.1007/978-3-030-02456-7_27

1   Introduction

Nowadays, problems related to the management and optimization of supply chains are crucial for industrialists who constantly seek, on the one hand, to increase their productivity and secondly, respond to various pressures such as the most stringent regulations, growing demand for quality and quantity of goods and services while minimizing the associated costs. Supply chain represents a competitive advantage that companies seek to perpetuate. It aims to optimize exchanges or flows that the company has with its suppliers and customers. It is then necessary to design effective optimization and decision-making tools adapted to the difficulties logisticians face in organizing supply chains. In fact, to solve supply chain problems, researchers have developed several optimization approaches for solving multi-objective problems, in order to find the most advantageous trade-offs between economic and qualitative performance. In this paper, we consider an optimization problem from a warehouse. Warehousing operations play a major role in supply chain management as they are related to the shipment of products from the warehouse to the customers while ensuring the safety of the products. A warehouse can be defined as a handling station dedicated to receiving, storing, order picking, accumulation, sorting and shipping of goods [1]. The cost of warehousing operations is comparatively high due to the existence of many non-value-added activities. Order-picking is the most expensive activity for warehouses, its cost is estimated at around 55% of the total operating expenses of the warehouse [2]. Therefore, the optimization of order picking activities immediately impacts on the warehouse efficiency, and also affects the performance of the whole supply chain. The faster items are picked from the warehouse, the shorter the time spent in order fulfillment will be; hence, the lead time required for delivering the product to the final customer decreases correspondingly [3].

Innovative strategies are currently used as a key element to gain a competitive advantage in real market sharing and acquisition of new markets. In this paper, we are interested in the use of innovation methods in solving problems in the supply chain, and more particularly to the theory of TRIZ. Indeed, TRIZ is the Russian acronym for "theory of inventive problem solving". TRIZ is one of the most powerful and widely accepted theories for adopting systemic innovation. TRIZ is a theory that has been widely used in multiple industries and fields to solve problems and find inventive solutions. TRIZ provides a set of methods and tools commonly used in preliminary technical product designs, based on dialectic and systemic. It allows users to adopt a dialectical style of thinking that helps them to understand problems as systems, to conceptualize the ideal solution, and to improve the performance of the system by solving the contradictions, which are descriptions of conflicts between the objectives of a problem. In a supply chain, the emergence of a conflictual situation between its objectives, such as costs, quality of products and services, may be associated with the notion of contradiction in the TRIZ theory. TRIZ refuses to make compromises and proposes to overcome these contradictions by proposing a solution that meets all the problem objectives. In general, solving a problem cannot be distinguished from the formulation phase. A respectable formulation of a problem which, in the case of TRIZ, involves the formulation of a relevant contradiction means the reconciliation of a solution. Thus, the identification and extraction of contradictions is the starting point for solving inventive problems. TRIZ was first proposed for solving technical problems related to product engineering design. Subsequently, it was extended to resolve other types of problems in other fields such as supply chains, service, education, and information processing. There are limited studies in the existing literature that deal with the application of TRIZ for problems in supply chain operations. A previous study [4] investigated the application of TRIZ to supply chain problems, particularly to inventory management problems. They demonstrated that there is no obvious or straightforward reason preventing TRIZ from being applied to all categories of supply chain problems, including warehousing problems. However, using TRIZ for solving problems is sometimes difficult because TRIZ lacks highly specific tools and methods to understand complex problems and formulate a related system of contradictions. For this reason, in this paper, we propose a method for solving supply chain problems and achieving a low-cost solution, based on complementarities between TRIZ and discrete event simulation and specific methods for solving supply chain problems.

The remainder of this paper is organized as follows. Section 2 introduces the materials and methods, including the algorithm for inventive problem solving, the notion of generalized system of contradictions, order-picking optimization methods, and the framework of the proposed method. Section 3 presents the result of applying the proposed method to a warehousing problem through a case study involving an automotive supplier producing electronic modules. A discussion and conclusive remarks are provided in Sect. 4.

2 Materials and Methods

2.1 Algorithm for Inventive Problem Solving (ARIZ)

TRIZ, which is the Russian acronym for the theory of inventive problem solving, was developed by Genrich Altshuller starting in 1940. Unlike problem solving methods that accept randomness in the innovation process, TRIZ is a knowledge-based systematic methodology, which provides a logical approach to develop creativity for innovation and inventive problem solving, while rejecting compromises between objective restrictions and specific situation limits [5]. ARIZ is the Russian acronym for the "algorithm for inventive problem solving", developed by the TRIZ creator Genrich Altshuller. ARIZ is a process that links the tools and techniques of TRIZ, in order to apply them in a structured manner, to evolve a complex problem to a point where it can be solved. ARIZ has been developed through several steps, and the last version of ARIZ accepted by Altshuller was ARIZ-85C [6]. The framework of ARIZ-85C, consists of nine algorithmic parts [7]. These parts can be selectively employed according to the practical situation of solving a problem, but parts 1 to 3 are mainly applied even for complicated engineering problems (Fig. 1).

These parts are dedicated to analyzing the problem situation by converting the initial problem into a formulated description, analyzing the problem model by identifying the existing resources for solving the problem, defining the ideal final result and the physical contradictions, respectively. Each part of ARIZ 85C has the following sequences [7]:

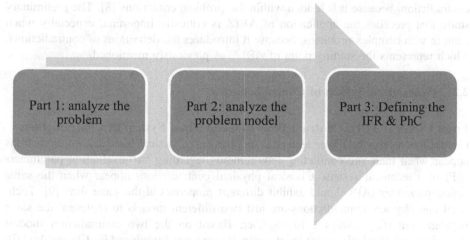

| Part 1: analyze the problem | Part 2: analyze the problem model | Part 3: Defining the IFR & PhC |

Fig. 1. Framework of ARIZ 85C (according to [7])

Part 1:

1. Reformulate the problem and its characteristics
2. Identify the conflicting elements of the system
3. Create a graphical schema of the conflict system
4. Select a graphical model of the system
5. Aggravate the main conflict
6. Formulate a problem model
7. Look for a standard solution

Part 2:

1. Analyze the operating zone (ZO)
2. Analyze the operating period (OP)
3. Analyze Su-field resources (SFRs)

Part 3:

1. Define the ideal final result (IFR-1)
2. Intensify the definition of IFR-1
3. Define the physical contradiction (PhC) at the macro level
4. Define the physical contradiction at the micro level
5. Define the IFR-2
6. Apply the inventive standards to resolve the PhC

It is important to note that ARIZ 85C only addresses the reformulation and resolution of the problem. However, contradiction is the pillar of ARIZ 85, and solving an inventive problem means solving the related technical and physical contradictions. A technical contradiction is the starting point of the whole problem-solving process using ARIZ. Sometimes, the technical contradiction within a problem is clearly evident, and at other times it seems that a problem does not contain any technical contradiction, because it is hidden within the problem conditions [8]. The preliminary study that precedes the application of ARIZ is critically important, especially when dealing with complex problems, because it introduces the definitions of contradictions, which represents the starting point of ARIZ, as previously mentioned.

2.2 Generalized System of Contradictions

From Classical TRIZ Contradictions to Generalized System of Contradictions

Contradictions can be either technical or physical. Classical technical contradictions appear when there are conflicting requirements regarding two evaluation parameters (EP) of a technical system. Classical physical contradictions appear when the same action parameter (AP) should exhibit different properties at the same time [9]. Technical and physical contradictions are just two different models to represent the same problem, but they always exist together. Based on the two contradiction models (technical and physical), a system of contradictions was introduced by Khomenko [10] to represent the causal relation between the AP and EP, as illustrated in Fig. 2. This system of contradictions is based on the existence of a contradiction of the parameter and a contradiction of the system, which justifies the need for two different states of the parameter [11]. The value of the action parameter must equal value 1 to satisfy the first evaluation parameter and value 2 to satisfy the second evaluation parameter. The desired result is to satisfy the two evaluation parameters.

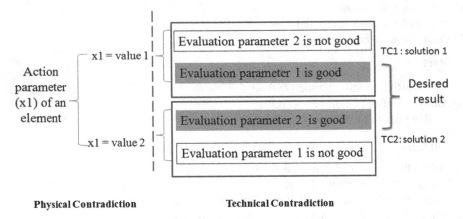

Fig. 2. Classical TRIZ system of contradictions

Example:

In an inventory management system managed by Kanban card system, we have the following problem (Fig. 3):

Technical contradiction 1 (TC-1):

If we have a big size of "The reorder quantity of kanban card", then "The stock breakdown" reduces, but "The stock value" increases.

Technical contradiction 2 (TC-2):
If we have a small size of "The reorder quantity of kanban card", then "The stock value" reduces, but "The stock breakdown" increases.

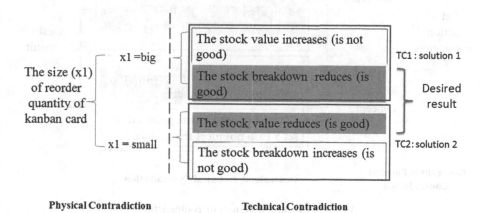

Physical Contradiction   Technical Contradiction

Fig. 3. Example of a system of contradictions

However, the classical TRIZ contradiction is limited by the number of evaluation parameters, which does not exceed two parameters. Indeed, when dealing with real and complex problems, this model cannot be used to represent the system of contradictions, owing to the problem multidimensionality. In order to represent the system of contradictions for a multidimensional problem, a generalized system of contradictions was proposed in [11, 12]. The generalized system of contradictions represents the generalization of the classical TRIZ system of contradictions, where two concepts based on a set of action parameters satisfy two sets of evaluation parameters. The desired result is then the simultaneous satisfaction of the two sets of evaluation parameters. The generalized system of contradictions is represented in Fig. 4.

2.3   Order-Picking Optimization Methods

Order picking involves several processes, which may include the scheduling of customer orders, assigning available stock to orders, releasing orders to the floor and picking the articles from storage locations [3]. Further, there exist five methods or ways to improve the order-picking operations: designing the warehouse layout, selecting the storage assignment policy, the picking policy and the routing strategy, and defining the material handling equipment to be used in the warehouse (see Fig. 5). The aim of these methods is to reduce the total time required to fulfill customer orders, by taking into account the constraints of available resources, such as workforce and material handling systems.

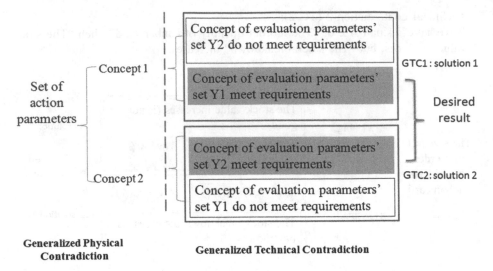

Generalized Physical Contradiction

Generalized Technical Contradiction

Fig. 4. Generalized system of contradictions

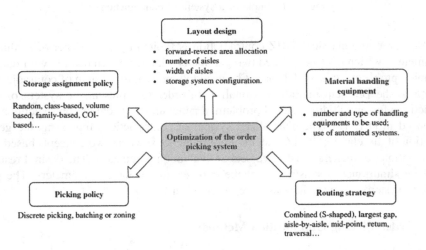

Fig. 5. Five ways to improve the order-picking operations

2.4 The Global Methodology Framework

Based on the integration and complementarity between the discrete event simulation, specific methods such as order-picking optimization methods, and the algorithm for inventive problem solving (ARIZ) given above, the proposed model is illustrated as follow:

Step 1: Optimize the System and Reach Its Limits

The main purpose of step 1 is to create a simulation model of the initial problem to optimize the initial problem and reach the system limits. The role of simulation in the proposed approach is to design and simulate the operation of the system to verify if there are optimal solutions that meet the objectives of the problem, or search for the limitation of the problem system. However, this step is an important step, because the optimization makes it possible to check whether the evaluation parameters (the problems objectives or constraints) of the problem are in a conflict situation or not. If they are not in a conflict situation, the problem must first be solved by introducing new constraints, to find the optimal solutions, which brings the evaluation parameters to a conflict state.

Step 2: Apply Specific Problems Solving Methods to Improve the Problem System

The purpose of step 2 is to apply specific problems solving methods, in order to go beyond the limits of the problem system, and expand the search space for solutions, by modifying the system description model and moving towards a space in which a solution can be found.

Step 3: Realize An Experimental Design to Extract and Formulate the Generalized Contradictions of the Problem

An experiment is a process or study that results in the collection of data. The results of experiments are not known in advance. Usually, statistical experiments are conducted in situations in which researchers can manipulate the conditions of the experiment and can control the factors that are irrelevant to the research objectives. The design of experiments (DoE) method is the process of planning a study to meet specified objectives, and determining the relation between the input and output parameters of a process, in order to optimize the output [13]. This method allows practitioners to make more informed decisions at each stage of the problem-solving process, and ultimately arrive at better solutions in less time.

The chosen simulation software (Witness 14) provides tools for random experiments, called 'experimenter' to realize a design of experiments and determine the relation between the parameters of a system.

In this step, we propose the realization of a design of experiments of the improved situation, characterized by (1) a set of action parameters $X = (X_1, ..., X_k)$, (2) a set of evaluation parameters $Y = (Y_1, ..., Y_n)$, and (3) a set of experiments $E = (E_1, ..., E_p)$. Each experiment Ei is characterized by a set of values $(V_{i1}, ..., V_{ik})$ attributed to the set of action parameters, and by a set of values $(Zi1, ..., Zin)$ taken by the evaluation parameters, as listed in Table 1.

Then, following the well-known concept of Pareto dominance [14], find the Pareto solution from the realized design of experiments. Finding the best generalized technical contradictions involves finding the existing conflicts between the evaluation parameters from the Pareto solution.

Step 4: Apply ARIZ to Solve the Contradiction

The main objective of this step is to propose concepts of solutions for the studied problem, through the resolution of the technical contradiction identified in Step 3. The identification of available resources may be useful for solving the problem. The ideal final result (IFR) and the physical contradiction (PhC) that prevents the achievement of the IFR should be formulated. The existing TRIZ principles should be used to solve the formulated physical contradiction.

Table 1. Design of experiments matrix

	X_1	X_2	...	X_{k-1}	X_k	Y_1	Y_2	...	Y_{n-1}	Y_n
E_1	$V_{1,1}$	$V_{1,2}$		$V_{1,k-1}$	$V_{1,k}$	$Z_{1,1}$	$Z_{1,2}$		$Z_{1,n-1}$	$Z_{1,n}$
E_2	$V_{2,1}$	$V_{2,2}$		$V_{2,k-1}$	$V_{2,k}$	$Z_{2,1}$	$Z_{2,2}$		$Z_{2,n-1}$	$Z_{2,n}$
E_3	$V_{3,1}$	$V_{3,2}$		$V_{3,k-1}$	$V_{3,k}$	$Z_{3,1}$	$Z_{3,2}$		$Z_{3,n-1}$	$Z_{3,n}$
E_{p-2}	$V_{p-2,1}$	$V_{p-2,2}$		$V_{p-2,k-1}$	$V_{p-2,k}$	$Z_{p-2,1}$	$Z_{p-2,2}$		$Z_{p-2,n-1}$	$Z_{p-2,n}$
E_{p-1}	$V_{p-1,1}$	$V_{p-1,2}$		$V_{p-1,k-1}$	$V_{p-1,k}$	$Z_{p-1,1}$	$Z_{p-1,2}$		$Z_{p-1,n-1}$	$Z_{p-1,n}$
E_p	$V_{p,1}$	$V_{p,2}$		$V_{p,k-1}$	$V_{p,k}$	$Z_{p,1}$	$Z_{p,2}$		$Z_{p,n-1}$	$Z_{p,n}$

3 Results

In this section, we present a case study to demonstrate the applicability of the proposed method. The case study focuses on the optimization of the number of operators working in the raw material store of a manufacturing company, specializing in producing electronic cards.

The raw material store feeds production lines 3 times a day (every 8 h). Seven operators (per shift) work in the store, and must ensure the supply of production lines at the right time. The store has 19 trolleys to fill. Operators must fill the 19 trolleys and then transport them to production lines. The trolleys are composed of a large number of empty slots (up to 280 places), which are characterized by the reference of the raw material to be put in place. The trolleys are placed in an area called "trolleys zone", and the raw material store is composed of several storage racks. To fill the trolleys, operators make round trips from the trolley zone to the storage racks to pick up the necessary raw material. To ensure his task, each operator is equipped with a reader gun that allows him to search the location of each reference. In these conditions, the seven operators need 7.44 h to complete the filling of trolleys. So they do not have enough time to bring the trolleys to the production lines. The store uses other external operators to help store operators accomplish their tasks at the specified time.

The store manager wants to reduce the number of operators working in the raw material store, as he assumes that the requested tasks can be done by less than 7 operators. On the other hand, the operator's team leader asks to add more operators, so that they can complete their work without the intervention of external resources. The store manager wants to reduce the number of operators in the raw material store while achieving the following objectives (Table 2):

Table 2. The problem objectives

	Initial situation	Objective to reach
PE1: delay to fill the 19 trolleys	7.44 h	<7 h
PE2: total load for operators	51.25 h	<40 h
AP1: number of available operators	7	<7

3.1   Step 1: Optimize the System and Reach Its Limits

This step presents the results from the optimization of the system problem. The model of the system problem has been implemented on a discrete event simulator (Witness 14), as shown in Fig. 6. The identification of the different parameters of the problem must be performed at this stage, in order to simulate the system. Thus, the evaluation parameters of the problem and the action parameters that influence them are:

PE1: delay to fill the 19 trolleys, is the time required for all operators to fill all the 19 trolleys

PE2: total load for operators, is the sum of the individual loads of each operator

PE3: total travel time of operators, is the sum of total travel time of each operator

PA1: number of available operators.

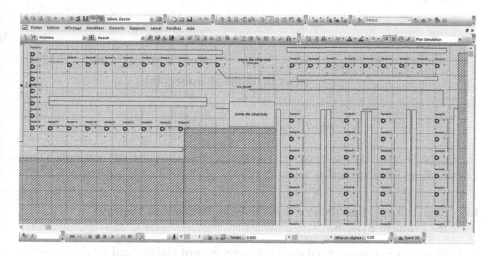

Fig. 6. Witness model of the warehouse problem

Then, we conducted an experiment which consists in varying the number of available operators in order to find the Pareto optimal solutions (while respecting the problem constraints). We illustrate the simulation results in the following graphic (Fig. 7) and in Table 3.

This figure represents the set of optimal solutions of the problem. None of the optimal solutions on the Pareto border meet the constraints of the problem. This means that the system has reached its limits, and needs to be upgraded or replaced by another, more efficient system that satisfies the objectives of the problem. On the other hand, we note that the two objectives of the problem (the evaluation parameters) are in a conflict situation, where one parameter improves while another deteriorates.

From Table 3, one concludes that to satisfy the problem objective, the system needs one more operator (8 operators per shift instead of 7). In addition to that, we identify that the required time to reach the picking location (EP3: 'travel time') is the most relevant contribution to the total picking time. In turn, the travel time is an increasing

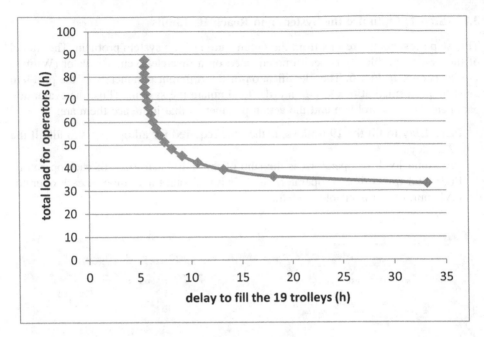

Fig. 7. Pareto front of the system

function of the travel distance, and thus minimizing the travel distance is the main lever for optimizing the total picking time.

3.2 Step 2: Apply Specific Problems Solving Methods to Improve the Problem System

With the ultimate purpose of reducing the travel time of pickers, and by using specific methods for order picking optimization in warehouses, we propose to change the order picking strategy, and make some changes to the warehouse layout to minimize the total travel distance. In the initial situation, an operator fills the trolleys of the raw material one by one, by moving back and forth from the location of the trolleys ("trolley zone") to the storage racks where the product to pick up is stored. In this situation, the operators adopt a random picking sequence or a round-trip sequence. Indeed, the order in which the products are picked up has no influence on the total workload of the operators. In the improved situation, we propose that operators adopt a traversal or an S-shape picking sequence by performing a warehouse tour between the storage racks and pushing the trolley to fill. The starting and ending point of this tour is the trolley area. The trolley must be filled in one journey between the racks. To achieve this, the picking sequence will be defined according to the locations of products in the storage racks. Thus, for each trolley an operator must have a pick-up list that indicates the order picking to follow, and the path followed by operators should be the shortest one through the storage racks. In this improved situation, the trolley becomes mobile, and the picking sequence becomes predefined. As part of the same improvement action, we make minor changes to the warehouse layout.

Table 3. Optimal solutions

Experiments	AP1 number of operators	EP1 delay to fill the 19 trolleys (h)	EP2 total load for operators (h)	EP3 total travel time of operators (h)
E1	1	33.15	33.15	12.37
E2	2	18.13	36.17	12.37
E3	3	13.15	39.19	12.37
E4	4	10.65	42.20	12.37
E5	5	9.15	45.21	12.37
E6	6	8.14	48.23	12.37
E7	7	7.44	51.25	12.37
E8	**8**	**6.97**	**54.27**	**12.37**
E9	9	6.61	57.26	12.36
E10	10	6.30	60.31	12.39
E11	11	6.09	63.33	12.37
E12	12	5.91	66.32	12.37
E13	13	5.76	69.34	12.37
E14	14	5.60	72.37	12.37
E15	15	5.51	75.38	12.37
E16	16	5.52	78.40	12.37
E17	17	5.50	81.41	12.37
E18	18	5.50	84.42	12.37
E19	19	5.51	87.41	12.37

3.3   Step 3: Realize an Experimental Design to Extract and Formulate the Generalized Contradictions of the Problem

In this step, a design of experiments of the improved situation was realized (see Table 4), to determine the relation between the input and output parameters of the new system.

From Tables 3 and 4, the colored lines represent the non dominated solutions for the initial system and the improved system, respectively. Finding the best system of contradictions involves finding the existing conflicts between the two non-dominated solutions. The formulated system of contradictions, described in Fig. 8, represents the existing conflicts between the system configurations from E8 (the initial system) and E25 (the best solution from the improved system). The objective of the next step is to address the generalized system of contradictions of the problem and solve the GPC.

3.4   Step 5: Apply ARIZ to Address the Contradictions

According to ARIZ, the algorithmic procedure for solving an inventive problem, based on the identified problem's system of contradictions presented in Fig. 8, is implemented as follows:

Table 4. Design of experiments of the improved system

Experiments	AP1 number of available operators	EP1 delay to fill the 19 trolleys (h)	EP2 total load for operators (h)	EP4 total waiting time (h)	EP3 total travel time of operators (h)
E20	1	21.78	21.78	0.00	1.00
E21	2	12.53	24.94	0.16	1.00
E22	3	9.56	28.20	0.42	1.00
E23	4	7.98	31.42	0.64	1.00
E24	5	7.23	35.04	1.27	1.00
E25	**6**	**6.61**	**38.48**	**1.70**	**1.00**
E26	7	6.22	41.73	1.95	1.00
E27	8	5.88	45.15	2.37	1.00
E28	9	5.66	48.72	2.94	1.00
E29	10	5.48	51.85	3.07	1.00
E30	11	5.35	54.89	3.12	1.00
E31	12	5.20	58.09	3.32	1.00
E32	13	5.04	61.41	3.63	1.00
E33	14	4.91	65.04	4.27	1.00
E34	15	4.83	69.02	5.24	1.00
E35	16	4.82	72.92	6.14	1.00
E36	17	4.81	76.40	6.63	1.00
E37	18	4.81	79.96	7.18	1.00
E38	19	4.81	83.38	7.61	1.00

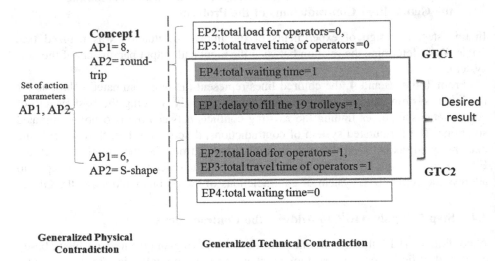

Fig. 8. Representation of the generalized system of contradictions

Part 1

The main purpose of Part 1 is the transition from an indefinite initial problem situation to a clearly formulated and extremely simplified description of the problem.

Problem Description:

The system <picking process>, whose main function is to change the position of the raw material from <position in the storage racks> to <position in the trolley> includes <operators, trolleys, location of racks, location of raw material, allocation of trolleys to operators, readers gun, raw materials, scheduling, barcodes, ...>.

- Contradiction formulation:

The problem is formulated as:

Generalized technical contradiction 1 (GTC-1):

If there are <six operators (AP1) who adopt a traversal or an S-shape picking sequence (AP2)>, then <the delay to fill the 19 trolleys (EP1) is good, the total travel time of operators (EP3) is good, and the total load for operators (EP2) is good>, but <the total waiting time behind stocks (EP4) is not good>.

Generalized technical contradiction 2 (GTC-2):

If there are <eight operators (AP1) who adopt a round-trip sequence (AP2)>, then <the total waiting time behind stocks (EP4) is good and the delay to fill the 19 trolleys (EP1) is good>, but <the total travel time of operators (EP3) and the total load for operators (EP2) are not good>.

- Desired result:

It is necessary, with minimal changes to the system, to satisfy all the evaluation parameters without increasing the number of available operators (AP1).

Problem Model:

(1) Conflicting pair:

<Tool: Operators and picking sequence> and <Product: queue, travel time, and loading delay>.

(2) Intensified conflict:

The adoption of a traversal picking sequence with mobile trolleys moving between the storage racks ensures a good travel time, but the presence of several trolleys in the storage racks causes the formation of a large queue.

It is necessary to find an X-element that has the ability to resolve the created queues, without deteriorating the travel time and loading delay.

Part 2

The main purpose of Part 2 is to identify available resources (space, time, substances, and fields) that may be useful for solving the problem.

Definition of the Operational Zone (OZ) and Operational Time (OT)

The operational zone is the space in which the conflict takes place. The OZ of the studied problem is the space in front of the storage racks or storage locations, where operators move with their trolleys to pick up raw material.

The operational times are defined by the time during which the conflict (T1) occurs and the time before the conflict (T2). The OTs of the studied problem are:

T1 = the waiting time of operators behind the desired storage location (in which the next article to be picked up is stored).

T2 = the moment at which the operator identifies the next location to move to from the pick-up list.

Define the Substance-Field Resources (SFR)

1. Resources of the tools:

   - The picking sequence (a pick-up list for each trolley)
   - The operators (their number)
   - The trolleys to fill with raw material (their number and size)

2. Internal resources:

   - Locations of the storage racks
   - Storage location of each reference of raw material
   - Allocation of trolleys to operators
   - Reader guns
   - The warehouse structure

3. The environmental (external) resources:

   - Production area
   - Information system

Part 3

The main purpose of Part 3 is to formulate the image of the ideal final result (IFR) and identify the physical contradiction (PhC) that prevents the achievement of the IFR. The ideal solution is not always achievable, but the IFR indicates the direction of the most powerful solution.

Formulation of the Ideal Final Results (IFRs) and Physical Contradictions (PhCs)

- IFR1:

Without complicating the system or introducing harmful side-effects, the X-element eliminates <queues behind storage racks> during the <operational time>, inside the <operational zone>, and preserves the tool's ability to provide <a good travel time, a good loading delay, and a good delay to fill the 19 trolleys>.

- Intensified IFR-1:

Without complicating the system or introducing harmful side-effects, the operator with his trolley eliminates <queues behind storage racks> during the <operational time>, inside the <operational zone>, and preserves the tool's ability to provide <a good travel time, a good loading delay, and a good delay to fill the 19 trolleys>.

- PhC for macro-level:

The physical contradictions are the opposing requirements for the physical state of the operational zone.

The <operational zone>, during the <operational time>, must <always allow operators to stand in front of the storage location and collect the raw material> in order to <eliminate queues of operators with their trolleys behind storage racks>, and must <allow only one operator with his trolley to stand in front of a location to collect the raw material> in order to <prevent blocking the passage to other operators who have to go to other stocks>.

Proposed Solution

By analyzing the formulation of the physical contradictions, we find that the space is a particular resource for this problem, and that the "separation in space," which is one of the separation principles for solving physical contradictions, could be applied. Thus, a new strategy is proposed based on changing the starting point for operators, in such a way that they take different paths. Initially, all the operators started from the same point simultaneously, and queues were created. If they start from different points and cross the store by taking different paths, this will positively affect the total waiting time.

Evaluation of the Solution and Synthesis of the Results

To evaluate the performance of the new system proposed with ARIZ 85C, we implement the concept of the proposed solution in the Witness simulation software. After simulating the impact of the proposed solution on the studied picking process, the results indicate that the proposed solution solves the formulated physical contradiction at the macro-level without deteriorating any of the evaluation parameters. The simulation results show that the solution removes the total waiting time, and has the following results: EP1: delay to fill the 19 trolleys = 6.31 h, EP2: total load for operators = 36.78 h, EP3: total travel time of operators = 1 h and EP4: total waiting time = 0.00 h. In addition, by optimizing the improved system from ARIZ 85C, we can reduce the number of operators from six operators to five. Thus, we gain 3 operators in total (for the three shifts).

The following table (Table 5) summarizes the results achieved from the application of the proposed method. As a result, the proposed method has reduced in total 2 operators per shift, working in the raw material store, which equals 6 operators in total (for three shifts). Thus, the raw material store can keep only 15 operators, to perform the same work that is currently performed by 21 operators, and without resorting to external resources.

Table 5. Synthesis of different states of the studied system

	AP1	EP1	EP2	EP4	EP3
Initial system	7	7.44	51.25	0.00	12.37
Optimized initial system	8	6.97	54.27	0.00	12.37
Improved system with specific methods for order picking optimization	6	6.61	38.48	1.70	1.00
Solution from ARIZ	6	6.30	36.78	0.00	1.00
Optimized solution from ARIZ	5	6.96	33.77	0.00	1.00

4   Discussion and Conclusive Remarks

In this study, we proposed a problem solving method based on the complementarities between TRIZ, discrete event simulation and specific methods for solving supply chain problems. A case study concerning the optimization of the number of operators working in the raw material store of an automotive company specializing in the manufacturing of electronic modules was conducted to verify the applicability of the proposed model. In this method, the creation of a witness simulation model of the initial problem is first done to optimize the initial problem and reach the system limits. Searching for optimal solutions that meet the objectives of the problem makes it possible to check whether the evaluation parameters (the problems objectives or constraints) of the problem are in a conflict situation or not. Specific problem solving methods are subsequently applied to go beyond the limits of the problem system, and expand the search space for solutions, by modifying the system description model and moving towards a space in which a solution can be found. Discrete event simulation allows for experiments on the system to be created and analyzed. Thus, an experimental design was developed to establish the cause-and-effect relationships between the parameters of the system in order to formulate a generalized system of contradictions. Then, ARIZ was employed to solve the formulated generalized contradictions and find innovative solutions that get as close as possible to the ideal final result.

In conclusion, this study contributes to existing knowledge by using the discrete event simulation in conjunction with the inventive algorithm ARIZ. The synergetic application of discrete event simulation and ARIZ and their complementarily with other methods, mainly specific methods for solving supply chain problems and design of experiments, allows for better results and a better performance to be obtained than by solving a problem using only simulation based optimization or ARIZ. The proposed model strengthens the weak points of both simulation based optimization and TRIZ by applying them in a complementary manner. Furthermore, this study highlights the application of ARIZ to solve problems with generalized technical contradictions. Further research could focus on extending the proposed method to supply chain areas other than the warehouse or to production management problems.

References

1. van den Berg, J.P., Zijm, W.H.M.: Models for warehouse management: classification and examples. Int. J. Prod. Econ. **59**, 519–528 (1999). https://doi.org/10.1016/s0925-5273(98)00114-5
2. Dharmapriya, U.S.S., Kulatunga, A.K.: New strategy for warehouse optimization – lean warehousing. In: International Conference on Industrial Engineering and Operations Management, pp. 513–519 (2011)
3. de Koster, R., Le-Duc, T., Jan Roodbergen, K., Koster, D.: Design and control of warehouse order picking: a literature review. Eur. J. Oper. Res. **182**, 481–501 (2007)
4. Ben Moussa, F.Z., Rasovska, I., Dubois, S., De Guio, R., Benmoussa, R.: Reviewing the use of the theory of inventive problem solving (TRIZ) in green supply chain problems. J. Clean. Prod. **142**, 2677–2692 (2017). https://doi.org/10.1016/J.JCLEPRO.2016.11.008
5. Ilevbare, I.M., Probert, D., Phaal, R.: A review of TRIZ, and its benefits and challenges in practice. Technovation **33**, 30–37 (2013). https://doi.org/10.1016/j.technovation.2012.11.003
6. Fiorineschi, L., Frillici, F.S., Rissone, P.: A comparison of classical TRIZ and OTSM-TRIZ in dealing with complex problems. Procedia Eng. **131**, 86–94 (2015). https://doi.org/10.1016/J.PROENG.2015.12.350
7. Altshuller, G.S.: Algorithme of inventive problem solving (1985). http://www.evolocus.com/Textbooks/ariz85c.pdf
8. Russo, D., Montecchi, T., Ying, L.: Knowledge based approach for identifying TRIZ contradictions. In: Proceedings of 2012 Design Engineering Workshop (DEWS 2012), pp. 134–140 (2012)
9. Fresner, J., Jantschgi, J., Birkel, S., Bärnthaler, J., Krenn, C.: The theory of inventive problem solving (TRIZ) as option generation tool within cleaner production projects. J. Clean. Prod. **18**, 128–136 (2010). https://doi.org/10.1016/j.jclepro.2009.08.012
10. Khomenko, N., De Guio, R., Cavallucci, D.: Enhancing ECN's abilities to address inventive strategies using OTSM-TRIZ. Int. J. Collab. Eng. **1**, 98–113 (2009)
11. Dubois, S., Rasovska, I., De Guio, R.: Interpretation of a general model for inventive problems, the generalized system of contradictions. In: Proceedings of the 19th CIRP Design Conference-Competitive Design (2009)
12. Dubois, S., De Guio, R., Rasovska, I.: Different ways to identify generalized system of contradictions, a strategic meaning. Procedia Eng. **9**, 119–125 (2011). https://doi.org/10.1016/j.proeng.2011.03.105
13. Ramakrishnan, S., Tsai, P.-F., Srihari, K., Foltz, C.: Using Design of Experiments and Simulation Modeling to Study the Facility Layout for a Server Assembly Process (2008)
14. Wang, F., Lai, X., Shi, N.: A multi-objective optimization for green supply chain network design. Decis. Support Syst. **51**, 262–269 (2011). https://doi.org/10.1016/j.dss.2010.11.020

Author Index

Printed in the United States
By Bookmasters